To the Extreme

SUNY series on Sport, Culture, and Social Relations
CL Cole and Michael A. Messner, editors

To the Extreme

ALTERNATIVE SPORTS, INSIDE AND OUT

ROBERT E. RINEHART
and
SYNTHIA SYDNOR
Editors

STATE UNIVERSITY OF NEW YORK PRESS

Published by
State University of New York Press, Albany

For information, address the State University of New York Press,
90 State Street, Suite 700, Albany, NY 12207

Production by Kelli Williams
Marketing by Jennifer Giovani

Library of Congress Cataloging-in-Publication Data

To the extreme : alternative sports, inside and out / Robert E. Rinehart
and Synthia Sydnor, editors.
    p. cm — (SUNY series on sport, culture, and social relations)
    Includes bibliographical references and index.
    ISBN 0-7914-5665-X (alk. paper) — ISBN 0-7914-5666-8 (pbk. : alk. paper)
    1. Extreme sports—Social aspects. I. Rinehart, Robert E., 1951–
II. Sydnor, Synthia. III. Series.

GV749.7.T6 2003
796.04'6—dc21   2002042646

10 9 8 7 6 5 4 3 2 1

For Nicholas Murphy and Alyssa Kathrene
R. E. R.

For Alvin, Mary, Jesse Francis, and Journey Elizabeth
S. S.

Listen: If we cannot do the superhuman we are lost . . .*

*Bertolt Brecht, "Wir Hören: Du willst nicht mehr mir uns arbeiten," Gedichte V, 8–9. Frankfurt-am-Main: Suhrkamp Verlag, 1960–1965, as quoted in Frederic Ewen, *Bertolt Brecht: His Life, His Art, His Times,* New York: Citadel Publishing Group, 1992, p. 327.

CONTENTS

EXTREME SKIING

SNOWBOARDING

Acknowledgments

When taking on a project of this scope, the support and enthusiasm of others become a valued entity. Throughout the inception and realization of this book, many individuals have facilitated my involvement: I therefore wish to express my personal gratitude to the Walker family; my son Nicholas and daughter Alyssa; Jim Rinehart, Karen Forcum, and Gabriele Rinehart; Kimmy, Wayne, and Jennifer Lang; to Harry, Gloria, and Kelly Rott; to Renee Echandi; to Vicky Paraschak; to Monica Papp.

For professional support, I am grateful to my colleagues in the Physical Education and Dance Department at Idaho State University: Mike Lester, Dave Bale, Ann Sebren, Sandra Noakes, Marcia Lloyd, Gina Lay, and Timothy P. Winter; to colleagues at California State University, San Bernardino: Clifford Singh, Chris Grenfell, Jennie Gilbert, Judy Powell, Joe Liscano, Greg Price, Jerry Freischlag, and Amy Wheeler; to the many students and athletes who have taught me about sport and relationships; and to Norman Denzin for his inspiration and faith. Finally, I wish to acknowledge the support of the Department of Kinesiology and the College of Natural Sciences at California State University, San Bernardino—particularly Dr. Terry Rizzo and Dean Paul Vicknair.

—R. E. Rinehart

I am grateful to the University of Illinois for a sabbatical leave that allowed me to begin this study of extreme sport. I have profited immensely from the ideas of Ed Bruner, Father Dwight Campbell, Michael Golben, Allen Guttmann, Stephen Hardy, and Joseph Kockelmans. Most of all, I would like to thank Robert Rinehart, for the book owes its genesis solely to him. These are earthly acknowledgments: I inscribe here also the names Blessed Peter George Frassati and St. Bernard of Montijoix, extreme athletes in a sense.

—S. Sydnor

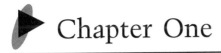 Chapter One

Proem

Robert E. Rinehart and Synthia Sydnor

Sports labeled "alternative," "extreme," "X," "gravity," "lifestyle," and "adventure" proliferate postcontemporary transnational times. Motifs associated with these sports are ubiquitous in everyday life—they decorate our backyards, street wear, language, lunch boxes, the Worldwide Web, MTV, ESPN, and advertising of every sort. In the summer of 1999, the US Postal Service issued 150 million stamps featuring extreme sports, and today over 10,000 Internet sites in English are dedicated to extreme sports.

This book centers on a few of the "extreme" sports: in-line skating, windsurfing, sky-dancing/surfing, BMX dirt-bike racing, mountain biking, Eco-challenge, whitewater kayaking, climbing, surfing, skateboarding, extreme skiing, and snowboarding. In order to interrogate a realm of alternative sport activities situated at various historical moments of invention, development, popularization, transglobal appropriation, reinvention, and perhaps even

Robert E. Rinehart is an adjunct professor in the Department of Kinesiology at California State University, San Bernardino. He has published a book, titled *Players All: Performances in Contemporary Sport,* and several research articles. His major research focus is in examining alternative sports forms, particularly forms that are on the cusp between popular culture and mainstream sports.

Synthia Sydnor is an associate professor at the University of Illinois at Urbana-Champaign where she holds appointments in kinesiology, criticism and interpretive theory, the interdisciplinary concentration in cultural studies and interpretive research, and the John Henry Newman Institute of Catholic Thought. Her research has appeared in a range of journals and books including *Quest, Journal of Sport History, Sport and Postmodern Times,* and *Games, Sports and Cultures.*

1

demise, we incorporated "older" extreme sports like surfing into this volume, as well as the newer extreme sports. Jake Burton, known as the prime creator of snowboarding, has written a chapter ("Snowboarding: The Essence is Fun") which sorts out an intricate historical foregrounding of snowboarding. Simon Eassom, in "Mountain Biking Madness," details the elaborate historical and technological lines which converge to continuously recreate and redefine forms of biking.

This book offers an interpretation of extreme sports from the standpoints of both the academic and the practitioner/extreme athlete. The scholars, who hail from cultural studies, anthropology, sociology, history, literary criticism, and other related interdisciplinary fields, are fascinated with some aspect of extreme sport in their research—their projects represent a range of methodologies and theoretical stances. The practitioners are all expert/elite athletes in their sport; some—such as Arlo Eisenberg—are renowned as the "Michael Jordans" of their sports, others are quiet grassroots participants. Some self-promote, some promote their sport, some try to warn the masses against their sport.

Our selection of particular sports and author-experts for inclusion in the book had to do with our quest to publish significant works of quality concerning the culture of extreme sports, and not a desire to forge a canon of particular sports or experts. The book is comprised of both "insider" and "outsider" information: juxtaposed with the athlete who bemoans frozen toes is the academic who categorizes risk-taking; intersecting with the daredevil, public scholar is the athlete who writes of his own cherished family. Beyond such binaries, readers can engage with the book at many levels—its contents evoke debates concerning theories of representation, authorship, dialogic narration, fieldwork, the avant-garde, "folk" sport, subculture, "whiteness," gender, danger/excitement, alternative and oppositional stances, and universalism.

There are surprises: the athletes-as-authors are eloquent writers, the academics are visceral performers. And the classic questions about sport are again confronted: What is sport? What is its origin? What is its use, value, function? Like the scholars, athletes, journalists, and poets who have long asked these questions, we also contemplate the essence of sport with a special eye toward understanding the "extreme" rejoinder to sport.

The labels "extreme" or "X" are everywhere these days. If someone wishes to convey radical, extraordinary, unusual properties to nearly any product, activity, individual, or lifestyle, these terms crop up. "Extreme" is linked today to soft drinks, health food, celebrity behavior, fashion and makeup, sexual technique, athletic shoes, cars, music, and of course, for the purposes of this book, to a relatively new (in the scope of human history of sport) form of sport. ESPN's Kevin Brooker characterizes it as "a combination of extraordinary individual achievement and unmatched personal enjoyment."[1] In Kyle Kusz's chapter, "BMX, Extreme Sports, and the White Male Backlash," the extreme discourse serves as exclusionary rhetoric for the dominantly-white "Generation X."

Though the cultural pop of a term like "extreme," when linked to sports, gives those sport forms a certain faddish panache, many participants are in for the long haul. They see these activities as lifestyle choices, with style, fashion, and aesthetics being just as important markers of participation as, for example, sponsorship and physical prowess. But Doug Booth's "Expression Sessions: Surfing, Style, and Prestige" shows how distinct lifestyles and tastes of surfers have evolved and remained authentic over the past 100 years.

The grassroots communities of surfers, in-line skaters, skateboarders, windsurfers, snowboarders, bicycle stunt riders, whitewater kayakers, extreme skiers, and orienteerers is certainly thriving and vibrant today. Proof positive: in a midwestern university town, Mosa Extreme Sports, a maker of protective gear and apparel for in-line skating, skateboarding, snowboarding, BMX bicycling, whitewater rafting, and air sports, went from $1 million sales in 1996, to over $6 million in 1998.[2] This is phenomenal growth, to say the least. *Street & Smith's Sportsbusiness Journal* highlighted this X sports boom with a series of articles titled in such ways as "An Extremely Profitable Niche" and "Cashing in on the Waves of the Future." Over 89 million US participants are registered in national associations, such as the National Off-Road Bicycle Association, American Sport Climbers Federation, and Aggressive Skaters Association.[3]

There are many ways that we can envision and study such athletes and their sports. As exemplified in some of this volume's writings, there are athletes who seek back regions, privacy, health and/or healing from their alternative sport ventures, who might not be included as 'registered' participants. Some athletes may practice their sports as regimens of asceticism, or outrightly decry the promotion of their activity into the mainstream. We might trace some of these philosophies back to New Games movements in the 1960s, American women's physical education philosophies of the early 1900s, or even prior to that, to the gymnastic systems and societies of nineteenth-century Germany and Sweden. Residual connections to New Age, Earth Day, and Green movements exist for some sports; others may embody urban sprawl and decay.

Whatever the venue or purpose, the fundamentally individual nature of these present-day alternative sports/activities remains. What are changing, however, as corporations and sponsors encroach upon and delve into the lucrative aspects of these cultural sport forms, are the twin aspects of money and control. Peter Donnelly, in "The Great Divide: Sport Climbing vs. Adventure Climbing," shows how the controversial balances between risk and difficulty in climbing may both resist and embrace institutionalization and commercialization.

The Disney Corporation, ESPN, ESPN2, ABC, MTV, the Discovery Channel, and large corporations such as Pepsi, Coke, and Nike have essentially appropriated and determined much of the electronic imaging of extreme sports to the world. Grassroots athletes are acknowledged by these imaging giants, but rarely privileged. Bob Rinehart's chapter examines some of the multinational strategies within in-line skating. Even the very word "extreme" in this context was engineered by these media corporations: "Extreme" was shortened to "X" by ESPN in 1996. *USA Today* reports that Ron Semaio, creator of the ESPN Extreme Games, changed the name of the sports festival to the "X Games" for fear that "someday 'extreme' would be . . . outdated. . . ."[4] Now, of course, the 'X' also prefixes other nouns and products' names so as to signify newness, shock appeal, or speed.[5]

The extreme athletes themselves recognize the inherent tangling of the media with the very nature of their sports and their sports as cultural commodities. In *Sick*, Susanna Howe has pointed out how "filmers" and photographers "create the dream that is snowboarding. It sells the lifestyle."[6] For much of snowboarding's existence, part of being a snowboarder meant to seek fame through rebel status at ski resorts and associations with "hardcore hip-hop and gangster style"[7] communities. This celebrity was pronounced to the world (or the athlete's small sub-culture of peers) visually, to eventually be used in advertising sports equipment, clothing or music. Belinda Wheaton, in her chapter "Windsurfing: A Subculture of Commitment," discusses insider/outsider statuses of participants. And Joanne Kay and Suzanne Laberge's "Imperialistic Construction of Freedom in Warren Miller's *Freeriders*" is valuable in providing an exemplar of critical analysis/interpretation of filmic narration of the rhetoric of class-related "freedom" as it is attached to images of extreme skiing.

Indeed, in addition to such commercial imaging, many extreme sports' growth is dependent on videography, for novice and experienced athletes alike watch videos of themselves, of others, and of experts repeatedly to learn basic skills and new tricks. There is also the subterranean world of sporting "zines," dilettante magazines in which creators seek to better control messages. Extreme sport 'zines are attempts to prevent the commercial mainstream from co-opting alternative culture.[8] Such films and 'zines are an archival gold mine for students interested in tracing the birth and techniques of postmodern folk games, for athletes today are particularly self-conscious of the history they are making.

The phenomenon of collecting and documenting "firsts," "landmark performances," or "records" of all facets of extreme sports is similar to what has occurred in mainstream sports such as baseball and basketball in the past century. In his classic work, *From Ritual to Record*,[9] Allen Guttmann points to this record-keeping as that which most sets modern sport apart from ancient and premodern sport. Bill Brown elaborates, commenting on the "fetishism for numbering" in American sports,[10] that baseball's enduring appeal resides in the "game's ability to orchestrate not individual and group, but scientific and narrative knowledge."[11] We see that this obsession with the record, with scientific and narrative knowledge, continues to mark many alternative sports; competing to be the best or to set speed, distance and/or performance records has many historical antecedents. But it is largely due to media influence that these activities have become "sport."

Likewise, broadcasts, advertising, and the mediatization of extreme sports echo post-millennial record-keeping, consumptive, and marketing strategies, and drive societal attitudes toward extreme sports. We might read of the birth of amalgamated "sports" such as skyrunning ("racing on terrain as high as 17,000 ft—forcing participants to brave dusty, rocky, and even snowy trails"[12]); of skyjumping from a plane while riding a water heater, wagon, golf cart, or automobile through the air at 120 mph;[13] of fifty-plus-mile swim races; or of lawn mower racing, toe skiing, or low-altitude parachuting. Participation ranges from the casual to the obsessed, from leisure/recreational enthusiasts to hard-core professionals, and from samplers to experts. One begins to realize that some of these athletes are simultaneously engaging in serious sport and making fun of canonical sport from this alternative sport vantage point.[14] In addition to these ranges of participant attitudes is the observation, as briefly noted above, that the units for most extreme sports are either individuals or dyads. Rarely—at least currently—are these extreme sports done as teams. This, of course, is in large contrast to the team-oriented sports of mainstream America. Football, basketball, volleyball, and so on—all are team sports, whereas most mediated extreme sports—such as street luge, in-line skating, skateboarding—are fundamentally individual sports.

Many extreme sports explode the 'canon' of mainstream sport in several ways. Grassroots extreme sports participants are not institutionalized with governing bodies; they have no eligible team roster, established practice times/locales, or coaches. Their activity is closely aligned with the precepts of 'play.' Alternative athletes in some X sports wear unique street apparel, uniforms by group consensus, not imposed from outside. There are no coaches. Sometimes the apparel references urban streetwear, hip-hop, "gansta rap," or grunge fashion. Drug-taking, alternative music, guns, and violence have been linked stereotypically to alternative sports participation. Of course, these caricatures of alternative sports are fraught with problems, much as mainstream American sports are unfairly typified as patriotic, clean-cut, and character building.[15] Yet, through various strategies and powers within culture, for the most part the history of alternative sports of the past twenty years show them to be eventually traditionalized to echo some of the stereotypical characteristics of mainstream sport.

The history of snowboarding's contested emergence into international Olympic competition is a case in point. Duncan Humphreys' "Selling Out Snowboarding: The Alternative Response to Commercial Co-Optation" sorts out strange juxtapositions of capitalism, punk, international federations, and the media as they decorate the culture of snowboarding.

Not only International Olympic Committee procurement or nationalism, but a corporate insistence on 'mainstreaming' these sports has encroached on them: in 1999, for example, contrary to the ethos of the single athlete (the "rugged individual"), the X Games contained "team" events where three in-line aggressive skaters performed routines simultaneously. Both formal and informal choreography for individuals is part of the everyday practices of these athletes, but working out routines with others is an attempt to capitalize on American-driven ideologies which privilege teamwork, interdependence, and trust.

There has also been a significant shift in the way sport is presented electronically. Filmic work in modernist sport work holds fast to centered wide-angle panning, with a large part of the field in sight of the television audience. Additionally, the whole contest is often broadcast. Extreme sports are, in contrast, intentionally conveyed as cutting-edge. Thus, an "MTV" approach—discontinuous shots, short (time duration) events, quick off-centered collage-type shots, blurred frames, super slo-motion cinematography, jolts of musical accompaniment, voyeuristic body shots, neon and holographic colors, and shocking up-close scenarios of sport-induced injury, illness, or 'crashes'—tend to predominate in extreme sports. In this way, such filmic stances and technologies have pushed sport closer to the realm of art. It has become highly "produced" sport—it is not in real time, but rather, taped and 'produced.'

Sport has always contained genuine artistic elements, but as C. L. R. James pointed out some forty years ago, "our enjoyment of it can never be quite artistic: we are prevented from completely realizing it not only by our dramatic interest in the game, but also . . . by the succession of movements being too rapid for us to realize each completely, and too fatiguing, even if realizable."[16] Now, our amazing technologies (and perhaps the insatiable energy of new times) enable us to bypass James's obstacles ("too fast," "too fatiguing") to realize sport as art.[17]

When the extreme sport event is shown to its conclusion on television or video, it is usually less than a minute in duration. X-athletes are as often interviewed by sports journalists concerning lifestyle choices[18] as about their athletic techniques or training. While ESPN and MTV Sports are forging a marriage between extreme sports and their presentations, they are also working to re-educate a whole new generation of sports viewers, to school them into new ways of looking at sports while borrowing heavily from successful strategies of mainstream sports.

The idea for this book—a collection of essays by both scholars and sport practitioners—stemmed from several sources. We were fascinated that new sports were being birthed before our eyes, and wanted as historians to document some of these alternative sports' origin stories. Too, we both are keenly involved in debates in qualitative work in sociology, anthropology, and cultural studies (to mention only a few areas) regarding "voice" of the "researched." Many strategies have been applied to this apparent dilemma, ranging from the old anthropological tropes of the emic and etic; participant observation; clandestine group membership; autobiography and biography; straight reportage; recording and transcribing; case studies; ethnographic performance work; and co-writing.[19] The list is seemingly endless. These are attempts to resolve an apparently

unresolvable crisis: that of knowing the 'other,' while simultaneously remaining the 'self.' Many scholars of sport have ignored
debates concerning power, authorship, and the other, and have been
quick to project expert hegemonic analysis upon the athlete, the
sport subculture, but slower to problematize and criticize their
own authorial stances. As editors, we considered that the best we
can do, perhaps, is *approach* the other (or others), brush up next to
her/him, and seek to better understand his/her experience(s).

Thus, we felt that readers might gain from a 'dialogue' between practitioners and academics. Our charge to contributors was
that they determine what they felt was germane to each sport and
to them, at this moment of their sport's evolution. With a few
authors, we discussed possible directions they might wish to pursue.
But, largely, the impetus for topics was generated by individual
authors. In some cases, practitioners and scholars discussed their
work: thus the constructed dialogue we editors had envisioned might
evolve from the book and be illuminated within it or upon publication found a reality prior to publication.

We worked to avoid a coffee-table type of book, yet sought
easy accessibility for readers. One might ask why we feel this, a
scholarly/popular culture book on alternative sport, matters, given
the current spate of books on extreme sports generally and each
sport form particularly. Of course, there is the standard, and very
sincere, reason given by all academics for the worthiness of their
topics: knowledge matters. To know more about our intricate,
mysterious lives on this planet enriches us. One of our authors,
windsurfer Bob Galvan, makes us privy not only to the matters of
his sport, but to the everyday ventures—finding fuel in Mexico,
trailer repair, the ordinariness of life—that come to make windsurfing *per se* so beautiful to him. Such knowledge matters because
it tells us what it is to be human: how wondrous, yet frightening;
how universal, yet particular. As sport sociologist George Sage
writes,

> . . . critical analysis implies a concern for identifying, scru-
> tinizing, and clarifying, and in this way helping over-
> come the obstacles to a complete understanding of the
> object of study. The purpose is to understand what is,
> and not present a detailed plan for what ought to be.[20]

This book is an attempt to identify *what is*, so that equitable
"control, production, and distribution of economic and cultural

power"[21] eventually may be effected, or at the least, noticed and discussed mindfully.[22] As well, to study extreme sports—inside and out—is to notice and discuss the achievements and problems of today's complex world.

This book also contributes to an ongoing scholarly discussion of authenticity within cultural studies, sociology, anthropology, history, and literary criticism. We believe there are continuum ranges, rather than binaries, of so-called authentic experiences. For example, to what degree is a young girl originary or derivative of actual experienced skateboarding culture (or cultures) when she imitates and rehearses a move she's seen performed on television? There may be, simultaneously, both completely authentic and no purely authentic conceptions of these sport forms. Anthropologist Ed Bruner amplifies this critique of authenticity in a way that we deem crucial for this collection's reckonings of alternative sport. He poses the questions:

> How is authenticity constructed? What is the process by which any item of culture or practice achieves an aura of being authentic? What are the processes of production of authenticity? . . . authenticity is something sought, fought over and reinvented.[23]

Jeff Howe's chapter queries these cultural processes in relation to power relationships of naming skateboarding; of naming self (one's biography most certainly helps shape one's interests); of labeling, and by labeling, of owning. In a world often bereft of continuity and stability, where on-line personalities play with the fluidity of their roles, where the thirty-some-year-old Super Bowl seems like an ancient tradition, the task of sorting out authenticity in anything is nearly impossible. Yet, the practitioner-athletes of this book actually participate in their chosen sport, and give their individual takes on that participation. Armed with the theories of cultural studies or not, they are 'authentic insiders.' As well, the 'invented' nature of these sports (like all culturally-laden artifacts) and the quickly evolving, emergent nature of them makes a discussion of 'authenticity' in these new sports by 'outsider' academics a valid and vital topic. In a sense, then, within this volume is a fluid museum of authentic alternative sports artifacts. For example, Tamara Koyn interweaves her poetic "Free Dimensional Skydiving" with authentic moments from her discipline, providing a postmodern pastiche of imaginaries and concrete experience.

There is an irony to extreme sports: that 'authentic,' alternative, 'pure,' avant-garde, forms quickly become mainstream and 'corrupted.' Consequently, associated alternative cultures also contribute to the growth and homogenizing of specific tastes of unique cultures into society. Many extreme athletes desire to be unique outsiders and nonconformists, yet, as Becky Beal and Lisa Weidman reveal, this too becomes an invented, 'conformist' rhetoric. As many note, the entrepreneurial business quickly elides into a multimillion dollar consumptive activity.

Extreme sports are sometimes connected to a new world order, a transnational village, the peaceful brotherhood of our planet. The beautiful choreography of X-sport scenes may evince an otherworldly utopia. And extreme sports are truly international. But extreme sports are also mostly 'white,' 'wealthy,' and exclusionary. Enthusiasts of many of the newer extreme sports must have funds, leisure time and access to specialized environments in order to participate for any length of time. Scholars—like Kay and Laberge, and Kusz—are beginning to investigate more deeply the extreme sport forms of the subaltern.

The paradigms used by scholars who treat the whole of culture and the things humans do in culture as 'travel' are useful for translating alternative X-sports into sites whose boundaries are queried in critical terms:[24] for example, we 'travel' within our lives from mundane work to extreme sport. Kristen Kremer, the extreme skier and author of "May 27, 1998" details such traveling between the real and imaginary realms of poverty, God's kingdom, an Irish pub, a world championship, paragliding, skiing, rafting, work, and play. In such 'travels' we may be equipped with unaccustomed power, freedom, or escape from existing social roles and obligations.[25]

Travel itself may characterize the postmodern condition and is certainly a form of conspicuous consumption. Like many tourists, the X-sport traveler seeks the exotic. Like many tourists, the X-athlete quests in his/her travels for signs (or markers) that they have found the authentic, the back region, or the perfect move.[26] "The tourist is interested in everything as a sign of itself. . . . To be a tourist is to dislike other tourists."[27] Certainly, for many participants, part of being an extreme athlete is to be less common than others, to privilege "insiders' expertise" and disdain mere "tourists" of extreme sport.

We know from classic studies in sport psychology, anthropology, and sociology that sport is universal in societies which are safe, peaceful, secure, and have capital and some divisions of labor.[28] Thus, at the beginning of the twenty-first century, alternative sports are not much practiced in diasporic or warring nations. And it is not only wealth or peace that complicates the practice of sport: today, people with new wealth have little time for leisure; conversely, the urban poor have much time, but little access to the equipment and spaces of most extreme sports.

Alternative sports are often articulated by their originators and media as moving beyond the old-world sport order. However, they occasionally reproduce the old typecastings. For instance, statements that belittle the female X-athlete such as "Awww, did you hurt your bottom?" or "Your hair got messed up on that one!" abound in extreme sports television.[29] One may counter that in extreme sports, anything goes, so that categories of difference may be magnified, altered, or blurred, and that stilted political correctness is unabashedly thrown out. Often, in alternative sport, the macho male athlete is exalted; Nazi and neo-Nazi iconography tattoos much of extreme sports equipment: clearly, in presenting an image of opposition, producers and entrepreneurs cater to an imagined adolescent audience.

In extreme sport, New Zealand is abundantly represented. Queenstown, New Zealand calls itself the "Adventure Sports Capital of the World," and many of our authors claim some tie to New Zealand. New Zealand boasts itself as the originary of bungee jumping; further, New Zealand's pioneering ideology insists that events like "adventure racing and expedition epics" have become a popularly-represented part of the histories that Martha Bell relates in her chapter.

"Board" sports (surfing, skysurfing, kayaking, skiing, windsurfing, snowboarding, et al.) are basic to extreme sports. Sydnor uses philosopher Gilles Deleuze's new cultural-aesthetic of sport— "the basic thing is how to get taken up in the movement of a big wave, a column of rising air, to 'come between' rather than to be the origin of an effort"[30]—to theoretically grasp the new sport of skysurfing.

Speed, time, and temporal issues are central to the ontology of alternative sport. Virilio states, "Speed is not a phenomenon but a relationship between phenomena."[31] In contemporary culture, there is increased speed of transmissions (that is, how fast we are witness to seeing, learning, and reading about alternative sports), increased speed of actions and exchanges (many alternative sports are performed at full speed, "fast"); increased "megalopolitan hyperconcentration"[32] (for example, our rapidly expanding cityscapes as venues for alternative sports, such as skateboarding or B.A.S.E. jumping). How, for example, does the Gravity Boarding Company's Hyper-Carve—a skateboard with a digital readout on the nose that indicates the current and maximum speed[33]—serve as an exemplar for theorizing new sports vis a vis "speed" at the beginning of the twenty-first century?

There is a moral and ethical discussion threaded within this anthology. All extreme sports are thrill-seeking activities to which psychologies of danger and excitement, and traditions of Judeo-Christian and Eastern theological and philosophical interpretation, may be applied. Do these sports put one's life in danger? Mounet and Chifflet's chapter examines the danger of white water sports, showing how a "standardized" sport paradoxically elides danger with the illusions of freedom and "extreme" for its "clients."

Is one of the main points of extreme sports to risk one's life?[34] And if so, is risking one's own life inherently wrong? In most cases, risking life might be a side effect of some extreme sports, and not the point of all extreme sports. To be courageous can be a vice or a virtue: rational and responsible training and performance in extreme sports, attempting to do a thing well, using talents to the fullest capacity of one's ability, entertaining others, fulfilling promoters' and fans' expectations, and even asceticism and self-mortification may characterize righteous and honorable dimensions of extreme sports for some participants. In many of the chapters of this book, authors are quick to point out that extreme athletes are not lunatics or daredevils, but meticulous performers, giving themselves to some lofty art form. Example: Brett Downs, in "Small Bikes, Big Men," writes, "we are just another group of athletes . . . we don't call ourselves Extreme. We are just riders."

Indeed, David Sansone's definition of sport includes "the ritual sacrifice of human physical energy"; the athlete is both sacrificer and victim.[35] Such a definition helps us to understand the universal essence of sport as it manifests itself today in versions extreme—and as it did in much earlier times, in mystic ways that connect the athlete and audience with ineffable meanings of life and universe. David Dornian evokes such noble associations when he writes of "climbers swimming against a universal current."

Self-exultation, self-centeredness, showing off, bragging and hedonism may frame the being of some extreme athletes and the ontology of the sport forms themselves. How do these attributes correspond to the virtues—such as humility, prudence, and preservation of life—central to the beliefs of many human groups today? For example, Tony Hawk, the infamous extreme skateboarder, has been positively featured in the Christian youth magazine *You!*[36] Is Hawk a sinner or a saint, or just a public figure in a private pose? Or note Arlo Eisenberg's "Psychotic Rant." His opening paragraph describes speaking of himself in the third person, and asks his family and friends to call him "god." Lee Bridgers' chapter, "Out of the Gene Pool and into the Food Chain," uses religious metaphors— "God of Extreme," "Church of Bike," "faith in Bike"—to speak of Bridgers' passionate devotion to risky sport.

X-athletes also describe the excitement of danger, the adrenaline rushes they get from their sports. Ron Watters relates the stories of three deaths on rivers, while simultaneously discussing the commercially-promoted oxymoron of "safe danger."

Within our proem and within this book, we've contemplated alternative sports, inside and out. But there is so much more in the cultural and physical spaces between the inside and out. Writing in 1908, philosopher Henri Bergson reflected upon these spaces of body, motion, mind, and spirit. He wrote of ideas and dreams:

> If the idea is to live, it must touch reality on some side; that is to say, it must be able, from step to step, and by progressive diminutions or contractions of itself, to be more or less acted by the body at the same time as it is thought by the mind. Our body, with the sensations which it receives on the one hand and the movements which it is capable of executing on the other, is then, that which fixes our mind, and gives it ballast and poise.[37]

Similarly, Jim Cotter takes the reader in and out of what he calls "A disturbing mix of hallucinations and deja-vu" as he describes his team's grueling 300 mile Eco-challenge.

What about virtual alternative sport, the cyberworlds of sport? There are already countless video and arcade games/experiences in which the participant's body is interfaced (through keyboard, cathode screen, dataglove, or datasuit) to an extreme sport contest/ performance. Similarly, the philosopher Paul Virilio calls the body the last urban frontier:

> Having been first *mobile*, then *motorized*, man will thus become *motile*, deliberately limiting his body's area of influence to a few gestures, a few impulses, like channel-surfing.[38]

Real space *is* giving way to virtual space. How will the glory of the physicality of sport of this past century be perfected in such space? In *Beyond a Boundary*, C. L. R. James anticipates this question. James writes:

> I believe that the examination of the stroke, the brilliant piece of fielding, will take us through mysticism to far more fundamental considerations than mere life-enhancing. We respond to physical action or vivid representation of it, dead or alive, because we are made that way.[39]

Other examinations—including studies of the physical inventions, evolution, materials, and technologies of alternative sports and sports equipment of recent decades—are likely to bear on the sports themselves. For example, in his account of his life-long surfing sojourn, Greg Page observes how telephones, faxes, pages, live videofeeds and knowledge of the world's surf and weather patterns make the odds of scoring big waves much better now than in the 1960s.[40]

The technologies are cutting edge. Just as running shoes revolutionized track and cross-country, kayaks constructed of the new material hypalon[41] and snowboard cores made of piezoelectrics instead of synthetic rubber are the stuff of the sport of our new times.[42]

Very soon, the above descriptions of cybersport, surf forecasts, new-age sports equipment and piezoelectrics will be dated and inconsequential (one time the bicycle was considered a revolutionary fusion of human and machine[43]). But for now, we can simply wonder at this fascinating thing, this dilemma called sport, this human spectacle-art-performance-contest-poetic that for countless centuries manifests itself on our Earth, and now also in our waters, skies, and virtual screens, in ways different, radical, and invigorating, afresh yet somehow also the same.

Notes

1. Kevin Brooker, ESPN. *Way Inside ESPN'S X Games* (New York: Hyperion/ESPN Books, 1998, p. 23). See also Dick Wimer (ed.), *The Extreme Game: An Extreme Sports Anthology* (Short Hills, NJ: Burford Books, 2001).

2. Debra Pressey, "Extreme Sports is New Name of Game: Firm Based in Champaign Supplies Protective Gear for Thrills and Spills Crowd," *The News Gazette*, Sunday January 25, 1998, pp. C-1, 3.

3. John Rofe, "An Extremely Profitable Niche: 'X' Sports Boom has Companies Eager to Ride on the Wild Side," *Street & Smith's Sportsbusiness Journal*, November 9–15, 1998, pp. 20–31.

4. Sal Ruibal, "X-tremely Overexposed? Burnout Likely Without Changes," *USA Today*, June 23, 1999, pp. C 1–2.

5. In summer 1999, the Disney Channel introduced "Z Games," a show that highlights crazy sports invented by kids.

6. Susanna Howe, *Sick: A Cultural History of Snowboarding* (New York: St. Martin's Griffin, 1998), p. 107.

7. Ibid., p. 114.

8. Stephen Duncombe, *Notes from Underground: Zines and the Politics of Popular Culture* (New York and London: Verso, 1998).

9. Allen Guttmann, *From Ritual to Record* (New York: Columbia University Press, 1978). Of record-keeping, Guttmann writes that it is "the marvelous abstraction that permits competition not only among those gathered together on the field of sport but also among them and others distant in time and space" (p. 51).

10. Bill Brown, "The Meaning of Baseball in 1992 (with Notes on the Post American)," *Public Culture*, vol. 4, no. 1, Fall 1991, p. 55.

11. Ibid., p. 57.

12. "Peak Performance," *Vogue*, March 1998, p. 95.

13. AXN, Fox Network, "The Sky is My Canvas," Nov. 28, 1998. For a larger list of alternative sport forms, see Robert E. Rinehart, "~~Emerging~~ Arriving Sport: Alternatives to Formal Sports," in Jay Coakley and Eric Dunning (eds.), *Handbook of Sports Studies* (London: Sage, 2000), pp. 504–519).

14. Recall the recent beer commercials that featured outlandish amalgamated imaginary sports such as sumo-diving and ski-jumping from a lazy-chair.

15. Andrew W. Miracle, Jr., and C. Roger Rees, *Lessons of the Locker Room: The Myth of School Sports* (Amherst NY: Prometheus Books), pp. 11–56, 221–229.

16. C. L. R. James, *Beyond a Boundary* (New York: Pantheon Books, 1963), p. 197.

17. See Walter Benjamin's essay "The Work of Art in the Age of Mechanical Reproduction," in *Illuminations* (New York: Schocken, 1969 [1936]), for an earlier examination of how technology impinges upon audience perception and production of life activities.

18. Example: "What music is going through your mind as you perform?" (answer: "Limp Bizkit"): 1999 live telecast interview of skateboarder at Summer X-Games. This technique, of humanizing the athletes, of course parallels NBC's strategy for Olympic broadcasts to show more human-interest stories.

19. For example, Carolyn Ellis and Arthur P. Bochner (eds.), *Composing Ethnography: Alternative Forms of Qualitative Writing* (Walnut Creek, Calif. and London: Alta Mira Press, 1996); Harry F. Wolcott, *The Art of Fieldwork* (Walnut Creek, Calif. and London: Alta Mira Press, 1995); Dennis Tedlock and Bruce Mannheim, *The Dialogic Emergence of Culture* (Urbana and Chicago: University of Illinois Press, 1995); Norman K. Denzin,

Interpretive Ethnography: Ethnographic Practices for the 21st Century (Thousand Oaks, Calif. and London: Sage Publications, 1997); Hélène Cixous, *Coming to Writing and Other Essays* (Cambridge, Mass., and London: Harvard University Press, 1991); Genévieve Rail and Jean Harvey (eds.), *Sport and Postmodern Times* (Albany: State University of New York Press, 1998).

20. George H. Sage, *Power and Ideology in American Sport: A Critical Perspective* (Champaign, Ill.: Human Kinetics Books, 1990), p. 11.

21. Ibid., p. 10.

22. See Ellen J. Langer, *Mindfulness* (Cambridge, Mass.: Perseus Books, 1989).

23. Edward Bruner, "Tourism, Creativity, and Authenticity," *Studies in Symbolic Interaction*, 1989, vol. 10, p. 13.

24. Robert E. Rinehart, *Players All: Performances in Contemporary Sport* (Bloomington: Indiana University Press, 1998); Malcolm Crick, "Representations of International Tourism in the Social Sciences: Sun, Sex, Sights, Savings and Servility," *Annual Review of Anthropology*, 1989, vol. 18, pp. 307–344; John Bale, *Landscapes of Modern Sport* (New York: St. Martin's Press, 1994); Judith Adler, "Origins of Sightseeing," *Annals of Tourism Research*, 1989, vol. 16, pp. 7–29; Umberto Eco, *Travels in Hyperreality* (San Diego: Harcourt Brace Jovanovich, 1986).

25. See Mikhail Bakhtin, *Rabelais and His World* (H. Iswolsky, trans.) (Bloomington, Ind.: Indiana University Press, 1984), for an especially penetrating examination of role reversal as a culturally historical trope.

26. See John Dorst, *The Written Suburb: An American Site, An Ethnographic Dilemma* (Philadelphia: The University of Pennsylvania Press, 1989). Dorst looks at the mundane as a site of potential discovery.

27. Jonathan Culler, "The Semiotics of Tourism," in Culler, *Framing the Sign* (Normal and London: University of Oklahoma Press, 1988), pp. 155, 158.

28. For example, Johan Huizinga, *Homo Ludens: A Study of the Play Element in Culture* (Boston: The Beacon Press, 1950); Bernard Suits, *The Grasshopper: Games, Life and Utopia* (Boston: David R. Godine Publisher, 1990; first published in 1978 by University of Toronto Press); Jack M. Roberts, Malcolm J. Arth, and Robert R. Bush, "Games in Culture," *American Anthropologist*, 1959, vol. 61, 597–605.

29. Such clearly sexist statements abound in merchandising like MTV Sports or ESPN X-Games highlights videos.

30. Gilles Deleuze, "Mediators," in Jonathan Crary and Sanford Kwinter (eds.), *Incorporations* (New York: Urzone Inc., 1992), p. 281. See also Ian Borden, *Skateboarding, Space and the City: Architecture and the Body* (Oxford: Berg, 2001).

31. Paul Virilio, *Open Sky* (Julie Rose, trans.) (London and New York: Verso, 1997), p. 12.

32. Ibid.

33. Bob Parks, "Fetish: Transition," *Wired*, April 1998, p. 51.

34. See "Cheating Death," segment on "Goin' Deep," Fox Sports Network, produced by Alex Flanagan; March 5, 2000.

35. David Sansone, *Greek Athletics and the Genesis of Sport* (Berkeley and Los Angeles: University of California Press, 1988).

36. "Hawk Man: Tony Hawk Doesn't Need Wings, He's Got Wheels," *You!* Nov./Dec. 1998, p. 14. The cover of this magazine declares: "Skateboarding's Not a Crime: We Asked the Expert Why." At the end of the one-page article, there was an editor's note:

> Tony's publicist informed us that he had a faith life; so of
> course we bit the hook. We were all surprised by his hesitation
> to answer faith questions . . . What about preparing for events
> physically, emotionally and spiritually, I asked. Well, he skipped
> the spiritual part.

37. Henri Bergson, *Matter and Memory* (New York: Zone books, 1991 [originally published 1901]), p. 173.

38. Virilio, *Open Sky*, p. 17.

39. C. L. R. James, *Beyond a Boundary* (New York: Pantheon Books, 1963), p. 203. Interestingly, one of James' chapters contemplates Tolstoy's famous question "What is art?" in light of sport performance.

40. Obviously, tow-in surfing, where jet skis tow a surfer to and rescue him/her from, gigantic waves, owes much of its existence to this technological leap for sport.

41. "Fetish," *Wired*, Nov. 1997, p. 80.

42. "Piezoelectrics absorb and dissipate vibrations that cause the snowboard to chatter and lose contact with the snow by converting vibrations into electricity that is dissipated through the board's core as heat and light; amazingly, the units are smart to selectively distinguish between harmful vibrations and good vibrations, such as subtle commands from the snowboarder's feet." Sean Wagstaff, "Street Cred: Smooth in the Crud," *Wired*, April 1998, p. 129.

43. Vernon Chadwick, Institute for the Living South, Memphis, Tenn., posted on April 28, 1999, to the cultstud-l@nosferatu.cas.usf.edu list.

ROLLERBLADING

 Chapter Two

Psychotic Rant

Arlo Eisenberg

This is my disclaimer. This is your warning. Arrogance has been so stigmatized that it is difficult to be successful or confident without feeling guilty or feeling compelled to apologize for it. I am confident, I have been successful, I refer to myself in the third person as "The Arlo," and I ask friends and family to call me "god." I make no apologies. What follows is an egocentric observation on the state of rollerblading.

I was lucky to discover rollerblading before it had really caught on. Of course, rollerblading was lucky that I discovered it because I devoted my life to making sure that it caught on. Inline skating by itself already had a lot going for it; it was fast, fun, athletic, graceful, and easy to learn. On just its intrinsic qualities alone, rollerblading would have gone far. It was destined to permeate every middle- to upper-class household in the world. But I saw an even greater opportunity in rollerblading. As long as there was a vehicle that was capable of infiltrating mainstream culture on such a major scale, why not project some not so intrinsic qualities onto it and try to affect mainstream culture?

Rollerblading's timing couldn't have been better. It is incredible, first of all, that an idea so inevitable as ice skating on dry land could have taken so long to come to market. After decades of suffering through clumsy, inefficient rollerskates, and despite the centuries that ice skating had been around and prospered, inline

Arlo Eisenberg is one of the most recognizable personalities in aggressive inline skating. He is a former X Games gold medalist, has served as the editor for the sport's most influential publication, *Daily Bread Magazine,* and co-founded Senate Wheels, the leading manufacturer of aggressive skating accessories.

skates became available to the masses only at the end of the 1980s. By all accounts, this concept was as big as bicycles (how many households don't have at least one bicycle?), yet it managed to avoid materialization all the way until the end of the twentieth century. Ice skating on dry land was a predictable, logical evolution of human recreation and transportation, and thanks to the proliferation of paved roads and the development of polyurethane there was nothing to hold the idea back.

Inline skates were released at the height of the media-saturated, trend-hungry, information age. Even bad ideas were able to prosper in this environment—remember those yellow signs hanging from car windows that read "Baby On Board" or "Jesus On Board," or "Baby In Trunk"? Imagine what would happen if you actually had not just a good idea, but a great one.

Inline skates landed on the world like a ton of bricks. It was a full-fledged phenomenon.

I predicted this. And I prepared for it.

By the time I discovered inline skates, when I was sixteen, I had already long since defined myself as a skateboarder. I was young and full of energy and aggression, so the physical act of skateboarding became my outlet for that. But what really drew me to skateboarding was its defiance. I loved how skateboarding was counterculture, how it criticized society and challenged convention—not just through the act of skateboarding, but by creating its own society, complete with its own language, its own music, and its own magazines. An entire culture evolved around the act of skateboarding.

Now skateboarding and its culture are indivisible. It is impossible to have one without the other. It is not enough to ride a skateboard to be a skateboarder—the culture of skateboarding is essential to its definition.

Some limitations of skateboarding were that it was so abrasive, and so antisocial, and it alienated itself so completely from the mainstream society that it made it near impossible to effect any kind of noticeable influence on any society other than its own. Also, aside from the abrasiveness of the culture, the actual act of skateboarding was very difficult, so it made it hard for people to be drawn to the scene in very large numbers.

People who are critical of rollerblading are always quick to point out that it is too easy. It is easier than skateboarding so it must rank lower than skateboarding in the mythical hierarchy of alternative sports, is the logic. It is my contention that accessibility is our greatest asset. When anyone says that rollerblading is too easy, they are actually saying that it is too easy to get into. It is impossible to measure rollerblading based on its limits because it is limitless. Everyone knows how to run, but that does not discount how difficult it is for Michael Johnson to run 200 meters in under twenty seconds. Just because something is easy to do does not necessarily mean that it is easy to take it to its extremes—it just means that you can take it further, quicker.

Unlike skateboarding, the rewards of rollerblading are immediate and consistent. The process of learning to skate on inlines is constantly gratifying so participants are encouraged to stick with it. Already rollerblading had one advantage built into it. But rollerblading was not skateboarding. There was no culture associated with it. It was just recreational activity. So what if the whole world started inline skating; what were the social ramifications of it? None.

Rollerblading—aggressive skating—was designed to be a mutation of skateboarding. The marriage of lifestyle to sport has been skateboarding's legacy and is a prerequisite to any contemporary action sport. Just like every other alternative sport before it and everyone after it, rollerblading took its cue from skateboarding. Unlike any other alternative sport, however, rollerblading has the unique opportunity to take the lifestyle/sport model to the masses.

The conventional wisdom in the unconventional circles of alternative sports is that acceptance by the mainstream is tantamount to death. My argument is that if we infiltrate the mainstream with new progressive ideas and change the mainstream, then we are doing society and ourselves a service. Through rollerblading we have the opportunity to take the ideals of all of the alternative sports to the world.

The social climate is ripe for new ideas. With the Cold War over and no real enemy to speak of, Saddam Hussein and Kenneth Starr notwithstanding, institutions designed to instill team values are no longer as relevant. Respecting authority and being a part of the team made sense when survival depended upon it, but in the absence of a universal evil to rally around, focus has moved away from the team and onto the individual. When it is a matter of life or death, there is a premium placed on winning; it is essential. If it is only a matter of life, then the premium is placed on more personal goals, such as enlightenment and gratification.

Success is no longer measured in terms of team, or wins. Success is measured by how much the individual enjoys the experience. In the football model the individual trains diligently and receives instructions from the coaches, and the reward is in the team's victory, if it should have one, and in the discipline the individual receives (assuming society values discipline). In skateboarding or rollerblading the focus is not on competition, so the goal is not to win and the concept of training becomes obsolete. The reward is in the enjoyment the individual derives from the act of skating and in the camaraderie of the lifestyle.

The success of alternative sports is a testament to this new social environment. Children are deciding in growing numbers that they prefer action sports to the team-oriented sports that their parents played. More than any other action sport, rollerblading is prepared to accommodate this influx of new participants.

Of all of the action sports, skateboarding, freestyle bmx, and rollerblading have the most mainstream potential because they can all be used for transportation and they can be used anywhere, unlike action sports such as surfing or snowboarding, which require an ocean or a mountain. Of all the "big three," rollerblading has the most mainstream potential because it is the easiest, and it has the most user-friendly image. Rollerblading's image is both an advantage and a liability, however.

Because rollerblading was new, we had the advantage of being able to review the action sports that came before us as we were attempting to define ourselves. We were able to borrow from what we thought were the best elements of the other action sports and we tried to steer clear of what we perceived to be weaknesses. In my vision, I wanted rollerblading to be rebellious. I wanted there to be an emphasis on the artistry of rollerblading as opposed to the athleticism. I valued style over difficulty. All of these qualities can be traced directly back to skateboarding. One thing that we tried to do differently, however, was to encourage as many people to participate in rollerblading as possible. We didn't want to undermine the built-in advantage of having such an accessible sport by making it an exclusive club like skateboarding.

For all of the advantages that our youth as a sport has afforded us, it has also been our biggest burden. Never mind the typical growing pains—the issues of credibility and acceptance from our peers will work themselves out over time. What we may not be able to recover from is the effect of the mainstream media on our identity. Without the advantage of decades of history to establish ourselves, we are the most malleable of all of the alternative sports. That fact, combined with the huge following rollerblading's unique accessibility has provided us, makes us a prime target for mainstream media eager to reach a new audience without losing an old one.

Since rollerblading was designed to infiltrate the mainstream, mainstream media is a necessary and valuable ally, but if the mainstream media is able to distort rollerblading's image to such a degree that it no longer represents the ideals it was designed to promote, then what is the value in the exposure? This dilemma has become the greatest challenge facing rollerblading.

As rollerblading's popularity grows, so do its pockets. Major sponsors eager to reach our coveted demographic are jumping in dollars first and they are making waves. The problem is not the sponsors or their money; we need them, in fact, if we want to grow. The problem is our age. Without a solid foundation to stand on, we always run the risk of caving in. When sponsors make suggestions or demands, without clearly defined parameters established through years of steady growth to fall back on, we are more susceptible to compromise. Compromise at a glance does not look like such a bad thing, but when it is compromise after compromise after compromise, eventually we run the risk of compromising away everything that we believed in.

Skateboarding's bastard offspring that had such lofty aspirations for the virtues of the alternative sports underground is now a sleek, high-powered, made-for-television machine. Rollerblading is reaching the masses all right, but what is it saying? Who is controlling it? The answer is disturbing. We are letting our sport be defined by the people who have the things that we think we want. We have become consumed with our success, and are so eager to keep it going that we have lost sight of how we used to measure success.

The television producers are defining rollerblading now; the corporate sponsors are. Our parents are defining rollerblading. What was once an alternative to football is fast becoming a replacement for it. The focus in rollerblading is moving away from the personal goals of the individual and quickly moving toward winning championships and training to win championships.

How do we get it back? First we have to want it back. We have to want to change the world rather than want to be absorbed into it. We have to value innovation above athleticism. We have to be confident and arrogant. We have to make demands. We have to not be afraid of challenging convention, but committed to it. We must not be content. We must challenge. We must fight. No one knows better than we do what we want, so why let anyone else try to give it to us? Turn off the television. Turn out the lights. Kill your parents. No apologies. No apollo jesus.

Chapter Three

Dropping into Sight

Commodification and Co-Optation of In-Line Skating

Robert E. Rinehart

> "Since the [X] Games, we're already seeing aggressive skating more in the public eye. I don't know if that's good or bad. It has created a whole professional class of rock-star-like people."
>
> Shura McComb,
> cited in Lisa Feinberg Densmore (p. 37)

Nobody really knows where it will peak—or even *if* it will end. There are guesses by journalists, by media moguls and corporate seers, by kids swarming like locusts over the urban landscape, gathering on the streets and in the parks and meandering in sanctioned and non-sanctioned areas, by people betting their livelihood on it and by people only marginally interested: when might this media blitz of alternative sports, of wakeboarding, barefoot jumping, sportclimbing, skateboarding, snowboarding, windsurfing, and in-line skating—and more—abate?

Is the cultural formation that is "extreme" sports a fad that will end with the maturation of Gen X, or might it prophesy a paradigmatic shift in how western societies view sport? Will a new sport ethic gradually supersede the current highly competitive one? Does extreme sport foretell a global sport ethic, or is it a Westernized phenomenon, pretty much confined to English-speaking, colonized sport culture? Does performing the sports—that is, the actual activities themselves—drive the *need* for the sports, or might this relatively new, alternative sport culturescape be driven by a cynical, mass-produced, media-oriented, economically-based cultural blitz that must have new and younger consumers in order to survive?[1] Are there significant differences among the new extreme sports, or do the sports follow similar patterns of status—emerging, resisted, grudgingly accepted, mainstreamed (or dominant), passé, obsolete—and are they merely at different stages of very similar processes?[2] Can we look at these sports as creating effects upon culture and in turn being created by cultural effects as profoundly as other cultural formations and artifacts have? Such cultural formations might include media, multinational corporations, or political/ideological movements. Obviously, alternative sports are interwoven with other cultural formations; any attempts to sort out the threads of each result in a less-than-accurate view of the alternative sportscape.

These questions are important ones, and, in this chapter, I can only hope to touch on them, primarily through the case of in-line skating.[3] The questions assume a complex 'constellation' of interrelationships, which I may only hope to better expose through discussion. As Walter Benjamin is said to have written to Theodore Adorno, "The great book of the future . . . will consist of fragments torn from the body of other work; it is a reassembly, a patchwork quilt of meanings already accomplished."[4]

My main 'reassembly' in this chapter will be to examine the intersections between individuals, groups, and corporations that were involved with in-line skating in the late 1990s and that resulted in the coproduction of a variety of commodities within this new alternative sport market niche. The process of commodification is surely not one-way (that is, for example, the "Big Bad Corporations" imposing structure on the solitary, rugged individual), nor is it necessarily even top-down in nature, with its effects percolating from the corporation to the individual. Rather, corporations produce commodities, and become inextricably linked with them; and individuals work, as, most consciously, did Michael Jordan in the NBA[5] and Tony Hawk in skateboarding, to establish their 'icon' status.

Though sports icons still are relegated to types, the generalized mythos of the westernized, Americanized 'hero' has lost a bit of allure, a bit of credibility, so that 'general truths'—in this case, stereotypes—slightly miss the mark for most consumers, and are thus replaced by more specific stories which reflect actual lived circumstances. Our heroes have been shown to be fallible. Indeed, the dynamic, mediated process between positive icon-making and negative destruction of the icon was standard procedure in the 1990s: from the capitalistically driven multinational media, both good and bad examples make for good 'stories.'

This is not to say that cultural tropes have ceased to exist (at least in the public's imagination), but rather, that the assumed homogeneity and totalization of audience is no longer a credible assumption, though an increasingly homogeneous media attempts to portray totalized audiences. As Kusz, in this volume, points out, the lack of discussion creates an impression of racial, ethnic, gender, and other standardizations that simply do not exist outside arbitrary partitions.[6] The tacit assumption that the audience is "like us" is fraught with problems which go beyond the scope of this chapter: however, as Fiske writes, "the networks . . . were irredeemably Fordist—they had grown and prospered by attracting the largest and least differentiated audiences possible."[7] And sport television followed the same strategy, though, as Fiske (1989) has also demonstrated, dominant or preferred readings are buoyed by resistant and oppositional readings of televisual texts.[8]

Individual Athlete and Corporate Strategies

> ESPN II is now broadcasting a two-and-a-half hour summary of the Games.
> The broadcasters sit in their chairs and tell the tale of the past week's events.
> They keep saying words like "rad" and "stoked."
> They can't help themselves sound like anything but a bunch of idiots.
>
> —Mike Opalek, 1997

The 'cult of personality,' which sport teams—and marketing agencies and their executives—are seeking to create, has changed much of the sportscape. As agent David Falk states, " . . . most of the professional leagues—certainly in America, in basketball, football, baseball—are really promoting the superstars, rather than promoting the institutions of the teams."[9] Sports writer Terry Pluto, in the same discussion, pointed out that

> sports agents . . . desperately want to turn their clients into these megastar, celebrity types who have their own television commercials for T-shirts or caps or Gatorade or any sort of products you could think, where you turn these guys into glorified hucksters.

The trickle-down effect of these mainstream-sport strategies upon more marginalized sports like in-line skating encourages athletes who want to remain viable in their sport to create their own marketing personality. Also, it encourages the very wealthy to hire agencies to help them with their commercial image. Within extreme sports, projected incomes make this very feasible for the top tier of recognizable sports stars.

For more individual sports (such as extreme sports as opposed to team sports like NBA basketball[10]), the strategy may be a good one, albeit decidedly calculated. The problems of this 'cult of personality'—or icon-making process—may be that the athletes literally give up their own 'agency' when they sign with agents, or when they sign with corporations. This, of course, may be antithetical to the claimed ideologies—like freedom, individuality, and an ethos proclaiming an aesthetic lifestyle—for many extreme sports and sport extremists.

Athletes occasionally emulate, without the strong ideological and historical backdrop of 'sanctified' sport (that is, mainstream sport—whose legitimacy is rarely questioned), professional wrestlers in their hucksterism.[11] Thus, they risk destroying the credibility that they may have spent much of their young adult lives fostering. As in sports television strategies, the athlete's personality becomes constructed, with shrewd aims at marketing strategies, for the least common denominator: that is, the largest market. And, ironically, athletes may be giving up that part of themselves that they most sought to find through alternative sports: their freedom.

Still, the processes of icon making and commodification are interdependent. In fact, many of the athletes *seek* to become commodities, finding lucrative careers through the process. This process is not unlike a symbiotic relationship, where companies, consumers, and individual athletes alike share (but not equally) in the profits. Many of the athletes, in fact, represent smaller corporations: for example, Arlo Eisenberg started Senate, and Angie Walton publishes *Daily Bread*. Consumers do get something from these relationships, not the least of which is a shared lifestyle with famous athletes (status), a use of product (identity), and cultural capital. But the consumer-athlete nexus is a constructed one, one in which both athlete and corporate strategies conspire to create a market of celebrity.

Even though snowboarding and other 'extreme' sports are clearly in different stages of their sports' commodification/incorporation than in-line skating—or, as Ingham, Loy, Guttmann, and Pearson put it more broadly, the sports' "institutionalization"—

some parallels do exist.[12] Jake Burton (of Burton Snowboards), himself a snowboarding icon, said, "We put a real premium on having athletes on our team that can give us input into and help us develop products and at the same time show people what the product is capable of doing."[13]

Whether enviously or deprecatingly (and therein lies the dilemma for in-line skaters), in-line skater/writer Mike Opalek commented that "when ESPN mentions skateboarding, Tony Hawk's name follows."[14] When individual athlete's names are recognizable, image becomes paramount. In an in-line skating magazine, the mention of just the first names of Arlo (Eisenberg), Chris (Mitchell), Aaron (Feinberg), and Brazilian female skater Fabiola holds for the skating generation clout similar to that which Cher, Madonna, and Elvis hold for babyboomers.[15] Thus does the corporation—ESPN, Disney, or X Games' sponsors Slim Jim, VISA, and the US Marines—sell individual 'image,' not unlike how Nike sells the "swoosh, [which] serves as a form of cultural capital."[16]

At the same time that the corporation deliberately builds up celebrity sportspersons, the athletes profit financially (albeit to a lesser degree) by utilizing cutting-edge technology, by remaining viable in their sport, and by increased opportunities for image-making and commercial exposure. But they also have done something differently from many mainstream athletes: they have become intertwined with the industry of extreme sports itself.

Arlo Eisenberg is a good (though certainly not singular) example: he formed Senate, worked as writer/editor of *Daily Bread*, has numerous sponsorship deals, is involved in video projects (for example, T-Bone Films), has traveled the world skating and promoting, co-owns his family's skatepark in Plano, Texas, and was even recognized by *Newsweek* magazine as one of the top 100 innovators for the new century![17] Most of the individual athletes I mention in this chapter are recognizable by the in-line skating community: by definition, they have intentionally or unintentionally become commodified. The groups—that is, companies, products, and images—as well, are in process of becoming solidified, defined, and reified by media and the strategies of multinational corporations (similar to the Nike "swoosh" emblem). But the trade-offs—for the individual consumers and athletes—clearly come with a price.

As professional skaters[18] find themselves involved more and more in doing the sidelight activities that help their careers, they find that they have less time to skate. This effect, not uncommon to successful mainstream athletes, might be termed the "book tour effect." Super Bowl, World Series, Stanley Cup, and NBA Championship winners annually bemoan this effect; however, in this regard, there is at least one major difference between mainstream and extreme sport: the perceived and real degree of 'play' versus 'work' to which athletes might admit. Mainstream athletes—pros—see their sport primarily as their work; alternative sport professionals still insist their sport is part of their lifestyle, thus still 'fun.' Thus, inliners might see that doing promotions for their sport, being involved in the culture surrounding in-line skating—all of the trappings of the sport—are considered extensions of the in-line lifestyle.

However, increased recognition and demands of secondary sources of income still can impact the actual skating. Skater Donna Dennis-Vano, writing about the women's portion of the 1995 X Games (herself a writer for *Inline*), said, "Angie [Walton, editor of *Daily Bread*] . . . has some of the most unbelievable airs and, in my opinion, the best style."[19] But Densmore is more candid: ". . . with more time at work than on wheels during the last six months, [Walton's] biggest obstacle was fatigue."[20] Despite the physiological downside, skaters Chris Mitchell, Arlo Eisenberg, Shane Coburn, Angie Walton, Brian Konoske, Jess Dyrenforth, Shura McComb, Donna Dennis-Vano, Brandon Hardin, National Master's Ski Championships winner Lisa Feinberg Densmore (crossover athlete)—just to name a few—all have supplemented their income by writing in, photographing for, editing, or publishing in-line magazines.

Skaters also promote themselves (and their sport) through in-person appearances and contests. In Manhattan Beach, California, the *People* Magazine In-Line Skating Spectacular is held annually. According to Esquire, skating entrepreneur Rick Stark,

> . . . whose company, Anywhere Sports Production, produced the show . . . [says,] "The industry has made a mockery of in-line skating. . . . [But] now it's a lot more relaxed and not as choreographed. . . . Our shows allow the skaters to do what they do best and still get paid at the end of the day."[21]

Of course, the insider information that the magazines seek, the efforts of both individual skaters and companies at wedding skilled performers with shows that work, and the authenticity that magazines provide their readership, is similar to product testing by pros. However, the efforts of athletes/skaters to expand their commodity status clearly cuts into their skating time.

But the skating culture—indeed, the 'extreme' phenomenon—as they once knew it is also morphing, changing to fit the demands of a seemingly voracious television audience. Because of this perception, liquor company Heublein dropped sponsorship of the beach volleyball tour in favor of a more cutting-edge, multiple-event amalgam called the Cuervo Gold Board-to-Board Challenge, which combines snowboarding and wakeboarding. Corporate spokesperson Scott Mueller says, "These events [pro beach volleyball] don't deliver the same message anymore. Alternative sports do, and that's where many of our consumers are now."[22] He might have added that future consumers, in the under-age population, are the potential market for Heublein as well. Thus, Heublein's sponsorship of extreme sports serves a double purpose: it educates the young in consumer behaviors regarding both alcohol use and extreme sport.

What is televised for in-line skating has changed, too. In the first X Games (in 1995), for example, distance (10K) in-line skaters were asked by ESPN to run a downhill race, at that time termed a "once-a-year carnival act for a TV event."[23] Since 1995, the views on whether the in-line downhill is appropriate or too dangerous have changed somewhat: Marvin Percival, of speed-skating company Sk8Deal (Andover, Massachusetts), recently explained that his own son is interested in what Percival calls the "extremely dangerous" downhill course. Coming from a speed-skating (as opposed to aggressive-skating) background, he says, gives the skaters and the company a "tremendous amount of credibility."[24] This, of course, translates into a greater acceptance of formerly inappropriate kinds of events like the massed downhill. (Thus are sporting events, over time, naturalized as normative.)

What of the larger corporations supporting in-line skating? What are some of their strategies for success? I e-mailed Roces, an Italian-based extreme in-line skating manufacturer, and the firm's International Team Manager Francesco Mattioli responded to my queries. He claims that the skating itself is what promotes the sport best: "It is always amazing to watch aggressive skaters pulling out incredible tricks on vert ramps or in the street. That is what most of our target [audience] likes and wants to see." Furthermore, "every single skater has [his/her] own character and personality and fits perfectly inside the [aggressive] team." Mattioli is, of course, speaking of professionals who are spokespersons for Roces and who skate using Roces gear. This strategy—of a 'cult of personality' for Roces' team members—is quite lucrative: the professionals' "image . . . can sell millions of dollars of products."[25]

Benetton (which owns Rollerblade® through its Edizione Holding and Benetton Group Spa) has determined that its "Colors of Benetton" image, commercial strategy, and world view, much like that of Nike, will provide social commentary on such issues as AIDS, HIV awareness, peace, and ethnic diversity/tolerance. Thus, Oliviero Toscani (1998) of Benetton writes on Benetton's Web page, "All commercial images have a social meaning and an impact. . . . advertising is very influential in the education of our young."[26] Lurking behind these rhetorically charged words is a (benign/malignant?) corporate strategy of coercion couched in the rhetoric of education. Yet it mirrors a strategy of constant change: "Research? We try to do the very opposite. We try to make ours ads personal."[27] This also reflects NBC's overt strategy to bring more human interest stories to the 1996 Atlanta Olympics television audience, and is clearly a corporate strategy of humanizing and making a more personal connection between advertiser and consumer.[28]

In this way, the company (using an artistic strategy of new and interesting—and newsworthy, notable, or shocking and revolting combinations—such as the photo of a nun and a priest kissing) pulls in audience (that is, potential consumers) that identifies with the *image* of the product—not just with the product. And the company drives consumers to identify with the people and social issues behind their product. Consumers, thus, can become satisfied, after the point of sale, because they did not merely buy sports clothing (which is marginally self-centered)—they contributed to a movement for world peace, or to tolerance between races, or to any of a vast array of socially conscious causes simply by buying the product. Additionally, they become emotionally linked to the stories of their own beneficence, and seek to regain positive affect again and again (in this way, former one-time consumers might become lifelong consumers). Products come and go: identification with image can last several lifetimes—and by ensuring identification with image (and, by extension, with the company itself), corporations seek to ensure long-term consumer loyalty.

Cole and Hribar (1995) have explored Nike's strategic use of feminism to gain North American women's product loyalty. They point out that Nike has created its own type of celebrity feminism:

In a historical moment marked by absence of movement feminism, celebrity feminism and popular feminism appear to fill the void by representing politics in the spaces where power and lifestyle intersect. (p. 365)

Nike, of course, has promoted similar social strategies with other groups, not the least of which was their P.L.A.Y campaign, presumably directed toward children (but really toward adult consumers in the name of children). P.L.A.Y. is an acronym for "Participate in the Lives of America's Youth," and is a strategy to introduce the Nike psyche to both present and future consumers. Where loyalty by athletes and fans used to be to teams (and vice versa), loyalty now is with and for products and the cultural capital that accrues from alignment with brands and images.[29]

And, of course, the in-line skating industry and its athletes understand the logic of successful marketing strategies. Thus, ESPN, Fox, and the skating magazines work to individualize and highlight successful in-line skaters like Aaron Feinberg, knowing that fans identify more strongly with people they feel they know; fans who identify with an individual are more likely to emulate the individual's purported use of brand products.

One of the differences between mainstream sports' stars endorsements of brands and in-line skaters' endorsements is the product itself. Mainstream athletes can endorse a vast array of product lines, so that former 49er quarterback Joe Montana (following Joe Namath) endorses Flex-All®, an analgesic balm. However, most in-line skaters' endorsements are for products/brands/images directly related to in-line skating. This may be due to the developmental stage of in-line as opposed to the ready acceptance of mainstream sports: in-liners need to continue to sell their *sport* rather than themselves.

But the distinction between 'counterculture' and resistant to more mainstream is quickly eroding. Often the personal strategies of in-liners—utilized so that athletes may remain involved in the sport, and marry their passion for in-line with their need for income—also reflect a more global strategy. Skaters believe that their sport is in its infancy, and that they must involve themselves in the direction it may take. Control over the sport is important to these athletes, yet it sometimes is in opposition to corporate aims.

Distinguishing Between Medias

Clearly, the impact of electronic media is quite different from that of the written media (newspapers, magazines, 'zines). The goals of the two are not necessarily similar, either.[30] While television and video are visual, the written media retell stories, presumably rely on more in-depth coverage,[31] demonstrate a more multivocal array

of stances, and find different angles to reanalyze what television
has provided sensorily and with immediacy.

Weaver discusses the standard news story, both on TV and in
the newspaper. He writes of a paradox of sorts: the television news
broadcast presents "a unified whole," a thematic block produced
for easy digestion, whereas the newspaper is made up of "a diverse,
numerous, often inchoate aggregate."[32] Newspapers are multivocal;
television demonstrates a univocal point of view. Despite this,
Weaver claims that television's "stories" are more in-depth and
experiential: television reportage

> is more analytical, which more consistently and insistently
> goes beneath and beyond the surface of events to exhibit
> the larger trends and meanings of current affairs, which
> achieves the more integrated and coherent exposition of
> the reporter's findings, and which constitutes the more
> flexible and sophisticated reportorial instrumentality.[33]

This depth is, of course, largely from an attempted singular point
of view.

While he writes about the differences between television and
newspaper reportage (and emotional involvement of the "viewer"),
Weaver does not, however, discuss affective difference between
magazine (whose temporal lag from the moment of 'news' is much
greater than that of both TV and newspapers) and television reportage. And Weaver reduces the discussion to unified audience stances.
However, a unified audience stance is a fiction.[34]

There are other differences, differences in strategies of the
media: for example, the 'hero-making' machines of both types of
media are qualitatively different. Skaters are aware of this strategy
for co-optation: *In-Line: The Skate Magazine* discussed the electronic media in a cover story titled "espn's extreme games baits the
hook with cash and credibility: the hero machine."[35]

However, Arlo Eisenberg says, "The hero you need for ESPN
is different than the hero for *Big Brother* [a skating magazine published by Larry Flynt]. Most people can identify with all the heroes
on ESPN. In the magazines, they still are [distinguishable] personalities."[36] In other words, on television, the icons/heroes have taken
on generalizable, more mainstream, status; in the magazines, they
are more niche types.

How does this difference possibly reflect any kind of reality?
In many ways, it doesn't (while simultaneously creating new reali-

ties and new approaches to old realities). For the most part, the images—of products, and now athletes as products or representations of brands—are media imaginings, images that have become almost caricatures of the athletes themselves. Still, they are viable and profitable methods of gaining audience—and selling product.

For television, whose raison d'être is to reach the largest number of potential buyers possible, privileging the dominant, usually nonoffensive sides of athletes is a solid strategy. Television's use of mainstream ideologies, with occasional "reality-enforcing" oppositions, attempts to position athletes as authentic,[37] while simultaneously accessible to a wider variety of audiences. This can be a difficult and tenuous proposition, yet, with the prior knowledge (and expectations) of the sports-television-viewing public, the amalgam of styles can be accomplished. Of course, the overall effect of a given broadcast—or a series of broadcasts—is what becomes mainstream: the totality of ESPN's *X Games* promotes an ideology of kids out having a good time, doing incredibly athletic moves on fairly new implements (in-line skates), and making their way through adolescence in a societally-benign manner. Individual skaters may be deemed "bad boys," or "outsiders," but of course that is a requisite stance for mainstream America: the underdog, the misunderstood teenager, the (usually male) kid who is trying to rise above 'his' anger. So, again, this 'type' is relegated into a larger 'multifaceted society' that is presumably reflected in the *X Games'* broadcasts.[38]

The strategy follows one the NBA and Nike and Reebok have used for years: show different 'personalities' of players to create fan identification with a pantheon of stars as reflected in a variety of lines (shoes being the easy example): David Robinson ("clean-cut All American US Naval Academy"), Michael Jordan ("the greatest basketball player ever"), Charles Barkley ("outspoken, honest to a fault, brash"), Dennis Rodman ("odd, hard-working role player who is always in trouble with authority but has a heart of gold"), and so on. But overall, the NBA and the shoe companies have submitted for consumer approval a picture supposedly reflective of American diversity and even, presumably, of tolerance for difference.

In-line skating has followed that strategy, though not so successfully, both globally (on ESPN and Fox Sports) and locally, within the 'subculture' of skating, and in the 'zines. In the skating magazines, the continual education of consumers is fundamental to their identification with any individual skaters. So, magazines have spent a lot of time establishing stars and potential icons. The profile is a staple of each month's issue. Magazines are currently—of course, informally—in the process of establishing rough hierarchies of these stars. And, as in mainstream sport, enthusiasts will claim that the hierarchies are solely based on the tricks each person can perform—but of course in establishing heroes in the magazines, personality, attitude, style all matter a great deal. Out on the street, performance and bravura matter more, but in the magazines, words reflecting mores are critical. Presentation of self in interviews establishes hierarchies. But a few stars have already become in-line role-niche icons: the ever-present Arlo Eisenberg ("one of the pioneers of skating"), the successful teenager Aaron Feinberg ("won the X Games on his sixteenth birthday—and bought a car"), and women's skater Angie Walton ("an entrepreneur who publishes *Daily Bread*").

Women skaters, not surprisingly but sadly, are not in great demand from corporate sponsors or from the media.[39] But, more distinct personality types—both men and women, boys and girls—are beginning to emerge as ways to establish identities for the skaters with which the consuming public may identify.

Mickey Mouse on Rollerblades®?

Though Benetton, Roces, and Nike all have sought product identification in the in-line skating industry, the Disney Corporation, by virtue of its sport-related media acquisitions (in 1995, ABC, ESPN, and ESPN2), seems to be the most highly-visible corporate player championing in-line skating. Why? Disney, as parent company (with its acquisition of Capital Cities/ABC), controls a vast array of product-dissemination outlets from its movie/product tie-ins with McDonald's (including Happy Meals) to its Disney *Adventures for Children* magazine to its Web pages for children to the chain of mall-related Disney Stores to its theme parks and sports concerns (not only ABC Sports, ESPN, and ESPN2, but also the California Angels and NHL Anaheim Ducks). Disney also paid $600 million for a five-year deal with the National Hockey League, which was 2.6 times the existing contract. Disney now has exclusive cable rights, "rights to more than 100 games for ESPN International . . . and use of footage at ESPN's restaurants and stores."[40]

Disney has consistently utilized a 'synergistic' strategy in which a variety of arms of the corporation intertextually promote one another, geometrically rather than additively increasing the whole of consumer exposure and recognition. The golden arches of McDonald's have combined with the silhouetted ears of Mickey Mouse, producing an extremely powerful, and relatively unchallenged, educational model for present and future consumers.

ESPN's presentation of extreme sports is pervasive, powerful, and persuasive. There certainly is competition for the 'image' of in-line within the competition for extreme sports themselves, from such various entities as multinational media corporations, including Disney, ESPN, and ABC, as well as Rupert Murdoch's Fox Network; from international and national publishers of fanzines such as *In-Line: The Skate Magazine, Daily Bread*, and *Speed Skating Times: International Inline & Ice Speed Skating News*; and from producers of equipment, apparel, and memorabilia such as Senate, Roces, Benetton, Rollerblade, Verducci, Nike, Fiction Clothing, T-Bone Films, and Salomon. However, Disney, through ESPN (and, of course, ESPN2), has effectively cornered the broadcast market for extreme sports programming.

In fact, in 1996, live attendance at ESPN's X Games was estimated to be 201,350; in 1997, the attendance increased to 219,900. Attendance is free: crowd shots are important for television to convey an image of ardent support. In 1997, between ESPN, ESPN2, ESPN International, and ABC's Wide World of Sports, the *X Games* were given thirty-seven hours of coverage; additionally, ESPN reached 71 million households; ESPN2 reached 48 million; and ESPN International was broadcast in 198 countries in twenty-one languages.[41] ESPN and ESPN2, respectively, pulled in 0.7 and 0.5 ratings for the 1998 *X Games*. ABC captured a 2.3 audience rating in 1997 and a 1.6 rating in 1998.[42]

ESPN's images of extreme sports (via the vehicle of the *X Games*) have gained cultural cachet and produced relatively homogeneous and dominant messages of what extreme sports constitute and how extreme sports (and their participants) may behave. But more specifically, the relatively less-established persona of in-line makes it an easier target for co-optation than other sports: "ESPN can come along and make Rollerblading what they want; they can't damage skateboarding."[43] And ESPN, while creating a singular and unified image of extreme sports as competitive, risky, and accessible, has also heavily influenced the image of in-line skating. This serves as an effective co-optation of the sport by a relatively univocal source.

George Trow explains how television has infantilized (and socialized) young people, creating a need, an ache, to become "adult" consumers. He writes, " 'adulthood' has been defined as 'a position of control in the world of childhood,' "[44] that adults are behaviorally just older children. Furthermore, the *appearance* of choice—of product choice, of freedom of expression—is seductive, thus problematic: "The permission given by television is permission to make tiny choices, within the context of total permission infected with a sense of no permission at all."[45] Within the medium of cable and network television, ESPN has served as the single most important agency that provides models for the alternative-sport audience, and yet, the nearly singular image that ESPN is providing, and the active disregard for the noncompetitive ethos of alternative sports in general and in-line in particular, provides for Trow's "tiny choices," of choices without any real choice.

But it is part of a larger sports-oriented marketing drive in the late twentieth century and the early twenty-first. Marketers have eschewed the former approach of sponsorship—"because a CEO or CFO 'had a great affinity for the sport' "[46]—in favor of a "brand-development approach" which Nike, Benetton, Roces, and Disney have all utilized successfully. Rather than the CEO being loyal to the sport (and by extension, the fans sharing in that loyalty—with nostalgia toward teams and individuals), the consumers are expected to become loyal to brands that cut across a variety of sportspeople. The brands themselves have become emblematic of the human contact with the sport. And the relationships of buyers to brands, and the affinity consumers have for the brands, have superseded thoughtful product choice, and have, in some cases, overcome the ethos that brought consumers to the product in the first place.

'Toons As Monopolistic Panopticon

There is, undoubtedly, a variety of 'kinds' of in-line skating, but I want to discuss the brand of in-line skating umbrellaed under the X Games of ESPN, which is a corporate arm of the Disney Corporation. In 1995, Disney acquired both ESPN and the American Broadcasting Corporation (as well as Miramax, "the Arts & Entertainment Network, Lifetime, and the History Channel,"[47] as part of the mega-acquisition of Capital Cities/ABC for roughly $20 billion.[48]

Within Disney, intertextual advertising is now seemingly benign (soft furry or rubberized creatures), most assuredly blatant, and, to a degree, symbiotically beneficial (that is, *The Lion King* movie is helped at the box office by Simba plush dolls, which are helped by Elton John's recordings, and so on).[49] However, it must be remembered that, like Disney's acquisition of Capital Cities/ABC (and ESPN), "mergers are driven not by coequal interdependency but by the reality of the absolute primacy of programming: the sovereignty of content over the manifold forms it can take."[50] Disney's intertextual advertising stems from a successful pattern and strategy of using "tie ins and licensing of spin-off merchandise from blockbuster films . . . in which the Disney marketing program [according to Hofmeister, cited in Barber] 'connects its book, movie, recording and theme parks' " together.[51]

And the strategies that worked so effectively for Disney now are, with slightly different packaging, working for Disney, ABC Sports, and ESPN—and their sponsors. As more recent examples: In an issue of *"Disney Adventures: The Magazine for Kids,"* three pages were devoted to "ESPN Action" previews of the 1998 Winter X Games.[52] The 18 January 1999 Web site for *Disney Adventures* contains a link for ESPN Action (Winter X Games): "ESPN's Winter X Games are back (January 14–17) in Crested Butte, CO." Also, for the X Games, sponsors such as VISA, Slim Jim, Taco Bell, AT&T, Mountain Dew, and Pringles receive "air time, on-site signs, a presence on ESPN International, an association with ESPN Magazine, and tie-ins to a special Internet site as well as to a grassroots multicity X Games Tour."[53] Synergy is in the air; mind-blitz is its main theme.

Interestingly, new technology (e.g., the Internet) has made the panopticon unobtrusive: when kids get on-line and 'hit' the Disney Adventures Web site, for example, the potential for demographic information is great. At the actual X Games in San Diego, similar—though less efficient—strategies were in place: at sponsors' booths, spectators were continually asked to fill out forms for entry into contests. Acquiring ABC and ESPN was consistent with Disney corporate strategy, and, in Disneyspeak, an "opportunity to use Disney's synergistic skills to aggressively expand ESPN's reach; to cross-promote among the three brands, Disney, ABC, and ESPN; and to use their combined leverage in the marketplace."[54] But the merger produced an increased ability for efficient surveillance of potential target markets.

Of course, in order to cross-promote effectively, Disney (ESPN) must have an oxymoronic product that is exciting yet controllable, that is thrilling yet safe—that is, in short, what one writer called "safe danger"[55] when referring, ironically, to extreme sports. What Eco terms a blend of the "reality of trade with the play of fiction"[56] for amusement parks like Knott's Berry Farm and Disneyland is a fitting description of Disney's (ESPN's) appropriation and reconfiguration of formerly outsider/extreme types of sports.

In-line skating (also known as Rollerblading[®57]) is an activity/ sport engaged in throughout the year by a variety of people in many different forms and forums. Many in-line sports events (such as the People Magazine In-Line Skating Spectacular (in Manhattan Beach, California),[58] the ASA-Sanctioned World Tour, and the National In-Line Skate Series (NISS)) proliferated during the 1990s.[59] In Raleigh, North Carolina, for example, ESPN's X Games Xperience, "a touring exhibition of the 3-year-old made-for-television competition," took up a weekend in April while touring the country and promoting ESPN's Summer X Games.[60]

Touring the country is an attempt to make contact with fans at the grassroots levels, and is a fairly inexpensive way to promote not only the sport but the product. It is not a phenomenon confined to in-line skating: for example, the three-member Colorado-based Schwinn Stunt and Freestyle Team "finished [its] Midwest tour at the Valparaiso [Indiana] Schwinn dealership" just prior to the 1998 X Games.[61]

Despite this spread of the sport—admittedly at the grassroots to localized levels—the dominant[62] in-line event, the one which burns in-line skating into a mainstream public consciousness, is and has always been the ESPN-driven and -produced image derived from the X Games and other ESPN-sponsored sports events. Of course, now there is competition with ESPN, ESPN2, and ABC for the extreme sports dollar, primarily from Fox Sports:

> Fox Sports Net uses "Rush Hour," a half-hour series that includes such shows as "Board Wild," "Crank," "The Extremists," and "Xtreme Sports," as the core of the network's extreme sports lineup.[63]

But largely, the initial and continuing image of extreme sports that the United States and the rest of the world see is via ESPN, though the United States is certainly not the athletic center of extreme sports. Through ESPN's aggressive promotion, the United States has most likely become the cultural and ideological center for extreme programming. This cultural/ideological hegemony fostered by ESPN came home to me while I was in Dunedin, New Zealand, watching snippets of ESPN brought to me by Sky Television. Still, there is resistance to this electronic dominance: New Zealanders claim to have been at the forefront of some extreme sports, most notably "bungy jumping."[64]

The industry sees the US market, and ESPN, as the dominant players, as well, with programming running through ESPN. ESPN owns, of course, the *X Games*, but also *Bikes, Blades and Boards,* and the *H2O Winter Classic*, which features pro snowboarders and surfers participating in both events on two successive days at Mammoth Mountain and Huntington Beach, California. However, "other alternative sports shows run on the network via barter deals."[65] Companies who primarily want to reach a teenage demographic choose to televise their fare through ESPN.

Why would I assume that ESPN's image of the X Games, and, by extention, of in-line skating, would predominate over, for example, images of "outlaw" skaters, or grassroots skaters, or other connotative derivations of skaters? According to Brockinton, "ad agency executives estimated that the asking price for a 'gold' sponsorship [for the X Games] would be upward of $2 million and for an 'associate' sponsorship, more than $1 million."[66] ESPN's intent is to combine the thrill of cutting-edge sport with the sedentary lifestyle of most of its viewers (watching television is by definition a relatively sedentary action). The 12-to-34-year-old male audience is the primary focus of advertisers, and ESPN's attempts to showcase the sports in a sport-literate fashion—while still paying homage to some of the lifestyle issues—is unique in sports programming. The sheer magnitude of exposure that ESPN brings to its image-making includes, in 1998, the fact that ESPN "was in 74 million homes at the time" of the Summer X Games and reached a rating of 0.7.[67]

The Mouse That Roared: Co-Optation of the In-Line Ethos

While paradoxically celebrating some of them, ESPN has worked to skew several of in-line's strongest ideologies. Its attempt to bring music to the X Games is, according to X Games founder Ron Semiano, a paean to the lifestyle and culture of alternative sports—music is interrelated with in-line skating. Of course, a somewhat more cynical view might be that, through music, ESPN could begin to encroach on cable networks like MTV with such shows as "X in Concert," and they could branch out with music offerings like the "X Games Soundtrack Album."

What are some of the ideologies that ESPN has ignored or displaced with a mass media ideology? That skating is a lifestyle, not a sport; that skaters are in charge of themselves and their lives (the western rugged individual mythos), rather than being regenerative human fodder for television; that skating is more an art form than a competition. In the sense that mainstream production values inculcate the alternative production, in-line skating is merely another sports product. Though the target market is 12-34-year-old males, and ESPN has utilized MTV style, quick-cut, choppy, handheld camera work (thus educating a new audience), the control struggles have created a few problems.

At the inception of the X Games, when no one knew if this extravaganza was going to be a success or not, reports from skaters were more critical of ESPN's handling of in-line. Some of the complaints included: not enough television exposure for women skaters ("If we had worn skimpy clothes, something a little sexier... would we have been televised? Probably."[68]), little activity provided for younger skaters after hours, change in formats ("There was no time to recuperate and get your nerve up again," said Jondon Trevena,[69]; and there was a double-elimination format, previously unheard of in in-line), addition of an event (the downhill), deletion of an event (a distance 20K), pressures from television schedules which made time a constraining factor, and too large a street final course, to name a few. Shura McComb, a skater who was head judge at the 1995 X Games, summed up the philosophical and lifestyle difference between the skaters and ESPN this way:

> The skaters had fun, but I don't think ESPN had a grasp on in-line skating. They didn't show any sympathy toward what the skaters believe in and didn't have much faith in us as professionals.[70]

In 1999, just four years later, many of the younger skaters were not talking so much about "fun" or about "what the skaters believe in": their concerns were more mainstream, more capitalistic. Younger skaters still write in to skating magazines asking how they might capture corporate sponsorship. One recent letter to the editor in *Daily Bread* engaged in this debate by listing reasons "Why I love being an un-sponsored rollerblader from Mt. Sinai, N.Y."[71]

But many skaters are savvy, involved in the issues, and vocal. One letter, from John Stevenson, encapsulates many of the dynamical arguments between the media-corporate and grassroots skaters' ideologies:

> I love seeing skating on T.V. even though I don't like the idea of corporations using our culture as a mass marketing ploy to sell to extreme mid-life crisis dads who like bungee jet skiing and other butt-pirate extreme sports. . . .

I started rollerblading because I can't play sports at all. I can't throw a ball, I can't swing a stick at it either, and I hated the rules and the enclosed atmosphere that kept me from expressing myself. Now, I am not planning to be pro, I probably won't. But, Picasso did not compete against Salvador Dali at art so why the hell should I!?!⁷²

Falling in Love All Over Again: Conclusion

The most successful celebrities are products.
Consider the real role in American life of Coca-Cola.
Is any man as well loved as this soft drink is?

—George W. S. Trow

Why is the fact that ESPN (along with the rest of Disney) serves as a monopoly over athlete image and icon-making a problem? Isn't sport—and entertainment—production a relatively benign entity when compared to, say, tobacco and gun manufacturing? As Benjamin Barber discusses it, the problem is not in capitalism itself. Nor is the problem in consumerism, or in those who would limit consumerism (as he calls it, the dynamic and dialectic between Jihad and McWorld). The problem with Disney cornering the American and international market for something as seemingly benign as alternative sports might be put this way, as Barber states it:

> The problem with Disney and McDonald's is not aesthetics, and the critics of mass taste such as Horkheimer and Adorno (and me) are concerned not to interfere with the expression of private taste, but to prevent monopoly control over information, and to interdict that quiet, comfortable coercion through which television, advertising, and entertainment can constrict real liberty of choice.⁷³

When one enters into watching television sport—any kind of televised sport—one has already allowed those agents—the network executives, the directors who decide on what one will see and which angle one will view it from, the marketing firms and agencies and arms of the networks who determine what products will sell with which programming, and the commentators whose oftentimes prewritten scripts fight hard to reinforce the sponsors' message—to "constrict real liberty of choice." This is one of the problems with previously resistive sport forms' "stars" seeking to become more and more cultural icons. They became celebrated because they represented, in a real sense, the outer limits of choice; but, having been swallowed whole into the mainstream culture, their presence is even more pathological than if they were clearly mainstream. They demonstrate the punishment that an individual may suffer if she/he chooses to remain individual.

Of course, one could argue, as does Rick Kushman, that pluralism does exist, at least under the umbrella that is cable television. He calls the programming "mostly niche shows," "one giant unpolished collection of our [America's] special interests."[74] Yet, the arguments remain that perhaps these niche shows—particularly those of the larger cable networks, like MTV and TNT and ESPN—create consumer needs, rather than reflect them, and only foster restricted choices within corporate giants (for example, Disney, ABC, ESPN, espn2, Classic Sports Network), while *simulating* a vast "liberty of choice." Many of the cable channels, too, have deliberately utilized broadcast television's successful strategies and have worked to broaden their appeal.

Notes

1. This strategy, one of "educating" youngsters to become lifelong consumers of a product, is reminiscent of the strategies recently brought to light by various states' attorneys general against the tobacco industry. Creating a lifelong commitment to one's product, obviously, guarantees corporate income for decades. In the case of the tobacco industry's seduction of American, and now third-world, youth, the product has been shown to be physically addictive and harmful. In the case of television viewing of sport and of new sport forms—indeed, the act of watching television itself—the product has been similarly demonstrated to be addictive but opinions vary on its degree of harmfulness. But if "religion is the opiate of the people," consuming sports television programming—through its logic of production—must be an opium derivative (see Richard Gruneau, "Making spectacle: A case study in television sports production," in Lawrence A. Wenner (ed.), *Media, Sports, and Society*, (Newbury Park, Calif.: Sage Publications, 1989) pp. 134–154. Similarly, ESPN and Fox and other sports networks have worked to create audience, and to create young consumers who will remain loyal consumers throughout their lifetimes.

2. For example, snowboarding is now a part of the Winter Olympics, though the first go-round (in the Nagano 1998 Olympics) was somewhat

fraught with problems for the International Olympic Committee. The US press declaimed, for example, the credibility of the sport when Canadian snowboarder Ross Rebagliati lost, then regained, the gold medal after violating the IOC's drug policy. The reinstatement found that the "IOC, lacking an agreement with the international ski federation on marijuana use, could not strip Rebegliati of his medal." (Sun News Services, "Notebook: Rebagliati regains gold on appeal," *The San Bernardino County Sun*, 13 Feb 1998, p. C3). John M. Glionna cites both snowboarders' marijuana use and the fact that "several boarders have become lost while venturing off and carving their own runs in unpatrolled wooded areas away from well-groomed ski slopes, prompting expensive and time-consuming rescue missions" ("Snowboarders shrug off outlaw rap," *Los Angeles Times*, 9 March 1998, p. A18) as evidence of the continuing outlaw status of snowboarders. And Austrian snowboarder Martin Freinademetz was "kicked out of the Olympics after a drunken party at a team hotel damaged a $4,000 switchboard" (Sun News Services, "Notebook: Wild party time," *The San Bernardino County Sun*, 13 Feb 1998, p. C3).

Clearly, however, snowboarding's incorporation into the mainstream Olympics was the result of not only a series of choices in which the IOC appropriated snowboarding by use of the International Ski Federation (FIS), which began a "snowboard tour to rival the ISF [International Snowboard Federation] circuit" and then weaseled its way (according to many of the ISF riders) into the mainstream (Chris Dufresne, "Culture crash," *Los Angeles Times*, 30 Jan 1998, p. C10). Many snowboarders, not willing to be so readily appropriated by the IOC, chose to boycott in 1998—but much of their reasoning was because they were sponsored by equipment and clothing manufacturers whose apparel they could not wear. Add to the mix the mass of professional snowboarders who did decide to compete, and also the extension of how many recreationalists (estimated at about 4 million in the US, but with up to ten trips a year per person, versus about two trips a year for skiiers, according to Greg Ralph, marketing director at Bear Mountain, Calif. are involved in the sport (cited in Pete Thomas, "Boarders take care of business," *Los Angeles Times*, 13 March 1998, p. C14). Critical mass of participants, thus spectators, was an important factor in the decision to "Olympicize" the sport, but also financial critical mass was vital: Sean O'Brien of Transworld Snowboarding Business Magazine (cited in Thomas, 1998, p. C14) says, " 'If it wasn't for snowboarding coming to the resorts, overall skier visitation numbers would be in the toilet.' "

But, snowboarding and in-line skating may not be two similar sports a decade apart: the choices that are made by participants, corporate sponsors, international organizing committees—and the lessons learned from snowboarding's experience—coupled with the lucrative nature of each sport (that is, how it catches on) may make, for example, snowboarding a mainstream sport with oppositional factions, and in-line a marginalized sport clamoring for mainstream status. As giant slalom snowboarder Lisa Kosglow says, "The sport went mainstream five years ago . . ." (cited in Dufresne, 1998, p. C10).

3. I do not, in fact, believe that they are either/or kinds of questions (though of course I have posed them in that manner), or that the simple binaries that they presume may be answered quickly and easily (cf., Claude Levi-Strauss, *Structural Anthropology* [Claire Jacobsen & Brooke Grundfest Schoepf, trans.] [New York: Basic Books, 1976]).

4. In Jay Parini, *Benjamin's Crossing* (New York: Henry Holt and Company, 1997), p. 192.

5. Jordan retired from professional basketball for the second time on January 13, 1999. According to a sidebar in the *San Bernardino County Sun*, Nike intends to continue to "[play] off Jordan's charisma rather than his jumper. 'Jordan has become a bona-fide brand and not just an endorsement,' Nike chairman Phil Knight said." ("Nike not out of air," *San Bernardino County Sun*, 14 January 1999, p. C6).

6. Kyle Kusz, "BMX, Extreme Sports, and the White Male Backlash" (Albany: State University of New York Press, 2001).

7. John Fiske, *Media Matters: Race and Gender in U. S. Politics* (Minneapolis: University of Minnesota Press, 1996), p. 116.

8. John Fiske, *Understanding Popular Culture* (London: Routledge, 1989).

9. Radio National, "Same game ... different attitude," in "Background Briefing," Australian Broadcasting Corporation Radio National (10 March 1996), http://www.abc.net.au/rn/talks/bbing/ stories/s10775.htm

10. But even this 'individual-sport' characteristic is changing in extreme sports. Corporations have insidiously inserted 'team sports' ethics and ethos into extreme sports. Witness, for example, the synchronized skating exhibitions, then contests, in the X Games. Perhaps this is an indication that extreme sports have indeed become mainstreamed, because fan identification with individuals is no longer seen as quite as important as it once was.

11. This is a point I have developed more fully elsewhere: see Robert E. Rinehart, *Players All: Performances in Contemporary Sport* (Bloomington, Ind.: Indiana University Press, 1998), ch. 4.

12. See Alan Ingham, "Occupational subcultures in the work world of sport," in Donald W. Ball & John W. Loy (eds.), *Sport and Social Order: Contributions to the Sociology of Sport* (Reading, Mass.: Addison Wesley Publishing Company, 1976), pp. 333–389; John Loy, "The cultural system of sport," *Quest* monograph *29*, Winter 1978: 73–102; Allen Guttmann, *From Ritual to Record: The Nature of Modern Sports* (New York: Columbia University Press, 1978); Kent Pearson, "The institutionalization of sport forms," *International Review of Sport Sociology 1* (14), 1979: pp. 51–60.

13. John Rofé, "Q & A: Jake Burton Carpenter: Industry giant scaled peaks 'my own way,'" *Street & Smith's Sportsbusiness Journal*, 1(29) 9–15 Nov 1998, p. 31.

14. Mike Opalek, "The X Games," *Box* 5(4), 1997.

15. "MTV [and, in sport, ESPN 2, at the least] is about the sound of American hot and American cool, about style and affect" (Benjamin R. Barber, *Jihad vs. McWorld: How Globalism and Tribalism are Reshaping the World* (New York: Ballantine Books, 1996): p. 10.

16. Cheryl L. Cole and Amy Hribar, "Celebrity feminism: Nike style post-Fordism, transcendence, and consumer power," *Sociology of Sport Journal 12*(4), 1995: p. 362.

17. "The century club," *Newsweek, 129*(16), 21 April 1997: pp. 34–42.

18. That is, those in-line skaters who receive money from product endorsements, from appearance fees, from successful competitions, from videos, and so on.

19. Donna Dennis-Vano, "Look out boys, here we come," *Inline: The Skate Magazine 4*(8) 1995: p. 28.

20. Lisa Feinberg Densmore, "Taking extreme mainstream," *Inline: The Skate Magazine 4*(8) 1995: p. 37.

21. D. Esquire, "In-line spectacular," *In-Line Skater, 2*(8), 1996: p. 18.

22. Cited in Sal Ruibal, "Crowds catching on to combination events," *USA Today*, 1 Aug 1997, p. 9C.

23. Pat Seltsam, "The games formerly known as Extreme," *Speed Skating Times: International Inline & Ice Speed Skating News* (July/Aug 1996), p. 15.

24. Personal communication, 18 Dec 1998.

25. Personal communication, 22 Dec 1998.

26. Oliviero Toscani, "Introduction to advertising," Benetton Web page, 17 Dec 1998: http://www.benetton.com/wws/aboutyou/ucdo/file1837.html

27. Ibid.

28. See Michael Hirsley, "Success, failure equally riveting on Games telecast," *Chicago Tribune*, 22 July 1996, sect. 3, p. 10.

29. This is not to say that the consumer is completely duped: witness Wheaton's chapter in this volume for evidence that windsurfers' resistance to multinational corporate strategies is a complex and often idiosyncratic response. But those pockets of resistance remain largely with extreme sports or activities typically marginalized even within extreme sports. Seemingly with little to lose (no corporations offering lucrative salaries, sponsorships, etc.), the core memberships needn't embrace corporate-loyalty strategies.

30. See P. H. Weaver, "Newspaper news and television news," in D. Cater and R. Adler, *Television as a social force: New approaches to TV criticism* (New York: Praeger Publishers, 1975) pp. 81–94.

31. Though Weaver (1975) argues that television is more in-depth, albeit from a univocal stance.

32. Weaver, "Newspaper news," p. 85.

33. Weaver, "Newspaper news," p. 86.

34. See John Fiske, *Television culture* (London: Routledge, 1987); Fiske, *Understanding popular culture*; Fiske, *Media Matters*.

35. *In-Line: The Skate Magazine*, Nov 1995.

36. Personal communication, 28 Oct 1998.

37. For participants' views, see Beal & Weidman and Wheaton, this volume.

38. See, however, Kusz's chapter in this text for an insightful discussion of the media-presented invisibility of non-whites in extreme sports.

39. However, there is a rising, insistent clamor for more press about female skaters from "letters to the editor," which reflects a *demand* for more equitably shared power.

40. Associated Press, "Disney plans profit on $600 million deal: Many believe it paid too much for NHL," *The Sacramento Bee*, 26 Aug 1998, p. C2.

41. ESPN Sportszone, 1997.

42. Langdon Brockinton, "ESPN, ABC ready X Games ad packages," *Street & Smith's Sportsbusiness Journal* 1(29) 1998: p. 20.

43. Arlo Eisenberg, personal communication, 31 Oct 1996.

44. George W. S. Trow, *Within the Context of No Context* (New York: Atlantic Monthly Press, 1997 [1980]), p. 50.

45. Trow, *Within the Context*, p. 51.

46. Clarion ad agency manager Gordon H. Kane, cited in Chris Roush, "A sports marketer with a mean curve," *Business Week 3389*, 12 Sep 1994, p. 96.

47. Michael Eisner (with Tony Schwarz), *Work in Progress* (New York: Random House, 1998), p. 382.

48. See Eisner, *Work in Progress*, pp. 355–380, passim. Coincidentally, the first "X Games," called the eXtreme Games, began in the summer of 1995, in Newport, Rhode Island.

49. "Disney is the most trusted brand name in the history of marketing. It hooks us when we're little and never lets go, this unshakable faith that Disney is the best at knowing what's best." Carl Hiassen, *Team Rodent: How Disney Devours the World* (New York: The Ballantine Publishing Group, 1998), p. 13.

50. Benjamin Barber, *Jihad vs. McWorld*, pp. 89–90.

51. Ibid., p. 65.

52. Phil Barber, "The chill of victory," *Disney Adventures: The Magazine for Kids* 8(3) (1998, pp. 53–55.

53. Brockinton, "ESPN, ABC ready X Games ad packages," p. 20.

54. Eisner, *Work in Progress*, p. 382.

55. Melissa Moxon, "Adrenalin rush tourism: Cashing in on a boom," *New Zealand Herald*, 28 Sep 1998, p. A8.

56. Umberto Eco, "The city of robots," in Thomas Docherty (ed.), *Postmodernism: A Reader* (New York: Columbia University Press, 1993), p. 201.

57. The folk-history of Rollerblade, according to Erik Spanberg ("For in-line skating, a brake on sales," *Street & Smith's Sportsbusiness Journal* 1(29) (1998), p. 26), goes like this: ". . . two hockey-playing Minnesota brothers [were] searching for an off-season training regimen . . . and began assembling early versions of in-line skates in their parents' basement, sawing off ice-skating blades and replacing them with tracks of thin wheels." At variance with this account is ESPN Books' in-house writer Kevin Brooker's account: "1979 Scott and Brennan Olson, two Minnesota hockey players, happen across an old in-line skate in a sporting goods store. They add urethane wheels and a rubber

heel brake and find it a good summer surrogate for ice-skating." (*Way Inside ESPN's X Games* [New York: Hyperion/ESPN Books, 1998], p. 80).

58. See Esquire, "In-line spectacular."

59. In fact, ESPN—among others—sponsors quite a few of these events. My point is more that the exposure on television creates a unified image of the sport, as opposed to the localized meanings tied to the events which move from city to city. Live events build audience, create fan identification with stars, and so forth. But the dominant image of in-line skating has been perpetuated and thus appropriated by ESPN.

60. Joe Miller, "Extreme sports: Passing fancy—or the future of sport?" *The News & Observer* (Raleigh, N.C.) 24 April 1998, *What's Up*, p. 15.

61. Diane Kubiak, "Stunt team spins through town," *Post-Tribune* (Valparaiso, Ind., 9 June 1997, p. B1.

62. I mean *dominant* in the sense Raymond Williams uses the term, but within an *emergent* sport-culture formation: " . . . what the dominant has effectively seized is indeed the ruling definition of the social" (Raymond Williams, *Marxism and Literature* [Oxford: Oxford University Press, 1977] p. 125). Of course, as Williams indicates, the interdependence of the dominant, residual, and emergent is incredibly strong, and the ebb and flow of the relationship[s] are what sustains them. Thus, ESPN (and Disney) are inextricably and dialectically linked to the local weekend events as well as to the NISS and ASA events. In point of fact, the ASA tour is broadcast on ESPN and ESPN2, while the Fox Network televises the NISS.

63. Brockinton, "ESPN, ABC ready X Games ad packages," p. 20.

64. Popular myth-making is quite insistent: "New Zealander AJ Hackett is considered the western father of bungy" (Jeff Neems, "Extreme sports," *Nexus* (University of Waikato, 15 Sep 1998, p. 15) and "its current popularity got its jump-start a decade ago in Queenstown [NZ]" (John Henderson, "Queenstown, the capital of action," *Los Angeles Times*, 8 Nov 1998, p. L17). These two quotes provide further evidence of the "cult of personality" and the sense of nationalism that pervade sport endeavors. Both, I suggest, are culturally constructed, not naturalized, spaces.

65. Brockinton, "ESPN, ABC ready X Games ad packages," p. 20.

66. Ibid.

67. Ibid.

68. Dennis-Vano, "Look out boys, here we come," p. 29.

69. Cited in Densmore, "Taking extreme mainstream," p. 33.

70. Ibid., p. 62.

71. Chris Sobik, "why i love," *Daily Bread* 26 (1999), p. 19.

72. John Stevenson, "Marketing Ploy," *Daily Bread* 26 (1999), p. 18.

73. Benjamin Barber, *Jihad vs. McWorld*, p. 297.

74. Rick Kushman, "Isn't that niche?" *The Sacramento Bee*, 13 Sep 1998, *Encore* p. 10.

WINDSURFING

Chapter Four

Journey To La Gringa

Bob Galvan

Baja Bob's Winter Vacation 1992–93

Last year we had a great time camping at Punta Chivato with my Dad's Ford pickup/camper. We planned to do a similar trip this year, driving my Ford van and pulling a rented house trailer. Dad's truck really likes premium gas, which, we found out, is not available in Baja except as aviation fuel. Also, he kept bitching about dust for months afterward, even though we had vacuumed and cleaned it several times during the month it took to get the camper windows replaced.

When I called CruiseAmerica in October to inquire, they assured me that the end of the year was a slow time and trailer rental would be no problem. So I didn't call back to reserve one until mid-December. I like to keep my options open. Of course I was too late. Every rental depot on the West Coast was plumb out of trailers except Tacoma, Washington. Well phooey—I didn't like their contract anyway: too many restrictions and not enough service. They wanted a $250 surcharge for going into Mexico, too. So I started calling smaller local outfits, and I jumped on the first house trailer I found. A small U-Haul franchise in Petaluma also rents some camping trailers as a sideline. I drove up to Petaluma to check it

---

Bob Galvan was born and raised in San Francisco. He spent all of his childhood summers swimming in the Russian River before starting to surf the waves of the Pacific as a teenager. After twenty years of paddling, he added a sail to his surfboard and started catching even more waves and doing more with them! Bob even works in the water, cleaning the bottoms of yachts in the many marinas of San Francisco Bay.

out on December 9. The 19' Terry looked perfect for Baja—already real worn-out and filthy. Low profile. Broken in. I put down my plastic and reserved for December 26 to January 9. Told them I was going to Arizona. Since they were closing for a few days around Christmas, I could pick it up December 23.

Good thing. When I got it home on the 23rd, I checked the taillights and found them all fucked up. Bad grounds, shorts, wired wrong in the first place, bum connections, the works. So I spent six hours outside in the freakin' freezin' cold figuring out and totally rewiring this tub's highway lights. But I got them right and bright, by God. This is after I spent a couple hours on the way home lengthening the trailer's wiring cable so it would reach my van's plug. The new plug I had mounted so securely right into the left end of my trailer hitch's main beam. The cable has seven wires in it and is an inch in diameter. A nontrivial job.

Meanwhile, Ting is having a shit fit over the trailer. She knows in her gut that this pile is headed for disaster. A wheel will fall off, the brakes will fail, the propane will explode, or something. She wants to cancel. My position is that it's all we can get, the contract is signed, I can make it work, and I will go with her or without her.

The next day she settles down, accepts her fate, reevaluates her faith in her Fixerman, and starts cleaning the trailer's interior—including taking the covers off the cushions and washing them. But she wants me to inspect the wheel bearings and brakes. OK, if that's what it takes. Damn.

I'm glad I have a big floor jack and an electric impact wrench. Thanks again, Dad! The wheels check out OK and I adjust the brakes a bit. Crisis averted. Let's load up!

Saturday, December 26, 1992

Today is my 43rd birthday. The girls make me a nice breakfast and a few presents appear, but the big deal to me is that we're leaving for Baja today. No deadline, no appointments, we leave when we're ready. I start the day by wrapping up my paperwork for the diving business, then switch to the business of loading the van. First the windsurf stuff—it all goes on the roof in the triple-tiered racks. Three boards, two masts, two booms, seven sails, mast bases and spare parts. Then wetsuits for three, including several types for me; sailing warm weather, sailing cold weather, and a thin drysuit for diving. This leads to the dive gear—masks and fins for all, speargun and tips, float, bag, fish stringer. I also bring one small scuba tank. Its primary function is to fill tires in a pinch, but I could dive with it if I felt so moved. Usually I am quite content to free dive while I'm on vacation. Only one bike this trip, Marina's kid-sized mountain bike. We can all ride it. I wedge it into the trailer's shower stall.

Last of the garage stuff is the tools and equipment check. Since we're taking my van, this is easy. Most everything is already in there. Lots of tools, a couple flashlights, jumper cables, Cylume® lights, a jack, duct tape, black tape, wire ties, electrical connectors, etc. Pack clothes—quick and easy. Warm stuff, cool stuff, lots of T-shirts, a couple of clean jeans.

Ting has been loading the trailer with food and housekeeping items. I don't even look, I just give it up to her. About 4:30 we are getting close to ready, and we're all out front futzing around the trailer. Our cat Mocha shows up and starts following Ting in and out of the trailer, kind of playing with us outside. It's new and different behavior for him. He finally follows me into the house for his dinner. Ting's sister Laurie will be house-sitting and cat-feeding while we are gone.

6 PM. *Listo.* (We are ready.) But it's dinnertime—what to do? We want to roll, not cook and clean, and we don't want to sit and wait in a restaurant either. We go over the hill to Strawberry Shopping Center and get High Tech Burritos *para llevar* (to go), tank up the van and head south.

The Central Valley is fogged in, so we opt for Route 101. It works out very well. Traffic is light, even through the city. Have you ever towed a trailer over Nineteenth Avenue? Middle lane, middle lane, middle lane, middle lane!

Give me space! I drive four hours to King City. We have some low fog around Watsonville, but break out of it as we enter the Salinas Valley. After pumping a tank and a half of gas, Ting takes over and gets us to Pismo Beach, another two hours down the road. On the best of roads we get up to 55 or even 60, but this is quite a load we are moving, and we must keep it slow to keep it under control. We are probably averaging 40–45 mph.

Sunday December 27, 1992

Midnight. We find a Farmhouse plastic coffee shop across from a shopping center with a huge, mostly empty parking lot. We pull into the lot and come to a stop, covering a whole row of painted "parking spaces." Stopping this rig takes advance planning: How you gonna get out? Please no backing up, don't block me in, is there enough room to make the turn?

Ting and Marina conk out in the van while I go in for a burger, a paper, and coffee. The *San Diego Tribune* and *LA Times* are really pretty good. The weather pages in particular put the *SF Chronicle* to shame. The restaurant is populated with the typical all-night coffee shop crowd: chain-smoking truckers, young lovers on hot dates, cops, and road warriors.

Fed and caffeinated, I get behind the wheel for another three hours, which brings us to Newbury at 4 AM. I think Newbury is on the northern perimeter of the LA metropolis—near Magic Mountain? Thirty more gallons of fuel, and I'm off again. I quit at the Camp Pendleton rest stop just north of San Diego—6 AM. I go lie down in the trailer—just open the door, walk in, and flop down. This is nice.

About 7 AM, Ting is ready to drive. She gets us into Chula Vista or some such community, where we make one last stop at the local version of Thrifty Drug. It's early and the parking lot is bare, so she puts us right in the middle of the parking lot. I bite my tongue and say nothing. The shopping list: broom, flares, disposable cameras, and call home to parents. We get it all, but it takes a while. Dad still has the three-week Killer Cold. Tutu is still freaked about banditos. Here the air is noticeably warmer than that frigid stuff we left behind. It feels almost like Southern California! By the time we are ready to leave, the store is busier, and we are blocked in because we parked too close to the front doors. We have to wait for one car to leave, then I have to back the rig and turn it to get out. In these situations I ask Ting to help me, but she invariably stands where I can't see her, and then feeds me information that is woefully ambiguous, too late, and often incorrect. I end up jumping in and out, alternately looking and driving, quietly seething as we depart.

Of course she can't find her way back to the freeway either . . . and a kid on a bike chases us down to tell us the trailer door is swinging open. "Welcome to San Diego," he says. The final US stop is in Otay Valley for fuel and MexInsurance. Last year we found the insurance right at the gas station. No such luck this year. We can't get into the gas station of choice because of the cars in there already and the fuel truck blocking the drive-through option. So we go next door to the hotel, find a big parking place in the back, walk three fourths of the way around the building in search of the front door only to be told at the desk that the dining room is for guests only. It's one of those deals where the breakfast is included with the room. By this time the traffic at the gas station is clearing up, so we drag the whole circus back over there and fill it. I pay for the gas and ask for 13 days of insurance, but they don't sell it. The clerk directs me back to the hotel next door. More quiet seething: I haven't had my coffee yet.

Ting takes us just across the border, then stops and we switch seats. I negotiate Tijuana, get us to the *cuota* and into Ensenada. We encounter light rain just north of Ensenada.

In downtown Ensenada there is a shopping center with a big paved parking lot. The anchor tenant is a store call "Gigante" (Giant). It's a Mexican version of K-Mart. Everything you could possibly want under one roof. We need to take a break anyway, so we pull in and park way up in the far corner of the lot. I go into Gigante (my first time in there) in search of motor oil, bread and cookies, bananas, limes, jicama. The girls hang in the trailer and draw. I find everything on my list, plus fresh tamales for lunch. Throughout our visit, DiscoLandia is blasting Mexican pop into the drizzly atmosphere. The trailer's head seems quite luxurious as we wash up and discharge our bodily fluids at will, in privacy, while camped out in this downtown parking lot.

I continue to drive through Ensenada and Manedero, and down the long, steep grade into the Valle de Santo Thomas, Baja's own wine country. We rotate drivers and I retire to the lie-down position in the back of the van for the rest of the afternoon. The raindrops get bigger as we travel south.

I sleep.

San Quintin, 4:30 PM. The dusty town has become the muddy town. We gas up and head south, but decide we don't want to struggle with pulling the trailer at night in the rain. Our trusty guidebook, "The Magnificent Penninsuia," shows Ceilito Lindo Motel and Trailer Park just south of town and a couple miles down a paved side road. It's out on a south-facing sandspit arranged much like Stinson Beach/Seadrift. So we hang a right and go where no Galvan has gone before. The road looks nice as it goes through a tunnel of cypress trees and past Hotel La Pinta.

And in a flash there is no more pavement! We are on it, and it is raining and it is real dark, and my only choice is to keep it all moving through the mud and the ruts, gingerly placing the wheels and babying the throttle as if my family's lives depended on it. If we stop in this mud, God only knows when we might become mobile again. On the other hand, does the road get better or worse farther and farther from the known universe? What to do, what to do? . . . .

And mercifully the eternal mud gives way to hard-packed sand, the road turns left, and the motel looms out of the darkness. OK, I feel better, now where's the trailer park? I see a sign that seems to indicate the trailer park is right across the road over here in the darkness, so I drive into what I perceive to be a driveway, only to find myself once again on a dark sucking-mud road into the unknown. I thank myself for installing "driving lights" just before we left. They are aimed just a hair higher than the low beams and are twice as bright. Flick them on and your rainy-night vision gets pretty good, for about 40 yards. Another eternity passes at 5 mph, and we come to a few dim and scattered lights and a cinder-surfaced parking lot. With very little exploration I choose a high and level spot and stop. But I fucked up: I put a puddle in front of the trailer door. And yes, it's still raining. The "trailer park" is in pretty sad shape. Dark as Hades, wet as the River Styx, and the shit/shower house is closed because the drains won't drain—use room 11 at the motel. (Paid guests only, $5 per night). We have no choice. This is it, home for tonight!

We all adjourn to the trailer for our first night in it. I have to go in and out a few times to fuss with propane and drains and pilot lights and such, and here I start to notice that these Wolverine boots I bought a couple months ago are keeping my feet totally warm, dry, and comfortable in these most stressful of conditions. I will rave more about them later. So we eventually get a dinner of pesto noodles with lamb on the table, and toss down some Ron Rico stress medication, and have family story time. We take turns reading a book about a swan that couldn't honk, and James Michener's autobiography. Marina is almost nine now and has become a voracious reader. At bedtime, Marina gets the upper bunk, Ting gets the lower (these two are across the forward end of the trailer), and I get the spare bedroom, the van. My room has a CD player and a new Eric Clapton double disk.

So the trip has begun. Twenty-four hours from home and here we are, up to our axles in adventure already. Buenos noches.

Monday, December 28, 1992

Dawn comes drippy and gray. Rain stops early, but the clouds persist. We get to check out our surroundings. Ceilito Lindo is on a marshy plain just behind the beach. The south-facing beach is quite nice—

moderate dunes, a very flat slope, nice little waves, prevailing wind cross-offshore. It looks like a surfer's paradise.

Back at the wagons, I decide to take advantage of the facilities and dump the holding tank. First I have to find a dump pipe that looks clear and has dry ground nearby, so I don't have to kneel in a puddle. Next, alert the girls and move the rig into position. Then open the trailer's "trunk" with my pocket knife (insert blade in key slot and twist) and wrestle the spare tire out so I can get at the long corrugated hose. Attach one end to the dump valve, stick the other down the pipe, pull the rod that opens the valve that allows the poop to flow. Uh, pull the rod. UNGH! OOOFF! WTF?! The rod appears stuck. I rest, reconsider, examine, and pull some more. Finally the plastic nut and the T-shaped handle depart the rod for a more satisfying relationship with my right hand. Now I'm *really* fucked.

About this time Ting calls my attention to the trailer hitch. It seems that the ball is lower than it was when we left home. Close examination confirms her contention. The brackets that connect the hitch to the truck have actually been TWISTED by the torques of the last twenty-four hours, so the tongue that holds the hitch ball is no longer level, but slopes slightly downward away from the van, putting the ball uncomfortably close to the ground. Just what I need right now—another major mechanical headache. This one will just have to wait; I have a load of shit to deal with first.

I dig into the repair kit for some "Plumber's Tape," a half-inch-wide strip of metal with many holes in it. It is commonly used to hang pipe. In my toolbox I find a nut that fits the threads on the dump valve pull-rod. I loop the Plumber's Tape into a circle, stick it onto the rod through two of the many holes, and twist the nut on. Now I have handle again, but I still need more force. I start to loosen the four bolts that hold the whole valve together, intending to decrease the friction on the sliding 'door' inside, but the first bolt snaps right off. Whoops, scratch that plan! A screwdriver inserted between the new handle and the valve body finally provides the leverage that leads to our great relief. Imagine our dismay as we watch brown puddles leak out of a dozen pinholes in the dump hose. All together now, "Shit!" The spare tire, thrown in the trunk as an afterthought, rode on top of the dump hose which was on top of the leveling jacks, and the hose got beat up.

So now it's decision time. What about this hitch situation? We could turn tail and run for the border—but I'm not ready to quit yet! We could ignore it and hope we don't bottom out too badly too often—that would be asking for trouble in this troubled land. Or we could try to get it fixed here in Baja—now we're entering new territory. Circumstances favor the third option. It's early in the trip, we're in a safe and mellow spot, and we are very close to a major town where it is likely we can get what we need. Here's the plan: leave the trailer and the girls here at Ceilito Lindo, Dad takes the van to San Quintin and gets repairs done. Ting agrees to that, *no problemo*. We unhook and I drive into town, about five miles away. It is maybe 11 AM. The dirt portions of the road look like slippery shit.

I make a bee-line for a *llanatera* (tire shop) I have done business with before, Servicio Enid. They refer me to Mofles Avina (Avina Mufflers) at the southern edge of town. Luckily for me, George is hanging out, and his English is very good—he has spent part of his youth in Sausalito. I explain the problem to George, and he translates to Senor Avina. I ask for two things: first, to burn holes in the hitch and the frame and pass long bolts through to strengthen the hitch and hopefully prevent the brackets from bending any more. Second, I want some way to raise the rear of the van since I don't think that disassembling the hitch and trying to straighten the brackets will be easy or quick. The brackets are half-inch-steel plate. Avina says he can put in a couple of extra leaf springs and do the bolt thing, but there are a couple jobs ahead of me. OK: I didn't expect instant service anyway. I'm just glad to find someone willing to help me today.

Here I must try to paint a picture of San Quintin and Mofles Avina. This is unlike any stateside business you have ever seen. San Quintin has few paved surfaces. It is alternately dusty and muddy, conjuring up recollections of Dodge City. The highway is the main street, and all manner of businesses line both sides. To park, you pull over into a chaotic sort of side street where you get either dry or wet dirty depending on the weather. In this parking area there are motor vehicles, pedestrians, dogs, food stands both stationary and mobile, and garbage. No sidewalk, except at the *zocalo* (town square). In many places the business level is 6 feet lower than the highway, so driving the transition means you either tip frighteningly sideways or you turn very sharply—and watch out for ruts and puddles. Mofles Avina is at one of these steep places. There are major mudholes on each side of his driveway. There is a cinderblock wall around the place, an overhanging half-roof, and a doublewide concrete pad with a grease pit in one side and an air lift on the other. There is also some nonpaved work area, and a large area where the trash (dead exhaust systems, oil filters, and other UFOs) is tossed, perhaps to be picked up later. It is one of the most substantial and modern-looking establishments in town.

While waiting, I seek out a cup of coffee. The best I can do is Nescafé at a little candy shop by the bus depot. It *is* hot, and there is real *leche* (milk) and real *azucar* (sugar), so I'm satisfied. I get it *para llevar* and walk across the street to explore the building materials store.

What they have is good stuff, but the selection is about 1 percent of what we are used to seeing back in Marin. I rest in the van, catch up on my journal, and snack a bit. Finally a kid of about 17 starts taking the rear wheels off. I get a lawn chair out of the back of my van, sit down, and watch. I am horrified when he starts to loosen the U-bolts that hold the springs to the axle with a mere box wrench. "Alto, un momento," I intercede, and dig out my half-inch-breaker bar, ratchet handle, and deep sockets. I have to show him how to use the ratchet handle. He uses my tools, but doesn't seem too impressed or even thankful. I know it makes the job go quicker at least. The extra leaf springs come from an old axle assembly in the back yard, where Avina keeps his house, his wife and his two-year-old son. It's relatively clean and neat back there. I make periodic trips to the yard to use the outhouse. At last the spring job is done, but Avina is still busy in the grease pit welding under a big truck.

Avina eventually brings his torch around to my trailer hitch. He has to burn four holes in the hitch and four in the van's frame. It's all right behind the bumper, but he doesn't want to remove it. He just lies down and works in the tight space, measuring and marking with a scrap of welding rod, lighting his torch with a Bic lighter, and burning without goggles or gloves. What a guy. He is actually quite likable—young, handsome, always smiling and in good spirits. After the holes are burned, he runs off to the other end of town and comes back with some threaded rod. I inform him that they have it across the street at Materiel Panamerica. Avina gets some *washas* (washers) and some *torques* (nuts) and we bolt it all up. *La cuenta*? (The bill?) *Un ciento.* (One hundred dollars.) Just what I was guessing.

Whew. I'm glad that's *finito*! I hop in and twist the key. *Nada.* I had not turned the ignition switch completely off. Well, what better place to need a jump start than an auto repair *taller* (shop)? "Senor Avina, una mas cosa. Mi batteria es muerte." "No problemo, amigo." A couple of guys get the funky old charger and fool with the plug. Sparks fly. I think they are pushing bare wires into the wall socket. The connections on the battery end aren't much better, but they get me going. I hit the road about 4:30, very happy to have accomplished my mission.

On the way back to Ceilito Lindo, there is a traffic jam at the first muddy section of road. Several vans and RVs are just stopped there, looking and wondering whether to proceed. I am forced to wait about five minutes until I can pass. The road looks just as soft as it did this morning, but traffic has torn it up more. Then I see what the rubberneckers were so concerned about. A fifth-wheel rig didn't make the turn as it left the motel, and is resting mostly in a field. I make it without incident. It is very nice to be back "home," such as it is. The girls have had a pretty good day. Ting serves me a well-deserved drink. Then I get the reefer going on propane for the first time, level the trailer, skip dinner and take a shower. We will get a good rest and try again tomorrow.

Tuesday, December 29, 1992

As we prepare for departure this morning, the trailer hitch is now a good six inches higher than it was before. This means that the trailer jack doesn't go high enough to hook up! Good thing I brought another jack. So we find a rock and jack and block and finally get hooked up. As the *gringo* who collects the camping fees makes his rounds, I ask his companion about wind here. "Yeah, it gets real windy in the summer. And there's a sand bar across the mouth of the lagoon. The waves there should be loads of fun." It sounds like an ideal windsurfing setup, with camping or motel right on the beach. I will be back.

The mud traverse on the way out is a real nail-biter. I drive the right edge of the road, the highest and driest part, but it also is not level. The trailer keeps sideslipping toward the center. Ting and I release copious quantities of adrenaline as we slosh along at 5 mph. Pavement never felt so good. We cross ourselves and give thanks.

Out on the road, I notice that now the gas gauge for the rear tank does not work. It's math time! I know I can safely get 150 miles out of a full tank and still have some gas left, so the strategy will be to use the tank with the dead gauge first and switch over to the front tank at a predetermined point. Checking the map, Catavina is 135 miles away. We will fill there and see how much gas it takes—in *litros*.

Tank capacity in *litros*:
20 gallons x 4 quarts/gal. = 80 quarts
1 quart = .95 litros
80 quarts x .95 = 76 litros

10 AM—El Rosario. We stop for ice, scrape mud off the vehicles, change drivers. We buy no gas. The new springs really do the trick. The ride is much better, but it feels a little swishier. Feels like the trailer is pulling to the center of the road. I check the trailer, even measure the hitch-to-wheel distances, find everything straight and aligned properly, tires good. Onward—averaging 30 mph now as we begin what I call the Catavina Pitch. It is the hardest section of Mexico 1, twisty and hilly and wild for about 200 miles.

At Catavina, we put eighty-one *litros* in the rear tank! I expected less than seventy-six. Either: 1. My tank holds more than twenty gallons (I have never pumped more than nineteen into it back home). 2. The pump is cheating us. 3. My math is wrong.

I suspect the pump. But here I also figure out why the gas gauge quit and fix it. It was just an electrical connector that was separated to avoid the welding torch. I sure am glad to lose that record-keeping and planning job! Those eighty-one litros cost me $33 (US). That's about $1.65/gallon.

Ay-yai-yai!

We have decided to modify our plans and go to Bahia de Los Angeles, 150 miles this side of Punta Chivato. This rig on this road is just too slow and tortuous. Bahia has been highly recommended, has wind, and we've never been there. So we hang a left at the junction.

The fifty-mile road from Mexico 1 to LA Bay is paved, but looks as if it has never been maintained. Pothole city. Darkness falls before we reach town, and I stop right on the road (no traffic at all) to aim all my headlights. Our angle of attack is different now with the new springs. An hour and a quarter after turning off, we bump, jolt, and roll into Bahia, as the locals call it.

We find a well-lit, jumpin' restaurant with happy gringos at the tables on the veranda, so we pull over and go in. We find clean rest rooms, lobster, rice, beans, tortillas, soup, margaritas, and info on the easy place to "camp" tonight.

Wednesday, December 30, 1992

We awake in a huge dirt parking lot next to the beach, across the road from the hotel. There are a couple dozen RVs in the beachfront slots, and a few more one row back. This place could hold a hundred vehicles no problem. People are cooking and fussing, dogs are roaming, generators are roaring.

It's too downtown for me. Our reefer is not cold, the ground is muddy, we're bummed and confused. We drop the trailer, and Marina and I go exploring while Ting rests. We head north out of town into desert-by-the-sea country. We drive some sandy tracks real close to the beach, and find many "campgrounds," areas where some local has put up a sign and maybe some white painted rocks. "Pedro's Camp, 2 Dollars a Night," "Park Here, One Dollar a Day." I don't find anyplace to my liking until we are about five miles out and there are no mo' damn signs and very little trash. I find a windsurfer camp and get encouraging reports from the four Santa Barbara sailors who come here often. They recommend the next campsite, where bored sailors in past years have moved rocks from the intertidal zone to make a nice launch ramp. It's large enough to accommodate the trailer too.

So we check it out and approve. We leave two lawn chairs and a beach towel to make the spot look occupied, and go back to town for Mom. After a fish taco lunch in town, we drag the trailer out to our campsite and settle in for some serious vacationing!

Still Wednesday, December 30, 1992

When we get to our campsite, it is more empty than we left it. Our two lawn chairs have vanished. We figure they appeared "left behind" to some local. The camp site is a level, sandy area just up from the beach, surrounded by low, thick brush. Just across the road is an immense area of classic desert flora, spaced widely apart for nice hiking. We do a bunch of site planning in order to get the trailer in a good spot facing the water, back to the wind, level, far back enough to leave us some front yard, and still be able to get the van out. That last part is tight. Parallel parking in sand can be hazardous.

Then I get to do the trailer service—unhook and perch hitch on some rocks, fool with leveling jacks (reefer doesn't work unless it's dead level), gray water drain hose, open propane valve, light two pilots.

Finally I climb up the van, untie a mountain of windsurfing gear, and hand it down to Ting. Where is she, anyway? Marina spends the afternoon setting up her fort in some trails through the brush. She is in heaven.

There is a hint of wind today and the clouds are thinning, but we haven't seen blue sky since San Diego. As evening falls, we rustle up a dinner of burger and potatoes, 'chokes and tofu, and the electric lights grow quickly dim. It becomes apparent that the trailer's battery is shot and cannot hold a charge, so I back the truck up a little and connect the two again. Now we have to be careful not to run the truck's battery down too far. Fortunately, all we need electricity for is some light and the water pump.

TRAILER SHIT LIST

- Tail/brake/signal lights FUBAR—6 hours to rewire.
- !Built-in ant colony!
- Battery dead—won't hold charge.
- Closet door pops open while on the road, dumping clothes on the floor.
- Pooper in poor condition. Flush water just runs down one side of the bowl, rather that rinsing all of it. Flapper doesn't seal watertight.
- Dump valve handle broke. Dump hose has pinholes (I taped them up).
- Window cranks dead, they must be pushed closed from outside.
- Dirty move-in condition.
- Foam cushions shot. You bottom out when sleeping.

Back in the downtown campground, I talk to some other RV folks, and they are having their share of troubles too, so I feel some consolation in not being alone. One group from Berkeley has a Dodge engine that is running very rough. They suspect a chipped tooth on the timing gear and a slipped timing chain. Another guy in a giant beautiful RV has a dying reefer. Another has ruptured a water tank. This evening Marina is walking on the beach, and the turquoise/silver ring I gave her for Christmas slips off her finger and disappears in the sand. She has the presence of mind to stop immediately and search for it. We can't find it but mark the spot well for a more intense search tomorrow.

Thursday, December 31, 1992

Today things are starting to click at last. The sky has cleared, the sun is out, the wind is picking up! I ride Marina's bike out to the point. I'm not sure exactly what "La Gringa" is, but the name is hung on this area. It could be the abandoned fish camp, or it might be the hill at the southern end of the clean gravel spit that separates the bay from Canal Ballena (Whale Channel). There are campers all over the place, though widely spaced—you have to make an effort to visit. There is a pretty even distribution of windsurfers, divers, fishermen, and kayakers. There are three large expedition-style kayak groups. They paddle over to the large and uninhabited Islas of Coronado and Angel de la Guardia for multiday camping trips.

I really like the spit—it's all smooth stones and very clean. On one side is the flat protected water of the bay, and on the other, just thirty yards away, are the big swells and bigger wind of the canal. I would like to camp out here on another trip.

On the way back I explore the abandoned fish camp. It was evidently quite a jumping operation at one time, as there are many dead trucks about, dead walk-in refrigerators and cleaning tables in a big building about 30 feet by 60 feet. The trucks and the plant are painted the same pale green, with some ornate but now unreadable lettering. There are also many wooden frames about 3 feet by 6 feet, with wire mesh stretched over them. Over at the base of the hills are the ruins of a shit/shower house with porcelain fixtures. I make mental notes on good stuff to scrounge for our camp, grab a sorry but serviceable lawn chair, and pedal back, knees flared out on the little bike, junk chair around my shoulder, looking funky, feeling right in my element.

Time to sail! I rig a 5.3 for Ting and a 5.9 for myself. The 5.9 is a new-to-me second-hand sail, a 1992 Waddell MonoSlalom, my first all monofilm (clear) sail. It is a different beast to rig from the SurfSlalom sails I have been using for the past few years, so I hassle with it for a while, but once on the water it is lovely. You can see right through the whole thing! What a view! And the power is just right for today's 15–18 knot wind. I sail pretty much all day in the flat water of the bay, sometimes with neighboring sailors, sometimes not. Once I carry my gear across the gravel spit way out into the canal. It is gorgeous out there, but just a little too windy for the sail I have. It is work to keep it under control, so I bore off and run downwind, blazing diagonally down the swells. I go far enough below the hill at the point to avoid its windshadow, then enter the bay and sail several tacks upwind to return home. An awesome ride.

Just before sunset I go on a firewood hunt in the desert, but don't get much. Everything is alive and happy—I need that dry dead stuff. I cook dinner while Ting and Marina walk to the point. After dinner we have a one-hour campfire, and stargaze with binoculars. I did some homework and know where to look to find some nebulae! One good spot that's easy to find is Orion's Sword. It's just loaded with fuzzy stuff that the naked eye can't see. It has been a very fine New Year's Eve. *Felize Ano Nuevo!*

Friday, January 1, 1993

In the morning Marina and I take a little drive to get away from camp—where firewood is more plentiful. We have some nice walks in the desert and come back with wood for days. I then take off in the van on my own for some more exploring to the north. I find the way to several more remote camps on the Canal Ballena, behind the hills and invisible from La Gringa. It is a real joy to have independent wheels down here at last. In the past, I've either been on trips where you fly down and stay in a hotel or boat, or I've been in a camper or camped out of/in the van. Once you set up camp in a camper or van, the vehicle becomes shelter and stuff is hung all over it, hidden under it, and spread around inside so you can't take it for a ride without disrupting camp. But with the trailer, home gets unhitched and parked at the campsite, and Dad can go cruisin'!

I check out La Gringa Point: I drive down the gravel spit to the base of the hill, get out and start walking around the eastern side. The gravel gives way to scramble-over rocks, and as I scramble, I encounter fellow gringos-on-vacation. I meet Irma, John, and Austin, a family from San Diego. Irma is a lovely young Chicana Mom, just straining her thong bikini and my good manners as we talk about our kids, both nine and looking for a friend. John, the Dad, tosses lures into the sea and reels 'em back. We can see some fish activity on the surface within casting distance. Around the next rock is a kayak group having lunch. They are returning from camping on Isla Coronado. The leader is a longhair surfer dude from Santa Cruz and we discuss windsurfing and spearfishing.

Continuing on around the hill, I am getting hot, so I find a lonesome place, strip nekkid, and take a short dip to cool off. This is halfway around, on the southern tip of La Gringa. The western side features more smooth clean gravel beach, with the bone and carcasses of many dead pelicans. Back at the van, I am happy to remember that I have most of a case of Pacifico in there. Time to crack one open!

I make another stop at the abandoned fish camp and pick up some more chairs and a heavy wooden fish cleaning table. Mind you, these pieces would be sent to the dump yesterday if they turned up in your alley, but here in the boonies, they add great comfort to a camp. I also bring back some carpet pieces and a frame with wire mesh stretched across it. Old carpet is a great way to make a clean spot for shoe and clothes changing. It cuts down on the sand quotient in the trailer and van.

This is turning into a hot day. I spend an hour in the tidepools prying oysters off the rocks right in front of our camp, and trying to find the clams that produce all those empty clamshells. Finally got it—you have to dig for the clams. They are about three inches down, below the little rocks that are jammed between the big rocks. They are hard to get.

Oysters are easier to pick, but harder to open. Fresh seafood for lunch. We all drive back to the point late in the afternoon. I go spearfishing while Ting and Marina watch and hang out. I see live Baja sand dollars, the kind with the hole in them, cruisin' around the sand. I stick two triggerfish, one little hogfish, and one other. The hogfish is very good eating, the triggers not so hot. We have a big long campfire with our Santa Barbara windsurfer friends—Steve, Eddie, and Joan. Plenty of chairs, stars, marshmallows. But the trailer runs out of water.

Saturday, January 2, 1993

Morning is cold, overcast, and wet with dew. I make oatmeal for Marina, taters/fish/coffee for me. Ting sleeps late in the van. She insisted on changing sleeping places because she was bottoming out on these dead cushions. I doubled them up and slept fine. The sun comes out after a while, and we sort things out for a trailer run into town. I find and fix a crooked rubber washer in the water hookup hose fitting. That's where much of the water dripped away.

Since the "graded" road is rough and tortuous, we try a sandy road and find it takes us to the "paved" road about mile outside town, via the dump. The ride is much better.

We get water at La Casita Blanca, a desalination plant next to the Pemex. The thirty gallons of pure water cost 7,000 pesos, or $2.30. A much better deal than the unleaded gasoline that I had to get pumped from a barrel on a flatbed truck. The Pemex only has leaded regular, so some entrepreneur trucks in fifty-five gallon drums of Magna Sin. Fifteen gallons cost me $36!

Tortillas are a buck a dozen, and go down Marina's throat real fast. We stop at a trailer park and dump the holding tank, and head back the way we came.

Since we are off the main route, it's a good opportunity to gather firewood. We make two stops and fill the trailer's entrance. My favorite wood is the remains of Old Man cactus. When the flesh dies, the wooden skeleton still stands, looking exactly like a set of smooth grey antlers.

We get the trailer parked and the van stuck in the sand. Much digging (I left the shovel home this time since we had a potty), some rocks, and tire deflation to 20 psi get it moving again.

After a well-earned lunch, Marina and I get serious about her lost ring. We set the wire screen on some rocks near the spot where the ring disappeared, and started scooping and tossing sand. Within five minutes, the ring pops into view on the screen! It is like magic. Yo—I am Dad!

We all three go on a long walk into the hills to the north. We wander through meadows of cardon, flush jack rabbits, and climb up some folded and metamorphed sediments standing on edge like the pages of a book, and we sit and soak in the view for a while— I brought binoculars, too. We amble back by way of 9-year-old Austin's camp, but they aren't home.

If the weather continues calm and cool tomorrow, we will pack up and head north in exploration mode, taking the back way to San Felipe through Laguna Chapala, Punta Willard, and Puertocitos; perhaps we'll continue home on the inland route via Mexacali, Salton Sea, and Bakersfield.

Late this night a big west wind kicks in. It is strong enough to make a lot of noise and blow things around, but this is not a sailing wind, this is some gusty, unreliable frontal disturbance. Feels like spirits.

Sunday, January 3, 1993

Still blowing west. Sky still gloomy. We eat, take showers, and pack up. Then the El Norte kicks in for real. Internal conflict here. The sky says "rain," but the wind says "fair and windy." While I confer with Campo Santa Barbara, a wind dummy hits the water on a 5.6. She planes. That's it—we stay! Back up on the roof, unload, rerig, yada yada. At least we hadn't moved the trailer yet! As I wrestle with our mountain of gear, a Canadian family with a 6-year-old girl and a 3-year-old boy walk down from their camp. They visit awhile (nonsailors asking standard questions) and invite Marina back to their camp to play for a few hours. Perfect! Ting

and I can both sail now and she won't have to worry about her
baby being alone on the beach.

The wind builds quickly, leading to the overpowered rerigging
frenzy. In two hours I have rigged the 5.9, 4.7, 4.2, and the 3.7 (I
can put two complete rigs up at once), and used all three boards.
There is clear sky to the north, advancing slowly toward us. Ting's
ride lasts about an hour, with Ting mostly getting beat up. I eventually get into the Canal Ballena with the small stuff, the 3.7 on
the Ecstacy (an 8-foot 4-inch wave board), and it is magnificent! I
am in a three-mile-wide slot between 1,500-foot-high mountains.

The island must be fifteen miles long. The water is clear and
blue and I know there is big marine life under me, though nobody
breaches or blows. There are three other sailors on the water, but
we have all launched from different places, and seem very far away
from each other. I only cross tacks with one other sailor one time.
He has a bigger, newer sail and smokes me. I have to pee, so I make
the crossing and land on Isla Coronado to take a break. The swells
on the far side of the Canal get more organized, good for jumping
and riding. There is some wind shadow at the beach where I land,
but the short swim is a small price to pay for admission to my own
private island!

2:30 finds me back at the trailer for heat and fuel. Instant
soup can be great stuff! At 3, I'm back out for round two, but on
the Seatrend (a straighter, floatier, faster board, 8 feet 8 inches) and
the 4.7 since the wind has abated a bit. I head straight for the canal
again, and sail alone for an hour. The sun finally breaks through
the clouds just before it dips behind the mountains to the west. For
five minutes, there is golden spray atop every swell and alpenglow
paints the peaks. This is my reward. I'm a happy camper.

The clear night brings a bright moon, a crackling fire, a fine
wine, a wonderful woman, and marital relations. I have been to
heaven. I can walk on water, too.

Southerlies at Dillon

February 6, 1999

I'd had my eye on this setup for 2 years. Now the sea, the sky, and
the soul converged and it was time to go. National Weather Service
was right on the money with their forecast for 20–25 mph southerlies on Saturday. My calendar was clear, my intention focused.
Time for another pioneering exploration.

Dillon Beach is at the mouth of Tomales Bay. It curves through ninety degrees to face due north at the channel and due west at the mainland side. Southerlies blow straight offshore, side-off, and straight sideshore depending on what part of the beach you pick. Waves arrive from the north through the west, the directions of power. During a southerly blow there is virtually NO wind chop because there is no fetch. There are high ridges on both sides of the bay so the wind could be venturied or gustified depending on subtleties of direction. Sailing out through the surf will be port tack, a situation I have little experience with, but coming in I'll be going left and facing the wave, a rare treat for these goofy feet in the northern hemisphere.

Saturday dawns pouring down rain. Remote sensors indicate building south winds from the buoys to the bay. I make a couple phone calls, load the van, and am rolling by 9:30. Questions arise and subside like koi in a pond. Will the wind be steady enough? Strong enough? Waves too big? Too gnarly? Closed out? I don't care. I just have to go and see for myself.

At 11 AM I am parked at a paved overlook above the beach. Spray is blowing sideways off the wave crests, the waves look evenly spaced and beautiful, not too big, and the water is smooooth! Steady rain. I put on my foulies and walk down the muddy trail to the beach to feel the wind at sea level and get another perspective on the surf. Wind feels smooth and steady, 4.7 and the little board!

Two more trips up and down, change suits, make a couple calls, chat with some other surfcheckers, and I launch off the sandy beach . . . only to flounder in that zone where "overpowered" intersects with "out-of-shape" and "new to this spot." I barely get up and hook in, mostly get the boom ripped from my grip. Another trip up and down, rerig and rest. Too warm in my layers of neoprene, and my tummy is too full of roast beef samich. Need to cool down.

Round two is much better. I pump it up and bear off for power, bang a couple curbs of white water, catch a little air, go down, say a few "oh shit's," get up, and get outside. Now I can cruise and catch my breath.

I'm hooked in and zooming over the 6-inch chop and the 6-foot swells. I look back at the shore and can barely see it through the rain. This is not the time to be doing distance runs, jibe ho! I'm on a big rolling swell right quick, and the spray blowing off the one ahead of me is impressive—OK, it's downright intimidating. This is one wave I'm NOT going to shred, I'm in cautious-exploration mode. I jam down the face and outrun this thick sand-sucking monster. Whew . . . I made it, but I'm getting a message from my body: "You're not in shape for this, Galvan!" The surf is bigger, thicker, more powerful than I had expected, and I hardly sailed at all last year.

Time to quit while I'm ahead. So I come to a huge inside arena of smooth water, wind just blasting, and I can't resist a long drawn out arcing jibe, sooooo sweet. Then I'm pointing back out into the surf of course, and I eat it at the first wave, lose my gear and start swimming. No rocks, no serious current, just a real clear sign that it's quittin' time.

So the place works. Bodies and gear need to be in top shape, small swell would be nice. Buoys were reporting 10 to 12 feet from the west that day. Oh yes, this is one of the sharkiest places in the whole damn Pacific Ocean! Enter the food chain at your own risk . . .

Chapter Five

Windsurfing

A Subculture of Commitment

Belinda Wheaton

Beyond Images

It is a common perception that windsurfing is a sport that takes place in serene environments and warm climates. While a gentle breeze is blowing, the windsurfer (person)[1] glides along effortlessly and gracefully on the board. However, the mainstream media, such as television advertising, often presents windsurfing as a high-action, glamorous sport, similar to surfing and involving the same breed of fit, blond, crazy, young, white, male participants. Both these images represent windsurfing, but they present two extreme "faces" of the activity.

The first image might represent the occasional participant, one who probably hires a board to use on the occasional trip, or on holiday abroad, and for whom windsurfing represents a recreation that participants enjoy in warm, gentle weather. Yet through my involvement in the sport it became clear that windsurfing is much more than just a recreation, or a craze; participants are involved in

Belinda Wheaton is a research fellow at the University of Brighton, England. Her research interests focus around the politics of popular culture, consumption, and identity. She has published a number of articles based on her doctoral research that examined the culture of windsurfing in the context of postmodern sport. She has also been a regular contributor to various specialist sports magazines and a columnist for a UK windsurfing magazine. She is an enthusiastic windsurfer, as well as a surfer, snowboarder, and skier.

a multilayered leisure subculture.[2] The latter image represents the apotheosis of the dedicated, often obsessive participant to whom windsurfing participation is more than just a sport; it is a whole way of life in which participants seek hedonism, freedom and self-expression. Participation in this lifestyle is manifest in a range of symbols from clothes and speech to the car and associated leisure activities. For core[3] members, windsurfing dictates their leisure time, their work time, their choice of career, and where they live.

These dedicated windsurfers form the basis of this chapter. According to survey research, there are 300,000–400,000 "regular windsurfers" in Britain, although not all of these could be described as active members of the culture.[4] Nevertheless, 15,000–20,000 around Britain avidly buy British windsurfing magazines each month,[5] and support a multi–million pound industry.

My personal involvement inspired the ethnographic research on which this chapter is based. An eighteen–month participant observation phase from 1995 to 1997 focused on a windsurfing community centered around Silver Sands beach on the South Coast of England,[6] one of the most popular areas in the UK.[7] As an active windsurfer, and a freelance journalist working for a British windsurfing magazine, I adopted a partially covert "complete participant"[8] role, based on my established position within the group, and my familiarity with the main setting.[9] The analytical themes[10] that emerged from this locality were developed with in-depth interviews with selected members of the British windsurfing community, as well as observations at other windsurfing communities in the UK and abroad.[11]

In this chapter, my focus is on 'commitment.' I will demonstrate the existence of a leisure culture with a value system that emphasizes commitment to the activity. Moreover, for core participants, this leisure activity serves as the basis for an entire lifestyle, and is so central to their sense of self that it constitutes a "culture of commitment."[12]

Subcultural Identity: Insiders and Outsiders

Active windsurfers identify with the role of 'windsurfer'; becoming 'a windsurfer' involves employing and proclaiming a subcultural identity through their leisure consumption and its attendant value system and lifestyle.[13] Dant observes the significance of the windsurfer's collective, subcultural identity: "There need be no names—no reference to personal identity, it is enough to be demonstrably a fellow windsurfer."[14]

The windsurfer's identity is marked by numerous visual signs, ranging from clothes and fashion and vehicles driven to the equipment used, which are distinctive and identifiable from both 'mainstream,' and other sports cultures.[15] However, other less visible characteristics, such as the value system which emphasizes commitment to the activity, and forms of 'insider knowledge,' are more important parts of the process of identity construction, particularly in the formation of 'taste' hierarchies within the subculture.[16] As Donnelly and Young outline, identity construction is "intended for two distinct audiences—members of the larger society and members of the subculture."[17] As the newcomer progresses from outsider to insider, the emphasis shifts from constructing an identity intended to signify his/her membership to the outside world, to ceasing to value that audience,[18] and concomitantly desiring to be valued by the inside world. In this analysis, I focus on the meaning and display of subcultural involvement and identification within the subculture's internal hierarchies of participation, knowledge and 'taste,'[19] exploring how in this seemingly image-based sport culture, commitment to the activity is central to 'insiders' ' meaning of 'authentic' subcultural identity.[20]

My point of departure is to briefly map the 'world of the windsurfer,' outlining the sociohistorical origins, context, and development of the windsurfing subculture.

A Culture of Hedonism

Bourdieu, in his article "Sport and Social Class," argues that the social conditions at the inception of a sport predetermine that sport's shape and direction; each sporting practice has its own "specific chronology."[21] Bourdieu suggests that windsurfing, like other "new sports," was invented by members of the "new" and "petite bourgeoisie," a "counter-culture," imported to Europe from the USA.[22] These sports stand in opposition to traditional sports practiced by the "dominant class"; they challenge the "standard attributes of bourgeois ritual."[23]

Bourdieu's hypothesis about "new sports" broadly reflects the British windsurfing subculture's ethos and values. Windsurfing portrays a public image that emphasizes individuality, freedom, hedonism and an anti-competition ethos, cultural values and ideologies it shares with many other "new sport" cultures, and specifically, the surfing culture from which windsurfing evolved. These ideologies are based in surfing's countercultural heritage, which emphasized surfing as a lifestyle, not the ethos of the bourgeoisie elites.[24] As Farmer argues, the hedonistic values of surfing culture, such as being "more interested in getting 'stoked' . . . than in working"[25]—and the lack of formal rules, regulation, and organization—distinguish it from dominant sports cultures. Yet the central question is how these values of counterculture, exhibited in surfing since the 1960s, have been appropriated and /or transformed in the different cultural space of windsurfing, and within the specificities of the sociohistorical moment of the mid-1990s. As I will illustrate, these characteristics also differentiate windsurfing from more traditional, institutionalized, rulebound, competitive, and 'masculinized' sport cultures, themselves marked by combative competition, aggression, and toughness.

Formation and Evolution of the Subculture

Windsurfing, or board sailing as it is sometimes called, originated during the mid 1960s. The windsurfer craft was based on designs and technologies adapted from the sports of boat sailing and surfing. While there is still debate and contestation over who "invented" the sport, by 1968, two Californian surfers, Hoyle Schweitzer and Jim Drake, had asserted their place in windsurfing history by patenting a product called the "Windsurfer" in America and Europe. By the mid-1970s companies were producing windsurf boards around the developed world (Europe, Canada, Japan, Australia). Windsurfing was Europe's fastest-growing sport in the mid-1980s—with more than half a million boards sold worldwide, Germany and France were the world's biggest producers and consumers.[26] The sport reached a period of maturation in the early 1990s, with equipment sales having peaked in the late 1980s;[27] as Turner argues, windsurfing is not a "fad or craze," it has established itself as a "genuine sport."[28]

Institutionalization

Windsurfing, like surfing,[29] has resisted regulation and institutionalization; as interviewees claimed, it was perceived to be a sport that "challenged the established way" [Scott]. In the early 1980s, the time when the sport became popular in the UK, windsurfing tended to be based around sailing centers or clubs. Sailors and other water users perceived that the windsurfers were "different," "more deviant"; they also tended to be younger. As Scott, who learned to windsurf during the early 1980s, argued,

It challenged the orthodox way of thinking about things, and traditional values and attitudes toward them. They [the sailors] looked at you with disdain.

In the 1990s, only a minority of windsurfers in Britain were members of organizations or associations.[30] Even among windsurfers who chose to participate in formal competitions, I observed a reluctance to join organizations. Likewise, although club membership was a prerequisite to gain water access in some (particularly inland) venues, few coastal windsurfing venues in the South had formal clubs. Windsurfing's "grass roots" resides with the casual weekend sailor.[31]

The Anti-competition Ethos

In 1984 windsurfing was accepted in the Olympic games as a class in the "yachting" events.[32] Nevertheless, the number of windsurfers who engaged in organized competitions was a minority; for example, only eighty British windsurfers were members of the IMCO class (International Mistral Class Association), the Olympic class board.[33]

When questioned about why they windsurfed, and in particular what had attracted them to the sport, the vast majority of participants of all abilities, sexes, and levels of involvement, stressed the individualistic and anti-competitive nature of the sport. Competitions opposed the freedom and expression of the windsurfing lifestyle, as Mike Waltz,[34] a professional windsurfer, explained:

It's one of the most powerful things about [wind] surfing; it's a free-spirited sport. It really wasn't based and built around a competitive thing, and although competitive [wind]surfing is big, it's still only a tiny piece of the world [wind]surfing scene.

Nevertheless, professionalization of the sport, particularly the formation of an international world windsurfing tour (which has attracted considerable corporate sponsorship, large prize purses, and media exposure), provided elite (male) windsurfers with a way to fund their activity. Entering national and international competitions became a stepping-stone to obtaining sponsorship, and for a few, a career. Yet, many windsurfers still tended to compete as a means to an end; to be able to windsurf year-round.[35] In national events I attended, many of the competitors competed to gain sub-cultural recognition, principally based around subcultural media publicity, which helped to secure equipment sponsorship.[36] The narratives of elite British wave sailors I interviewed illustrated both the continued existence of the anti-competition ethos, and this contradiction in their individual motivations to compete:[37]

> No, I think it [competition] sucks, I am not into compe-titions . . . it is just not for me, I have enough stress coming [here] for one contest, I am more of a "soul surfer," that's what I would like to get into a bit more. [British wave-sailing champion]

Furthermore, some resistance to this institutionalization and commer-cialization process existed, particularly from the anti-competition wave sailors (characterized as the "soul surfers"), who perceived that these "professional" organizations represented "self-interested individuals" who wanted to "bleed their sport." A professional windsurfer publicly condemned the Professional Windsurfing Association, claiming:

> They're fending for themselves . . . so that they can pro-tect their money-earning potential . . . they are not inter-ested in performance, improving the sport as something that kids can get into. . . . Competition doesn't promote good sailing. It doesn't promote talent—it promotes com-panies. I'm not into that. [Mark Angulo][38]

Professional windsurfing, windsurfing in its most commodified form, co-exists with the "soul-surfing" ethos that pits an indi-vidual against the environment (the wind, sea, and waves), not other people. For example:

> I have never been very keen on face-to-face competitive sport. When you deal with the sea, it is very different because you have to do it—you can't let it beat you. If you mess up, you'll pay the consequences, and I quite like that. [Michael]

Furthermore, competition in windsurfing takes several coexistent forms including self-improvement, or personal development, the self against the environment, and in particular gaining peer respect.

Diversification and Fragmentation

Windsurfing expanded rapidly during the 1980s, the catalyst being technological developments, particularly new materials with higher strength-to-weight ratios which have resulted in much lighter, more efficient and durable boards and rigs (the sail, mast, and boom) which are easier to use, carry, and transport. Windsurfing became a popular and fashionable sport. Yet, with this increased participation and popularity, the exclusivity of the windsurfing subculture and the uniqueness of its identity decreased.[39] Accordingly, the windsurfing subculture became more fragmented;[40] in the 1990s (when this chapter was written) the generic term *windsurfing* encompassed several different forms of the activity, ranging from long-board sailing to freestyle, speed sailing, and wave sailing in surf. 'Subworlds' and 'scenes'—such as wave sailors—have re-created exclusivity among themselves, found new locations, and reappropriated signifiers of subcultural status in distinctive ways. Despite considerable overlaps in 'subworld' membership, each defines itself in relation to other groups or cliques of windsurfers, creating an exclusionary process within the subculture, as well as between insiders and outsiders. Nevertheless, these subworlds retain their identity within the subcultural whole, and share similar characteristics, attitudes, and values. At the core of the windsurfing subculture, there are similarities with surfing cultures, and despite a degree of animosity between the two cultures (which has arguably developed around competition for space in the surf),[41] they share locations and the industries that have developed around the sports.

Local and Global Patterns

Windsurfing, like other new sport subcultures, extends beyond nation states;[42] popular in many industrialized nations, its centers are Europe, Australia, and North America (particularly Hawaii). Despite the relative dearth of organizations or clubs, informal small group interactions such as "surf safaris," competitions, car boot sales, trade shows, and fairs all encourage links between different groups and communities of windsurfers, helping retain the conformity in information and cultural characteristics of the windsurfing subculture. Travel, whether for the weekend or longer holidays or trips, is an integral part of the windsurfer's lifestyle. Thus, as John, one of the keen participants at Silver Sands explained, he often bumped into the same people on his windsurfing holidays, regardless of how far afield he traveled:

> Well I met one bloke, a guy that I first met in Cabarette. He was an estate agent then, and then I bumped into him again in Fuerteventura, and also at Longbridge car boot sale, and sailing at Silver Sands. This was over a number of years. And when I turned up in Hawaii, . . . he was at Camp 1 the next day, which was weird.

Specialist windsurfing magazines and videos, although produced nationally, have much wider audiences, which serve in the exchange of ideas such as the latest techniques and other forms of 'insider knowledge.' The windsurfing industry itself, based around the production of windsurfing equipment, accessories and clothing, has importer/distributors in many countries, producing standardized products and promotional materials.

To summarize, the windsurfing subculture in England is part of a wider subculture, in which "the various means of communication . . . serve to link them into a subcultural whole."[43] As one interviewee put it, windsurfers worldwide have "a common bond." Although local differences exist, this ethnography, based on several settings in Europe, Hawaii, and the Caribbean, indicated that there were many similarities in cultural characteristics in all the settings observed, ranging from attitudes and values to subcultural style. In the following section, I will outline important facets of this value system that delineates the subculture, and specifically the centrality of 'commitment' to subcultural status.

Subcultural Status: "Beach Cred"

One issue that is crucial in the subculture is skill:

> Well, status is how good you are. If you can do a water start, carve jybe, you have a certain status because of that. [Male, core, intermediate windsurfer]

Status in the windsurfing culture is achieved primarily by being a "good windsurfer"—the better the windsurfer, the higher the subcultural status. Being good—or, in subcultural argot, a "hot" or "rad" sailor—is based primarily on level of skill. Those who perform the most difficult maneuvers, with the most style, are considered the most skilled: "If they are a good sailor, they are treated with respect "[Jenny]. However, other attributes are important to gain beach status, or "beach cred," such as having a "go-for-it attitude," being willing to attempt hard and dangerous maneuvers ("being rad"), even if they fail, and being prepared/able to go out in all conditions, particularly on the windiest days, and in the most dangerous sea conditions:

> I mean, you look at people who are really good at what they're doing, but also very brave in what they are doing as well, so you really admire people who go out in difficult conditions and things like that. [Debby]

Windsurfers watch each other—but mainly they watch the best windsurfers at the beach, termed the local "hot shots":

> I mean we all watch, don't we. We go down the beach and look out, and say, "He's quite good, oh yes." It's like going to an art exhibition and saying, "That's quite a good painting." [Jo, female]

"Being looked at" or "watched" is a recurring part of the windsurfers' narratives. The gaze of the (male and female) spectators I observed, as well as other (predominately male) windsurfers was focused on the more advanced windsurfers out on the water. Men, who formed the majority of participants,[44] and specifically the more proficient men, were under this gaze of other men.[45]

Despite the anti-competition ethos, "beach credibility" is gained by outperforming the other sailors at the beach. At all beaches that I observed, the better windsurfers competed to be the "local hot shot":

> Silver Sands is a vast beach, yet people see it necessary to perform in one area, again vying for status . . . it happens where ever you go—everyone wants to be the hot shot on the day. [Alex]

Jo's analogy of the "art exhibition" is also informing, as it highlights the subjective dimension to windsurfing prowess. The aesthetic and subjective character of being 'a good windsurfer' is especially apparent in wave sailing, which is the closest form of windsurfing to regular surfing. Elite wave sailors frequently refer to other wave sailors' "styles"—an individualistic way of performing and expressing maneuvers. This subjective element contributes to competition over status in the subculture. However, competitiveness over status predominates toward *men* at the core; those men whose sense of self is most firmly embedded in windsurfing, and younger men whose masculine identity is most fragile. This competitiveness between elite men to demonstrate their sporting supremacy contributes to the exclusivity of the culture based on 'prowess,' alienating and excluding participants who are less skilled, less committed and less "go-for-it," as well as reducing camaraderie and support among the men.[46]

"Just Do It"

The other value central to attaining subcultural status was commitment to the activity:

> The next group of people who always get respect are those who try, however experienced or inexperienced they are. The ones you notice are those you see improving— they gain an enormous amount of respect. [Emma, core female reflecting on status at Silver Sands]

Windsurfing is a notoriously hard sport to learn, and to become proficient requires considerable commitment in time, effort, and money. The majority of elite windsurfers are very committed; as Scott explained: "You've got to put the time in, and make the effort to improve." Commitment and skill level are connected.

"Hard core" is a term used by the windsurfer to signify high subcultural status, as well as connoting a particular attitude and image.[47] Nevertheless, terms like "total respect" or "hard core" depend on the individual's positioning in the subculture—his/her ability level, age, and gender. For example, nonelite and particularly older individuals who try hard are seen to be "having a go," are respected. However, if a younger person claims to have "total respect" for an elderly windsurfer, the younger one admires the older one's commitment and his/her ability to keep windsurfing. But as John clarified, it is a different type of respect from that for elite windsurfers:

> Yeah. I mean—you'd notice it, and you'd think, "Ya, I'd like to do that when I'm 65," but you'd be more

interested . . . in watching the other guy, because it's going to be more exciting to watch, and, you might learn something. [John]

As more committed and proficient windsurfers have higher status, corresponding forms of windsurfing that require more skill, and more commitment in time to achieve that skill level, are ascribed a higher status, particularly "short-board sailing." Those forms of windsurfing that are hardest to learn (requiring the most commitment in time) and perceived to be the most hazardous, such as wave sailing, are considered the most exclusive,[48] extreme 'sub worlds.' As Stephen, an elite racer, affirmed: "Wave sailors as a whole have my utmost respect, because it frightens the life out of me." Varying statuses create divisions between subgroups of windsurfers, types of windsurfing, and different geographical locations (this last division reflected in the term "localism"), which seem to be partly attempts to retain the exclusivity of their part of the subculture.

"All the Gear, no Idea"

Windsurfing, in common with many other 'new,' individualized sports, is based around the consumption of objects, in its case the windsurfing equipment or kit, which is both expensive and often fetishized.[49] The windsurfer (board) has a subcultural symbolic value, which is greater than its functionality.[50] Certain brands of boards have more status than others, which members with high subcultural capital are able to differentiate: "People are very good at being able to sort of pick out what the 'in' boards are" [Debby]. Yet, despite the centrality of windsurfing equipment to the activity, and the expenditure required to get involved in the sport, members can't 'buy' their way into the core of the subculture. In Bourdieu's terms, the relationship between economic capital and (sub)cultural capital is more complex than a direct exchange. An anti-materialism ethos is evident from the windsurfers' attitudes toward those individuals who purchase equipment deemed beyond their proficiency, or try to demonstrate their subcultural membership or status by displaying their equipment. Every interviewee declared that a visiting windsurfer with the most up-to-date board, sail, and wetsuit might turn heads on the beach, but prestige in the group was based on performance alone[51]—who was "good," and who "went for it"[52]: "They have tried to take the check book route into windsurfing, and that is a definite no" [male, core windsurfer]. Although newcomers often perceived that having the most up-to-date or the most technical equipment intended for more skilled sailors signified that they were "real" windsurfers,[53] the core windsurfers viewed it as a "novice blunder"[54]—a mismanagement of the identity construction process. Emma, for example, recounted with embarrassment that, as a beginner, she wanted to be proficient enough "to sail the shortest possible board," the type of board used by more advanced windsurfers. In her enthusiasm to gain and demonstrate her sporting proficiency, she incorrectly assumed that the shorter the board she used, the higher her status. As Donnelly and Young observed in the climbing subculture, the conspicuous display of "equipment" and other symbols of identification is the first stage of identity construction.[55] As participants become more experienced, they realize that "overt display is a rookie error that highlights the subcultural values of coolness and understatement."[56]

Likewise, windsurfers' terms for such individuals include "fashion victims" and "equipment junkies." Nevertheless, there are variances and contradictions in this anti-consumption ethos, which for example, varies according to the type of windsurfing activity, and between geographical locations.

A "Culture of Commitment"

You do it all the time, you are out all the time, talk about it, think about it, it is the main driving force in your life. [marginal participant, addressing a core windsurfer]

Commitment, as I have demonstrated, is a central value in the windsurfing culture, and essential to subcultural status. However, this commitment to windsurfing extends to become an organizing principle in participants' whole lives. For "core" participants, for whom windsurfing is "serious leisure,"[57] commitment to windsurfing affects their whole lifestyle. This relationship between subcultural identity, lifestyle, and commitment is central to understanding the internal distinctions and stratification of subculture members, and the meanings they give to their new sport consumption.[58]

Indicators of Commitment

Donnelly suggests that friendship patterns, time, and money are key indicators of commitment to a particular subculture and its associated lifestyle.[59] Examining these and other indicators of commitment in the windsurfing subculture—for instance: lifestyle rituals (such as watching the weather forecast), where participants live, how far they drive to the beach, and the effect of their windsurfing career on employment and career development—all illustrate the extent to which dedicated windsurfers attempt to organize their whole lives around this leisure activity. I will discuss some selected examples.

However, before doing so, it is important to emphasize the intense physical and mental pleasure that participants gain from the activity.[60] Interviewees in this study argued that once they were "bitten by the bug" or "hooked," windsurfing quickly crescendoed into a vital part of their lives—it was a "psychological high" they needed:

> It's almost a spiritual thing . . . the feel-good factor is so high—even if you've had a bad spell, it's better than not sailing at all—you know, like the buzz I get, the endorphin sort of buzz. The simple physical feeling it gives you is great, I think, and the mental spin-off . . . I don't know a single other sport that's been able to give me those sorts of things. . . . So, I think it's just, it's terribly life-enhancing. [Lisa, core female]

Without a comprehension of this sociopsychological dimension to the activity, it is hard to comprehend why windsurfers devote seemingly excessive amounts of time, money, and 'self' to this leisure subculture, at the same time as expressing extreme frustration about their involvement.

Social Activities and Friendship Patterns

Core and keen windsurfers tend to socialize mainly with other windsurfers.[61] The participants contend that the type of people who windsurf are cognate; they have "a similar viewpoint on life" [Scott]. However, the strong friendship networks and communities that develop between windsurfers exist because of their commitment to a lifestyle adapted around windsurfing.

Core windsurfers are prepared to put their 'whole life on hold' just waiting for that one windy day. Keen windsurfers that I observed willingly 'sacrificed' or postponed other social or sporting commitments and opportunities if the wind blew up. As their commitment to windsurfing increased, they found it increasingly hard,[62] and were less likely, to continue their friendships with nonwindsurfers. So committed windsurfers tended to 'hang around' together outside of the beach environment.

Stephanie, a female in her early 40s, was one of the most committed people I interviewed, and in her own words an "obsessive" windsurfer, yet she was by no means atypical of core windsurfers. Stephanie argued that she would not obligate herself (or her husband, who was also a windsurfer) to any social occasions, just in case there was a chance she could be windsurfing. Windsurfing, as she vividly described, dictated almost every aspect of her life:

> Most of our best friends are windsurfers. It's like people who don't windsurf are from another planet really, or, you know they have to tolerate you, or you tolerate them. But like my family, you know, Christmas is all around the weather forecast . . . and they just have to want to know what you are doing at New Year, and I said, "Don't know yet, depends on what the weather is doing. . . ." I just refuse POINT BLANK to have a meal in the middle of the day. I will NOT. I mean I am terribly selfish about it, and they just—I think all his family think I'm selfish. . . . I mean, sitting around in the middle of the day eating a meal if it's windy is my idea of HELL, you know. I won't do it. . . . They'd be hurt, yeah, absolutely, well I just tell people that I put windsurfing first, and that's it, and if you don't like it, stuff it. You know it's an addiction and it's a way of life, you know. If they can't cope with that, then they're not really worth bothering with. [Stephanie]

To the less serious, and particularly non-, windsurfers, the total commitment demonstrated by the core, especially by female participants, was often perceived as antisocial and selfish.[63] Michael, a marginal participant who socialized with core windsurfers, reflected that they were exceedingly single-minded, and that in their "own little world" this "selfishness" that the windsurfing lifestyle perpetuated became accepted, the norm. He highlighted a particular incident:

> Two or three years ago, a whole bunch of you were meant to be somewhere and you didn't turn up because it was windy. And someone had gone to loads of trouble—it was someone's party, and nobody turned up. And no one ex-

pected them to turn up. And it was just bizarre, because this whole party had been organized and nobody bloody came until they got off the beach. And no one was kind of bothered. Windsurfing is an excuse for ignoring a lot of social commitments—and that is universal. [Michael]

Michael's commentary is not an exaggeration. Core windsurfers, who in the majority are male, put their windsurfing before their families and partners. Men expect their partners to understand and accept their commitment to windsurfing. Alex, a male core windsurfer in his twenties, told me:

I say [to new girlfriends] if you ever ask me to choose between windsurfing and you, it will always be windsurfing. . . . How many relationships have failed because of windsurfing? In a past relationship, my girlfriend used to stop me going windsurfing . . . She used to say, "Right, you are windsurfing one day this weekend." I would just miss out on days. We broke up.

Clearly, not all participants are so committed to windsurfing. As Donnelly suggests, those individuals whose level of commitment is low are only partially recognized as subculture members by more committed members.[64] A common subcultural career pattern is that, as participants get older (typically from their mid thirties), their total commitment to windsurfing decreases, and other parts of their lives, such as careers and family, take precedence. As Claire explained, windsurfing was no longer a compatible lifestyle option, as she was so "jealously guarding of [her] spare time."[65] It was at this point that many windsurfers become marginal or occasional participants, or stop completely.

Economic Resources: Money

Windsurfers around Great Britain tend to be socioeconomically-privileged men[66]; there is a bias towards AB males, particularly the professional classes, although participants in the Profiles survey represented all socioeconomic groups. Irrespective of the anti-materialistic attitudes, the more-involved participants spent much greater amounts on the activity, namely on equipment, transport, and travel. Although some interviewees claimed that windsurfing was not a particularly expensive leisure pursuit, particularly in relation to other urban-based consumption activities, economic status did exclude many potential participants from windsurfing, especially disadvantaged groups. As Young and Gallup suggest in the North American context, the cost of the equipment clearly plays an important "gate keeping function."[67]

Nevertheless, despite the expense, many of the less advantaged people I observed did find a way to continue to windsurf. Irrespective of their economic capability, serious windsurfers prioritized spending on windsurfing. Economic status restricts but does not necessarily prevent participation in consumer culture.[68] For instance, teenagers who could not afford their own windsurfing equipment worked at the beach, or for local windsurf shops for "slaves rates" in return for the loan of equipment. Some became instructors in holiday centers abroad. James, an elite windsurfer and student, claimed: "I sacrifice everything to windsurf. I'm skint, £900 overdrawn, all my student loan is gone—I had 3 of them, so I have debts." [James]

As Bourdieu hypothesizes in relation to "new sports" more broadly,[69] the exclusion of those without the financial means is more subtle than an exclusively 'class'-based analysis acknowledges. "Economic barriers—however great they may be ... are not sufficient to explain the class distribution of these activities. There are more hidden entry requirements."[70] For example, windsurfing is a very time-intensive activity, which women in particular find hard to sustain: "Windsurfing takes up half a day, or a day. Aerobics you can go down to the gym—fit it in—hubby or partner will baby-sit, so windsurfing is a problem" [Lesley]. At Silver Sands almost all of the women who windsurfed were "privileged women," predominately well-educated, between 20 and 40 in age, many with their own income.[71] While they did find the equipment expenditure a financial drain, none of their narratives suggested that the cost of windsurfing was so prohibitive as to make them stop. However, almost all the interviewees indicated that "lack of time" was particularly effective in restricting their participation, especially for those women who lived a considerable distance from the water, or who had young children. Windsurfers need lifestyle flexibility.[72]

Lifestyle Flexibility

Farmer's research highlights that surfers brag about the unrestrained and "free" life they lead, epitomized in the bumper sticker "No job, no phone, no money, and no address."[73] Likewise, Crosset and

Beal highlight that sailboarders, like surfers, are highly regarded in their subculture if they "drop out" of the dominant culture to devote more time and effort to their sport.[74] While they warn that "dropping out" does not necessarily constitute resistance or opposition to the middle-class values of the dominant culture, this degree of commitment is indicative of the ways in which the dedicated surfer and windsurfer sets up his/her life to be able to drop everything when the conditions are right. Having lifestyle flexibility is essential for commitment to be a serious windsurfer:

> It's a lifestyle thing. I'm willing to spend my whole year and set up my life so that when that day happens, I'm ready and I can go. The true surfer is that way. He'll work in the restaurant at night, he'll do whatever he can so that when the day comes and the surf is good, he's surfing. I think a lot of windsurfers are like that, they like that side of it. [Mike Waltz[75]]

In the UK, coastal windsurfing is dependent on wind direction and strength, as well as the sea-state (wave size, tide, and so on). This unpredictability is a continual source of frustration for participants, particularly those who live some distance from the windsurfing venue. My research revealed numerous examples of the ways in which serious windsurfers adapted, or attempted to find ways to fund continued activity, which also gave them the versatility and time to windsurf when the weather conditions were right.

"Office Job? No Way": Employment and Career

Although the employment patterns of the core subculture members is very varied in terms of the range both of professions and of income levels, a commonality is that those who are able to, organize their employment to allow them to windsurf as often as possible.

The 9-to-5 office job represents the antithesis of the freedom of the windsurfing lifestyle. Part-time, occasional well-paid work, being a student, even being on unemployment benefits are all appealing options. One teenager I met washed dishes in a bar and allegedly "nicked car radios" to fund his windsurfing. Another lived in his panel van right through the winter. He had a university degree but chose to pick daffodils and conduct other menial tasks to pay for his food. Young and Gallup make a similar observation on the occupational status of windsurfers in the USA:

> We contend that for each teacher and doctor there is
> what Reiss (1984:40) has called an Okie(s) . . . i.e. a per-
> son who resides in his/her vehicle and eats peanut butter
> (at least during the sailing season) so they can afford to
> windsurf.[76]

Having ample 'free time,' and flexibility in the work sphere
are the most valued commodities among serious windsurfers. For
many of the privileged middle-class participants at Silver Sands, it
was not money that constrained their ability to windsurf, but lack
of time. As Sue claimed, "It is fitting everything in—that's the
trouble, finding time." Emma, a part-time general practitioner,
explained that she had chosen the GP route, rather than being
trained as a surgeon, a higher-status position within the medical
profession, to enable herself to have the time and flexibility to
windsurf:

> Time to do other things, sportingwise, has always been
> important to me. So as soon as I qualified, I directed my
> career, through jobs I applied for, to fit with windsurfing.
> There is no way I would do a job more than 10 miles
> away from the sea, because I would just go nuts. [Emma]

For many of the committed windsurfers in this research, irrespective of their class background, gender, or educational level,
employment was adapted to fit with their leisure activity and the
need for flexibility, often at the expense of earning more money.
Thus, as in the surfing culture, material wealth was not valued
unless it also enabled the participant to windsurf.

Quality of Life: "Dropping Out"

John and Debby were both professional people in their mid to late
thirties with high incomes. They had bought a house on the coast,
initially, as a weekend home, but had since sold their London flat
and moved to the coast. For both of them, the move involved a
drop in income, and in John's case, a change in career. However,
moving to the coast symbolized more than just increased opportunity to windsurf. Debby explained their rationale:

> Then it was really John saying, "Actually, I don't want
> to do this job any more—I want to do something com-

pletely different," and we don't want to live in London. So buying the house was part of saying to ourselves— we're not going to be in London anymore, I don't want to work five days a week, I don't want to work in a sort of the regimented hours I do at the moment. So I want to do something which is totally flexible, which means if I want to piss off and do something different for an afternoon, that's fine. . . . I mean, it would be windsurfing because that's what we'd both do. But yah, it's really about trying to organize things so that you can actually do what you want, when you want, not that you don't work because you have to work anyway, but just not to be tied down by it.

Interviewees outlined that windsurfing, and nonurban living, represented an escape from the constraints of the city "rat race"; it presented a lifestyle in which having leisure *time* was more highly valued than high incomes and material goods.

As Booth argues in discussing the surfing culture in Australia:

Mass consumer capitalism created the conditions under which the middle-classes revised traditional ideas about leisure as an adjunct of work: leisure became an autonomous social practice based on individually chosen lifestyles.[77]

This attitude of work as an adjunct to leisure was widespread, particularly among the younger windsurfers, or those who had become dissatisfied with professional career paths and had the economic stability to be able make such choices about their careers.[78]

Nevertheless, there was a degree of lip service among these professional people at Silver Sands, who claimed that "money didn't matter." Without doubt, those individuals who had *both* flexible employment and economic wealth were envied, especially individuals whose lifestyles enabled them to take extended holidays or trips abroad.

Conclusions: Serious Leisure and Subcultural Commitment

This ethnography has shown that identities in the windsurfing subculture are constructed around leisure consumption, and that, for the very committed, subcultural status and identity are central to their sense of self. The research supports Chaney's claims that increasing numbers of people "choose their type of work, and how it is organized, in order to be consistent with their lifestyle values."[79] Contrary to the (typically modernist) view of leisure as peripheral to "the serious business of life,"[80] the concept of "serious leisure" helps to reconceptualize the changing nature and meaning of work-leisure relationships. For some, a commitment to windsurfing resulted in a reduced interest in pursuance of a particular career; almost all of the committed windsurfers declared a need for "lifestyle flexibility."[81] In post-industrial society and specifically among the "(new) middle classes," it has been suggested that the "new struggle" is for control over time, and the "the temporal location of work and leisure,"[82] not just economic wealth.

While the common perception of alternative or 'lifestyle' sports such as windsurfing is that they are spectacular and very visual, dominated by commercial consumption, eclipsing 'authenticity' of experience,[83] I have shown that the existence of a 'culture of commitment' contradicts this view. Leisure identities are based around subcultural commitment, as demonstrated by the conspicuous use of time, not solely conspicuous consumption. In these individualized, privatized, and seemingly market-driven cultural spaces, subcultural communities have been created that express—in their own terms—a sense of subcultural 'authenticity' and localized 'resistance' to conspicuous consumption, institutionalization, and materialism.

Notes

Publishing note (August 2001): This chapter was written in 1997. Some sections of it, in amended forms, have been published elsewhere. In particular see Belinda Wheaton, "Just Do It: Consumption, Commitment and Identity in the Windsurfing Subculture" *Sociology of Sport Journal* 17 (2000): pp. 254–274.

Acknowledgements: I am grateful to the Economic and Social Research Council (UK), whose postgraduate studentship (ROO 429334379) made the doctoral research on which this paper is based possible. I would like to thank the editors and Tim Dant for their useful comments on earlier drafts.

1. *Windsurfer* refers to both the person and the object of consumption, the windsurfing board. See also Tim Dant, "Playing with things—Objects and subjects in windsurfing," in *Journal of Material Culture* 3 (1998).

2. The theoretical use and applicability of the term *subculture* both in the sports context and within popular culture more broadly remains

contested. For a discussion of these issues, see for example: Todd Crosset and Becky Beal, "The use of 'subculture' and 'subworld' in ethnographic works on sport: A discussion of definitional distinctions," in *Sociology of Sport Journal* (1997): pp. 73–85; see also, Sarah Thornton, *Club Cultures: Music, Media and Subcultural Capital* (Cambridge: Polity Press, 1995). While acknowledging these limitations and problematics, my use of subculture in this context is both as an analytical and descriptive category.

3. Peter Donnelly, "Towards a definition of sport subcultures," in Hart, Birell, and Marie (eds.) *Sport in the Sociocultural Process* 3rd ed. (Iowa: Brown, 1981), pp. 565–87.

4. The sources are: BMRB, British Market Research Bureau, TGI index (1995), and Profile Sport Consultancy, The United Kingdom Windsurf Report. A joint publication between the Profile Sport Market Consultancy and the Royal Yachting Association; March 1994. However, due to the unrestricted/unorganised nature of the windsurfing sport, participation figures tend to differ between sources, and tend not to differentiate between the 'casual' and committed windsurfers I have identified. It is likely that the committed members are only a small percentage of all recreational windsurfers.

5. *Boards* and *Windsurf* magazine audience figures, 1996–1997. These are the two windsurfing magazines published in the UK.

6. For purposes of anonymity and confidentiality, some place names, dates, and all the names of respondents are changed.

7. Geographical proximity to coastal and inland waters, as well as socioeconomic factors, affected this distribution pattern.

8. Martin Hammersley and Paul Atkinson, "What is Ethnography?" in *Ethnography: Principles in Practice* (London & New York: Routledge, 1983), pp. 1–25.

9. Clearly there were ethical considerations, in that I was partially concealing my true intentions from the group. These issues are discussed in Belinda Wheaton, "Covert Ethnography and the Ethics of Research: Studying Sport Subcultures," in Alan Tomlinson and Scott Fleming (eds.) *Ethics, Sport and Leisure: Crises and Critiques* (Aachen: Meyer & Meyer Verlag, 1997), pp. 163–72.

10. In the wider project a number of themes are explored ranging from: the existence of a sport subculture; gender relations and identities (masculinities and femininities) within the group; to exploring the significance of "postmodern" leisure lifestyles in cultural identity formation in late modernity. See Belinda Wheaton, "Consumption, lifestyle and gendered identities in post-modern sports: the case of windsurfing" (Ph.D. thesis, University of Brighton, 1997).

11. Notably I visited the island of Maui in the Hawaiian Islands, the windsurfer's Mecca and home to an international community of 'hard-core' windsurfing addicts. A total of twenty-four interviews were conducted.

12. The term "culture of commitment" is a useful term I adopt from Crouch and Tomlinson, which they use to describe the culture that

surrounds "serious leisure" activity. Serious leisure stems from the Canadian sociologist Stebbins. See, Robert Stebbins, *Amateurs, Professionals and Serious Leisure* (Montreal: McGill Queen's University Press, 1992); Alan Tomlinson, "Culture of Commitment in Leisure: Notes towards the understanding of a serious legacy," in *World Leisure and Recreation* 35, No. 1 (Spring 1993): pp. 6–9; and David Crouch, "Commitment, enthusiasm and creativity in the world of allotment holding," *World Leisure and Recreation* 35, No. 1 (Spring 1993): pp. 19–22.

13. Although in this chapter my focus is on commitment, in the wider project the multiple ways in which windsurfers create identities through their leisure consumption and its attendant lifestyle are explored. See also Belinda Wheaton "Just Do It: Consumption, Commitment and Identity in the Windsurfing Subculture," in *Sociology of Sport Journal* 17 (2000): pp. 254–274.

14. Tim Dant, "Playing with things," p. 5.

15. The specialist subcultural media, particularly windsurfing magazines, play an important part in this process.

16. See Thornton, *Club Cultures*.

17. Peter Donnelly and Kevin Young, "The construction and confirmation of identity in sport subcultures," in *Sociology of Sport Journal* 5 (1988): p. 224.

18. Ibid.

19. Thornton, *Club Cultures*.

20. While authenticity has many meanings, I am referring here to a set of subcultural norms and values that give meaning to the subculture and an individual's (subcultural) identity. A full examination of these complex and often contradictory processes is beyond the scope of this chapter, in particular that the 'uniqueness' of the subcultural identification of the committed windsurfer is not based on subcultural style.

21. Pierre Bourdieu, "Sport and Social Class," in *Social Science Information* 17, No. 6 (1978), p. 821.

22. Pierre Bourdieu, *Distinction: A Social Critique of the Judgement of Taste* (London & NY: Routledge & Kegan Paul Ltd, 1984), p. 220.

23. Ibid.

24. See Douglas Booth, "Surfing 60s: A case study in the history of pleasure and discipline," in *Australian Historical Studies* 103 (Oct 1994): pp. 262–79; and Kent Pearson, *Surfing Subcultures of Australia and New Zealand* (St. Lucia, Queensland: University of Queensland Press, 1979).

25. R. Farmer, "Surfing: motivations, values and culture," *Journal of Sports Behaviour* 15, No. 3 (Sep 1992): p. 242.

26. S. Turner, "Development and Organisation of Windsurfing," *Institute of Leisure and Amenity Management* 1 (1983): pp. 13–15.

27. Profile Sport Consultancy, The United Kingdom Windsurf Report, p. 23. For example, in the mid-1980s, the peak of windsurfing in the UK, 27,500 boards were sold there, compared with only 9,000 in 1993. However, these figures do not reflect the larger secondhand market.

28. Turner, "Development and Organisation of Windsurfing,"pp. 13–15.

29. See Booth, "Surfing 60s," pp. 262–79; Douglas Booth, "Ambiguities in Pleasure and Discipline: The Development of Competitive Surfing," in *Journal of Sport History* 22, No. 3 (Fall 1995): pp. 189–206; and Kent Pearson, *Surfing Subcultures of Australia and New Zealand* (St. Lucia, Queensland: University of Queensland Press, 1979).

30. Profile Sport Consultancy, The United Kingdom Windsurf Report.

31. Turner, "Development and Organisation of Windsurfing," pp. 13–15.

32. Women and men competed together, although by 1994, separate women's and men's classes were established.

33. Profile Sport Consultancy, The United Kingdom Windsurf Report, p. 13.

34. Interviewed in *Boards* (No. 101, 1993), p. 70.

35. Windsurfers who did compete had a "relaxed attitude to competition"; competition did represent "work" but "having a good time" remained an important motive. The exception were the "racers" who competed in long-board racing, the form of windsurfer closest to the sailing culture, and furthest from the surfing culture. They had a more conventional attitude to competition; the racing "subworld" was closer ideologically to those of mainstream "athletes."

36. Some individuals gained sponsorship without competing.

37. Booth discusses similar tensions between "pleasure and discipline" within professional surfing; the alternate philosophy of the "soul surfer" who rejected competition, commercialism and any bureaucracy, and a "new generation of perspicacious Australian surfers who recognized that professional competitions offered an avenue to eternal hedonism" (Douglas Booth, "Surfing 60s," p. 278). Booth argues that "soul surfing" emerged in the surfing culture (during the 1960s) as a reaction against competition, and "as an oppositional cultural practice symbolising the idealism of counterculture." Soul surfing was a reaction against competition and commercialism. Likewise, in the windsurfing subculture *soul surfing* was subcultural argot (appropriated from the surfing culture) to describe the type of windsurfing (usually wave sailing) that pitted an individual against the environment, not other people; the anti-competition ethos (and, as I argue more fully elsewhere, the anti-commercialism) discouraged windsurfers from engaging in formal competition.

38. Professional windsurfer interviewed in *Boards* (No. 101, 1993), p. 71.

39. As subcultural theorists have suggested, the more removed the subculture is from the parent culture, the higher the value of that subcultural identity. See Peter Donnelly, "Sport Subcultures," in *Exercise and Sport Sciences Review* 13 (1985): pp. 539–78.

40. Furthermore, as Donnelly argues (drawing on Toffler [1970]), the larger the subculture, the greater the likelihood of diversification and

fragmentation. Donnelly, "Towards a definition of sport subcultures," p. 571.

41. These hostilities between the subcultures of windsurfing, surfing, and other water users is well documented in the surfing subcultural media. Historically, surfers have been quite antagonistic toward windsurfers— for example, they call them "wind wankers." In Hawaii, the epicenter of windsurfing, and surfing, a local by-law prohibits windsurfers from going on the water before 11 AM. However, in Hawaii, the tensions between the wealthy white 'colonialists' and the Polynesian surfers is well documented. (See Mike Doyle, *Morning Glass: The adventures of a legendary waterman* [Three Rivers, Calif.: Manzanita Press, 1993].) Surfing has played an important part in Hawaiian culture for centuries, both as competitions and as part of harvest celebration. (See Greg Noll and Andrea Gabbard (eds.), *Da Bull: Life over the edge* [Berkeley: North Atlantic Books, 1989].) Yet despite the prevalence of Polynesian surfers, few windsurfed. The majority of windsurfers were white, or "haloes" as the Polynesians term them. Thus, although the antagonism between windsurfers and surfers in Hawaii (and elsewhere) is played out as competition over space, it seems likely that economic status and ethnicity are also contributing factors.

42. Donnelly, "Towards a definition of sport subcultures," pp. 565–87.

43. Ibid., p. 577.

44. The British windsurfing and its culture were clearly dominated by men, specifically white, predominantly middle-class men aged between 15 and 60. BMRB, British Market Research Bureau, TGI index (1995), and Profile Sport Consultancy, The United Kingdom Windsurf Report. From 80 to 90 percent of the windsurfers who used Silver Sands and other coastal locations nearby were male, even a higher percentage in the winter, although according to the survey research cited, women constitute up to 30 percent of regular windsurfers around the UK. Despite the emphasis on the young male portrayed in the media, survey data illustrate that only 16 percent of British windsurfers are under age 20 (ibid.).

45. See Shaun Nixon, "Check out the beef! Masculinities, the body and the contemporary men's magazines," in *Body Matters: Leisure Images and Lifestyles* (Eastbourne: LSA, 1993), pp. 73–78; and Toby Miller, "Sport, Media, Masculinity," in David Rowe and Geoffrey Lawrence (eds.) *Sport and Leisure: Trends in Australian Popular Culture* (Sydney: Hardcourt Brace Jovanovich, 1990).

46. This discussion about competing masculinities is explored more fully in Belinda Wheaton, " 'New Lads?' Masculinities and the New Sport Participant," *Men and Masculinities* 2 (2000): pp. 434–456.

47. 'Hard core' is not specific to the windsurfing subculture but used by surfers, skateboarders, and snowboarders. See, for example: Farmer, "Surfing: motivations, values and culture," pp. 241–57; Ian Borden, "Another Pavement, Another Beach: Skateboarding and the Performative Critique of Architecture," in Ian Borden, J. Kerr, Jane Rendell, and A. Pivaro

(eds.), *The Unknown City: Contesting Architecture and Social Space* (London: Wiley), in press.

48. See also Donnelly, "Towards a definition of sport subcultures," pp. 565–87.

49. Likewise, a content analysis of windsurfing magazines highlighted that they give prominence to, perhaps even fetishizes the equipment that windsurfers use, particularly the boards and sails.

50. See also Tim Dant, "Playing with things: How a windsurfer realises leisure," draft paper. Fiske likewise notes the symbolic value of the surfboard; see John Fiske, "Reading the Beach," in *Reading the Popular* (London: Unwin Hyman, 1989).

51. Of course, proficiency, particularly at the elite level, tends to reflect access to resources—especially the time and money to participate.

52. Likewise, a cardinal sin was to posit a commitment to windsurfer by talking about it, and going through the motions of "being a windsurfer," but not actually windsurfing.

53. See also Dant, "Playing with things."

54. Donnelly and Young, "The construction and confirmation of identity," pp. 197–211.

55. Ibid.

56. Donnelly and Young, "The construction and confirmation of identity," p. 230. Core windsurfers adopted other forms of such "impression management." For example when recounting a particular sailing session, it was important to downplay the size of the waves. Novice wave sailors tended to exaggerate the size of the waves, signifying their 'fear' and inexperience to the more expert wave sailors.

57. Stebbins, *Amateurs, Professionals and Serious Leisure.*

58. Conceptualizing the relationship between lifestyle, commitment, and identity is also a focus in Donnelly's theorizing of sport subcultural membership (ibid.), and other research surrounding Stebbins's conceptualization of "serious leisure." For example, studies of serious leisure have underlined that a lifestyle is developed around an activity that emphasizes commitment and provides a collective social identity. See Stebbins, *Amateurs, Professionals and Serious Leisure;* and Robert Stebbins, "Social World, Life-style and Serious Leisure: Toward a mesostructural analysis," in *World Leisure and Recreation* 35, No. 1 (Spring 1993): pp. 23–26.

59. Donnelly, "Towards a definition of sport subcultures," pp. 565–87.

60. I discuss this "commitment to pleasure," and how it is embodied, in Belinda Wheaton, "Consumption, lifestyle and gendered identities in postmodern sports: the case of windsurfing" (Ph.D. thesis, University of Brighton, 1997). Contrary to Bourdieu's suggestion that the common feature of "bourgeois sports" is that they are mainly pursued for their "health-maintaining functions, and their social profits," people windsurf primarily for short-term gains. This commitment is to the 'felt,' not 'displayed' body, to physical and

mental pleasure, or self-actualization. What binds these communities is a shared understanding of the pleasure of windsurfing; the excitement, the buzz, the thrill of blasting along the water at 30 miles an hour, or jumping ten feet into the air.

61. Many windsurfers talk incessantly about windsurfing. Windsurfers have their own jargon to describe the windsurfing experience as well as techniques and equipment. Some of this patois is unique to the windsurfing subculture, but many forms of expression are shared with the surfing culture; for example, the numerous terms to describe waves and wave breaks. Language, as Fiske argues, "signals subcultural membership," it demarks the (surfing) culture, and vitally functions to exclude the outsider. ("Reading the Beach," p. 60.) Windsurfers are stratified according to who has most knowledge of this jargon—those at the core having the most knowledge and subcultural status. Outsiders/newcomers whom I observed did not understand the subcultural argot—to the extent that it was hard for them even to socialize with windsurfers.

62. Compounded by the weather-dependent, and thus in the UK, very unpredictable nature of the sport.

63. See Belinda Wheaton and Alan Tomlinson, "The Changing Gender Order in Sport? The case of windsurfing," in *Journal of Sport and Social Issues* (Aug 1998).

64. Donnelly, "Towards a definition of sport subcultures," p. 572. Donnelly argues that "marginal members" are those member for whom the subculture is a relatively minor part of lifestyle. In this study the majority of marginal members were those individuals who were in the process of exiting the subculture.

65. Many marginal participants suggested that as they got older, the time commitment was hard to sustain (see on), and the unpredictable, weather-dependent nature of the sport became unbearable.

66. See endnote 45.

67. Kevin Young and K. Gallup, "On Boardheads: Windsurfing, Bourdieu and cultural capital," paper presented at the NASSS conference, Washington (Nov 8–12, 1989).

68. Celia Lury, *Consumer Culture* (Cambridge: Polity Press, 1996).

69. Bourdieu, *Distinction*.

70. Ibid., p. 217.

71. Although Silver Sands is located in a particularly affluent part of Britain, survey data gathered nationally suggested that British women who windsurf regularly, tended to be middle class, and in particular professional women (Profiles, ibid.).

72. Feminists have demonstrated the nexus of structural, material, practical, and ideological constraints that severely limit the opportunities for women to indulge in active leisure and particularly sport. See for example, Eileen Green, S. Hebron, and Dianne Woodward, *Women's Leisure, What Leisure?* (Basingstoke: Macmillan, 1989). While I have focused on

time and economic factors, many others of these factors constrain women's involvement in and enjoyment of windsurfing.

73. Farmer, "Surfing: motivations, values and culture," p. 242.

74. Todd Crosset and Becky Beal, "The use of 'subculture' and 'subworld' in ethnographic works on sport," pp. 73–85. The authors draw on Young and Gallup's (ibid.) study of sailboarders (windsurfers) in the USA.

75. Professional windsurfer interviewed in *Boards* No. 101 (1993), p. 70.

76. Young and Gallup, "On Boardheads," p. 11.

77. Booth, "Ambiguities in Pleasure and Discipline," p. 189.

78. Those without the ties of domestic commitments or careers planned lengthy trips abroad. Traveling in a van was a popular option; it was cheap and offered the freedom that typified the core windsurfers' ethos.

79. David Chaney, *Lifestyles* (London & NY: Routledge, 1996), p. 15.

80. Stan Parker, "Editorial," *World Leisure and Recreation* 35, No. 1 (1993): pp. 4–5.

81. Young and Gallup's research on windsurfers in the USA illustrates a similar relationship between subcultural commitment and work-leisure relations. Specifically, they cite championing sailing careers over jobs, taking leave of absence or resigning, and having "wind clauses" written into job descriptions, which allowed the individual to skip work when it was windy, working instead on weekends or evenings. (Young and Gallup, "On Boardheads")

82. Breedveld (1996), p. 81.

83. David Crouch and Alan Tomlinson discuss these characteristics of postmodern leisure more broadly in "Collective Self-generated Consumption: Leisure, Space and Cultural Identity in Late Modernity," in *Leisure, Modernism, Postmodernism and Lifestyles, Leisure in Different Worlds*, Vol. 1, Ed. I. Henry, LSA publications No. 48 (Eastbourne: LSA publications, 1994), p. 312.

SKY DIVING/DANCING/SURFING

Chapter Six

Free Dimensional Skydiving*

Tamara Koyn

Introduction

Three-dimensional skydiving includes a group of skydiving disciplines that encompass some of the more creative aspects of skydiving. Today, these include freestyle, skysurfing and freeflying (which can also be referred to as vertical relative work). In freestyle skydiving, the skydiver performs maneuvers that resemble dance and gymnastics while freefalling at speeds ranging typically from 110 mph to 180 mph. In skysurfing, the skydiver attaches a sky board

---

Tamara Koyn *(http://www.Koyn.com/CloudDancer)* received a bachelor of fine arts degree in teaching dance with movement science background and media communications: film/video production from Webster University in 1991. She has been a freestyle pioneer since 1985 with more than 1,800 freestyle jumps and 500 vertical relative work jumps. She was the 1992 World Freestyle women's champion, and attained a 234 mph head-down average fallrate as the fastest woman in Skydive Arizona's first-ever freefall race in 1995. Tamara has instructed freestyle, pre-skysurfing, and freeflying courses around the world since 1988 and judged international 3-D skydiving disciplines since 1993, and is the author of the first books on freestyle, *Freestyle Notes* and *More Freestyle Notes*. With Tony Loper, she produced *A Video Guide to Freestyle*, the first instructional video on freestyle. The author writes personal essays and maintains a Web site to share material with the skydiving community. You can visit her site at: http://www.koyn.com/CloudDancer

*See glossary at end of chapter for definition of terms unique to free-dimensional skydiving.

to his feet prior to exiting the aircraft and then, while freefalling at speeds ranging from 100 mph to 160 mph, he or she performs maneuvers resembling acrobatics. A camera flyer, a skydiver carrying one or more cameras attached to his or her helmet, will freefall along with a freestylist or skysurfer to capture all the action on video. Freeflying is the newest discipline in three-dimensional skydiving. Freeflyers are a group of two or more skydivers who freefall together and perform an assortment of three-dimensional maneuvers while flying relative to one another. Typically, they will be head-down or head-up and can connect with each other to build different formations. Freeflyers fly over and under one another in fluid transitional movements as well. Additionally, a camera flyer will freefall with the freeflyers to capture all the action on videotape. The future of three-dimensional skydiving is vast and more disciplines will develop in this area.

Section I: Freestyle

Background: *In 1992, Tamara Koyn and her camera flyer, Jamie Paul, won gold in the women's division of the World Freestyle Championships held in Eloy, Arizona. In preparing for the world championships, Tamara traveled from St. Louis to train at West Tennessee Skydiving's monthly "Boogie Till-Ya-Puke" events. The skydiving center, located one hour's drive east of Memphis, operates the fastest-climbing high-performance jump plane in the world. At the "Boogie Till-Ya-Puke," skydivers pay a flat fee for all the jumps they can make in one weekend. The following is prose that Tamara wrote about her training at West Tennessee Skydiving in preparation for the World Freestyle Championships in 1992.*

Training Till-I-Puke

> 4:45 a.m.
> My alarm sounds off.
> I frantically grabbed it, shutting it off.
> I typically snooze but not this time.
>
> I knew that if I wanted to become a better freestylist,
> I needed as much freefall practice time as possible
>   and that meant getting on every lift possible,
>   starting with the first lift.

I went to the manifest desk carrying my rig,
holding the metal hardware silent with my other hand.
I feared waking up others, creating a frenzy at the desk.

I stood on the grass runway, still wet with dew, for the first lift.
I enjoyed the sweet sound of the turbine props spinning up.
It reminded me of the image that only the stars from movies,
such as *From Wings Came Flight*,
jump from this type of luxury aircraft.
I felt good and that, someday,
I'll be able to skydive well enough for some big project.

With the power of a jetliner,
the plane surged forward and I watched the ground peel away.
"Concentrate," I thought to myself.
I closed my eyes, rehearsing every detail of the dive.
"Pinwheel launch, shifting the weight straight forward out the door,
staying upright, believing in the relative wind,
then bringing my right arm forward to stop back looping,
and assume the side stag position . . ."
I knew that I had barely enough time to mentally practice the
dive twice
before performing my last gear check.

Seven minutes later, I was in the air.
How well I mentally practiced was put to the test.

Running from the landing area, I mentally go over the last dive.
"Good leg spread going through my Chinese backloop,
need less momentum to finish my cartwheel . . ."
Approaching the door of the indoor packing area,
breathing hard,
my legs almost collapse beneath me.

———

I made four jumps and it felt like 4:00 p.m.
I looked at the clock.
11:50 a.m.
I felt glad, the day was quite young.
It will be a long day.
I sighed.

I proceeded to manifest.
I was directed to immediately go to the runway.
"Oh ——, what's my next dive?"
I frantically reviewed my training syllabus compiling my next dive.
"Front layouts to standing stag pirouette,
              this time keeping my weight centered
    Then into an Arabian with my knees straight,
              they were bent on the dive before last,
       And . . ."

I ran with my rig to the runway.
As it initiated its descent after dropping the load before me,
    the sound of the diving King Air seemed to tear through the sky.
I never ceased to be amazed by the power of the plane.

Sunday

5:00 a.m.
My alarm sounds off.
Shutting it off, I grabbed my rig with one hand on the metal
    hardware and forced my stiff sore body to the manifest desk.
It was still completely dark outside.
I groaned.

Half asleep, I watched the remainder of the line form behind me.
I wondered what motivated the other fun jumpers at this hour.
Pushing to this extent didn't seem like the fun
    pleasure jumpers would be looking for.
My desire to improve my freestyle was more than enough motivation.
And I loved the mental and physical challenge of the boogie.

While I was awake, my body was not.
I proceeded to stretch and do other exercises,
    stimulating relaxation and circulation in the muscles,
        reducing the stiffness I felt.
I felt somewhat better, physically awake, and ready to jump.
"Puke," I should say.
It felt good to lie down on the carpeted comfortable floor again.

"Lift 1, go to the runway," the PA announced.

"Get my tired sore body to the runway," I groaned to myself.
I made my way through the wet grass to the runway.
I was nervous but felt expectant.
This dive will be a test to see if I really did learn
    what I thought I learned yesterday.

"Exit, exit, exit." the pilot announced.

I stood in the doorway
    and the morning sun hadn't yet touched the ground.
Poised in the frame, I made eye contact with Wings Field below,
    centered my weight,
        and established a clear calm focus.
Achieving a smooth controlled exit required my best concentration,
    similar to that of a springboard diver.
I nailed the exit,
    a full twisting stag front layout to the T position.

From my third dive of the day, I ran from the peas (as usual).
It was a good dive
    and it was obvious that I was driving my learning curve.
With my adrenaline pumping and my spirit on fire,
    a chill sneaked up my back.
"I love it," I gasped to myself feeling vibrant energy,
    as I burst through the door into the packing area to pack.

———

3:20 p.m.
I just manifested having finished my fifteenth jump of the boogie.
I had a short wait, allowing me to take a short rest.
"Damn it, I missed my finish at the standing stag,
    wobbled as I rolled onto my side,
        couldn't control my heading in the side stag..."
In other words, I ——— up big time.
Feeling discouraged and wondering if I was crazy,
    I lay on the floor and briefly cried.

My dance instructor repeatedly explained to me that:
"You'll receive your toughest challenges in the dance studio."
I quietly and humbly acknowledged to myself that
        I was now at my freestyle studio (West Tennessee Skydiving).
"When it is time to perform, you will find it easy," he explained.
He was correct.
Given my one dive chance,
        my performance came easily at the 1991 freestyle competition.
And again,
        my performance came easily before McGowan's cameras.
"In class, you should always seek to push yourself to the limit."

I made my way out to the runway for the sixteenth jump.
I was tired.
I recalled more of my dance instructor's advice:
"You might think you're tired,
        but there is always something a little extra deep inside yourself
                —you just have to reach for it."

Seven minutes later . . .

I leaped from the door frame feeling fresh and energized as ever.
I made a clean stop at the Chinese split,
    clean cartwheel, and . . .
While standing in the compass position,
        I reached for and held my foot with my hand.
To my astonishment and surprise,
        I stayed in control of this seemingly impossible maneuver!!!

I felt like a little kid
        who was given free rein in an ice cream store.
I leaped into the hanger to pack.
Again, again, again . . .

After frantically finishing my log from my previous dive,
        I raced with my gear to the runway.
My last move of the dive involved the T position.
The air felt nice as I relaxed into the stable position.
It became apparent that even the T was now physically difficult.
A little voice crept into my head.
        "You trained well. Good job, kid."

I was manifested for my twentieth jump of the weekend.
I knew this would be my last dive.
I needed to give myself a break from trying so hard to do well.
I had a few interesting new ideas I wanted to try.
Just for a more relaxed type of fun.
A Chinese cartwheel into a side reversal back to the split again . . .

From standing in the door,
　　I stepped out facing the relative wind, making an easy exit.
The King Air, silhouetted in the setting sun, dove downward
　　away from me,
　　　　leaving me suspended in space.
It seemed as if I had stepped into the twilight zone.
I folded my legs, sat up and continued to watch the King Air,
　　now just a small speck in the orange sky.
I tried the new maneuver, expecting it to fail
　　(because of its extreme difficulty).
To my astonishment, it happened!
I did it again!
In delight, I wavered my arms and legs
　　dancing about like a kid discovering a new toy.

————

The next morning, I woke.
It seemed that the weekend was a dream.
I knew it wasn't because I was terribly stiff and sore.

　　I examined my logbook. I had clearly learned much material. Usually, it took me approximately five weekends of jumping to cover this amount of material. Before "Boogie Till-Ya-Puke," I never experienced such a condensed learning curve and intensity in my jumping life. I admit that with each subsequent boogie, I became increasingly more spoiled and "addicted" to the BTYP experience; and my hunger (and need to remain competitive) to learn new freestyle grew proportionally.

Section II: Skysurfing at the 1997 World Air Games

Background: *In 1997, Tamara participated as an international judge for freestyle skydiving and skysurfing at the first-ever World Air Games in Efes, Turkey. In this section, Tamara shares a personal essay on the aspects of the skysurfing event that intrigued her artistically.*

Competition Overview

The first International Parachuting Committee (IPC) World Freestyle and Skysurf World Championships were held at Efes, Turkey, September 13–21, 1997. A total of 55 teams—four women's skysurfing teams from four countries, twenty men's skysurfing teams from fifteen countries, sixteen men's freestyle teams from ten countries, and fifteen women's freestyle teams from twelve countries—competed. A team consists of one camera flyer and the performer (a skysurfer or freestylist).

During the compulsory rounds, competitors were required to perform five different compulsory sequences. During the free round, skysurfing teams could perform anything that they imagined in a fifty-second routine. Free rounds are evaluated for execution, artistic impression, difficulty and camera flying. Competitors performed three compulsory routines and seven free routines in the course of the ten-round competition.

One of the most exhilarating aspects of the competition was the inspirational nature of the routines the competitors performed.

The Skysurfing Compulsory Rounds

Four teams competed in the women's division in skysurfing.

Viviane Wegrath of Switzerland, the top woman skysurfer, performs the zigzag movements of the slalom maneuver very well. While performing the slalom movement, a skysurfer assumes the tracking position and changes the direction of the track by 90 degrees. In the case of this competition, skysurfers were required to change the direction of their tracking four times. She actually changed the direction of her track by a complete 90 degrees and actually traveled in that direction before changing to the next direction. In the video, a viewer could see her actually shifting back and forth in front of the scenery behind her.

The skysurfing compulsory round did not finish without humorous entertainment. After performing a compulsory sequence, one skysurfer quickly had to pull up his pants when they fell down.

The Skysurfing Free Rounds

Once the first two compulsory rounds were complete, the skysurfers were free to release their creativity. Skysurfing teams shredded the skies, performing techniques seen on ESPN's X Games. Mihail from

Russia performed a number of the skysurfing moves popular in the X Games such as the Helicopter and the Hen House Surprise. Many skysurfers included the Hen House Surprise in their routines. The more advanced skysurfers found some way of adding additional flare and finesse to the maneuver. During his Hen House Surprise, Mihail places his left hand on his hip. Oliver of Team Pulse from Switzerland performs the maneuver holding his left hand over his head pointing at the ground.

In skysurfing, there is a growing trend toward performing high-speed spins. For example, Oliver performed the Tidy Bowl in the Hole maneuver, during which he included a wicked-fast rotating Helicopter. The Invisible Man is another high-speed spin in which the skysurfer, while standing, rotates so rapidly that it is difficult to make out any body features of the surfer himself. The Invisible Man has been performed at five revolutions per second. Valery Rozov from Russia performs this move with an especially fast rotation in his red and white vibrant suit, and Mike Frost of England finishes his dive with this move. A number of other competitors also included the Invisible Man in their routines.

Pierre Chaford from Brazil, wearing the colors of his country, green with black and white accents, choreographed his routine well as one cohesive whole, performing many of the popular skysurfing moves from the X Games. As he performed an Invisible Man, the black stripes on his arms created a very pronounced strobelike effect. Pierre finished one of his routines in a head-down pose, moving out of the top of the frame. To me, it looked as if Pierre were playing the drums with his hands as he moved out the top of the screen, while another observer saw that he was scaling an invisible rope.

The skysurfers came up with some new creative moves as well. For example, Csaba from Hungary performed a bent-knee Helicopter while crouching at the hips and grasping the folds of his knees with both hands. He transitioned into this move from a standard Helicopter and then out of this move, accelerating again into another Helicopter.

During one jump, Scott Smith of the United States transitioned into a Galleon and dropped below his camera flyer, Peter Raymond. Then, suddenly, Scott presented his board flat to the relative wind into a head-down bent-knee spinning position. Peter suddenly fell past and then was filming looking up at Scott's spinning head with the sky in the background. The video looked impressive to many.

Even the more intermediate-level skysurfers found something creative to perform. For example, Gökhan from Turkey performed a face spin with the skyboard positioned on his seat and with a rail grab—one hand behind his back to reach the board.

To finish his routine, Hilton from South Africa performed back layouts as he traveled from the center of the screen off to the left side. And camera flyer Mick from Australia framed a close-up of Milton's head as he performed a Helicopter to finish his routine.

Docking Maneuvers

Many skysurfing teams ranging through the entire skill range included some form of docking (hands to hands, hands to feet, hands to board, etc.) in their routines.

During a skysurfing exit, camera flyer Rob from Australia grabbed the nose of Chris's board. Chris sat, leaning back some, as they rode the hill together entering a slow horizontal rotation. Mick and Mike, another Australian team performed some kind of Butterfly action for their exit. Their Butterfly move, during which the camera flyer and skysurfer hold hands and tumble around each other, spun with oscillations. Starting off another round of competition, Skysurfer Mike made a diving exit hanging onto Mick's legs with his board trailing behind. Mike finished his routine by taking a double-handed grip on Mick's foot.

Apparel and Board Designs

In general, the apparel and board designs are becoming more and more creative. In other words, there were more variations on the designs painted on the board. For example, Josef from Austria painted the bottom of his light blue board with a white squiggle line from the nose to the tail and the top of his board white with a light blue squiggle line. However, this year, no skysurfer used any unusually shaped boards. But board size did vary among the competitors. Nothing in the rules indicated that a competitor couldn't use a small board. Thus, the board size was considered in the difficulty score.

Men's world champion skysurfer Oliver from Team Pulse wore an orange and red jumpsuit, had a board comprised of diagonal orange and red stripes, and had dyed his hair a bright red. He finished his last round of competition by releasing smoke from his board. As he spun and twisted through the various moves, the smoke actually twisted and rotated as it would from aerobatic planes in an airshow.

Damian from the USA wore white shorts with a black spiraling stripe and a black shirt with white vertical stripes. The barber pole effect this outfit created when he performed a Helicopter would have been much stronger if he had been wearing pants. During another round of competition, I glanced up from the computer screen where I was entering scores at the time and just missed the end of a move. Did I just catch him performing a Helicopter with the camera flyer presenting a sideways view of the move?

Camera Flying

Camera flyers often rotate around the camera to perform a camera roll. Because they try to keep the camera in place and rotate their bodies around the camera, this is more difficult to perform than simply performing a cartwheel-type action about the center of gravity, especially when flying close to the subject. If the distance between the performer and camera flyer is greater, then it will be less visible if the camera flyer's rotation is not centered on the camera. Also, if the camera flyer is flying face down, it's easier to perform such a roll as the camera is already on the axis of rotation. When the camera flyer makes a camera roll in exact timing with a performer's looping rotation, the team move is commonly referred to as a synced roll.

In skysurfing, Mike and Andy from Great Britain showed some strong teamwork nicely punctuated with synced rolls. First, Mike exited by backing out of the tailgate of the Casa and smoothly making a half backloop into the head-down position into a Helicopter. From a standing position facing to the left, Mike performed a back one-and-a-half twist, repeated the move, and then on the third rotation, Andy performed a synced camera roll along with Mike as he made a single simple backloop.

Dangers

Several small incidents reminded anyone that skysurfing is dangerous. For example, near the end of a dive during a head-down move, Robin Berg's board came off one foot. Having one foot break loose from the board can cause a broken leg if the board is not released promptly. In Robin's case, it turned out that the worn shoe laces on one foot had broken.

Section III: Learning to Freefly

In December 1993, I went to Skydive DeLand, one of the world's top skydiving centers, located in Florida. My original intention was to develop a slower-falling freestyle suit while working with a jumpsuit manufacturing company, but my plans quickly changed when I started jumping.

Philippe Vallaud, a French skydiver, invited me to try *chute assis* with him. It started out that I would just make a jump or two to try it out. *Chute assis* is relative work performed while standing up plus more! We left the plane standing and facing each other. First, he leaped over me, and then it was my turn to leap over him. After I leaped over him, he transitioned into the Olav Frog Position, a head-down dive position with the legs and arms spread, while I flew standing next to him. (This basic head-down position for controlling relative flight was named after its pioneer, Olav Zipser.) I looked at his smiling face and was astonished by this very unusual visual predicament of flying relative in these positions. While tracking away, I was out of breath, and I continued breathing hard in my excitement all the way into the hangar area and then fumbled with packing my parachute. I was hooked!!!

He invited me for another jump. During this jump, we were to fly standing facing each other, and then I was to ascend (slow my fall rate a little) and stand on his shoulders to make a Totem formation with him. In the air once more, I was above him slightly and I made my approach. My feet made contact with his shoulders. It surprised me that I didn't feel much of his burble. It was odd to look at him below me and to feel the air clean enough for controlled flight. Suddenly, there was a sense of height and the possibility of falling. (For a moment, consider standing on someone's shoulders on the ground looking downward without holding on!) But I didn't fall. In fact, I floated off his shoulders as he descended. It was a perplexing feeling.*

Later, during one of the evenings, while I was walking among the runways, I felt a strong sense that it would be natural to just be floating along the taxiways while upright—almost as if I believed it could happen! Of course, I knew better than this.

In the following days, Philippe continued to surprise me and welcome me to skydive with him. By this time, I was very grateful

---

* We discussed freeflying techniques. Further information can be found at:
http://www.koyn.com/CloudDancer/articles/TamarasFirstVRW.html

and astonished by his kindness in sharing the sky with me and continuing to teach me *chute assis*. I felt sure that I was only a low-time freeflyer to him. He has over 2,000 *chute assis* and 4,500 total jumps!

Looking at me intently, he explained the next dive to me. "If I get more than five meters from you, you lose!" He said he would do anything, duck under me, jump over me, dash around me, float or sink on me, back away from me, or flip . . . During the climb to altitude, I was nervous and was sure that I would lose—I am just a novice. I felt he was expecting me to perform. We left the plane and faced each other while standing, the starting point for the game to begin. My reflexes were wired and I reacted with the excitement of a child in a game of tag. He ducked under me and I pivoted to chase him. Then, his arms went down and legs came together—I knew the fall rate would quickly accelerate and I immediately dropped, accelerating with him. Huffing and puffing, I landed just totally wired with excess energy, and I didn't know what to do with it.

Twenty jumps later, my skills had improved and the challenge of the dive tasks had increased. But this time, he wanted me to hold the Olav Frog! I flipped over and was looking straight at his face and the world both upside-down. "Totally cool," I wrote in my log. Then his face descended under me and out of sight. I rotated about my spine until he was in sight again. It felt perfect. I was on balance sightseeing the world upside-down and just wanted to stay that way. It was pleasantly comfortable and easy.

At this point, I realized that I was suddenly doing things that I hadn't been able to do before because now I was being pushed beyond my limit. For example, I suddenly did all the relative control necessary to chase and stay within five meters of him. I'd never been able to master the Olav Frog position on solo dives. But when I tried it with Philippe, I did it! During my previous attempts at performing this head-down position, my legs kept buffeting and, when I tried to do pirouettes, I couldn't rotate about my spine as the axis, and it would turn into a spiraling dive. But now that I had to learn relative control in the Olav Frog position, I held it and pirouetted perfectly about my axis.

On one of the last dives, I did a half front loop from standing to the Olav Frog Position. Again, I was looking at him and the world upside-down. The "way cool" part was the visual effect as I was trying to learn to fall straight down. In a series of over-corrections, I saw myself approaching and backsliding to and from him. Seeing the distance change while upside-down was very strange, almost disorienting, and wild!

A Few Years Later . . .

When I was first learning to control my proximity and level with respect to another freeflyer, I would correct only one of the two parameters at any given time. This meant that each time I got level with my partner, I'd see that I was too far way. Once I adjusted my distance, I'd realize that I hadn't stayed level with my partner. However, as I gained experience, I learned to correct both simultaneously.

Once I learned how to side-slide while head-up or head-down, I was then very poor at side-sliding while simultaneously adjusting my proximity and level relative to a partner. In other words, my flying was still two-dimensional, making it hard for me to dock with anyone who was moving even just a little bit.

Meanwhile, as I would visit different drop zones to teach freestyle seminars and preparation courses for skysurfing, I'd say to others in casual conversation that someday I would like to try landing an airplane. When I was in Washington DC teaching a freestyle course I mentioned, in casual conversation, trying to land a plane to Peter Farbish, an interesting new friend who also hang glides. He said "Come with me, we can do it right now!" He was renting a C-152. Knowing that I could easily learn to land without help on the controls, Peter signed me up for a flying lesson with an instructor he knows. "The yoke is yours! Land the plane!" I turn to final approach staring at the runway in front of us and, suddenly, reality jerk me by the back of my collar as I watch the runway seesaw during a fifteen-knot crosswind as I manipulate the control inputs. "Oh, god . . . What the hell am I doing?"

A few years later, in the summer of 1997, I was more frequently invited by my friends to fly the C-150 or C-152 and practice landing. In early July, my friend Jim set me up with more flying lessons with his instructor than I was mentally ready to handle. During my final approach, I had trouble keeping my airspeed correct while at the same time maintaining my accuracy on the numbers and center line. I messed up my alignment and was low over the runway near its right edge. With the instructor doing nothing to help me, I radically banked the plane to the left and right, drifting from side to side just above the pavement, still trying to get lined up. The total scene of the tilting horizon and sideways shifting pavement beneath me seriously resembled a video game. I barely got the wavering stopped and the plane level as I planted both wheels down. Whew! I took a deep breath through my dry mouth and took off to practice more landings.

Eventually, I started learning to finesse my landings, practicing a variety of different techniques and trying it in different wind conditions. Not thinking that it would really be possible, I mentioned to my friend Hubert Trimmel, a captain for Vanguard Airlines and a certified flight instructor, that it would be special to maybe do my first night landings at Kansas City International! He said that he would be waiting for me to come in on my Southwest Airlines flight with the C-150. Just as it felt strange to me to put on my skydiving gear in the night before a night jump, it felt strange to me to be taxiing the plane in the night. I told myself to ignore my funny feeling and to just follow the yellow taxi line with its green trail of lights.

Once airborne, I turned the plane back around onto final approach, during which the runway's lighting scheme had its maximum intensity, and lined up to the centerline of yellow lights. There, before us, was the runway outlined in yellow lights with the green threshold lights clear across the entire width at the start of runway 19L and a grouping of lights on the right and left side of the first portion of the runway. Naw, this couldn't be real. No. It was unreal to me. Overlooking the scene and actually setting up to land, I had the feeling that maybe I was experiencing a virtual reality or something. It couldn't be the runway of an international airport—BUT IT WAS!! I was conscious of making small corrections, spaced relatively far apart in time—the leg muscles of one leg (or the other) pressed a rudder pedal slightly in advance of a yoke adjustment. And, then getting closer to the runway . . . feeling a complete sense of stillness on my final approach path, I felt a mental calmness during which my mind was completely empty of any thought. I've felt this feeling before when positioning myself still in the door of the plane before a competitive freestyle skydive involving complex timing of high speed movement.

In preparing to land, I had the feeling of raising the airplane's nose in one fluid, continuous motion (rather than my usual series of somewhat jerky adjustments). As the flight path curved to a flat glide, I adjusted the airplane's heading slightly with the rudder pedal. The night air just seemed so smooth as the plane felt almost as if it were flying on silk just above the centerline of lights. I noticed that

my breath was following along with the timing of the flare. In retrospect, I *think* it was one nice gentle great big long exhale.
Sssssssssssssssssssssssssss
Contact.

It was late at night. The other air traffic at Kansas City International was dying off, and I made more landings. Just as for night jumps, I find something serene, almost seductive, about being in the night air—the sense of awareness and feeling changes, providing some sense of mental calmness yet focus.

The very next day, I performed my first Spock formation with fellow freeflyer Pat Works seemingly as if by magic. Once we had exited the airplane, I was freefalling in a position above him at a 45 degree angle and achieved a completely stationary position relative to him. With the same feeling as that landing flare, I moved smoothly and accurately in a straight line to my slot over his head in one continuous movement. It felt easy to me in that instant and I extended my hand and placed it on his head. The Spock formation was totally stable, and I got excited springing back out of the formation again.

Suddenly, over a series of just eight to ten jumps spanning one month, I noticed an ubelievable increase in my ability to control my side-sliding smoothly while controlling level and proximity relative to a partner (particularly while flying head-down).

At the 1997 World Freefall Convention held in Quincy, Illinois, I jumped with Jessica, silver medalist in the intermediate division of the 1996 US Freestyle Nationals. She performed various freestyle poses and maneuvers all just several feet in front of me. The live performance was very dynamic and that feeling was enhanced by the sensations of following her fall rate as I was freeflying to stay with her. Following freestyle is seriously like an elevator ride. As she moved into a faster falling position, I stood up, feeling the drastic change into a faster fall rate, and started running and playing with my legs. She saw me and then mimicked. It was great fun to actually be able to play and flip while in control of my relativity.

On my last jump with Jessica, I really took notice that my freeflying skills had suddenly improved. Jessica wanted to perform a standing stag and for me to dock on her hand. I wasn't sure if I could do it as I had problems with being able to follow even a slightly moving subject for making actual contact. We left the plane and after making a graceful spinning exit, she stood up in her Compass pose and then a Stag, and I went head-down. Adjusting simultaneously all three parameters (proximity, levels, and lateral movement) to accurately match her flight path, I took her hand!

Since she just wanted to touch me, she was satisfied, pulled away and moved on to her next freestyle move.

After some reflection, I realized that my sudden gain in skill was connected with my practicing landings in the Cessna. When flaring the plane (and, mind you, this is after you have learned and can establish a good final approach), you have to adjust the plane's attitude to regulate your altitude over the runway, turn the control wheel to be lined up with the centerline, and use the rudder (foot) pedals to keep the nose of the plane pointing down the runway. When flying level just above the runway's surface like this, you *have* to control all three parameters as the plane slows and settles onto the runway. This practice forced my mind to deal with controlling three parameters at once, and that transferred into freeflying as simultaneously controlling proximity, level, and lateral movement. What's even more astonishing is that when I allow my legs to relax with my knees dropping to the side in the plane, I am using almost the same muscle groups for manipulating the rudder pedals that I would use to control side-sliding while head-down in freeflying! Skydive University training programs make use of isometric exercises that target the usage of muscle groups that are used in the actual skydiving skill being taught. If you are not relaxed, it is more difficult to control the different parameters simultaneously for landing the plane with any degree of finesse.

The November 1997 FreeFly Festival at Skydive Arizona

That fall, I went to the November 1997 FreeFly Festival at Skydive Arizona. For the most part, I focused on dives with one partner and experienced my first "points" in sequential VRW. Nearly all of the sequential VRW required my ability to control proximity, level, and lateral movement all at the same time. My timing in practicing landings in the airplane relative to the development of my freefly skills at that time exaggerated the positive effect it had and prepared me to do well at the freefly festival.

With Marcos from Brazil, I experienced my first stable vertical Compressed Accordion. Marcos was standing. I was head-down and, upon reaching my position beside him, I took my grip on his ankle. I felt his hand grip on my leg as I was looking out into the empty space in front of me with the sky and patchwork ground in the wrong places. Strangely this time it wasn't a solo dive. I was actually docked with someone and the formation was surprisingly stable with absolutely no tension. It was very cool. On a following dive, we made the vertical compressed accordion again and we smoothly rotated the piece.

I experienced my first real VRW sequential dives with Chris Rimple from freestyle team Nitros when he took a break from his training. We both launched into the head-down position with a right hand shake. We let go and did a left hand shake. We both rotated head-up and made two Fish Bone moves in which I went over the top on the first one and he went over the top on the second. Then we encircled each other continuously facing each other and repeatedly flying over each other. To finish, I was upright and swiveling around to make a vertical Compressed Accordion with him while he was head-down with us both facing the same direction. Just before taking grips our Dytters (audible altimeters) beeped and I saw Chris arch backwards with his head disappearing beneath his shoulders as he took off into his track. We repeated the dive, making refinements, and for the first time I found myself concentrating again as I had for freestyle training. "Do this action here, finish like that, accelerate fall rate here . . ."

Later in the week, Brad Chatellier, from SSI Pro-Tour team Mad Style, showed up and we did more VRW sequential dives. After practicing some skydives in which we went over and under each other, Brad and I performed what I could call the head-down Daffy Cartwheel transition block. Both of us were head-down. I docked with my hand on Brad's foot while he was in a head-down Daffy, he made a cartwheel, and then I redocked on his foot. It all seemed unreal to me to actually smoothly and delicately touch his foot and to let go again. Then we changed roles. We finished the dive with me head-down and making a Spock, this time by positioning an arm forward of my torso to touch Brad's head while he was head-up. I was really close, so close that I felt that we were about to kiss each other! To my amazement, the formation was stable.

For our last two-way together, we started with a cool back diving exit. As we rode the hill backward, I looked at Brad with the horizon at an odd angle behind him as we gradually proceeded into a head-down position together.

In yet another surprise, the Z-Airtime champion team members invited me on some two-way dives. "Have a look at our Destination Xtreme Tour Stop #2 jumps and choose from the menu!" So off the end of the sky ramp I went looking backward going head-down to make a 69 dock with Rob Mahaffey, who was head-up for my first-ever point on the hill. I was head-down facing Rob and taking grips on his ankles. It felt neat, fun and weird. Then, I Spocked him, we made half-cartwheel transitions, and he Spocked me. Even though our level and proximity control felt sloppy to me, the points still happened—we are both skilled flyers. It was amazing to me to actually experience a relaxed dive with points.

With Brian Germain, another one of the champion Z-Airtime team members, I get to try the Monkey Wheel and Inverted Spock. We launched into a head-down facing each other with grips on each other. I, then, swiveled to head-up, maintaining my grip on his chest strap. The Monkey Wheel, in which we front-looped while holding onto each other, went quickly and easily. In the Inverted Spock, I was head-up adjusting my fall rate, and it was quite perplexing to see someone actually doing a head stand in my hand! In terms of my physical strength, I could never do something like this on the ground.

Glossary

Boogie—Special skydiving events are often called "Boogies" within the skydiving community.

Burble—The region behind a freefalling skydiver has turbulent wind flow because his body breaks up the air as he falls through it. The burble is smaller when freefallers are head-up or head-down when they are freeflying.

Crosswind—The wind component that blows across the runway. As a pilot is landing an airplane, the crosswind is acting to push the plane sideways off the runway, and the pilot must adjust the controls so that it does not.

Flare—When landing a plane or a square-type parachute, the forward speed is reduced and the descent rate is briefly arrested before final touchdown. This action is referred to as flaring. Under a parachute, it is accomplished by pulling both steering handles downward with the correct timing. In a small airplane, it is accomplished idling the engine and pulling the yoke, control wheel, or stick backward. The exact details of the techniques vary according to the model of parachute or airplane.

From Wings Came Flight—a sixty-minute music video with a variety of skydiving disciplines featured in coordinated colors produced by Norman Kent, a well-known professional freefall cinematographer.

Galleon—A skysurfing maneuver in which the skysurfer is head-down with the tail of the board tucked tightly to his seat. The knees are bent and the nose of the board points to the sky while the tail of the board points toward the ground. A Galleon may or may not rotate. Among skysurfers, the Galleon is also called a Torpedo.

Head-down Daffy—A head-down position in which a freeflyer positions one leg forward and the other leg backward.

Helicopter—A skysurfing maneuver during which the skysurfer is head-down and spinning with the bottom of the board towards the sky.

Hen House Surprise—A skysurfing maneuver during which the skysurfer is head-down and spinning. The knees are bent and one hand holds the board.

Hill—The apparent direction of the relative wind shifts as the skydiver's motion changes from the forward motion of the aircraft and accelerates towards the ground. Skydivers refer to this as the "hill" or exit transition.

In the air—A prepositional phrase that refers to the idea that the jumper(s) is (are) in freefall. It is also used to mean that the jumpers have already taken off in the aircraft to make a jump.

Lift—The ride to altitude in the jump plane.

Manifest—Location in a skydiving center where a jumper can sign up for his or her next jump. The attendant will then tell the jumper that he or she is on a certain load number and will be boarding the plane in a certain amount of time.

Mike McGowan—A camera flyer well-known for his numerous videos, which he makes available to skydivers. He also does photography for parachuting magazines around the world. McGowan's work is also featured on TV and in publications for the general public.

Peas—The landing target is a circular area comprised of pea gravel.

Point—When relative work skydivers make a formation and then separate to make another, each formation they make together is referred to as a point.

Rail grab—A skysurfing move involving a rail grab is one in which the skysurfer places a hand or hands on an edge of his or her skyboard.

Relative wind—The apparent wind or air that the skydiver feels when in freefall as a result of his or her motion through the air. When exiting the airplane, the motion is forward at first and then accelerates toward the ground. Thus, for a skydiver, the relative wind appears to come from the direction in which the plane was flying and then shifts to come from the ground.

Relative work (RW)—When two are more skydivers are in freefall together, they can fly relative to one another, hence the term *relative work*. When the term *vertical relative work* or *freeflying* is used, the relative workers are flying primarily in a standing or head-down orientation rather than face-down into the relative wind.

Rig (or gear)—A parachute harness and container system with main and reserve parachutes.

Sequential VRW—During a freefall skydive, relative partners may come together to make a variety of different formations. For freeflyers, this is sequential VRW, and for skydivers flying in a face-down position, this is sequential RW.

Spock Formation—A formation involving two freeflyers. One freeflyer is standing up while the other is head-down. The head-down freeflyer is directly over the other freeflyer with his hand placed on the head of the standing freeflyer.

Tidy Bowl in the Hole—A skysurfing maneuver that involves both the skysurfer and camera flyer in the performance of the maneuver. The Tidy Bowl in the Hole was made popular by Rob Harris and Joe Jennings at the first skysurfing competition in ESPN's X Games television program in 1995. In this move, the skysurfer enters a Helicopter while the camera flyer flies over the skysurfer into a head-down position and begins orbiting around the spinning skysurfer.

Track (or tracking)—a maneuver in which a skydiver travels horizontally across the sky.

Vertical Compressed Accordion—In this freeflying formation, one skydiver is head-up and the other is head-down. They are side by side with each having a one-hand grip on the other's ankle.

Vertical relative work (VRW)—See *relative work.*

Wings Field—The proper name of the airport where West Tennessee Skydiving is based.

Chapter Seven

Soaring

Synthia Sydnor

> *Today, curiously, a growing number of adepts share the attraction of the void and the extreme sensations it offers, through bungee jumping, skysurfing . . . Suicidal experiments on the inertia of a body . . . the relative wind of dizzying displacement, with no other aim than that of experiencing the heaviness of the body.*
>
> —Paul Virilio, *Open Sky*

Skysurfing/dancing is astonishing.[1] A human leaps from a plane from the top of the sky at 13,000 feet, falling to earth, surfing through the sky, while another, the camera flyer, videotapes the choreographed descent with a helmet-mounted camcorder.

> For the first 50 seconds of a 65 second freefall, they're "on," moving vertically at about 120 mph and horizontally at 50 mph, surfing the ultimate wave, the wind . . . [They] deploy their canopies 3,000 to 2,000 feet above the earth for a one to five minute canopy ride to the ground. The skysurfer releases and steps out of the skyboard bindings just before touchdown.[2]

The athlete valiantly dances the descent either without a board, or flipping, twisting and hanging upside down with feet strapped to a custom skyboard.

> Most are made of honeycomb aluminum and graphite. Novice skysurfers start out using very small boards and

move up to larger boards as their skills increase. Skyboard size is measured by the ratio of the board's surface area to the skysurfer's height . . . Skyboards weighing more than 0.6 gram per square centimeter of surface must have their own miniature parachute recovery system. . . . Average cost per board is $600–$750.[3]

And the camera flyer contributes to the performance through his or her own creative and athletic skills:[5]

The camera flyer is more than a "human tripod" or impartial observer. He or she must not only be a creative videographer, but an expert-level freestyle flyer who literally flys circles around the skysurfer. The camera flyer has to use his or her freestyle flying skills to follow the skysurfer through the sky, keep the athlete in the frame, go for the creative camera angles, even fly over and under the skysurfer to give the viewer the most exciting viewpoint. . . . Some camera flyers have the helmet custom-molded to the head; others wear motorcycle or BMX helmets with the chin bridge shortened toward the chin to increase peripheral vision. Cameras are mounted on a flat platform on top of the helmet. [Some helmets] can simultaneously carry a video, still and motion-picture camera . . . camera flyers wear slick or fast-fall suits so they can fly even faster [than the sky surfer], but their suits feature wings from the wrist to the waist or hip so they can slow quickly. The zero-porosity wings become rigid when the camera flyer extends his or her arms out and forward, and gradually collapse as the arms are tucked in. Some camera flyers eschew wings . . .[5]

Skydancing/surfing movements consist of twisting layouts, tracking with the camera, helicoptering (flying upside down), sitting spins and other spinning maneuvers, the presentation of front, back, and side moves on film,[6] bent-over pirouettes, piked stand-ups, flat spins with twists, tracking cartwheels, tucked pirouettes, and tracking barrel rolls.[7]

Soon we will have to learn to fly, to swim in the ether.[8]

As noted above, the filming of the performance is as much a part of the sport as is the performance itself (in competitions such as at the Extreme Games, the scoring is 75 percent for the skysurfer and 25 percent for the camera flyer), and for this reason alone, skysurfing is postmodern: aesthetics of photography, the design/engineering/technologies of flight, the surmounting of "outerspace," and the "urbanization" of the body[9] are fused into a daring sky-art performance.

> Jumpsuit should have low drag, skin tight legs and a high drag cloth on the arms.[10]
>
> Costume: A surfer who wore an attractive purposefully coordinated jumpsuit and had a board with appropriate/stylized graphics received the full point.[11]
>
> Skysurfers usually wear "low drag" bottoms such as Lycra sport tights . . . To counter the drag of the board, most wear "high drag" tops . . . cotton (moderate drag) and widewale corduroy (more drag). The skysurfer can create further draft with under-the-arm "winglets" of fabric that fill with air, and mesh vents, also under the arm . . . higher drag means more muscle work is required to maintain control . . .[12]
>
> Showmanship: good face shots with smiles/camera geeking, gesturing with the arms, and other acts directed specifically at viewers . . .[13]

What have humans of the late twentieth/early twenty-first century wrought? A future-oriented present.[14] A sport so extreme that only twenty years ago it would have been inconceivable. The human dream to fly is accomplished and more—no awkward flapping or premature crashes to the ground—the sky dancer as visible angel soars and drifts to earth in a magnificent symphony to the visual-performative-celebrity-speed centric culture of postmodern humankind.[15] Or, from Christianity's standpoint, sport-as-sin, for sky dancing is prideful, vain, suicidal, narcissistic.

> Creativity/Communication: Showmanship . . . Did the camera flyer do interesting movements about the skysurfer and/or film from interesting angles? . . . posi-tioning of the skysurfer within the boundaries of the frame, focus, etc. Things getting into the frame such as the camera flyer's own hands or something flapping up into the frame . . . docked the score . . . Was the camera flyer chasing the skysurfer or did he successfully stay with the skysurfer? . . .[16]

Skydancing/surfing is so beyond the realm of the traditional canon of sport that it is perhaps blasphemous to hand it over to sport scholars. For they would debate its "characteristics," "context," and trivial facticity, asking of skysurfing questions such as: Is it sport? What are its antecedents and consequences? What are its origins? its history? its ethnography?

> For the modern mind, space and time are the basic forms of hindrance.[17]

I will not taint skysurfing in such a way. Instead, here I try to dream in my written text about skysurfing, and offer as my product this scholarly fantasy of skysoaring.

We academics are afraid of heights, speed, and falling. We fear that the chute (canopy) won't open, that we will crash into another, that the plane will interfere with our jump, that a heart attack will render us unconscious in the sky. We have no body awareness, no ability to coordinate landing, no timing. We are dizzy and in disarray. Our throats involuntarily moan death—uhh—uhhh. Our stomachs churn and spew.

> So it is with philosophy: if it exists, it is anywhere but in the works of philosophy. And the only exciting thing is this anamorphosis, this dispersal of philosophical forms into all that is not philosophy. The whole world has become philosophical. . . . All of philosophy and poetry come back to us from places where we no longer are expecting to find them.[18]

As sport scholars, what do we tell each other about sports such as skysurfing, and what do we reveal about ourselves? The way we frame our *questions*, the *issues* we define, the epistemological and ontological methods and theories we construct to deal with these questions and issues—our tellings, our stories—precisely situate ourselves in the context of our times, of a modernity on the brink of becoming something else.[19] We tangle in our works with binaries wrought in the Enlightenment and after—myth/reality; feminist/misogynist; amateur/ professional—analyzing the intricacies of deviance, gender, technology, nationalism, consumerism, and violence upon sport cultures; our works and lives about these are sometimes tinged reminiscences, nostalgic about how it should be, how it used to be, how it should not become . . . culture is doing us; we are not doing culture.[20] Scholars of sport studies dissect specific aspects of particular sports; we create scales, interview techniques, and questionnaires; we document, save, frame, and display; we produce findings, counts, conclusions.

Yet, our work on sport and culture—any intellectual work— advances through divergent vocabularies, contrary attitudes, outlandish imaginings; intellectual work in the humanities—as much of our work about sport is—advances in part because we experiment with the poetics of our research. We contribute these twists because we know that otherwise, conversations about the human condition—about sport culture or things such as skysurfing—become stale and irrelevant when these are tied to certain languages.[21]

> The Federal Aviation Administration does not approve of debris falling from the sky . . . However, this . . . does not prohibit the dropping of any object if reasonable precautions are taken to avoid injury or damage to persons or property . . . when you land, take care not to overfly the crowd . . . Sky surfers must avoid accidentally dropping their sky boards after opening . . . There is no doubt that if one of these landed on someone, injury would result . . . no dz [drop zone] will last long in a community where the citizens have any reason to believe that falling debris could land on their property.[22]

To analyze skysurfing means to weaken the boundaries between the cultural spaces of sport/sport studies/sport culture/performances/participants/artifacts/artists/advertisers/consumers/researchers/media. To analyze the dream of skysurfing is to make more fluid the definitions of *sport* itself and open up the production, theorization, and circulation of our scholarship (by which I mean sport history, sociology, philosophy, anthropology, Olympic studies, etc.) into popular culture at large, as the contributors of this book have attempted.

In so doing, I forward another possibility of the text of sport studies. I have wanted to show that it is possible for the "writing-up"—the written text— of sport studies to be sensuous abstraction, to be performative, visual. I use the tactic of the list, montage; I decorate my text with mellifluous quotations. My endeavor is perhaps like art criticism:

by describing the sites of fascination, where meaning is supposed to implode with a great flourish, you bestow beauty on that void and give meaning to what shouldn't have any. And yet there is no contradiction in this, since its clear that the literary endeavor . . . is, quite simply, art criticism.[23]

Contrary to popular belief, we're not hard-core thrill seekers. We're pioneering a new form of art . . . [24]

Hence, I recognize that how I talk about sport, how I watch sport, how I write about and study sport is invented, selected, narrated, performed, collected, labeled, protected, pillaged, duplicated, reenacted, reproduced, copied, and remembered in certain ways. Culture, history, sport, skysurfing—*whatever*—are always in the act of becoming—our acts of research, writing, presentation, publication, are always, too, in the process of becoming. This *whatever* is the word of Giorgio Agamben, from his beautiful, provocative book, *The Coming Community*.[25] Agamben's *whatever* coincides closely with the philosopher Walter Benjamin's take on "doing" philosophy, history. Using this thought, we would understand that to write or study something like skysurfing "does not mean to recognize it the way it really was. It means to seize hold of a memory as it flashes up at a moment of danger."[26] These are Benjamin's words paraphrased from "Theses on the Philosophy of History."[27] In every sport history/anthropology that I create, I cite Benjamin's words to remind me of the fleeting vocation of all cultural activities. Benjamin ruled out claims to a binding authority or obligative truths, replacing them with "what was in some sense significant or interesting."[28] He kept thousands of word passages, poetry pieces and "wish images" that he juxtaposed, fit and disassembled to archive the arcades of the world through which he wandered.[29] Benjamin was both "ponderer and collector."[30] He insisted, "I have nothing to say, only to show."[31] The world was a phantasmagoria[32] for Benjamin, a term Marx used to "refer to the deceptive appearances of commodities as 'fetishes' in the marketplace."[33] But for Benjamin, the phantasmagoria was revolutionary. He wrote:

In reality, there is not one moment that does not bring within *its own* revolutionary possibility—it wants only to be defined as a specific one, namely as the chance for a totally new resolution in view of a totally new task.[34]

Benjamin's phantasmagoria was a "magic lantern show of optical illusions, rapidly changing size and blending into one another.[35] All of the phantasmagoria was of purely representational value—it was made of everything desirable that held the crowd enthralled; with Baudelaire's *flâneur*, Benjamin marveled at walking among, yet above the crowd; he was awed by the activity of window shopping, at "charging time with power like a battery, at [empathizing] himself into the soul of the commodity."[36]

Using Benjamin as the ontological and epistemological foundation for this treatise on skysurfing, I preface skydancing/surfing as part of a theoretical and real phantasmagoria. The words that portray and express skysurfing are by nature only and always fragmented and juxtaposed, the postmodern essences of speed, daring, contest/agon, aesthetics, form, celebrity, flight, etc., encapsulated in skysurfing's illusion. The space/terrain[37] of soaring, dreaming, heaven, desire, enthrallment, is vital to my analysis.

A century ago, philosopher Henri Bergson scrutinized terrain in terms of bodily spaces that give what he called "ballast and poise" to the mind. In his major work, *Matter and Memory*,[38] Bergson argued that "space, by definition, is outside us, yet the separation between a thing and its environment cannot be absolutely definite and clear-cut; there is a passage by insensible gradations from the one to the other."[39] This abstraction of insensible gradations from bodily spaces to environmental ones was consequential for later thinkers, and too, I argue, for the ways in which scholars read 'new' extreme sports such as skysurfing. For example, following the philosophical line that Bergson and Benjamin drew, Gilles Deleuze's introduction to "Mediators" ruminates on the categorical spaces of sport, forwarding a unique touchstone for not only the biomechanical analysis of sport, but also the cultural and aesthetic study of sportlike activities such as skysurfing:

> Running, throwing a javelin and so on, effort, resistance, with a starting point, a lever. But nowadays, I see movement defined less and less in relation to a point of leverage. Many of the new sports—surfing, windsurfing, hang-gliding—take the form of entry into an existing wave. There's no longer an origin as starting point, but a sort of putting-into-orbit. The basic thing is how to get taken up in the movement of a big wave, a column of rising air, to "come between" rather than to be the origin of an effort.[40]

In addition to using such analysis to interpret a sport like skysurfing, we can also use the metaphors of "getting taken up in the movement," "to come between rather than to be the origin of an effort" as metaphors for a way of doing sport studies, of traveling betwixt and between sport, culture, philosophy, pedagogy—rather than being the origin of an effort.[41]

As you can see, I am layering this essay with both discussion of the practical, how-to of skysurfing, and with contemplation of our disciplinary studies of sport.[42] As skysurfing has accomplished in terms of the deinstitutionalizing of sport, I am attempting to write in a space different from that of origins, efforts, and how-to's. To help me, I am also disposed to draw on Homi Bhabha's founding work of the third space. Bhabha suggests in his work *The Location of Culture* that theory, being, and history exist in a timeless space of unmeaning he calls the Third Space, which is beyond control. Bhabha:

> We should remember that it is the "inter"—the cutting edge of translation and negotiation, the *in-between* space— that carries the burden of the meaning of culture.[43]

Third spaces are liminal, meaning borderlands, threshold, in-betweenness. Victor Turner from Van Gennep called the liminal *"betwixt and between."*[44] Liminality is "a realm" where there is a certain freedom to juggle with the factors of existence. The liminal can apply not only to rites of passage of individuals or groups, but to the liminal spaces, the "not here, not there," that are in theory, in writing, in culture at large, in the surfed sky, all at the same time. Bhabha again:

> This is the space in which the question of modernity *emerges as a form of interrogation* . . .[45] . . . What is crucial . . . . is the belief that I must not merely change the *narratives* of our histories, but transform our sense of what it means to live, to be, in other times and different spaces, both human and historical.[46]

The idea of liminality is also at the forefront of MIT professor Sherry Turkle's work. Her *Life on the Screen*, influenced by Victor Turner's conception of the liminal moment (Turkle was a student of Turner's), describes present-day times and the activities of those new times (such as skysurfing) as infused with new meaning and great cultural creativity.[47] Turkle states:

if your culture is going through a liminal moment, don't hide it . . . celebrate it. Understand it for what it is. Victor Turner taught me to rejoice in the liminal moment. . . . we are dwellers on a threshold, poised in the liminal moment, a moment of passage when new cultural symbols and meanings can emerge. Liminal moments are times of tension, extreme reactions and great opportunity. These moments shimmer with new possibilities. They are painful, tough, full of hard choices—and they provoke anxiety. But they can be exhilarating.[48]

Sports such as skysurfing/dancing are transformative, liminal features of these times of new meaning and cultural creativity. The epistemological and ontological standpoints offered by such sport transport us, as scholars, into liminal spaces and spaces of freedom.

Accordingly, without excuses, the aesthetic-choreographic regard of sport performance in photography, videography, literature, cinematography (in journalism, television, film, personal computing, music videos, advertising, and the like) is critiqued and displayed, made into genre. As Benjamin ended his "The Work of Art in the Age of Mechanical Reproduction," "mankind's self-alienation has reached such a degree that it can experience its own destruction as an aesthetic pleasure of the first order."[49] These aesthetic pleasures are evident in ad campaigns that use skysurfing images.

The release handle that activates the release system of the sky board should be located near the hip. (A release handle located near the feet can be impossible to reach due to the centrifugal force of high speed spins.) . . . Cut a hole and affix the soft part of the Velcro to the suit just above the hole. Place the hooks of the Velcro of the release handle into the two lips of the soft Velcro and feed the cable into the hole down the leg of the jumpsuit to the board. Most of the release cable should be inside the jumpsuit, i.e. not flapping loose in the relative wind . . . to catch on the door of the plane . . . other aerial teammates, etc. The release handle should be mounted so that it is facing forward.[50]

Agamben says that "there is a good that humanity must learn to wrest from commodities in their decline." This good involves linking "together image and body in a space where they can no longer be separated, [thus forging] the *whatever* body."[51] Just here, within the confines of this essay, consider the skysurfing body to be the *whatever* body.

> To appropriate the historic transformations of human nature that capitalism wants to limit to the spectacle, to link together image and body in a space where they can no longer be separated, and thus to forge the whatever body, whose physis is resemblance—this is the good that humanity must learn to wrest from commodities in their decline. Advertising and pornography, which escort the commodity to the grave like hired mourners, are the unknowing midwives of this new body of humanity.[52]

Now metaphorically poised at the plane's door, I write and perform my way around, through, and out of the sport scholarship of the early twenty-first and twentieth centuries. I have tried, as the American sociologist Laurel Richardson says, to write theory so thick that it no longer looks like theory.[53] Cathartically,[54] I have endeavored to disintegrate sport studies into the raw materials of postmodern life. Skysurfing disintegrated some of the canonical frame of sports—team, male, nationalistic, bounded playing field—from its performance. But it has also captured and celebrated the essences—good and bad—of our time. Skysurfing is phantasmagoric, raw, dangerous.

VII. PARACHUTE MALFUNCTION PROCEDURES
    A. For a canopy malfunction, keep your board . . . (Do not release the sky board because it can fly up into your face.) . . .
    C. If the pilot chute deploys between legs, cut away the sky board immediately to avoid serious injury to your back/legs . . .
    I. Pilot Chute deploys in front of your arm. Raise BOTH arms overhead (Raising one arm is asymmetrical and can cause a spin).

IX. LANDING EMERGENCIES
    B. Power Lines—. . . drop the board by pointing your feet and prepare for a power line landing.[55]

In sport studies we can dissolve boundaries, recognize the phantasmagoria, blend dance, choreography, technolanguage, music, sport, consumerism,[56] sport philosophy, sociology, history, anthropology, our lives as keepers and generators of sport studies, our lives as sport fanatics, our lives as parents and athletes, our philosophical sorrow, joy, nihilism[57]—to name some—together into bold, zealous sport studies.

As the athletes do in skysurfing, scholars are reconfiguring their bodies and senses to move quickly across vast cultural spaces. There is a synergy between us and the geographical-cultural-liminal phantasmagoric world as we "trill across the structures"[58] of our world.

To do these things is—perhaps most dangerously for scholars—to hand over to, or at the least, share, our work with storytellers, dancers, transnational corporations, filmmakers, streetpeople, athletes, advertisers, virtual players—who in many cases, as exemplified by the author-athletes of this book, are already doing a better job of studying/interpreting sport than is the academy.

Notes

1. E.g., http://www.cruzbayvillas.com/Skydive.html; http://www.perigord.com/para/ffp disc us.html; http://espnet.sportszone.com/editors/xgames/surf/history.html; ftp://ftp.afn.org/skydive/gifs/skysurf1.gif; http://w3.restena.lu/al/pub/indivs/manncath/skysurfing.html; http://www.gate.net/~barry/equipmnt.html; http://w3.restena.lu/al/pub/indivs/manncath/rules.html; http://www.skysurf.co.nz/aboutus.html; http://192.52.88.43/GIFS/TSW/PRIVATE/SKYDIVE/documents/SkySurfInfo.html; http://home1.gte.net/ssipro/frame.html; http://www.3000.com/surf-flite/2.htm; http://www.qni.com/~tnt/wffc.htm; http://www.cruzbayvillas.com/main3DU.html; http://www.pointofinsanity.com/adthis.html

2. Dina Hernandez, "Overview of Pro Skysurfing at the Extreme Games," (27 Dec 1997) http://www.frc.ri/cmu.edu/~belboz/skydive/skysportif/overview.html.

3. Ibid.

4. Ibid.

5. Ibid.

6. "Skysurfing with Troy and Vic," http://viruszine.com/virus2/skysurfers/skysurfers.html

7. Tamara Koyn, "More Skysurfing" (10 May 1993), http://www.afn.org/skydive/usenet/1993/may/0052.html

8. Paul Virilio, *Open Sky* (Julie Rose, trans.), (London and New York: Verso, 1997), p. 3.

9. Ibid., p. 11.

10. Tamara Koyn, "Skysurfing" 3 Aug 1994), http://192.52.88.43/GIFS/TSW/PRIVATE/SKYDIVE/documents/SkySurfInfo.html

11. Koyn, "More Skysurfing," http://www.afn.org/skydive/usenet/1993/may/0052.html

12. Hernandez, "Overview of Pro Skysurfing at the Extreme Games," http://www.frc.ri/cmu.edu/~belboz/skydive/skysportif/overview.html

13. Koyn, "More Skysurfing," http://www.afn.org/skydive/usenet/1993/may/0052.html

14. See Joseph Francese, *Narrating Postmodern Time and Space* Albany: State University of New York Press 1998.

15. For example, Virilio, *Open Sky*, p. 12, on speed: "Speed not only allows us to get around more easily, it enables us above all to see, to hear, to perceive and thus to conceive the present world more intensely."

16. Ibid.

17. Dean Kuipers, "The Need for Speed," *Wired* (Oct 1997), pp. 108–110.

18. Jean Baudrillard, *Cool Memories II: 1987–1990* (Chris Turner, trans.), (Durham: Duke University Press, 1996), p. 65.

19. "The hero is the true subject of modernity."—Walter Benjamin, "The Paris of the Second Empire in Baudelaire," in Walter Benjamin, *Charles Baudelaire: An Epic Poet in the Era of High Capitalism* (Harry Zohn, trans.), (London: New Left Books, 1938, reprinted 1988), p. 74; as quoted by Peter Osborne, "Small-Scale Victories, Large-Scale Defeats: Walter Benjamin's Politics of Time," in Andrew Benjamin and Peter Osborne (eds.), *Walter Benjamin's Philosophy: Destruction and Experience* (New York and London: Routledge, 1994), pp. 59-109. See also Pierre Missac, *Walter Benjamin's Passages* (Cambridge, Mass. and London: The MIT Press, 1995), pp. 83–129.

20. See Jack Sands and Peter Gammons, *Coming Apart at the Seams: How Baseball Owners, Players and Television Executives Have Led Our National Pastime to the Brink of Disaster* (New York: Macmillan Publishing Co., 1993); special issue of *Quest, Perspectives on the Modern Olympic Games* 48, Vol. 1 (Feb 1996): Michael R. Neal, "The Postmodern Olympics: Technology and the Commodification of the Olympic Movement," and Peter J. Arnold, "Olympism, Sport and Education"; and Thomas P. Rosandich, "USA Versus the World Sport Structures—A Comparison," *The United States Sports Academy News*, Spring 1996, Vol. 18, No. 2, p. 3—all of whose point is to argue how sport in postmodern times is errant and must mend its ways.

21. For example, J.G. Ballard's "Project for a Glossary of the Twentieth Century," in Jonathan Crary and Sanford Kwinter (eds.), *Incorporations* (New York: Urzone Inc., 1990), pp. 269–279; glossary entries, twists of "typical" sport studies, are relevant to discussion of sport and culture:

Aerodynamism: Streamlining satisfies the dream of flight without the effort of growing wings. Aerodynamics is the motion sculpture of non-Euclidean space-time.

Time and motion studies: I am both myself and the shape that the universe makes around me. Time and motion studies represent our attempt to occupy the smallest, most modest niche in the surrounding universe.

Also, Charles Jencks, *The Architecture of the Jumping Universe: A Polemic* (New York: Academy Editions, 1995), who reinvisions the profession of architecture in a way similar to my call, as quoted in Brendan Gill, "Dear Darling Cosmos," *The New Yorker*, 19 June 1995, pp. 93–94:

Members of the profession should adopt instead an "aesthetic of life," which consists of undulating movement, of surprising humour, of catastrophic folds and delightful waves, of billowing crystals and fractured planes, of layered glass and spiraling growth.

Also, Rem Koolhaas, *Delirious New York: A Retroactive Manifesto for Manhattan* (New York: The Monacelli Press, 1994), pp. 152–159.

22. Koyn, "Skysurfing," http://192.52.88.43/GIFS/TSW/PRIVATE/SKYDIVE/documents/SkySurfInfo.html.

23. Baudrillard, *Cool Memories II: 1987–1990*, p. 35. See also Arthur and Marilouise Kroker, *Hacking the Future: Stories for the Flesh-Eating 90s.* (New York: St. Martin's Press, 1996), pp. 31–64.

24. "Skysurfing with Troy and Vic," http://viruszine.com/virus2/skysurfers/skysurfers.html.

25. Girgio Agamben, *The Coming Community* (Michael Hardt, trans.) (Minneapolis: University of Minnesota Press, 1994), 49.0.

26. Benjamin, "Theses on the Philosophy of History," in *Illuminations,* New York: Schoken Books, 1968 p. 255.

27. Ibid., pp. 253–264.

28. Benjamin, *Charles Baudelaire: A Lyric Poet in the Era of High Capitalism,* p. 40.

29. For example, as Buck-Morss, *The Dialectics of Seeing: Walter Benjamin and the Arcades Project,* Cambridge, Mass: MIT Press, 1993, p. 33, describes:

Arcades, fashion, boredom, kitsch, souvenirs, wax figures, gaslight, panoramas, iron construction, photography, prostitution, *Jugendstil,* flanêur, collector, gambling, streets, casings, department stores, metros, railroads, street signs, perspective, mirrors, catacombs, interiors, weather, world expositions, gateways, architecture, hashish, Marx, Haussmann, Saint Simon, Granville, Wiertz, Redon, Sue, Baudelaire, Proust.

30. Ibid. p. 241.

31. From Benjamin's filing system, *Konvolut V,* p. 574 (Nla, 8), as archived by Buck-Morss, ibid., p. 222. All *Konvolut* references below refer to Benjamin's files as archived by Buck-Morss.

32. Benjamin, "Paris—The Capital of the Nineteenth Century," in *Charles Baudelaire: A Lyric Poet in the Era of High Capitalism*, p. 165. See also Buck-Morss, *The Dialectics of Seeing*, pp. 66, 81. From Konvolut V, p. 1056 (f°, 3), as quoted by Buck-Morss, *The Dialectics of Seeing*, p. 66.

33. Buck-Morss, *The Dialectics of Seeing*, pp. 81 and 212.

34. Benjamin, Notes to the "Thesis on History," I, p. 1231, as quoted by Buck-Morss, *The Dialectics of Seeing*, p. 339.

35. *Konvolut V*, pp. 698–707, 1049, as archived by Buck-Morss, *The Dialectics of Seeing*.

36. *Konvolut V*, p. 162 (D2a, 4), as quoted by Buck-Morss, *The Dialectics of Seeing*, p. 105. On *flânerie*, see Ibid., pp. 344–346.

37. For example: David Harvey, *The Condition of Postmodernity* (London: Blackwell, 1990), pp. 211–239; Michel de Certeau, *The Practice of Everyday Life* (Steve Rendall, trans.), (Berkeley: The University of California Press, 1984), pp. 91–130; Edward Soja, *Thirdspace: Journeys to Los Angeles and Other Real and Imagined Places* (London: Blackwell, 1996), pp. 53–82.

38. Henri Bergson, *Matter and Memory* (N.M. Paul and W.S. Palmer, trans.), (New York: Zone Books, 1896, reprinted 1991), p. 173. Benjamin read Bergson. See Benjamin, "On Some Motifs in Baudelaire," in Benjamin, *Illuminations*, p. 180.

39. Bergson, *Matter and Memory*, pp. 202 and 209.

40. Gilles Deleuze, "Mediators," in Jonathan Crary and Sanford Kwinter (eds.), *Incorporations* (New York: Urzone Inc., 1992), p. 281.

41. See also Henri Lefebure, *The Production of Space* (London: Blackwell, 1991).

42. See also Synthia Sydnor, "A History of Synchronized Swimming," in *Journal of Sport History*, 25 (1998) Special Issue: *"The Practice of Sport History,"* Steve Pope [ed.], 252–267.

43. Homi Bhabha, *The Location of Culture* (London and New York: Routledge, 1994), p. 38.

44. Victor Turner, *The Forest of Symbols: Aspects of Ndembu Ritual* (Ithaca: Cornell University Press, 1967), pp. 106 and 93–111.

45. Bhabha, *The Location of Culture*, p. 245.

46. Ibid., p. 256.

47. Sherry Turkle, *Life on the Screen* (New York: Simon and Schuster, 1995). On Turkle, see Pamela McCorduck, "Sex, Lies and Avators," *Wired*, April 1996, pp. 106–110 and 158–165. See also Edward W. Soja's early "The Socio-Spatial Dialectic," in *Annals of the Association of American Geographers*, Vol. 70, No. 2, (June 1980), pp. 207–225.

48. McCorduck, "Sex, Lies and Avators," pp. 109–110.

49. Benjamin, "The Work of Art in the Age of Mechanical Reproduction," in *Illuminations*, p. 242.

50. Tamara Koyn, "Skysurfing," http://192.52.88.43/GIFS/TSW/PRIVATE/SKYDIVE/documents/SkySurfInfo.html.

51. Agamben, *The Coming Community*, 50.0.

52. Agamben, *The Coming Community*, 49.0; note the similarity to Benjamin, "The Storyteller: Reflections on the Works of Nikolai Leskov," in Benjamin, *Illuminations*, p. 83.

53. It used to be that sport studies academicians were consultants to forums such as *Sports Illustrated, Vogue, The New Yorker, Fitness.* Now we use these magazines to teach and as primary sources for our own research. See also Laurel Richardson, "Writing: A Method of Inquiry," in Denzin and Lincoln (eds.), *Handbook of Qualitative Research,* Thousand Oaks, CA: Sage Publications, Inc. 1994 pp. 516-529.

54. See Elin Diamond, "The Shudder of Catharsis in Twentieth-Century Performance," in Parker and Kosofsky Sedgwick, *Performativity and Performance,* London: Routledge, 1996, p. 16: "The problematic of catharsis lives on in contemporary performance, given the connections it articulates between seeing and feeling, between word and body."

55. Tamara Koyn, "Skysurfing," http://192.52.88.43/GIFS/TSW/PRIVATE/SKYDIVE/documents/SkySurfInfo.html See also Virilio, *Open Sky,* p. 129:

> From the exocentration of a body in flight above the ground we suddenly swap to egocentration: the centre is no longer located outside; it is its own reference, its 'driving-axis' > The inertial centre serves as the world's axis, but of a small inner world which turns protruded man into a *planet,* though a living planet, launched into the void of a cosmic time and not, as often claimed, into the space-time of the intersidereal universe.

56. See Bruno Latour, *We Have Never Been Modern* (Catherine Porter, trans.), (Cambridge, Mass.: Harvard University Press, 1993); Paul Virilio, *The Art of the Motor* (Julie Rose, trans.), (Minneapolis: University of Minnesota Press, 1995); Lewis Mumford, *Technics and Civilization* (New York: Harcourt, Brace, Jovanovich, 1948).

57. See esp. Michael Novak, *The Experience of Nothingness* (New York: Harper & Row, 1970).

58. Dean Kuipers, "The Need for Speed," *Wired,* Oct 1997, pp. 108–110.

BMX

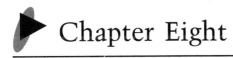

Chapter Eight

Small Bikes, Big Men

Brett Downs

Did you happen to hear an explosion in the bicycling world several years ago? It resonated from ESPN's 1995 X Games. While scarcely promoted behind "legitimate" mountain biking, BMX dirt jumping and freestyle hit the public as the greatest spectacle since professional wrestling. America turned to see young men hurling themselves and their bicycles through the air over ridiculous dirt mounds and ramps. It was a daredevil extravaganza with almost assured carnage. Surely a ratings grabber if there ever was one. All of a sudden my sport became "extreme" and the public became aware of what I have been doing all these years. This media exposure is what enables me to write this chapter, yet it has nothing to do with why I ride or my values. While television presents stunts with a few riders, the soul of the sport is what makes it truly great. In order to understand what I mean by soul, you must get some background to BMX and freestyle riding.

Brett Downs started jumping his bicycle off curbs at the age of five in 1972. Never stopping, except for injuries, he continues to perform in shows on the East Coast and compete nationally in both the ramp and flatland classes. Brett has appeared in several magazines, videos and commercials as well as performing in NBA and NFL halftime shows. His sponsors include Adidas, Contraption Devices, Infinity Cycles, ODI grips and Odyssey components. Off the bike, Brett received a B.S. degree in education from Millersville University of Pennsylvania. A junior high school teacher and carpenter, Brett has written articles for BMX magazines and Web sites, assisted in producing and promoting events and videos, and designed bicycle components. A recent father to son Henry, Brett is currently looking for a freestyle baby carriage and extra small helmet.

It is safe to say that since the dawn of bicycling there have been riders trying some type of stunt or trick. Nearly everyone has said the immortal words, "Look Ma, no hands!" Some of us simply never stopped. The number of riders is greater than you might think. Television presents only the top professionals, but there are thousands of riders worldwide. If you look carefully, you can probably find them in your own neighborhood. We are an invisible army—for the most part—but we can be found if you pay attention. We are called BMX'ers, freestylers, or trail riders. Mostly, we simply consider ourselves riders.

To help the nonrider understand what we are doing, I must first take a moment to differentiate the types of riding. BMX stands for bicycle moto-cross racing. This is when a group of up to eight riders races around a dirt track over jumps and through bermed turns to cross the finish line first. A trails rider is a person who may or may not race but spends his time jumping over dirt mounds perfecting his skill and the smoothness of his riding at midair tracks. A freestyler is a trick rider who either rides ramps of all shapes and sizes or does spinning and rolling tricks on flat ground. The public uses the label BMX to describe all types of riding on 20" (wheeled) bicycles. Not that it really matters what they call us, but there are differences among the different forms of riding. While most riders generally specialize in one type of riding, there is a lot of crossover into the different styles. The bikes appear similar but they have specialized designs or components for each specific use. The specialization in bicycle design is the easiest way to tell what type of riding is the most common for a rider.

Now, thanks to the X Games, BMX/freestyle riding has become popular with the general public. This isn't the first time BMX has approached the big time. In the 1980s BMX and freestyle had a boom and thousands of aspiring riders hit the pedals—and the sports skyrocketed. After booming for about three years, BMX and freestyle quickly died, as most fads do. The first contact with the mainstream has a great impact on how riders view this age of "extremism." With this surge we riders are once again growing in ranks, yet there is an air of apprehension. We do not want to be treated as the next big hype or fad. Riding has got roots and deserves more credibility than it was given before.

In the eighties' BMX boom the sports were controlled by large corporations that either manufactured bikes and products, were sanctioning bodies for competitions, or were part of the print media. These companies generally excluded the actual riders from the direction in which the sport would progress and what was available to ride. Eventually the sport all but died out. Due to overmarketing there wasn't anyone left to buy new bikes. Too much structure from big money corporations imposing their will on the riders prompted many to quit altogether. The new riders who had started riding because it was a fad also left when they realized that the tricks actually were harder than they appeared. Magazines that were the lifeblood of the sport and connected riders around the world folded due to the withdrawal of advertisers who could not sell enough product. One reason they couldn't move their wares was that those left riding had transcended the limits of their bicycles. Without heeding the advisement of riders, the manufacturers took design advice from marketing experts looking for the next fad. This made it extremely difficult to keep riding, as the quality of bikes declined. The best bike frames, costing close to two hundred dollars, could break in less than six months.

The riders were faced with producing their own bikes and componentry. Many homegrown companies started with experienced riders who were sick of breaking their mass-production bikes. Taking their practical knowledge of what not to design, new companies such as Standard Industries and S & M Bicycles revolutionized the bikes and enabled the sports to continue. The control of the sport was slowly shifting back to those actually riding. This control would continue to impact not only bicycle design but the whole industry— from the media, to competitors, to riders' attitudes.

The void in the media was filled as riders made videos to present their local scene to rest of the BMX community or created underground 'zines and distributed them among friends. Eventually new magazines were formed and distributed by mail-order bike shops to their customers. Freestyle competitions were revitalized as riders promoted their own series and restructured the way contests were held and judged. The sanctioning bodies in BMX racing learned to make racing more exciting and fun with better tracks and easier access to the stars of the sport. The riders gained control of the sport through hard work, perseverance and dedication.

With the new "extreme" boom we riders see the control of our sport going back into the hands of big business. The scene is being manipulated by people who never swung a leg over a bike. ESPN is controlling the major contest series, and companies such as Taco Bell and Slim Jim are sponsoring them. Not that this is altogether bad, but it is usually to the detriment of the rider. Taking a back seat to those putting on the show for mass consumption, the riders are often treated as talent in a huge media event. (Generally at these contests we are not allowed to practice in the competition area, or practice starts at 8:00 am so as not to get in the TV schedule's way.) Can you imagine an Olympic skier getting only one or two practice runs six hours before he lays it on the line? Or how about if after the skier races down the mountain, he is asked to leave the area and has to pay a spectator's admission fee to watch the rest of the event? Both of these absurdities have happened to me. The professional riders are also making paltry amounts from putting themselves on the line for television while the corporate sponsors and networks are doing millions of dollars of business. While the sponsors spend thousands of dollars for the ramp riders' riding zone, the flatland riders usually are forced to compete in a dusty and bumpy corner of a nearby parking lot or to dodge ramps in the middle of the street course. The amateur class has been pushed aside to the day preceding the competition and exists only due to the insistence of Matt Hoffman, the rider who originated the contest series. The way I see it is, while ESPN and the other sponsors are primarily producing a television show, they too realize they are also running our competition series. They are here because we ride. We should be respected as athletes are in most other sports. As long as these competitions continue to treat us as unwanted stepchildren, rider support will decline. Currently, several of the top pros are considering joining together to take an organized stand against this type of corporate disrespect.

As things were getting out of control in the late eighties, a new type of riding took over. It was called street riding, and it was basically riding around town performing bike stunts on whatever obstacles were found. Riding left the competition format. Stairs, curbs, banks, walls, and loading docks became the arena for BMX and freestyle. Through street riding, riders revolted against the rules and structure of organized competitions. Today there is an upsurge in trails riding in which the emphasis is placed not on competing or celebrity but in digging out jumps in secluded locations and riding for the sheer enjoyment of it. Again the riders have found a way to revolt against the establishment. The next boom heard in bicycling may be from the implosion caused by BMXers and freestylers again running away from those trying to control the destiny of the sport.

Why then are we out practicing for hours on end? Why do we spend all of our money on the upkeep of our scoots? Why do we face certain injury with a seemingly careless disregard? Plain and simple: it's fun. The thrill of a trails rider bobbing through a series of ten closely packed jumps is similar to that of the best roller coaster you have ever ridden, only you are in control. A flatland freestyler treats a parking lot the way a figure skater treats the ice, spinning and gliding across the surface, striving for a nirvana of technical skill and grace. A vertical freestyler launches himself off a half-pipe and upwards of thirteen feet over the coping and callously tosses off limbs, spins the handlebars or flips before dive-bombing kamikaze-style back into the ramp. The adrenaline rush is matched only by the sense of satisfaction. We are at our best when on a bike and wouldn't have it any other way.

The tremendous pride in riding comes at a price, though. Most of society sees us as a bunch of deviants who don't fit into the established structure. We dig up the empty lot in the neighborhood to build jumps. We are the older guys practicing flatland at the park while parents keep a skeptical eye on us because they are sure we are there to sell their precious Billy drugs (or worse!). We are the trespassers who invade the hidden parts of your town known only to security guards because there is a fun bank or rail to ride. Those around us cannot understand why we spend all of our time on those "little bikes" instead of doing something more mature like working overtime at our jobs or going to the bar for happy hour at the end of the day.

All types of people ride, yet our riding separates us from the flat-footed public. Riders are anomalies to most people, homegrown Evel Knievels, so to speak. We do not have a place in normal society. The average Joe is always there to remind us, too. Everyday when I am practicing my flatland tricks, some redneck has to yell something along the line of "HEY FAGGOT!" as he is waiting at a red light. I walk into the bike shop and ask about a frame, and the shop owner asks me don't I feel silly riding a little kid's bike and why not get a mountain bike instead. Years of experience and dozens of friends around the country will agree with me on these points. This is another reason why in the BMX/freestyle community there are hesitant feelings about going mainstream. Those who cheer us at the X Games cannot always be trusted. The beer-swilling frat boys watching an ESPN contest at their spring break resort are often the same ones who chase us all over town trying to run us down with their cars. "Thanks fellas, glad you liked my contest run. See you at home next week."

Aside from the actual riding, the lifestyle of a rider is another amazing feat. Many professionals, the best the sport has to offer, do not work. They ride. Day in, day out. It is a paradox that those with the most expensive bike bills are often the poorest of all as they are always riding. Although a few riders do work "real" jobs, pulling weeds or the graveyard shift at 7-11 is a common way for a pro to procure bike parts and food. This dedication to a sport is comparable to that of any other professional athlete. The only difference is pro bikers usually cannot win enough to support themselves. Only in the last couple of years has an elite professional group been able to make a comfortable living from riding.

Another amazing aspect of the lifestyle is simply being out of the house and being a part of the world. Riders are out in the streets everyday witnessing all the typically invisible wonders. But we see the homeless and the crazy people in our towns. We see the drug deals going down. We see car accidents and back seat romances. We see kids getting hit by their moms, and we get chased by dogs. Each rider has his own stories about the unreal. They fill in the blanks on rainy days when we must resign ourselves to the couch with our friends. Here are some of my favorites:

My friend Joe was a nationally-competitive flatlander. He usually placed in the top three at contests. He practiced in the parking lot of an old skating rink. One day a car pulled in and parked in the shadows at the other end of the lot. Joe kept on riding as the driver sat and watched for over an hour. Firing up the engine, the driver approached the practice area. Joe was called over to the driver's window. He rode over and was ordered "Do your best trick" as he found himself staring down the barrel of a gun. Joe did a double whiplash and got the hell out of there.

One night about ten of us had gathered after a freestyle show in Rockville, Maryland. We were all friends from different parts of the country, so we had a session until late into the night at a local industrial park. Calling it a night, we headed back to our hotel. Suddenly an old model sedan drove by and turned into the parking lot. The occupants started yelling the usual epithets as the car sped towards us. We were riding in a pack when the car barreled straight down the middle, splitting us the way a bowling ball goes through pins. We all yelled at the maniacal motorist and made the requisite hand gestures. Locking up the brakes, the drunks decided to teach us a lesson. They spun around and charged again. What they didn't know was that one of us was a factory-sponsored rider and got free bikes. When the car reached our group, it had to be doing at least forty. At the last possible second Dave leapt off his bike and threw it at the car. The sound of bicycle and automobile colliding broke the silence of the night. The windshield was shattered across the laps of the passengers, Dave's bike was snapped in two, connected only by a brake cable. We all stood in amazement at his sacrifice. As the car disappeared into the distance we erupted into cheers.

My friend Bob is a dirt jumper. Every spring, he and his friends have to build new jumps to replace those destroyed by winter. This year they found some secluded woods about 100 yards from a cemetery. While digging the track, his friend felt the shovel hit something solid. With a flick of the wrist he unearthed the obstruction and threw it into the dirt pile. When they looked to see what it was, the object stared back at them. They had found a human skull. It was just the face from the upper lip to the forehead, but it was more than enough to freak them out. When Bob told me this story, I told him he better call the police or something. Bob said he knew they should but then the cops would destroy their new jumps by investigating the scene. It was decided that the best plan was to quietly rebury the skull and christen the spot as the Dead Trails. Ride in Peace.

Call it BMX, freestyle or stunt-biking Tom Foolery, the riding is what unifies all these stories and those involved. The stories are about overcoming obstacles. While not the usual type of tale, these stories coincide with any mainstream sports hero's trials and tribulations in pursuit of success. We are just another group of athletes (I am using the term loosely) who do what they love no matter what hinders them.

With all these rewards and detractions shaping a rider's personal experience, it is understandable why we do not like being called extreme BMXers. We don't call ourselves extreme. We are just riders. The nonriding public who sees us on television calls us extreme. To have the society which rejects us or big money corporations that won't compensate us for our talents label what we do for mass consumption is degrading. The last thing we want to do is ride for anyone but ourselves.

Now with the onset of extreme sports phenomena the future of BMX/freestyle is up in the air. As in the past, the market may get saturated, the production may get out of control and the riding may get too difficult for all those following trends to keep up with it. Then again, riding may get more acclaim and exposure and, while never being truly assimilated into the big-time sports world, it may find a home. If the riders, manufacturers and promoters all decide to work together and treat one another with mutual respect, things could work out.

I think that riding will follow in the footsteps of its long-lost ancestor, skateboarding. Starting originally as a fad in the 1960s, skateboarding gained sudden popularity and then died. A resurgence in the 1970s came as a result of better equipment and new skateparks giving more people a chance to start. After another recession in skating, the new styles of skateboarding in the 1980s brought back a refreshed interest. Currently skateboarding is at another peak after a few lean years. Like skateboarding, the popularity of BMX and freestyle may waver over the years; but there always will be a core group of riders to carry the torch for the next generation to pick up and claim as their own. Personally, all I am completely certain of is that as we proceed through the new millenium, no matter the direction the sport takes, I will still be out riding in my parking lots as you drive by staring at me.

Chapter Nine

BMX, Extreme Sports, and the White Male Backlash

Kyle Kusz

BMX bike riding is one of the sports which has enjoyed a resurgence in popularity with American youth due to the creation of ESPN2's X Games. The popularity of the X Games has been instrumental in, if not creating the desire for new 'alternative' sporting activities, at least cultivating the growth and popularity of these athletic pursuits. Like skateboarding and in-line skating in their "extreme" forms, BMX riding is performed on a half-pipe and street course, but unlike the former, there are other forms of BMX competition such as flatland competitions and dirt jumping. BMX has become one of the marquee sports of the summer X Games, with its top performers (TJ Lavin, Matt Hoffman, Jay Miron, Denis McCoy, Ryan Nyquist, and others) some of the central figures frequently used to represent the ethos of "extreme" sports. The ethos of this media-created conglomeration of 'nonmainstream' sporting practices is characterized by the valorization of risk-taking behaviors; the emphasis of creativity, individuality, and marking oneself as "different"; and the participation in activities individually performed but practiced in small groups that value a sense of community.

Kyle Kusz is currently a lecturer in the Department of Kinesiology and Physical Education at Northern Illinois University, where he teaches undergraduate and graduate courses in the sociocultural study of sports. He is also completing his doctoral dissertation at the University of Illinois at Urbana-Champaign. His research examines the conjunctural politics of various representations of white masculinity in American sports, film, and popular culture.

BMX riding, in its 1990s "extreme" form, features riders performing daredevil spins and flips off obstacles which can launch riders as high as fifteen to twenty feet in the air, as well as executing difficult technical maneuvers and tricks in flatland competitions and on street courses. The representations of BMX riding help to generate and legitimate the adoption of particular values, attitudes, affects, investments, identifications, in its participants and spectators, while simultaneously subtly reproducing particular relations of power and discursive knowledges about race, gender, youth, sport, etc. More specifically, BMX is a cultural activity which valorizes overcoming one's fears and taking risks; BMX performers are frequently represented as individuals who love taking risks, who love pushing their bodies to their physical limits, who demand our admiration because they are brave enough to take chances and willing to risk significant injury in order to successfully pull a trick. The creativity and the desire to be original and to display a unique individuality are narrative tropes through which BMXers are frequently represented. Broadcasts of BMX street and half-pipe competitions always involve the commentators lauding or criticizing riders for their ability (or lack thereof) to invent new stunts or to develop new lines to traverse a street course so that they can grab bigger air or pull a trick that has never been imagined before. Additionally, BMXers often represent their participation in BMX (as it is represented by others) as a "lifestyle." Within these stories, BMX is forwarded as the determinate force through which participants constitute identities. The move to represent BMX as a lifestyle is a representational strategy used to assert and authenticate the BMXers' cultural difference. It is important that we understand BMX and extreme sports as being represented through the categories and representational logics of a youth cultural practice itself constituted by the logics of style, lifestyle, and signifying difference.

My perspective in examining BMX as an "extreme" sport is as a white, male, twentysomething sports enthusiast who remembers watching the first "Extreme Games," as they were first named, and being somewhat fascinated by these sporting activities and their "alternative" ethos and values, yet whose greatest bike trick in the early 1980s was "popping a wheelie." I was uncertain then what it was that fascinated me about these activities and the competitors who performed them. At least in part, my initial interest in extreme sports stemmed from the way in which the early representational strategies of the Generation X discourse[1] were employed to make sense of (and to sell) these commercially invented "extreme sports," particularly to American youth.

But, through the writing of this chapter, I have come to see extreme sports in a radically new way. No longer do I read this sporting formation as a politically benign cultural formation which can be lauded for devaluating competition while emphasizing the cooperation and community that participants display. Rather, my interest in extreme sports relates to how, as a popular cultural site, it has become involved in a reactionary politics of representation which seeks to represent a strong, proud, confident, unconstrained, and unapologetic white athletic masculinity whose characteristics, investments, desires, and practices would appeal to white males. These white males, in the 1990s, were said to have been experiencing a crisis of confidence, self-esteem, social status, and identity— as white males came under critique in the 1990s.

My concern in this essay is to take a critical perspective of some specific contemporary representations of BMX culture and extreme sports. More specifically, I want to make explicit the political, social, cultural, and economic forces and conditions of the context of the United States in the early 1990s which are responsible for invisibly shaping the forms and contents of the images being displayed and narratives being told about extreme sports. I construct this context in order to explain how representations of extreme sports can be read as sites involved in a reactionary representational politics which attempts to constitute and foreground images of whiteness as disenfranchised, nondominant and marginalized. To obscure, discredit, and disavow the social, economic, cultural, and political privileges of whiteness is a response to the critiques of people of color, multiculturalists, feminists, and others who, in the late 1980s and 1990s made visible and criticized the way in which whiteness operates as an invisible, normalizing force within the social formation of the United States.

On the one hand, examining extreme sports as a cultural formation involved in the production of whiteness does not seem to be a very profound exercise because even the casual observer of these activities can see that the performers and spectators of extreme sports are mainly young white males. But, if we agree that one of the characteristics of whiteness, as a racial identity, is its ability to make itself invisible to the everyday, uncritical gaze (mainly of whites) or to construct itself as a racially unmarked category as whiteness scholars have asserted,[2] then exposing extreme sports as a site of whiteness becomes somewhat of a significant and necessary first step in the critical examination of this specific form of whiteness. With this in mind, I wish to situate this examination of some representations of extreme sports and the BMX cultural formation within the relatively recent, and ever-expanding, list of critical studies of whiteness.[3]

Critical Studies of Whiteness

This growing body of the critical study of whiteness begins by conceiving of whiteness not as an unproblematic biological category but as a socially-constructed category shaped by historically specific social, political, cultural, and economic forces, conditions, and discourses.[4] Dyer points out that although a person's whiteness appears to be easily discernible simply by looking at one's skin color, a number of other signifiers, codings, and factors are influential in how one's racial identity is comprehended. For Dyer, factors such as "the shape of nose, eyes and lips, the colour and set of hair, even body shape may all be mobilised to determine someone's 'colour.' "[5] Beyond the physical markings of one's body, racial identity is also signified through one's mannerisms, speech patterns, sartorial styles, or affective identifications and investments (that is, taste in music or other cultural activities). For communications scholar Raka Shome, who is concerned with examining the strategies used to represent whiteness, whiteness is "the everyday, invisible, subtle, cultural, and social practices, ideas, and codes that discursively secure the power and privilege of white people, but that strategically remains unmarked, unnamed, and unmapped in contemporary society."[6] This notion of whiteness and its representational strategies are crucial to my readings of some fairly recent mainstream media representations of extreme sports and the fifteen-minute "underground" BMX video titled "Live Fast Die."

Another facet of the critical study of whiteness is an effort to particularize whiteness, that is, to expose whiteness as a historically specific social construction which is frequently constituted to appear as though it is transhistorical or universal. Critical scholars of whiteness have shown that the racial category of "white" has a history; which is to say that who is constituted as white has been different throughout history and that whiteness, as a racial identity, cannot be unproblematically read off one's body. David Roediger's study of how Irish immigrants in the United States in the early twentieth century came to be understood as "white" is a good exemplar of making visible the historicity of whiteness.[7] Studies like Roediger's that particularize whiteness have shown that whiteness cannot be conceived as a static transhistorical phenomenon. By recognizing and making visible the historical, cultural, and social particularities and complexities of whiteness, we are able to move beyond definitions of whiteness that attempt to essentialize it as a monolithic site of domination, oppression, and exclusion. Whiteness always exists in multiple forms within one specific historical moment. The examination of whiteness must include a concern with how factors such as class, gender, age, geography, sexuality, and nationality shape the various ways in which whiteness is represented. By keeping in mind that there are multiple forms of whiteness, one can avoid simplistically and reductively accepting the popular understanding of whiteness as being, in all cases, a site of domination, superiority, and privilege.

But while acknowledging the need to not reductively essentialize whiteness as always being a site of privilege and domination, cultural workers must maintain a critical perspective in their examination of all forms of whiteness. This is especially true within the contemporary historical moment where there has been a noticeable increase in representations of poor whites or "white trash" and working class whites within mainstream popular culture.[8] Representations of "trashed" whites have been read as symptoms of a reactionary racial politics which seeks to represent whiteness as deprivileged, powerless, and located on the margins of society in order to undermine the arguments of feminists, multiculturalists, and others who have identified whiteness as exclusionary, dominating, and oppressive. Newitz's critical examination of "the largely white [and male]" "alternative rock" scene in the early 1990s is one such study of whiteness which maintains its critical gaze even when encountering representations of a youthful white masculinity whose disadvantage, alienation, self-deprecation and marginalization are represented as "naturally" and "authentically" (through the commonsense understanding of the category "adolescent") constitutive of its identity. Newitz argues that we should understand the self-deprecating lyrics of songs such Beck's *Loser* or The Offspring's *Self-Esteem* as functioning to enable the white male youths who produce and consume these texts to avoid the criticism of others (because no one can criticize them any worse than they criticize themselves) and to reconstruct a sense of superiority (because no one can criticize them as well as they can) which has been destabilized by global economic processes. These processes

have radically changed the domestic labor economy, and the increased emphasis on 'cultural difference' has challenged the superiority and sense of normality previously experienced by white
males. Newitz insightfully argues that this form of white masculinity—which, at first glance, may seem to express an authentic or
legitimate claim to powerlessness and a deprivileged, marginal social position—can actually make possible a set of social relations
and a cultural space that allows these white male alternative rockers to reclaim a sense of superiority and insusceptibility to criticism. So, in the critical study of representations of whiteness, it is
crucial to maintain a trenchant gaze even on those representations
of whiteness which may appear, at first glance, to be marginal, un-
oppressive, deprivileged, and otherwise somewhat powerless for they
may also function to re-secure the dominance, normality, and centrality of whiteness in unique ways.[9]

Finally, the recent research on whiteness has also called attention to the invisibility of whiteness, the way in which whiteness (for whites) often goes unnoticed as the invisible norm, how
it acts as "the unraced center of a racialized world."[10] Research on
whiteness illuminates representations of whiteness in cultural sites
in order to expose how individuals are constituted as white and
how whiteness is represented "as the norm in the dominant social
and cultural structures of western societies."[11] This research has
called attention to the ways in which representations of whiteness
are often unproblematically conflated with the categories of humanity[12] and/or nation within popular culture.[13] The invisibility
and normativity articulated with whiteness enable it to maintain
its privileged position within the racialized world and its normative power as an often unconsidered, yet pervasive, invisible political force which organizes everyday cultural practices, social
relations, and representational practices. This critical exposition of
whiteness includes illuminating the discourses, social practices and
relations, and the material conditions which can obscure and dis-
guise the dominating effects of whiteness.[14]

Whiteness in the Context of the 1990s United States

Having identified some of the main themes of the research on
whiteness which shape my analysis of representations of BMX
culture and extreme sports, I think it is also necessary to understand that the contemporary academic concern with whiteness
within the United States is an effect of a unique set of social,

cultural, political, and economic forces and conditions in the early 1990s. The method of inquiry I utilize in this study is that of a conjunctural analysis. Within this theoretical optic, one assumes that the meanings of cultural forms are not pre-given or natural, but are the complex effects (and instruments) of particular, complex, and politically strategic combinations of cultural, social, political, and economic discourses, forces, and conditions that operate within that historical moment. The meanings articulated with cultural forms are always to be understood as political effects, in that they often reproduce dominant knowledge about subjects (men and women; youth and adults; blacks and whites) and uneven relations of power along lines of race, gender, class, age, sexuality, and nationality. In order to situate my readings of some specific representations of BMXers and extreme sports as a whole, then, let me first briefly outline some of the crucial forces that have contributed to the shaping of the form and content of representations of white males in the cultural formation of extreme sports.

The contemporary focus on whiteness in the early 1990s can be understood, in large part, as a result of the pervasive logic of identity politics[15] that emerged from the Civil Rights, student, women's, and Gay liberation movements of the late 1960s and early 1970s. These social movements disrupted and challenged the mythical sense of consensus that organized the American popular imaginary prior to these protests. Within dominant understandings of the way in which identity politics works, historically marginalized groups such as nonwhites, women, and homosexuals argue that they have been discriminated against by the overt (and covert) practices and relations within dominant culture: normative structures, values, knowledge, and ideologies work in favor of whites, men, heterosexuals, and the middle class. These groups point out how their voices and perspectives have long been silenced and marginalized by mainstream representations of "American" history. By the 1990s, these subordinated groups argued it was time not only for their increased representation and voices, perspectives, and knowledge in American popular culture, but that the United States should right the oppressive and exclusionary wrongs of its past (exclusion, discrimination, violence—both real and representational) by taking steps to eliminate the practices, privileges, policies, and assumptions[16] that led to the history of discrimination against these groups. In short, they charged that it was necessary for the United States to "expand citizenship to people of color and other subordinated groups."[17] In their critiques of the American social formation, these groups have called attention to the ways in which whiteness operates as an invisible, yet influential, normative force that constantly works to produce and reproduce its own centrality, normality, and dominance.

As the privileges and normativity of whiteness came under attack by groups such as multiculturalists and feminists,[18] a conservative white backlash developed to contest their challenges of dominant American culture and their representation of whiteness as a site of oppression, domination, and superiority. American media culture (by this I mean the news media, popular television, movies, and music) has been particularly instrumental in the generation, mobilization, and legitimation of this white backlash discourse. Popular culture operates as a vitally important pedagogical site which shapes and influences the forms and contents of this reactionary white backlash. The rhetoric of conservative whites such as talk radio host Rush Limbaugh; mainstream Hollywood films such as *Falling Down, Disclosure*, and *The Fan*; and news stories like *Newsweek*'s 1993 cover story titled "White male paranoia" are popular cultural sites that have been instrumental in reflecting the paranoia that white males are increasingly represented as feeling. Additionally they have also significantly contributed to generating the self-images, the feelings, and experiences of this growing group of "angry White males."

Within the discourse of the "angry white male" that emerged in the 1990s, white males are represented as increasingly feeling "threatened" and "paranoid" over being identified as the universal oppressor of "feminists, multiculturalists, P.C. policepersons, affirmative-action employers, rap artists, Native Americans, Japanese tycoons, Islamic fundamentalists and Third World dictators, all of them saying the same thing: *You've been a bad boy.*"[19] The figure of the "angry white male" is almost always coded as middle-aged (anywhere from mid-thirties to mid-fifties), with populist values and characteristics,[20] whose class position is ambiguously (and strategically) portrayed as middle or working class. Acting in response to the critiques of white male privilege made by nonwhites, feminists, postcolonialists, and others, the discourse of the angry white male makes the claim that white males have become the victims of a hypersensitive, politically correct context. This discourse alleges that affirmative action programs and efforts to culturally diversify workplace and educational settings by expanding opportunities for nonwhites and women have not simply leveled the economic playing field so that nonwhites, women, and white men compete evenly for such things as jobs and educational opportunities, but these measures have *unfairly* operated against the favor of white males. The discourse of the angry white male is a reactionary representational strategy where white males are constituted as the victims of a historical era in which the complaints of a small group of militant multiculturalists, feminists, and other "minority" groups have threatened the traditional values the United States was founded upon, and the very future of the nation.[21] As Giroux explains, ". . . in an era of unprecedented unemployment, poverty, and diminishing opportunities for most Black Americans, right-wing Whites have convinced themselves of their own loss of privilege."[22] Thus, on one level, the rhetoric of white male paranoia pre-emptively dismisses any consideration or claim of white privilege in order to forward a narrative that not only seeks to disavow the racial privilege of white males by offering representations of white males as disempowered and disadvantaged. It also goes even further by constructing white men hyperbolically as victims who are under siege "in their jobs, in their neighborhoods, in their homes, and in their schools."[23]

These critiques of whiteness have led to an increased number of popular representations of white males that portray them as experiencing feelings new to American white men in the post-World War II era: vulnerability, uncertainty, lacking confidence, being conscious of their racial identity, and experiencing an unstable sense of social status. In the 1990s, as a part of this reactionary discourse of white males, there was a prominent increase in the number of representations of white American men as being anxious and fearful, marginalized, powerless, and disadvantaged. Films such as *Falling Down*, *The Fan*, and *In the Company of Men* are organized by the discourse of the angry white male and display the anxiety, guilt, fear, and threat to his identity he is said to be experiencing. They represent/legitimate a particular resentful reaction by the white male which manifests itself as a violence that seeks to negate the identity of the nonwhite and female others who have challenged his cultural position and engendered his "identity crisis."[24]

The point of outlining the context of the United States culture in the early 1990s is to constitute it as being a time of increasing racial anxieties and animosities between whites and blacks which was organized, at least in part, by the logic of identity politics. It was an era in which whiteness became increasingly visible as a racial identity and was critiqued, both in scholarly journals and the popular press, as a frequently oppressive, exclusionary, normalizing, and dominating social force operating against non-whites. The popular versions of these critiques of whiteness identified white males as the main beneficiaries of white privilege. Within this context, a white conservative backlash formed which attempted to defuse the challenges to the dominant-hegemonic position and authority of whiteness by appropriating the logic of identity politics to construct narratives where white men were cast as vulnerable, powerless, and disadvantaged victims of a social formation that celebrated "cultural difference" and increasingly identified them as the "universal oppressors."[25]

White Backlash Politics and Extreme Sports

Baker and Boyd point out that within this era where more attention was given to the study of popular culture, there was, curiously, a relative lack of attention given to mediated sport culture as a site of popular culture open to critical inquiry.[26] I think this oversight can be understood, at least in part, as an effect of the pervasive idea that sport is a set of "relatively autonomous"[27] cultural spaces and practices largely immune to or unaffected by broader sociocultural, economic, and political dynamics. Such conceptions of sport seem to abstract it from its larger historico-cultural context and often mystify how it is a prominent culture site where differential power relations and discursive knowledge about gender, race, class, age, and nation are produced and reproduced. My examination of extreme sports, however, attempts to show how the constitutive forces and conditions of the historical conjuncture of 1990s America shaped the representation of extreme sports and its athletes.

Grossberg, writing about the social, cultural, political, and economic circumstances that contextualized late 1980s and early 1990s America, argues that popular culture became "the ground, the tactics, and the first stake of hegemonic struggle" for the "new conservatism" in the United States during this time. For Grossberg, the new conservatism has been successful in extending its views and constructions of reality through the subtle organization (and re-organization) of the "ways [popular cultural texts] are presented and used, how they are taken up, and the forms of people's commitments to them."[28] Grossberg emphasizes that the most important part of the project of the 'new conservatism' involves the subtle rearticulation, or the "re-ideologization" of the "ownership, anchorage, and territorialization" of popular cultural sites so that new social maps that support the aims of the new conservatism (of which the "white male backlash" is understood to be an instrument and effect) are established in the place of previous maps, codings, and narratives that organized the popular representation of these cultural sites and practices.[29]

Grossberg's insights on the hegemonic operations of new conservatism provide us with a starting point from which to make sense of the way in which representations of BMX and extreme sports were drastically reideologized or rearticulated in the 1990s. Through the examination of a specific selection of representations of BMX culture and extreme sports, I want to show how BMX and other extreme sports have been rearticulated and infused with new meanings and new affective investments which constitute them as politically productive activities. As such, they express quintessentially American values of rugged individualism, risk taking and creativity and they are implicated as a part of a reactionary project which seeks to resecure the hegemonic position of white males. My argument relies on the critical analysis of three texts: the first, "Live Fast Die," is a BMX video produced by BMX youth for an intended audience of other BMXers; second, a June 30, 1997 *US News & World Report* cover story which attempts to explain the rising popularity of extreme sports in the late 1990s; third, a December 6, 1997 *Sports Illustrated* "special report"/cover story titled "What Ever Happened to the White athlete?"

"Live Fast Die" is a fifteen-minute video[30] which not only showcases the amazing athletic abilities of BMXers performing their spectacular aerial tricks, but also offers the viewer an unique 'inside' look at the ways BMXers seek to construct their identities and how they represent their culture. The video is evidence of the way BMX has been represented (and represents itself) as radically different in its values, investments, and meanings from other 'mainstream' sports and cultural activities for youth. "Live Fast Die" is a representative text of the way in which BMX and extreme sports were predominantly imagined in the early to mid 1990s through the category of a subcultural formation.[31] Because BMX was imagined through the category of a subculture, it was imagined as a socially marginal activity practiced by youths (frequently white and male) who espoused anti-establishment values that set it in opposition to middle-class norms and values. Its subcultural representation further enabled BMX, and extreme sports as a whole, to be read as different from and marginal to 'mainstream' sports, which are represented as building character in men and teaching them the virtues of discipline, teamwork, and competition to make them 'productive bodies' for the needs of American capitalism.

"Live Fast Die" also exemplifies the derogatory connotations that were articulated with BMX and some of the other extreme sports (for instance, skateboarding, snowboarding, and in-line skating) prior to their more recent re-signification, which I will discuss later. In "Live Fast Die," countless images show white male BMX youth participating in rebellious activities by consuming large amounts of alcohol, smashing beer bottles on their heads, setting hair on fire, blowing up aerosol cans, and obstructing traffic by riding couches and shopping carts down the middle of busy city streets. The absence of an adult presence, the frequent use of images of BMX riding at night, the Generation X 'grunge' sartorial style worn by BMXers, and the loud, disruptive skate-punk musical score operate to legitimate the marginal identity of these youth and of BMX culture. A recent description of skateboarding as a sport of the X Games in a mainstream newspaper article provides a summary of the different and marginal identity the images of "Live Fast Die" are meant to express to the viewer about BMXers and their culture:

> "In general, most people still look at skateboarding as something I really don't want my son to be doing, hanging out at the park, smoking cigarettes," says Sasha Steinhorst, a pro skateboarder. . . . "That's the image of skateboarding. Punks out of control. . . . What remains the same as 10 years ago is the way the world looks at skateboarders. Through disapproving eyes."[32]

In terms of a critical perspective on whiteness, the video's representation of BMX identifies it as a cultural practice performed almost exclusively by white male youths (aged from the mid-teens to mid-twenties).[33] Although this is the case, the issue of the racial identity of BMXers is almost always unnoticed or seemingly not of interest to many observers (whether academic or lay) of the sporting activity.[34] Thus, the representations of BMX youth and its culture corroborate recent studies that show that whiteness is invisible to most (whites) and often exists as an unmarked term.[35] But, what is most germane is that, on the surface, "Live Fast Die" presents images of white male youths who do not seem to be reaping the economic benefits of 'white privilege' and whose values, desires, characteristics, and investments are represented as worlds apart from those of the politically dominant, economically secure and advantaged, and culturally pervasive "angry white male" figure constructed in popular critiques of whiteness.[36] Because this image of white masculinity is rather commonly read and accepted as authentic (that is, one can find empirical evidence of the existence of such white male BMX youth), it can be mobilized within a white male backlash politics desperate for cultural representations of white males as unprivileged, nonnormative, and economically unstable or disadvantaged. Thus, the extreme athlete becomes a strategic white masculine figure who can be employed in discussions of the validity of white male privilege as an example of a white male who is not the site of normality, economic privilege, and/or political power.

In order to see how extreme sports and the white male extreme sport figure get mobilized within such a conservative representational politics, we may turn to *Sports Illustrated*'s (December 6, 1997) special report, which "investigates" the increasing absence of the white (implicitly male) athlete in American professional sports. One need only look at the cover photo to read the report as being deeply shaped by the representational logics of the white male paranoia discourse constructed by the media and popular culture.[37] Four clean-cut, affable white basketball players are presented, each kneeling with one hand on a single basketball. From their crew-cut hairstyles, to their white Chuck Taylor sneakers, to their white uniforms, to their big ears and optimistic faces, to their hands amassed one on top of the other on the basketball (signifying an investment in the "team"), the image transcodes a nostalgic desire for a less complicated and more innocent time (read: a period absent of whites' perceptions of the annoying constraints of political correctness and the need to recognize and live with difference—especially, in this case, racial and ethnic difference—which is often popularly imagined in 1990s Americaq as: 1950s "consensus" America). The photo invokes a nostalgic desire for a time when these smiling white boys were atop the American professional sports world (read: when the culturally hegemonic position of white males as the embodiments and arbiters of normality was not popularly challenged).

Immediately, this special report can be read as an instrument and effect of the representational politics of the white male backlash. This reading is reinforced throughout the article, with its repeated representation of white male athletes as vulnerable,[38] insecure,[39] and as having a marginal identity[40] within the spaces of professional sports. Within this narrative, the racist implications of investigating the declining place of the white athletes is rational-ized (ineffectively) through statements such as, "that a white ma-jority calmly accepts [then why the special report?] minority status in one of its most cherished social institutions is itself a measure of progress."[41] In the guise of hard-hitting investigative reporting—through its use of "empirical" evidence such as data involving the sport participation patterns by white and black youth and survey information about white and black youths' investments in becom-ing professional athletes—the tone of the report, one of lamenta-tion over the increasingly marginal position of white male athletes in American professional sports, reveals the reactionary politics that organize its construction. The narrative has what Scott calls a "paranoic"[42] quality in its depiction of white male athletes as vulnerable and threatened by the overwhelming success of black males in American professional sport. White male athletes are portrayed as the innocent victims of black athletic superiority, while black male athletes are represented as a dominant, discriminating, and exclusionary force whose success has unfairly constrained the life possibilities of white male youths by driving them to abandon their dreams of being professional athletes. Incredibly, this narra-tive is able to repress long histories of racial inequality, institu-tional racism, and white privilege while simultaneously asserting, like many whites' perspectives on affirmative action policies in the 1990s,[43] that in the world of sports, white (male) athletes are the disadvantaged social group.

Within this special report, extreme sports are invoked as the activities young white males are increasingly flocking to as a result of the supposed diminishing opportunities for athletic success for white men in "mainstream" sports such as football, baseball, and basketball:

> Unsure of his place in a sports world dominated by blacks ... the young white male is dropping out of the athletic mainstream to pursue success elsewhere .... He is increasingly drawn to ... alternative athletic pursuits that are overwhelmingly white.[44]

The popularity of extreme sports for white male youth is explained as the reflection of their desire to find a sporting practice where they can not only be successful but hold a superior and dominant position.

As opposed to the white masculine identity of the "extreme" BMX athlete as represented in "Live Fast Die," where he is depicted as desiring to authenticate a culturally different identity through the appropriation of styles, attitudes, dispositions, and investments that inscribe it with the oppositional markings associated with the category of "marginal youth," *Sports Illustrated*'s representation of the extreme athlete characterizes this form of white masculinity as desiring a space where it can reconstruct a sense of superiority and psychic stability by investing in a cultural space and practice it can claim as its own. The desire of the white male extreme athlete to constitute himself as culturally different is not more accepting or tolerant of cultural differences, but seeks an identity cloaked in the codes of cultural difference to relieve itself of its feelings of vulnerability, inferiority, and instability and to reclaim its imagined sense of cultural superiority and normality. It is important to understand that the construction of the white masculine BMXer in "Live Fast Die" as "authentically" marginalized and different implicitly operates to legitimate the logic of *Sports Illustrated*'s construction of innocent white athletic youth as turning to extreme sports as a result of its inability to find success in "mainstream sports."

Finally, *US News & World Report*'s June 30, 1997 cover story on extreme sports demonstrates how the meanings articulated to these white male extreme athletes (who were previously imagined as subversive, disenfranchised types who consciously defined themselves—and were defined—in opposition to middle-class American norms and values) have undergone a significant reideologization and become reconstituted as the embodiments (white male bodies) of a set of values and affective investments represented as traditionally American. The extreme athlete is also constructed in this text through the codes of a traditionally American strong, confident image of white masculinity whose predecessors are said to be such (white) masculine icons as Indiana Jones, the Old Spice sailor, and the American frontiersman.[45] Although the article's explicit purpose is to explain the popularity of extreme sports, a reading informed by critical whiteness studies may view the text as exemplifying how "notions of race are closely linked to ideas about legitimate 'ownership' of the nation, with 'whiteness' and 'Americanness' linked tightly together."[46] Additionally, the article's construction of extreme sports and its athletes enables one to see how the extreme athlete is being mobilized, in a recoded form, within the project of the white male backlash for the purpose of discursively attempting to reassert and resecure the culturally normative and hegemonic position of white masculinity in the United States.

In order to read critically how the representational politics of the white male backlash seem to be shaping representations of extreme sports and its athletes, I must first show how extreme sports and the extreme athlete are subtly recoded in this cover story. The first sign of the recoding of extreme sports can be found in an examination of the images that accompany the article. An entirely new set of images and sporting activities is used to represent extreme sports. The largest photos show active individuals[47] practicing extreme sports in natural settings: people battling white water rapids in a raft, climbers scaling spectacular ice formations, and BASE jumpers leaping off beautiful rock formations. Only within significantly smaller frames (which are also fewer in number) are the activities that frequently come to mind with the mention of extreme sports displayed: an in-line skater captured at the height of a flip and an "aggressive" all-terrain skateboarder traversing down a hillside. The photos visually demonstrate the way in which the article accomplishes its project of reideologizing the extreme sports formation by first displacing the position (and with it the oppositional meanings) of skateboarding, BMX, and in-line skating—the activities that ESPN2, in its first broadcasts of the "Extreme Games," featured as exemplifying the ethos of extreme sports—and re-presenting as the sporting activities that are tied more closely to nature and practiced individually as the center of the extreme sports formation.

The article's selection of these images and sporting practices to represent extreme sports is instrumental for yet another reason. The scenic photos of isolated individuals (all of the participants represented are white men) in natural settings are used to visually reinforce the article's narrative, which seeks to articulate the extreme athlete with the rugged individualism embodied in the simulated figure of the American frontiersman. The article represents the extreme athlete as an offspring of the American frontiersman (racially coded as white) as both are said to have an insatiable appetite for risk, a thirst for adventure, and a desire to be the embodiment of strength, coolness, and confidence. The article argues that the popularity of extreme sports and extreme athletes reflects a particular desire on the part of "those wishing to put that Man With No Name swagger in their step."[48] Unavoidably, this "Man With No Name" must be read as a code word for white males. Additionally, the quote elucidates how whiteness (here, white masculinity) is represented as desiring to be able to be both invisible as a racialized identity, but confident, centered, and secure within the racialized world. The above quote (and the way in which it was euphemistically represented by the author) elucidates how whiteness often goes unmarked in cultural representations and how an implicit facet of white masculinity (without necessarily essentializing it) is the desire to always hold a culturally hegemonic position. Further, we can read that the desire to be a "Man With No Name," to wish whiteness to be always invisible, as a historically specific desire felt by United States white males in the 1990s which is a result of the popular critiques of whiteness and the increased emphasis on racial cultural diversity in post-civil rights America.

Critical examination of *US News & World Report's* construction of the extreme athlete also allows us to see how the logic of the discourse of the angry white male shapes the article's construction of the appeal of the extreme athlete. This article attempts to distance the identity of the extreme athlete from the figure of the angry white male represented in *Newsweek's* 1993 cover story.[49] As opposed to Gates' article, where American white males of the 1990s are represented as experiencing excessive amounts of racialized fear and anxiety and a newfound self-consciousness about their whiteness, the *US News & World Report* article goes to great lengths to constitute the extreme athlete as different. The article employs the scientific "authority" of professor of psychology Keith Johnsgard to implicitly establish the extreme athletes' difference from the angry white male: "These people [extreme athletes] are really emotionally stable people, not moody at all. They don't suffer from a lot of fear or anxiety or depression."[50] Extreme sports are said to be a practice that allows one to achieve a "freedom from excessive self-consciousness."[51] Although the article attributes the excessive self-consciousness to concerns about one's body shape and appearance and unstable economic times, I contend it is better understood as symptomatic of how the increased visibility of whiteness has forced white males to become more conscious of how their racial identity shapes their everyday lives, how whiteness operates as a normalizing social force, and how white privilege works institutionally. So, although the extreme athlete is discursively distanced from the simulated figure of the angry white male in the article, the former relies on the latter in order to gain its meaning. Although the extreme athlete is being distanced and marked as different from the angry white male, his difference in this narrative is not that of having been shaped by different socio-political forces and conditions but that of representing a different response for white masculinity to these conditions. The angry white male, due to the timing of his representation, experiences fear and anxiety in this era of identity politics, while the white male extreme athlete, being an instrument and effect of the representational politics of the white male backlash, which appropriates the logic of identity politics to make visible and invest in forms of whiteness that can make a claim to holding an authentic marginal identity, is figured as overcoming these feelings of fear and insecurity through this practice, which allows him to resecure his manhood and to once again see himself as superior in this racially homogenous cultural site of extreme sports.

Conclusion

In this chapter it was my intention to extend the critical study of whiteness to the study of sport as a site of popular culture by taking as a test object some specific media representations of extreme sports. Part of this project has been to disrupt the way that whiteness is frequently represented as a racially neutral category by making visible the 'whiteness' of the extreme sports formation in terms of the individuals who practice these activities and the representational strategies used to construct images and narratives. Another implicit concern of this essay has been to read how these images of whiteness offered in extreme sports and its athletes cannot be understood as existing prior to or apart from other categories of identity such as gender, class, age, and nationality. Finally, I have attempted to fix a trenchant gaze upon the white masculinity of the extreme athlete whose represented values, desires, and attitude are said to have become enormously popular not only for American (read: white middle class) youth but have also been used to sell products for corporations such as Nike, Chevrolet and Pepsi. Even the United States government has jumped on the extreme bandwagon by representing service in the Marine Corps as an extreme activity.[52]

I have also tried to take seriously Frankenburg's point that whiteness as culture must be examined "as practice rather than object, in relation to racial formation and historical process rather than as isolable or static."[53] With this in mind, I attempted to locate the creation of extreme sports within the historical context of the 1990s United States, where the forces of identity politics, multiculturalism, popular critiques of whiteness, the reactionary white backlash, the Generation X representation of American youth, and diminished economic expectations helped to give shape to the representations of extreme sports and its athletes. More specifically, I have argued that representations of extreme sports and its athletes have become instruments and effects of a white backlash politics of representation which seeks to align itself with or to constitute forms of whiteness that can somehow make an 'authentic' claim to being marginal, disenfranchised, innocent, abnormal, or poor. This representation of whiteness as 'other' enables it to reassert its cultural authority (which it only imagined having lost in order to legitimate 'crisis' narratives—whether of nation [US], of community [suburbia], or of identity [white males]), to reclaim its invisibility, and to constitute itself as universal norm as a 'victimized' identity in this era of identity politics.

Notes

1. I say early representation of Generation X because the narratives and characteristics used to depict Generation X changed, as one would expect, throughout the 1990s. On the one hand, this initial representation of Generation X functioned to escalate and 'legitimate' conservative narratives of the United States and its traditions being in a state of crisis by representing youth coming of age in the late 1980s and 1990s as uneducated and politically apathetic 'latchkey' kids whose inarticulateness, poor work ethic, and "alien" attitudes and styles were the visible proof of the conservatives' claims of disintegrating families and "family values" and an educational system more concerned with building self-esteem than upholding educational standards. On the other hand, this discourse also organized the formation of a marketing category and youth style which drew on the dominant codes and tropes of youth and adolescence to appeal to American youth of the 1990s (ESPN, Extreme Games, Summer 1995).

2. See Richard Dyer, *White* (London: Routledge, 1997); bell hooks, "Representations of whiteness in the black imagination," in Lawrence Grossberg, Paula Treichler and Cary Nelson (eds.), *Cultural Studies* (New York: Routledge, 1992), pp. 338–346; and Matt Wray and Annalee Newitz (eds), *White Trash: Race and Class in America* (New York: Routledge, 1997).

3. These studies of whiteness were particularly influential in my reading of extreme sports: Hazel Carby, "Encoding white resentment: *Grand Canyon*—a narrative for our times," in Cameron McCarthy and Warren Crichlow (eds.), *Race, Identity and Representation in Education* (New York: Routledge, 1993) pp. 236–250; Richard Dyer, *White* (London: Routledge, 1997); Ruth Frankenburg, "Introduction: Local whitenesses,

localizing whiteness," in Ruth Frankenburg (ed.), *Displacing Whiteness: Essays in Social and Cultural Criticism* (Durham: Duke University Press, 1997) pp. 1–34; Henry Giroux, "White noise: Racial politics and the pedagogy of whiteness," in *Channel Surfing: Race Talk and the Destruction of Today's Youth* (New York: St. Martin's Press, 1997) pp. 89–136; H. Giroux, "Rewriting the discourse of racial identity: Towards a pedagogy and politics of whiteness," *Harvard Educational Review* 67(2) (1997): pp. 285–320; bell hooks, "Representations of whiteness in the black imagination," in Grossberg, Treichler and Nelson (eds.), *Cultural Studies* (New York: Routledge, 1992), pp. 338–346; A. Newitz, "White savagery and humiliation, or a new racial consciousness in the media," in Wray and Newitz (eds), *White Trash: Race and Class in America* (New York: Routledge, 1997); Fred Pfeil, *White Guys: Studies in Postmodern Domination and Difference* (London: Verso, 1995); Leslie Roman, "White is a color! White defensiveness, postmodernism, and anti-racist pedagogy," in McCarthy and Crichlow (eds.), *Race, Identity and Representation in Education* (New York: Routledge, 1993), pp. 71–88; Raka Shome, "Race and popular cinema: The rhetorical strategies of whiteness in *City of Joy*," *Communication Quarterly*, 44(4) (1996), pp. 502–518; Wray and Newitz, *White Trash*.

4. Wray and Newitz, *White Trash*.

5. Dyer, *White*, p. 42.

6. Shome, "Race and popular cinema," p. 503.

7. David Roediger, *Towards the Abolition of Whiteness: Essays on Race, Politics, and Working Class History* (London: Verso, 1994).

8. Newitz *(White Trash)*.

9. Ibid.

10. Ibid., p. 3.

11. Shome, "Race and popular cinema," p. 503.

12. Dyer, *White*.

13. Thomas Nakayama and Robert Krizek, "Whiteness: A strategic rhetoric," *Quarterly Journal of Speech* 81 (1995), pp. 291–309.

14. Wray and Newitz, *White Trash*.

15. By identity politics, I borrow from McCarthy's notion of particular political mobilizations that deploy a "discourse of group distinctiveness in everyday struggles over political representation and scarce resources" Cameron McCarthy, "The Devil Finds Work: Re-reading Race and Identity in Contemporary Life," in *The Uses of Culture*, ed. Cameron McCarthy (New York: Routledge, 1998) p. 136.

16. Such as better enforcing affirmative action programs implemented decades earlier and by embracing cultural diversity in education and the workplace.

17. George Yudice, "Neither Impugning Nor Disavowing Whiteness Does a Viable Politics Make: The Limits of Identity Politics," in *After Political Correctness: The Humanities and Society in the 1990s*, eds. Christopher Newfield and Ronald Strickland (Boulder, CO: Westview Press, 1995).

18. Giroux, 1997.

19. David Gates, "White Male Paranoia," *Newsweek*, 13 March 1993, p. 48.

20. This is a middle-aged male who exudes familial and national pride, nostalgic longing for an imagined past where difference was less visible and the cultural centering and normativity of white males was unquestioned.

21. Listen to Rush Limbaugh's radio show for more exact examples of this rhetoric.

22. Giroux, 1997, p. 286.

23. Lois Weiss, Andria Proweller, and Craig Centrie, "Re-examining 'A Moment in History': Loss of Privilege Inside White Working Class Maculinity in the 1990s," in *Off White: Readings on Race, Power, and Society*, eds. Michelle Rine et al. (New York: Routledge, 1997), p. 212.

24. C. McCarthy, "The devil finds work: Re-reading race and identity in contemporary life," in C. McCarthy's *The uses of culture* (New York: Routledge, 1998), pp. 135–146.

25. Gates, "Paranoia," p. 48.

26. Aaron Baker & Todd Boyd, *Out of Bounds: Sports, Media, and the Politics of Identity* (Bloomington: Indiana University Press, 1997).

27. See Pierre Bourdieu, "How Can One be a Sports Fan?" in *The Cultural Studies Reader*, ed. Simon During (London: Routledge, 1993), pp. 339–356, for an example of an examination of sport which essentially argues for sport having its own constitutive logic which somewhat isolates it from the broader forces and conditions of a historical conjuncture.

28. Larry Grossberg, *We Gotta Get Out of This Place* (New York: Routledge, 1992), p. 255. For Grossberg, the "new conservatism" represents a popular conservative sensibility which seems to have taken hold in the US in the 1980s and 1990s and has growing numbers of Americans taking up conservative positions on matters of social equality and the distribution of economic resources. It also refers to a largely unorganized coalition of forces, including the 'New Right' and the 'Religious Right,' whose origins have been traced to the presidential campaign of conservative Barry Goldwater and whose apogee, as of this writing, appears to have been the presidency of Ronald Reagan.

29. Ibid., p. 260.

30. I want to thank Brett Downs for allowing me access to this video, as it is a part of his personal collection, and want to make clear that I represent "Live Fast Die" as an insiders' video, mainly through my conversations with Brett about the video and who would have access to it.

31. Sarah Thornton, "General Introduction," in *The Subcultures Reader*, eds. Ken Gelder and Sarah Thornton (London: Routledge, 1997), pp. 1–7.

32. Gary Fallesen, "Skateboarders Find X-ceptance at Games," *Democrat & Chronicle*, (23 June 1997), p. 6D.

33. No non-whites represented in the video and only one white female skateboarder turns up in any of the footage.

34. The scholarly work of Duncan Humphreys, "Shredheads Go Mainstream: Snowboarding and Alternative Youth," *International Review for the Sociology of Sport*, 32, 2 (1997), pp. 147–160; and Robert Rinehart, *"Cyber-sports: Power and Diversity in ESPN's The Extreme Games,"* Paper presented at the annual North American Society for the Sociology of Sport Conference, (November 1995), Sacramento, CA, as well as, popular representations of extreme sports like Brendan Koerner, "Extreme Sports: Why Americans are Risking Life and Limb for the Big Rush," *U.S. News* and *World Report*, (30 June 1997), 50–60, exemplify how the racial identity of these performers has gone largely unnoticed and/or un-interrogated.

35. Richard Dyer, *White* (London: Routledge, 1997).

36. The article by David Gates, "White Pale Parnoia," *Newsweek*, 121, 13 (March 1993), 48–53, offers a good example of this white male figure.

37. In this image and the corresponding story, white masculinity is constituted as innocent, non-oppressive, and subordinate within contemporary professional sports. This representation of white masculinity is the polar opposite of the meanings articulated with the image of white masculinity produced in texts like: David Gates, "White Male Paranoia," *Newsweek*, 121, 13 (March 1993), pp. 48–53, or the film, *Falling Down*.

38. S.L. Price, "Whatever Happened to the White Athlete?," *Sports Illustrated*, 87, 23 (6 December 1997), 32–51.

39. Ibid., p. 44.

40. Ibid., p. 34.

41. Ibid., p. 33.

42. Linda Scott, "The Campaign Against Political Correctness: What's Really at Stake?" in *After Political Correctness: The Humanities and Society in the 1990s*, eds. Christopher Newfield and Ronald Strickland, (Boulder, CO: Westview Press, 1995), p. 113.

43. Lois Weis, Andria Proweller, and Craig Centrie, "Re-examining 'A Moment in History': Loss of Privilege Inside White Working Class Masculinity in the 1990s," in *Off White: Readings on Race, Power, and Society*, eds. Michelle Fine, et al. (New York: Routledge, 1997), pp. 210–226.

44. Price, "Whatever," pp. 31–32.

45. Brendan Koerner, "Extreme Sports: Why Americans are Risking Life and Limb for the Big Rush," *U.S. News & World Report*, (30 June 1997), p. 59.

46. Ruth Frankenburg, "Introduction: Local Witnesses, Localizing Whiteness," in *Displacing Whiteness: Essays in Social and Cultural Criticism*, Ruth Frankenburg (Durham, NC: Duke University Press, 1997), p. 6.

47. Identifying how these images of extreme sports feature individuals rather than groups participating in these activities is important because it is through these images that the individualist ethos which Extreme sports are said to represent is transcoded.

48. In the written text, we see the same project of displacement when the first description of the youthful Extreme sports enthusiast who predominantly practices and spectates these sports forms occurs in the last paragraph of the article.

49. Brendan Koerner, "Extreme Sports: Why Americans are Risking Life and Limb for the Big Rush," *U.S. News & World Report*, (30 June 1997), p. 56; David Gates, "White Male Paranoia," *Newsweek*, 121, 13 (March 1993), pp. 48–53.

50. Cited in Koerner, "Extreme Sports," p. 59.

51. Ibid.

52. The US government's use of the discursive logics of Extreme sports to sell the Marine Corps is further proof of the way these formerly marginalized sporting activities which were marked as unproductive and somewhat deviant have been rearticulated as productive and quintessentially American practices.

53. Frankenburg, *Displacing Whiteness*, p. 20.

MOUNTAIN BIKING

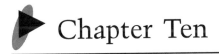

Chapter Ten

Out of the Gene Pool and into the Food Chain

Lee Bridgers

Yesterday, while driving back from leading a group of raw novices on a tour of the White Rim Trail, I came across a familiar sight: parked alongside the base of the cliff below the infamous Portal Trail was a line of emergency vehicles, arc lights, and long-faced mountain bikers. The Portal Trail is Mother Nature's way of making mountain bikers pay for her treats, and on this day she was collecting the bloody toll.

The single-track Portal Trail runs along a narrow ledge 700 feet above the Colorado River where the Moab Rim, a sheer cliff along the western edge of the Moab Fault, is broken by the river gorge. Here the river crosses the fault and the Moab Valley, continuing on its way, carving a massive channel through solid rock as if the formidable obstacles of the valley and the rift of the fault were not even there. The snaking Portal Trail, along the cliff face just below the rim, allows hikers coming up from the river and bikers concluding the Poison Spider Mesa or Gold Bar Rim Trail to

---

Lee Bridgers founded, owns and operates Dreamride LLC, the hardcore mountain bike vacation, sales, and film service in Moab, Utah. A mountain biker long before the sport had a name, Lee authored the mountain bike guidebook *Mountain Bike America: Moab*, published by Globe Pequot Press. Before settling in Moab, Lee ran the nation's oldest media center, the Rocky Mountain Film Center, and directed and taught in film programs at the University of Colorado in Boulder, the San Francisco Art Institute, and Piedmont Community College. Lee's motivation is to ride faster than people half his age so as to avoid having to talk to them.

179

experience scary exposure and spectacular views of Arches National Park and Moab, Utah—the former outlaw town, uranium mining paradise, and mountain bike Mecca I call home.

There is a spot on the Portal Trail just before the scenic overlook that is two feet wide. On one side is a vertical rock wall, on the other a drop of 700 feet down to Potash Road. A smooth round rock a foot and a half high juts into the trail at this point, leaving you less than 10 inches of trail surface on the edge of the scariest vertical exposure you can imagine. The exposure is so frightening that foolish bikers who ride this section have a tendency to high side by hopping over the rock. It is a simple trick, but if you biff, you die. This little rock has taken the lives of three riders over the past decade, two within the last year. There may be more, I don't know. I'll bet if we scoured the cliff face we'd find some bones and a couple of beat-up bikes stuffed into cracks a couple of hundred feet above the road. Some folks have the gumption, think they have the skill, ignore better judgment, hit a pedal or a chain ring on that little rock, and . . . well, you can imagine the rest.

Just in case you have no imagination, I will let August Brooks, a longstanding member of Moab Search and Rescue, describe one cliff jumper for you: "He looked like a bloody sack with sharp sticks poking out everywhere." The fall is not straight down. You bounce off a few rock ledges on your way to heaven. I say heaven, because anyone who falls from the Portal is frankly not smart enough to get into hell, where Jimi Hendrix plays third guitar and Janis Joplin couldn't make the choir.

Moab Search and Rescue volunteers see the results of stupid behavior day after day. Their familiar frustrated faces along the roadside said everything as I shuttled my group past the sobering scene. It is no fun to retrieve broken bodies from this steep and unforgiving cliff face. If Search and Rescue is lucky, the body falls into the road. Most of the time, however, the bloody mess is 200 or 300 feet up on some godforsaken rock outcropping—accessible to only the most experienced rock climbers. There is one good thing about retrieving a fallen cyclist from the Portal's grasp, though: No hurry!

My novices, a group of investment bankers from New York City who had just pedaled themselves along the White Rim into the land of Dizzying Low Blood Sugar, began to ask questions. "Why would anyone ride such a dangerous trail?" queried Ethan, a shy and gentle Jewish fellow. "How far did he . . . uh, fall?" whispered Steven, Ethan's brother, a hair's width from total exhaustion, barely able to speak.

"Far enough," I answered.

Tom, a stockbroker and amateur photographer, asked Miki, who assists with novice groups, "You don't ride that trail do you? Please tell me you don't ride that trail."

Miki said simply, "I just hope it wasn't a woman."

I understood that statement to mean that a woman would ride that section of trail only if goaded by a boyfriend. Women are smarter than men, if you didn't know that already. However, they do get stupid when accompanying a man. Testosterone is contagious. Michael, who booked this Dreamride mountain bike vacation[1] for himself and his friends, added, "And on the first day of the Fat Tire Festival. It's really sad."

"No, it isn't sad at all. We should rejoice! It's NATURAL SELECTION! Only an idiot, poisoned by his own gonads, trying to impress his girl or his buddies, is stupid enough to ride that section of trail. Just be thankful that he is no longer able to breed." This came out of my mouth without a thought to preface the impulse to judgment.

Nervous laugher barely masked the shock at hearing such an insensitive statement, but frankly this kind of thing just makes me mad . . . bunnyhopping mad! I recalled an incident for the group, so that they could understand the stupidity it takes to be unaware of one's mortality when staring at the drop along the Portal Trail. I began, "Once upon a time I was sitting on the overlook, enjoying the view, after walking my bike along the exposed section of the Portal. I had passed a mixed group of college-age lads and lasses on the way up Poison Spider Mesa, and, as I sat staring at the valley below, at peace with the world, amazed once again that I lived in this beautiful place, here they came, a confused bunch, some riding, some walking the exposed single track . . . a fatal accident waiting to happen."

"The first rider demonstrated admirable skills on the bike, cleaning the section with snotty flair. He wheelied off the last three-foot ledge to where I was sitting and let out a hoot, 'Yaaahooo!'—like the search engine. What the fellow did next made me want to throw him off the cliff. He turned and taunted his friends, 'Come on, man, you can make it!'

I went ballistic, screaming at him, 'You stupid jerk, do you want to kill your buddies? Do you want to live the rest of your life knowing you killed one of your friends? Go back and ride it again. You can do it, you hooting college student asshole!' "

Let us all pray that the "asshole" was the one who fell this time and not one of his buddies or the "girlfriend."

Ironically, I am more akin to the fellow who falls from the Portal than to the wealthy Wall Street financiers I had in tow, worried about the volatility of the stock market and wheezing from the effort of cruising along a nearly flat dirt road. Back home, these stock-broking dudes have their own risks. I hear they will take a plunge with the market, but as a professional mountain biker my risks are tangible, scenic, and if they don't kill me, I get stronger. Jumping off a four-foot ledge is not a risk, it's damn fun. One day these stockbroker tourists may end up jumping off a fifty-story building. Where's the fun in that? If I jump, it's to clear a gap in the rock, not to clear my accounts. I understand the allure of the Portal's technical, dangerous single track. I'm just too damn smart to let it kill me.

The big difference between me and the unfortunate idiot who falls from the Portal is that I never ride that section of the Portal Trail. It's just too narrow and the little technical thingie with the foot-and-a-half round rock is just too obvious a spot to die on. Clearing a foot-and-a-half rock is no challenge. I always walk this spot, and take the Portal route only when lightning is threatening to fry my clients on Poison Spider Mesa, or we are simply too bushed from thrashing the extremely technical Gold Bar Rim to ride down Poison Spider. The Portal is a great hike, a convenient emergency exit from the mesa, but, because of the exposure, it has only one rational attraction as a fun single-track ride: It's damn fun.

What is the difference between an organ donor and an extreme mountain biker? Skill and luck, and sometimes a brain. I have ridden with a handful of the best extreme riders in the world, and not one has ever displayed a hint of shame at walking that tiny section of the Portal Trail. These guys would never goad anyone into doing something they didn't *feel* like doing.

Nate Toone is a fellow from Salt Lake City whom I ride with, sponsor, photograph, and hire to lead extreme skills clinics. We both love "bikesurfing," a style of mountain biking unique to Moab, where you swoop, dive, and jump in huge sandstone bowls and chutes. Some of us swoop. Some dive. Very few jump like Nate.[2]

Bikesurfing is sort of like half-pipe riding, but much more twisted and dangerous. You cannot practice this sort of thing, because blowing a move means you will probably end up in Intensive

Care or the morgue. You must work into it slowly, always within your skills and the bike's structural limits. There is a lot of deadly exposure on the smooth Secret Entrada Slickrock. Imagine riding on the outside of a half-mile-wide basketball made of rock. All around is a drop of 100 to 200 feet.

Nate remarked once, as we were hanging it out over a huge rolling dropoff, "The big drops don't bother me. It's those 100 foot drops that make me queasy. The fall is scary. Dying is scary, but I can handle that. The thought of being maimed, lying down there with no hope of anyone finding me, is not my idea of fun."

Nate Toone is undoubtedly the best extreme slickrock rider in the world, will go off a twenty-foot ledge onto solid rock or do a 100-foot wall ride for my camera, but he walks the exposed portion of the Portal Trail above the 700-foot drop. He can ride it, no problem, but he knows it's like Russian roulette. One out of every thousand times he may have to put a foot down, but more importantly, it's just no fun to risk your life for a stupid eighteen-inch bunnyhop over a little rock. It is better to risk your life on a thirty-foot drop-off for one thousand bucks and a cool picture.

"Man, you could die on that little section," Nate says with a nervous laugh and reverent respect. With head bowed, he contemplates the Mother of All Easy Bunnyhops, but after tiptoeing, with downhill rig in tow, over that little rock, onto the viewpoint beyond, he races down the quadruple-black-diamond grade on the other side as if it's a cakewalk. Nate is beautiful to watch, the Marilyn Monroe of mountain biking, but he gets out of sight really fast, a rocket with human intent, doing things and making outrageous moves that not only seem impossible, they *are* impossible. I dismount to watch him dive into the deep, loose, jagged rocky slots and twisted drop-off switchbacks, disappearing down the trail ahead of me. After I walk half the trail down to the road, there he is, leaning against his forty-pound machine, grinning. There is respect in his smile, because I am riding within my limits and will be there to ride with him tomorrow. No ego crap. No competition between friends. Only competition with fear, rocks, death, ledges, and Natural Law.

Since Nate leads skills clinics for my company, Dreamride, I get to learn from him, over and over, never tiring of his wit and uncanny ability to articulate the act of being one with a mountain bike. Standing on the slickrock in front of a group, he'll do a seemingly obscene hop, holding imaginary handlebars, demonstrating a jumping technique, then show them the specific muscles it takes to do the job. Nate is not a muscular guy, mind you. He just has the *right* muscles, like the little muscle at the elbow that bulges upward. I've seen that muscle in tennis players, but Nate doesn't play tennis. He got it from bunnyhopping a mountain bike. With this little muscle he can stand on flat ground and pick both wheels of a 40-pound downhill rig up by the handlebars. Try it sometime.

As a survivor who made it past his younger years of testosterone dares, serious injuries, and the thrill of going way fast when he couldn't foresee the consequences, Nate instantly judges relative danger against relative risks and rewards. Extreme mountain biking is populated by very few guys like this, who work in bike shops and have lots of scars. Their eyes reveal the latent fear that reflects the sting of serious injury. They have been to the ER, spent time in IC, learned from mistakes, and are intimate with their limits. Despite past catastrophes, they still rock hard, at least until they get injured again. Shit happens.

Everyone who worships the God of Extreme and is a card-carrying member of the congregation of the Church of Bikesurfing knows that one mistake can mean death and that injuries at this level of skill are almost always caused by mechanical failure. Our religion is based on a litany of rituals—rituals of checking the equipment over and over: Wheels shall be strong and true. Bars shall be stout and tight. Brakes shall be flawlessly adjusted. Wheels shall be twisted on really tight. Body armor shall be worn like the pope wears that shovel on his head. Faith, hope and charity, but most important of these is *faith in your bike.* Faith in my equipment. Hope to survive. The charity is provided by tons of suspension travel. We need forgiveness! We need enduro rigs. We need bikes that are as forgiving as Jesus, and as strong, light and kick-ass as the Archangel.

Worship is attention. I pay a lot of attention to my bike. I preach biking. August Brooks once told me, "I see you out there preaching extreme biking, and I've got to tell you that all it means is that I will be out on the Slickrock Bike Trail scraping some poor schmuck off the rock with a snow shovel."

I can't help it. The passion for speed and danger snuck up on me like a desert cat digging for the energy bars in the day pack of a mountain-biking organ donor. It was like all of a sudden people were describing me as extreme. My clients point it out to me daily. Sometimes I wonder why. Maybe it has something to do with a Freudian quest for self-destruction. Hell, I have certainly seen it in quite a few of my clients. The line between just plain old mountain biking and extreme mountain biking is a fine one, but what finally made me understand my own sick view of mortality was the time I was aerial scouting for the IMAX film *Everest*.

While we were cruising along in the Cessna, angled to get a good shot of the terrain below, the small plane lost its grip on the air cushion, broke loose and side-slipped like piece of paper sliding off a desk. The pilot turned white and screamed as he fought to get the little plane under control. He shook like a martini mixer all the way home, but I was cool as ice. Honestly, the thought that went through my mind as the ground grew closer and closer was, "Well, at least I'm not going to die of cancer."

It was two years ago that I coordinated the mountain bike segment for *Everest*, scouting and acquiring Moab locations, bikes, and riders, as well as handling Moab crew and logistics. The film, and its making, are perfect examples of the quandary the sport of mountain biking is in, let alone the sport of mountaineering, which is obviously way out of control.

When first contacted to set up the mountain bike segment, I was told by the producer, "We don't want the doubles doing anything that the subjects, Ed and Paula Viesturs, can't do. This is not an extreme sports kinda thing we are doing. It's a training sequence." Oh, sure.

I didn't believe the guy for one second. Anyone who would fake a documentary with stunt doubles obviously had no qualms about lying about the subjects' abilities, and anyone making a movie about brain-atrophied climbers stepping over frozen yuppie stiffs, taking a step every five minutes in hip-deep snow, passing survivors with their noses and hands frozen off, was in desperate need of speed, or this big-screen flick was going to be as depressing as a visit to the dentist.

As a result of my suspicions, I secretly went into extreme mode, hiring the best riders I could find, despite the meager budget for the doubles, and acquiring the heaviest, sturdiest downhill bikes I could dig up, despite the cross-country training theme of the segment. These deeds paid off the very first day of shooting when the director asked the doubles to ride an unpermitted and unrehearsed section of trail without a practice run. High on adrenaline, speeding along at forty miles an hour, a throbbing eggbeater at their backs, the riders discovered that an insignificant little jump in the trail was followed by a blind 90-degree turn above a deep, rugged wash. The heavy, ugly, long travel bikes instantly saved them from serious injury, and saved the director from losing the entire Moab budget in one stupid move. The ignorant fellow didn't even have the sense to thank me for that one. These movie dudes just didn't know and didn't want to know.

Later in the week of shooting, the director ended up sending these guys down slopes so scary that the women doubles simply couldn't or wouldn't ride the descents at speeds the director required. The director, who got the money to make IMAX films from making car commercials, solved the problem by dressing one of the men stunt doubles as a woman and sending two men down the cliff face of Amasa Back Trail, almost killing one of the riders in the process when they hurried the shot without an equipment check. All this happened on an illegal, unpermitted section of trail in designated wilderness, House Resolution 1500. I was away securing permits for the following day's shoot, so when I saw the rushes that night I went ballistic, as I am known to do, but this time I was cussing out the fat cats, calling them idiots and assholes.

So much for my movie career.

I mention this incident to drive home the idea that people who know nothing about mountain biking and the natural world are in the process of defining the sport as extreme for the wrong reasons—ego gratification, greed, and ignorance. These deadly sins, when combined with an uncaring attitude toward the environment and blatant disregard for youngsters who might emulate what they see in the media, are a deadly cocktail. These user-people, even if I work for them and feed my family off their dribblings, are recklessly portraying extreme mountain biking as regular old mountain biking.

Yes, *Ed and Paula Viesturs ride like this every day.* (While in reality, Ed and Paula wouldn't be caught dead riding along the cliff on the edge of Amasa Back one thousand feet above Jackson Hole at forty miles an hour just to train for a stupid climb of Mt. Everest for Hollywood Buick commercial guys.)

That's why they hired me!

It makes me sick, and ironically, it also makes me money. It also sends inexperienced riders off the Portal Trail and trashes the environment that makes Moab such a great place to ride. The single most important draw of riding a mountain bike is NATURE—not the environmentalist, tree-hugging, untouchable nature of Sierra Club twits who try to make themselves look like caring people by keeping you off the grass so they can buy a three-million-dollar home and have the mountains untouched in their picture window—but the nature that you can just dive into and have sex with. The challenge is to treat her right.

Just a week ago I rode the 24 Hours of Moab Race Course. As part of the Behind the Rocks Trail, this piece of terra firma is very dear to my heart, and literally a hell of a ride. The full trail is rife with deep sand, gnarly ledges, nasty transitions, technical slickrock, steep, sandy and loose rocky hills, an overdose of babyheads, as well as dangerous solitude, but the race course loop is simply a hard ride that loops out of the Behind the Rocks area onto the Back of Behind Trail, a boring dirt road into some stunning scenery.

I took a single client, Mark O'Donahue of Boston, out there to introduce him to the evils and insensitivities of mountain bike racing in the desert. We were not disappointed. The race course, from the highway side entrance of the Behind the Rocks Trail, starts with a mellow upslope, becoming more and more technical as you approach the Bee Hive rock formations that are the rocks in Behind the Rocks. It gets really sandy, rocky, difficult, and dangerous, drops into a great downhill, and dumps you onto a wide dirt road for a fast and easy downhill to the staging area.

Early on, in the most technical area of the course, there were some racers pre-riding the track. I stopped at a particularly difficult section to show them the faster line—a line necessary for any chance of winning the race. I watched them walk down the trail picking up loose rocks and throwing them out of the way, then walk back up, and try to ride the section back down. The testosterone was flowing freely and I began to feel like the jerk who beckoned his friends to death along the exposed section of the Portal Trail.

Leaving these fellows to kill themselves, Mark and I traveled further out onto the course. We came across a flattened lizard, turned into waffle by deep knobby tire tread, and an archeological site recently unearthed by traffic on the road. It was a series of small rock circles, not fire rings mind you, but a symmetrical ring of individual circles made of cut and angled stone. We were both blown away that racers were zipping over them without so much as a glance.

After marking the site for the BLM, who now consider this site to be their most important untouched site in canyon country, we resumed our journey around the course, discovering that the race promoters had built a new spur around Prostitute Butte. Now remember that this is a desert, and it takes up to two hundred years for the flora to regenerate. Frankly, we don't need *two* roads around the butte.

Prostitute Butte is a rare gem—a gigantic rude stone formation that resembles a naked lady beckoning a bit of sodomy. More than that, it is home to a couple of beautiful sandstone arches, one of which is square! It was in a cave in Prostitute Butte that I first spent time in the Moab area with my family. It used to be pristine, a rarely visited spot where middens, arrowheads, and stone tools were scattered about on the ground. I used this spot as a base to scout the trail network above Kane Springs Canyon, and spent many an hour timing myself on runs around the butte, through the Junipers and Piñon, past a variety of flowering cactus. Now every tree within 100 feet of the cave at the eastern end of the butte is cut down. The area looks like a pitcher's mound. Marlboro shot a commercial on the west end of Prostitute Butte a few years back and trashed the area so bad that it nearly makes me cry every time I pass it.

Now Granny Gear Productions is doing more damage with their 24 Hours of Moab Race, with help from their sponsors, the right-wing, secret government propaganda tabloid that used to be Newsweek magazine, and Patagonia, the disgustingly hip outdoor clothing line that is a well known joke to thin-walleted hippies, anti-New Age professional beer drinkers, rednecks, and mountain bikers. I wish I had a dollar for every time I heard the putdown, "It's just too . . . too . . . Patagonia." This can be in reference to a restaurant, a house, a car, a person, or any other thing with a hollow, vacant, creepy, New Age vibe.

From Prostitute Butte we passed through the staging area, buzzing with bikers and promotions. I noticed that Granny Gear Productions had staked out a new trail parallel to the road as part of the course. Mark and I dipped in to check it out. Of course, this new trail was completely unnecessary due to the fact that it parallels an existing road. Under our tires was freshly crushed cryptobiotic soil crust that will not regenerate for over 250 years. Crypto is the plankton of the Moab desert. Without it the place is just a mound of drift sand. Everywhere broken cacti were mushed up and mixed into the deep sand. As a sand rider I like the advantage long stretches of this deep stuff give me in a race, but as a lover of the desert it made me want to kick the promoters square in the ass. I had to contain my anger as we road past the Granny Gear Productions van. It took extreme effort not to give these early worms the bird.

The day of the race Granny Gear Productions decided that the new trail was too difficult and used the road anyway.

I offer up a prayer. Let us bow our heads.

May these people ride the Portal, refuse to dismount for the Mother of All Little Bunnyhops, biff on the rock, fall over the edge, hit every ledge on the way down, and land in the road so that Search and Rescue can find them easily.

Notes

1. For pictures of, and information on, Dreamride mountain bike vacations in Moab, Hawaii, Colorado, North Carolina, Virginia, and California for riders of *all* skill levels, visit *www.dreamride.com.*

2 . For pictures of Nate Toone in action and information on extreme, cross country and downhill racing skills, visit *www.bikeskills.com.*

Chapter Eleven

Mountain Biking Madness

Simon Eassom

I own a mountain bike.[1] It is a pretty good one, with high quality 'gear' and a very good frame, although slightly 'retro' by today's standards: I've owned it since 1980. Ironically, I bought it in Coventry (near where I lived), a place famous for little other than being the city where bicycle manufacture first began in earnest in the 1860s. I've done some pretty extreme things on it, if cycling off-road over Alpine passes, crossing bits of Australian desert, and regularly bike-packing hundreds of miles in remote places count as extreme actions. The only mountains I have cycled up are smallish ones (unlike the Crane cousins, who did much to promote the fashion for these things in the 1980s by cycling up 19,000 foot Mt. Kilimanjaro in Tanzania), and I obviously haven't cycled down many that I haven't cycled up; although I must admit to taking the odd cable car and funicular railway in the Alps before enjoying the freewheel back down again. Extreme mountain biking, as it is

Simon Eassom is Head of Sports Science at De Montfort University in Bedford, UK. He is the author of numerous articles and book chapters in the areas of sport philosophy, ethics, and history. He is currently Director of the Centre for Applied Sport Philosophy and Ethics Research at DMU and has recently been awarded a Teaching Fellowship of the University for outstanding teaching in his area. He is a retired extreme sports aficionado, limiting his current activities to off-piste skiing. In the past he has climbed throughout North and South America and in the European Alps, specializing in winter ice climbing in Canada and Scotland. He has sailed across the Atlantic, parachuted, and scuba dived. His mountain biking expeditions have included a tour of Mont Blanc and an off-road north-south traverse of Australia.

understood to mean, involves something more hair-raising than twiddling one's bottom gear over the Col de la Forclaz or riding 160 miles in a day, in torrential rain, fully laden, to catch a plane home (both of which count as pretty extreme in my mother's reckoning). But, having owned a mountain bike, which I've used to service my adventurous wanderlust in ways that my old drop-handlebar touring bike could never do, I've done the odd mountain-bikey kind of thing, as one does. It is a bit like eventually taking one's V8 all-terrain behemoth off the Tarmac and into the conditions it is designed to cope with. It can be a lot of fun. It can be addictive. But to claim that extreme action is why these vehicles exist is mistaken. Function rarely precedes invention. Extreme mountain biking, like four-wheel-drive off-roading, owes as much to fashion and consumption as it does to any inherent desire within us all to do such crazy things (and to invent the apparatus to enable us to do them).

I am going to play fast and loose here with the term *extreme*, despite the obvious suggestion given the overall content of this book that mountain biking is included here as an extreme sport because of the pretty radical, outrageous, unbelievable, dangerous, technically demanding, psychologically damaging, technologically enhanced, and media-entranced feats of the cable-TV-megastar-in-the-making "yo-hey-dude" punks who are supposedly the real mountain-bikers. Any analysis of the current mountain biking subculture gives us only a partial picture. Indeed, I am not sure that there is just one mountain biking subculture. Extreme mountain biking takes many forms. In principle, it is any action that utilizes a bicycle in mountainous terrain to push the function of that bicycle to the extreme. In other words, leaping out of an airplane wearing a parachute and strapped to a bicycle does not constitute extreme biking of any kind, mountain or otherwise. But then, what is a bicycle? What is its function or form? What constitutes an extreme use? My focus will be on these questions and not on the current subcultures represented in fanzines and on cable TV shows.

You cannot get much more extreme than the early riders of the "ordinary" bicycles in the 1870s (the so-called "penny-farthings" with one small wheel at the back and one enormous wheel in front atop which the rider would sit), who served an apprenticeship of fire just learning to get on board their ridiculous machines. It was not uncommon to fall over and onto the rotating wheel at the expense of the odd broken or even removed finger. Charles Spencer, owner of one of the earlier bicycling schools in London, describes how to mount the high-wheeled bike:

> Hold the handle with the left hand and place the other on the seat. Now take a few running steps, and when the right foot is on the ground give a hop with that foot, and at the same time place the left foot on the step, throwing your right leg over on to the seat. Nothing but a good running hop will give you time to adjust your toe on the step as it is moving. It requires, I need not say, a certain amount of strength and agility.[2]

Once on board, all was not easy. The ordinary was direct drive: there was no crankset or chain and no freewheel mechanism. The wheel rotated at the same revolutions as the pedals, and the pedals rotated the same as the wheel. Freewheeling downhill required the rider to take his or her feet off the pedals and hang them over the handlebars and, presumably, hang on for dear life. Going head over heels over the handlebars was an occupational hazard. And then there were the roads. Decades of expansion of the new transport system, railways, had led to the rapid decline of roads. We would not recognize them as roads today. They were more like tracks—rutted dirt paths along which a coach and horses would bounce and shake, taking three days to cover the 200 miles from London to Manchester. Bitumen was a new invention in the late nineteenth century: MacAdam had invented a process for applying molten tar mixed with small stones over wooden railway sleepers to create a smooth(ish), water-resistant, and durable surface: hence, Tarmac. So, think again about those early pioneers on their "ordinaries." All cycling in the 1860s and 1870s was off-road by today's standards. From the outset then, bicycle users have explored the extremes of their usage. In the early days of any technological innovation, the parameters of its usage are contained almost entirely at the failure point of that machine. Prototypes are always extreme machines.

Am I simply equivocating here about the use of the term *extreme?* I don't think so. What I am trying to do is find a way into the beginning of my analysis of this mountain biking madness. To understand it requires us to understand something of what a bicycle actually is and how and why it ever got invented. That process requires an explanation that can account for several essential facets of sociotechnical change. To begin with, the 'working' of an artifact must be understood as *explanandum*, not *explanans*: the utility of any machine is a result of its sociotechnical development, not its cause. In other words, mountain biking exists as much to make mountain bikes what they are, as a result of what they can do post hoc, after the fact of their existence. The mountain bike is a composite of its users, its makers, and its own existence. Moreover, any analysis of the development of the artifact needs to allow for the agent-oriented and contingent aspects of social and technical change as well as of the structurally constituted aspects. The mountain bike is a product of its time. Its conception is not a mark of pure thought. It is a cross-fertilization of cultural influences of the 1970s, '80s, and '90s. There is not really a great deal of difference between the early days of the bicycle and the early days of the mountain bike in terms of their evolutions as products of social change and technological infusion. So, to begin this process we must have at least a little history.

It is reasonable to suggest that the mountain bike has been the single most significant development in the history of the bicycle in the last 100 years. Its development and evolution from the 1960s into what it is today reflects a genesis similar to that of the "safety bicycle" (with standard diamond-frame and two equal-sized wheels that we would all recognize as a 'bike') from the 1860s to the 1890s. As the early bicycles went from driveless scooters to direct-drive big-wheeled "ordinaries," to the chain-driven equal-wheeled "safety," the progression was not a linear process directed towards some sort of a priori conception of what this thing was or should be. The arrival at the "safety bicycle" was a push from behind with two pulls from above and a few sideways nudges. As the bicycle developed, different social groups became interested in its conception for different purposes and had profound influences on redirecting its path to a completed product. For decades after the emergence of the safety bike, little changed in the bike manufacturing world to alter the basic design of the bicycle. Minor modifications were made to braking mechanisms; new materials and technologies allowed small changes to frame and wheel construction; and the invention of, first, hub gears and then the derailleur helped to improve the efficiency of the bicycle but did little to alter its basic dynamics and appearance.

The earliest bicycle-like inventions were what we might call "running machines." There is evidence that Leonardo da Vinci had considered the possibility of a two-wheeled humanly-propelled transport mechanism. Interestingly, the drawing in his Codex Atlanticus, probably done by his pupil Salai around 1493, shows a bike with a crank and belt drive mechanism powering the rear wheel. He was ahead of his time. The first machines in production did not arrive until the 1790s and had no power train: they were in effect wooden rocking horses with the rockers removed and replaced with wheels. The Comte de Sivrac's Celerifere (circa 1791) and von Sauerbronn's Draisienne (circa 1817) both required the rider to sit astride a frame suspended between the wheels and to "run" with a cross-country skiing type action. Heavy steel toe-capped and hob-nailed boots were a necessity for starting and stopping. Steering was impossible. The utility of such a vehicle is highly dubious. It was a novelty, a new fashion accessory. Some were used by postmen, but generally they were something of an eccentric hobby. Blacksmiths complained about the threat to their livelihood if bicycles ever replaced horses and were known to smash up any they found in their villages. They were uncomfortable, inefficient, and ill-suited for anything that a modern bicycle might tackle. Why did such a vehicle ever come into being? Despite the obvious drawbacks, two-wheeled self-propelled vehicles of one kind or another were here to stay. By the 1860s, the velocipede, as it was patented by Pierre Michaux in France and Pierre Lallement in America, became the first bicycle driven by pedals describing a rotary action. Commonly known as the "Boneshaker," this is, quite literally, what it did.

Manufacture of the velocipede escalated in the 1860s, largely in England and America. The Coventry Sewing Machine Company Limited saw an opportunity to diversify its struggling business into the design and construction of velocipedes. While it was still a quirky fashion accessory, James Starley and William Hillman (both famous names in the later development of motorcars in England) set out to market their new designs with a spectacular promotional feat. In 1871 they rode nonstop from London to Coventry in one day—a distance of nearly 100 miles and still a creditable achievement even by today's standards.[3] What is more interesting is that they rode atop their new "Ariel," a high-wheeled "ordinary," fitted with an ingenious braking device that saved them from the perils of freewheeling out of control on the steep downhill sections over the Chiltern Hills. The Ariel was launched in 1871, at the bargain price of eight guineas (about $15), considerably cheaper than the $200 first required for the early velocipedes. The bicycle succeeded as a sport machine. By the end of the 1870s most developed countries had cycling clubs and associations for enthusiasts. Long-distance cycling became commonplace and track racing sprang up in London and the various manufacturing centers of the Midlands (Coventry, Birmingham, Wolverhampton, and Leicester).[4] By the end of the century, bicycles had been used to circumnavigate the world.[5]

It is ironic that the success of the only bicycle emerged when its sporting use superseded its utility as a mode of transport even though its potential as a vehicle of transportation fueled the early inventors. The dual essence of the bicycle, freewheeling roller and efficient load carrier, has been at the heart of the tensions between bikes for sport and bikes as transport that led to the near terminal decline of the cycle industry 100 years later. The bicycle has two wheels. It will not stand up without support. It has no power supply of its own. Its two wheels turn whilst supporting a metal frame capable of carrying a relatively large weight but at the same time requiring that weight as an energy source to turn the wheels. The eccentric Frenchman Bernard Magnaloux, throughout his five-year cycle ride around the world, traveled with a bike and baggage weighing over 75 kilos. The North Vietnamese men and women who kept their soldiers supplied with food and munitions during the America-Vietnam conflict would carry up to 75 kilos of goods supported by their bicycles as they pushed them doggedly along the Ho Chi Minh Trail. Together, bike and rider are considered more efficient as a transport mechanism, in terms of distance covered for energy used, than birds, horses, cars, planes, or any other "fuel"-burning machine. This is the bicycle's only essence or nature: a machine that rolls and rolls, requiring relatively little effort from its rider. A rolling machine: light in weight; moderately fast. A workhorse: weight bearing; continuous and long-lived. It has carried hundreds, maybe thousands, of people around the world in search of adventure. Millions commute to work on one. Nearly as many use one as cheap haulage to get their goods to market. But these uses have little connection with why the bicycle was invented and are far removed from its raison-d'être, either 100 years ago, or today, as a leisure and recreation vehicle. With the mountain bike, as with the safety bike, different user groups hijacked the emerging machine and pulled its development forward from their position of need and desire. In both cases, the bike's essence is found in its meaning and not in its value.

It is for this reason that, regardless of the millions of bicycles in use around the world, the cycle manufacturing industry in Europe and America was on the verge of collapse in the 1980s. How could it be that a vehicle so useful and so ubiquitous as the bicycle could be in such low demand that giant manufacturing companies such as Raleigh, Saracen, Bluemells, Coventry Eagle, Pashley, and Dawes were struggling to survive? Its value as a functional tool is secondary to its meaning as a cultural artifact. To understand the reasons behind the crisis that hit bike builders, and to understand how the mountain bike saved the whole business, is also to understand something of the phenomena of the bicycle and its existence *in extremis* in the guise of the mountain bike. It took another revolution in bike design and marketing, a century after Starley and Hillman, to get manufacturers to realize what cycling is all about.

In the 1960s, cycling was all bicycle clips and yellow plastic parachute rain capes, Philip Larkin-type bowler-hatted gents commuting to their civil service jobs from sleepy suburbs. The bicycle itself was largely unchanged in appearance from the end of the last century. It had a "diamond" frame (the shape described by the tubing from the headset along the top tube to the seat, down the stays to the rear hub, back along to the bottom bracket and up to the front forks), heavy-weight steel tubing, raked front forks, and conventional head and seat tube angles providing predictable handling. Development stagnated, not because the bicycle was complete or finished or fully evolved, but because the social groups whose imaginations could see beyond its function to its meaning and the technological development necessary for radically shaking the complacency from its form did not exist at one and the same time.

Some powerful user groups made minor inroads into the bicycle's basic design but specialist bikes were expensive, often custom-made, and in demand only for sport cyclists engaged in racing and time trials. For decades the bike was predominantly cheap transport. Apart from in Africa, the Indian subcontinent, and China, where it remained so, the bike was all but superseded by the motorcar. The car had virtually killed off the bicycle as a leisure vehicle for adults. The only group of the population riding for fun were children—and then it was something most were expected to "grow out of." The only adults still riding their bikes for fun were slightly cranky eccentric types.

Through the '70s and '80s various new children's crazes—choppers, the Raleigh Grifter, BMXs—revitalized a stagnant industry, but few made much of an impact on diminishing markets. Adult bikes were not cheap: $50 in 1970 bought a racing bike look-alike with a one-year guarantee of rusty wheels, bent spokes, buckled wheels, rattling gears, seized cables, squeaky brakes, and a sore backside. By 1980 the same machine cost $160. I spent four years commuting to work every day on such a machine, a 25-mile round journey, with weekends used up cleaning, oiling, greasing, and straightening wheels. If I could have afforded a car, the bike would have been consigned to the garbage.

If the bicycle industry was to survive and expand, it had to reproduce the factors that led to its huge growth 100 years previously: it had to appeal to the main consumers, adults. If it could no longer do so as necessary transport, then it needed to have the attraction of being a sport vehicle.[6] The bike metamorphosed as a result of various cultural and historical factors that, almost by chance, placed the mountain bike (just as the safety bike had done a century before) in the public consciousness as a new "must-have" piece of sports equipment. Between the late 1960s and the 1990s the mountain bike changed and evolved (not necessarily in any linear progression) from the California "clunkers" of Marin County to the sophisticated hi-tech machines of today. That development was due to a combination of various factors: personalities, changing features of consumer culture, altered perceptions of the environment, changing psychologies of identity and image, and increased leisure time. The mountain bike is a product of now and now is a product of the mountain bike. In many ways, the mountain bike is an icon of new times.

In 1986 the neophyte bike company Muddy Fox launched a stunning advertisement campaign for its new range of off-road bicycles. Set against the backdrop of the Snowdonia mountain range in Wales, a bike stood upright, unassisted by a rider, on top of the flat, calm water of Glaslyn, reflected in the mirror-clear surface. It was a stunning image for its time, an idea that has been used repeatedly ever since: an impossible image of a product doing the impossible. Muddy Fox bikes could go anywhere. They could even ride on water. Saracen relied heavily on the endorsement of the Crane cousins, always seeking new "unbelievable" adventures to raise money for Third World technology projects. Apart from the Kilimanjaro expedition in 1986, they cycled up and down England's, Wales,' and Scotland's highest peaks. Perhaps their biggest adventure was the epic "Journey to the Center of the Earth": a 5,000-kilometer ride from the estuary of the Brahmaputra, over the Himalayas, across Tibet, and into remotest northwest China to the point on the globe furthest from the sea (the center of the earth). And they carried nothing with them but a sleeping bag each and the most minimal tool kit.

For such images to succeed, the underlying symbolism required the reader to already recognize the signification of wilderness, adventure, freedom, and exclusivity that gave meaning to the bike as other than bike. The mountain bike's appeal grew because of three main signifiers that radically altered the image of cycling:

- Hi-tech specifications
- Exclusivity
- Adventure appeal

All three are inextricably linked with the growth of consumerism in the 1980s and the trend toward conspicuous lifestyle choices.

The mountain bike has become, more than ever before, a gear freak's heaven. Bicycles have always appealed to enthusiasts, particularly those who like to dismantle things, rebuild them, maintain them, improve them. But technically they have been the simplest of machines. Other than endless talk about gear ratios and ideal chainset combinations, the safety bicycle (even in racing bike form) offers little for the techno junkie. The mountain bike changed all that. At last, the enthusiast could revel in the latest componentry. Ultralight materials such as high-grade alloys of various kinds and titanium were used for gears, brakes, cranks, seat posts, and chainsets. Epoxy resins replaced brazing for bonding together thinner and lighter tubing. Reynolds 531 double-butted steel tubing became 'old hat,' and companies such as Cannondale experimented with aluminum. The bicycle became another victim of space-age fetishism. Moving parts got Teflon, clothing got Kevlar. Old fuddy-duddies kept their leather Brookes saddles; everybody in the know luxuriated on gel-filled, crotch-friendly ergonomic marvels. None of this happened overnight, but it was there from the outset. Everything got extreme. Specifications suddenly mattered: twenty-one gears, Deore XT, Mavic rims, Shimano, everywhere Shimano. These became the watchwords of credibility in the late '80s and early '90s. American-made bikes from manufacturers such as Giant, Trek, and Alpine Stars were sold in Europe through an appeal to techno-fetishism. It suddenly mattered that one's bike was shod in particular kinds of tires. Labels had to have the ring of West Coast surf-shack-style backyard cottage industry: esoteric, in the know, and made by the experts who were out there doing the stuff. Pseudo mountain bikers bought off-the-peg Japanese-equipped machines. Real mountain bikers wanted everything made-in-the-USA. Such changes helped to create the image of the bike as an acceptable adult toy. It wasn't just a bike: Don't you know the difference? It's a mountain bike.

Punters rarely rode their new bikes up or down mountains. For the most part they transported them on the back of their new four-wheel-drive designer vehicles. Range Rovers, Shoguns, Cherokees sported mountain bikes on racks in the summer, along with windsurfing boards and downhill skis in the winter. The mountain bike was exclusive, and this is what the consumer wanted. The bike had to signify knowledge, education, drive, determination, and perhaps most of all, money. My first mountain bike, sporting top-of-the-range Deore XT components, was twice what a hand-built touring bike would cost. Off-the-peg bikes hit the $1,000 mark early in the 1990s. The mountain bike became a tool both of social differentiation and identification. It differentiated those who owned one from those who didn't want one, as people in the know, fashion conscious, trendy, young, going-places kind of people. The bike became a visible statement of identity. I might ride my bike around town during the week but, hey, on weekends I'm an all-action, outdoors, thrill-seeking hedonist who lives life on the edge. Of course, a lot of people rode mountain bikes because they were comfortable, efficient, practical, and a lot of fun. But such fashion victims were largely passive consumers of an image already well-enough established to make the mountain bike a viable marketing tool.

Few people knew what to do with all this new technology. New magazines sprang up monthly with tech-tips and reviews of the latest must-have components. Articles sprang up teaching users how to hop their bikes over logs, boulders, steps, curbs. Wheelies and donuts were essential tricks of the trade. Whilst the new magazines led the development in certain ways, in others ways they were always one step behind the times. It's the nature of the beast. Magazines sell to bulk audiences that attract advertising dollars. They have to appeal to what's already established as fashionable. New British magazines in the early '90s, such as *Mountain Biking UK* and *Mountain Biker*, tried to keep up with all that was new and radical whilst trying to create their own market by promoting mountain biking itself to new consumers. They were often one step behind the times. In 1990, I wrote to the editor of one of these magazines offering my services as a freelance journalist with articles on how to go about planning a real "adventure" with one's newly-acquired go-anywhere machine. I had just returned from cycling part of the Tour du Mont Blanc and had previously ridden off-road across a large part of the Italian Alps. He did not think that the majority of his readership would be at all interested in such exploits. He was probably right, but that is not because I had wrongly gauged mountain biking and mountain bikers. In his own way his perceptions and his magazine's focus were part of the ongoing process of shaping what mountain biking was to become. In retrospect there is no doubt that the appeal of the mountain bike is its go-anywhere potential. For me, go-anywhere meant taking my bike across deserts, through jungles, and over Himalayan passes. Equally compelling were those visions of do-anything potential. The mountain bike could ride over bumps, power up the steepest slopes, and hurtle down heart-stopping inclines. I got hung up on the environment, others craved technique. Years later not one edition of the monthly mountain biking magazines is published without a photostory of some wild trip into the heart of Laos or a charity ride across the Atlas mountains and on into the Sahara. This is now just as much a part of what mountain bike owners want to do with their bikes. There are many different interpretations of *extreme.*

The mountain bike fitted the times. It grew up in an era of psychobabble and know-thyself pop philosophy. It fitted the general exodus from the cities to rural and wilderness adventure. Everybody wanted their own bit of freedom, to be their own frontiersman doing something daring and esteem-enhancing. Owners had to live up to the declaration on their decals: Trek, Specialized, Discovery, Stumpjumper, Craghopper, Dirtgrinder, Buttbuffer. The mountain bike fitted any trend that was going. It was environmentally friendly, a green machine. It was nondiscriminatory (no "mixte" frames for women in skirts here). Businesses sprang up to feed the fashion. Bike hire services boomed. Couriers and dispatch riders off-loaded their motors and got aggressive on a bike (shades, day-glo, gloves, and load whistle compulsory). The police swapped their horses for wheeled steeds. And park rangers did the rounds in a different kind of saddle.

Whilst all this emerged in the 1990s, the mountain bike itself still had no definitive nature. It did not arrive as some incarnation of a Platonic ideal. Its only essence was and is that of any other bike: it rolls (on its own downhill, powered by its rider uphill). What makes it a "mountain" bike is its capacity to cope with the conditions found on mountains. Well, kind of. It does not do icefalls and crevasses too well, nor glaciers (even though extreme riders have tackled such things). Do mountain bike riders find new challenges to test their bikes or do they find new bikes to test their challenges? Is the extreme mountain biker a cyclist or mountain descender? Of course, he or she is both and neither. There are those who have rediscovered ordinary (?) cycling after owning a mountain bike and those who have taken up climbing, sky-diving, and other adventure sports. Mountain bike riders are not a homogenous group.

The development of new technologies that have shaped the mountain bike (suspension systems, shock-absorbing wheels and tires, better brakes, stiffer frames, stronger gears) have determined what extreme riders can do and also been determined by what those riders want to do. Mountain bike technology, like that of surfing before it, has been led by those out there doing the stuff. It's necessarily initiated by do-it-yourself enthusiasts sourcing their own components and starting up small-scale industries, supplying other enthusiasts. These are the extreme mountain bikers, like their ancestors riding prototype velocipedes and ordinaries using their own bodies as crash-test dummies.

But still it is not clear what exactly constitutes "extreme" mountain biking. I can only offer the following thoughts. The bicycle rolls. It will roll downhill continuously unless brought to a stop. This much is obvious but also hidden. Steering the bicycle, braking, jumping over things are all extraneous features of riding. They exist to enable the rider to keep on going without losing control, to keep on rolling despite the terrain, the curves, the obstacles, and to roll faster and faster. As the bicycle is a rolling machine, it is a machine that in conception knows no limits to the speed at which it rolls. It is not a flying machine. It must gather its momentum by the turning of its wheels by gravity or by rider input. The ultimate is to roll and never stop. The extreme mountain biker explores this essence and understands the meaning of rolling through pushing his or her limits of control over the bicycle by taking it down steeper hills and over terrain that challenges the desire of the machine to just roll and roll. The mountain biker is no more an "extreme" athlete than those who first climbed aboard their "running machines" and high-wheeled "ordinaries." The mountain biking sport competitor is no more "extreme" than the wilderness traveler. To be extreme on a bike is to explore the bike's meaning in ways that compromise one's own being. It is to exist with the bike and become part of the bike in the action of traveling at speed and/or over great distances and difficult terrain. Those of us that do so have the same sort of motivations that compel skydivers, skiers, and surfers. Without our intents the bike has no meaning. It is nothing but tubes and cables and rubber. And the rest—the TV dollars, the punk radical chic, the techno-babble— these are merely sideshows.

Notes

1. I will use the term *mountain bike* throughout to refer to all variants, such as: all-terrain bike, off-road bike, ATB, MTB, etc.

2. Charles Spencer, *The Modern Bicycle*, cited in J. Woodforde, *The Story of the Bicycle* (London: Routledge, 1970), p. 110.

3. G. Williamson, *Wheels within Wheels: The Story of the Starleys of Coventry* (London: Geoffrey Bles, 1966).

4. W. F. Grew, *The Cycle Industry: Its Origins, History, and Latest Developments* (London: Pitman, 1921).

5. A. Ritchie, *King of the Road: An Illustrated History of Cycling* (London: Wildwood House, 1975).

6. This is not to suggest that any one group set out to create a new market or product. Thus, it would be quite wrong to suggest that any one individual or group of individuals 'invented' the mountain bike in order to sell a product.

ECO-CHALLENGE

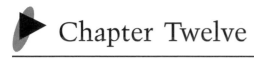

Chapter Twelve

Eco (Ego?) Challenge
British Columbia, 1996
Jim Cotter

> A journey into nature.
> Push yourself until the pain comes and then go on,
> until you think you cannot survive.
> Here the ego will let go.
> Here you will be purified.
>
> —Lilloet vision quest

The sequence of horse riding, running, mountaineering, canoeing, mountain biking, and rafting across 300 miles is finally revealed to us in the late evening. The safety officials each promise their section to be tougher than the preceding one. Yeah, yeah, we think. But unfortunately they are soon to be proven right. By the time we pack for the first stage and double check that we've included all compulsory personal and team equipment, there's less than two hours for sleep before boarding the buses.

Jim Cotter earned his Ph.D. in Exercise/Environmental Physiology in 1998 from University of Wollongong. He also holds a master's degree in physical education (distinction) from the University of Otago, and bachelor's degrees in physical education (distinction) and science (physiology) from, respectively, the University of Otago and the Universities of Otago & Canterbury. He has nine peer-reviewed papers published in the field of exercise physiology. As well, Jim has ten years' participation in multisport, orienteering/rogaining and adventure racing, including the Southern Traverse, Coast-to-Coast, Eco-Challenge, and all major Australian multiday, multisport events (JLW, Winter Classic, Cradle to Coast, Three Peaks). In his athletic endeavors, he has finished in the top five every time but once.

As we stumble down the road and arrive at the convoy of yellow school buses, it strikes me that this is essentially my (movie-influenced) impression of an American summer camp; young people heading away with anticipation and nervous excitement, on an adventure—on these distinctive yellow buses. Maybe the only real difference between those youngsters and us, apart from the unsociable hour of departure (c. 3 AM), is that we have more experience in the outdoors and therefore our drive for adventure simply requires a greater physical challenge. After all, our personal and team objectives for Eco-Challenge are to compete at a high level with good friends, while having fun and adventure. Because the personal commitment and experiences are so overwhelming, it seems rather blinkered to place much focus on being first to reach the finish line. Obviously, we'll put all our energy into it, but with each of the 300 miles having its own challenges, we must be prepared simply to accept what we face.

The convoy eventually rolls off the highway and we emerge into the predawn cold in a large paddock containing several helicopters, a corral full of horses, Lycra-clad athletes, cowboys, camera crews, and those yellow school buses—hardly your average gathering, but colorful nonetheless. Our transport for the next twenty-three miles is partly our decision, though our choice consists only of running or riding horses. There are two horses per five-person team, with no doubling allowed on the horses.

Judging by the instructions from Mark Burnett, the race director, he's keen to liven things up from the outset. Specifically, two team members are on horses on one side of the paddock, while the remainder of the team stand on the other side, and we're instructed to form into our team of five before exiting the paddock via a narrow track, 1,000 yards away. True to prediction, the 7 AM start is the catalyst for mayhem, with 140 horses and 210 runners converging near the middle of the paddock. Fortunately, our initial riders, Eric and Bill, don't suffer the unceremonious dismount of some other riders, and we manage to gravitate into a team before reaching the far end of the paddock. Predictably though, we've begun with a hiss and a roar, despite wisdom dictating that we should begin slowly. Wisdom takes back seat amidst this chaos. Once the initial, pent-up energy is flittered away, no one will run any meaningful distance, and if they do, it's usually to escape an animal that is stumbled upon.

We'd practiced running behind horses and holding onto their tails, but the Western saddles used in this event have good hand holds, so we run alongside. Most of our gear is in two packs, carried by the riders. This works well, although I soon find it awkward trotting my trusty steed (Jasper) with a pack on, and resort to alternating between a canter and a walk—a pattern that produces fairly intense interval training for the runner and nearly causes our disqualification when a roving cowboy determines that we're galloping (which is illegal). During the subsequent walk section (to minimize hoof damage), Jasper is unhurried, and several teams overtake us. Therefore, when we leave the horses to cross the swollen, glacially-fed Lilloet River at the end of this stage, there are many teams already lined up in front of us waiting to cross. Fortunately, this activity is under safety supervision, as we're appalled at the lack of cohesion and poor river-crossing technique shown by most teams, with many requiring rescue by the officials. This is our first real chance to observe the dynamics and skills of other teams, and it is no surprise that 56 of the initial 70 teams are destined not to finish the event.

That's enough of being harsh on the qualities of other teams, because early in the subsequent mountain trekking stage, we (or mostly I) make a blunder by misinterpreting the race notes, causing us to miss a trail and costing many hours of mind-bending struggle through slide alder. Most ultradistance races seem to have at least one section that is either stone-dead monotonous or incredibly frustrating. Eco-Challenge is no exception. The 1996 event requires trekking through several valleys filled with slide alder—a densely-packed, almost impenetrable shrub, made more so because we're carrying ice axes. Once into the alder there are few chances to glimpse the terrain ahead, and progress is gauged largely by the interminably slow movement past the peaks that tower above the valley sides. The alder often contains prickles, mainly stinging nettle and club foot, and bee hives. After hours of struggling in alder, nobody is in the mood to appreciate the intrinsic beauty of local fauna such as bees, so the hives have just one positive impact: if somebody stumbles into one, they leave a decent swath through the alder while struggling to escape. However, the down sides are that the escapee doesn't always flee in the direction we're trying to go, and Kristina is left with a massively swollen face after scoring nine stings in one episode.

Since the walking trail isn't on our map, we don't realize that many other teams have gained literally miles on us until we stumble across it near the head of the valley at midnight on day one. The race is only one day old, and already we're shattered: physically, from battling through slide alder at a snail's pace after the morning run/ride, and mentally, by the realization that our valuable energy expenditure of day one has largely been in vain. After dragging out the sleeping bags and scoring nearly three hours sleep, we're revitalized and keen to make up some ground. The remainder of this first mountain stage leaves us no more tired, but with several great memories. The fatiguing progress of further slide alder and several more thousand feet of climbing valley walls and snowfields is quickly forgotten. Even the cold wind and discomfort of trying to sleep for an hour on a rock ledge above a glacier (4 AM on the second night) is remembered less clearly than the view of an orange moon sliding up the side of a peak silhouetted above the blackness of a valley far below. This stage is otherwise highlighted by chatting to friends or friendly individuals from other teams whom we occasionally mingle with, by long periods of roped team travel across snowfields encircled by peaks, by mountain lakes and lush meadows in full bloom, and by beating the other three teams in our proximity out of the bush and down the forestry road to the trek-to-canoe transition area. Not that we're competitive!

Our top-notch support members[1] have a hot meal already prepared—no easy feat when we could just as easily have arrived this time last night or tomorrow night. It's 11 PM, sixty-four hours into the race, and we're held in transition by news that race organizers are rescuing a team who've capsized a canoe while paddling the six miles of river at the beginning of this fifty-two-mile canoe stage. That leaves forty-six miles of canoeing "down" a lake— definitely a strong contender for the brain-dead component of this year's course! That is, monotony is guaranteed when paddling long distances on flat lakes, mostly because you can see the next corner for so long before arriving, and after rounding that corner you're faced with more of the same. The tedium is complete if you're in physical pain—usually it's your bum or your back. I suspect it's like driving a car across a desert while stuck in first gear.

My teammates use the spare hour to catch some sleep, but there's too much going through my mind, and sleep just doesn't happen. It never does if you're the last one still awake. Because of the capsize we leap frog into fourth place, but this bonus is paled by the fact that two friends (one of whom is very experienced) are in that ill-fated team. For them, the balance has abruptly switched from adventure to misadventure, as being tossed into a bone-chilling river in the pitch blackness of a moonless night would be terrifying. Nevertheless, ostensibly we are adults who are appropriately experienced in the outdoors, and are participating in the Eco-Challenge under our own consent and common sense, so the responsibility for misadventure arising from our choices and actions should reside squarely with ourselves.

While on this topic, I was irritated by the misaligned egos and apparent blamelessness of several Eco-Challengers who loudly derided Mark Burnett for being quick to accept their entry fee while setting an absurdly difficuly course. If only those individuals were prepared to consider one harsh possibility: that the gap between their egos and their teams' capacity for wilderness travel might be rather wide. In prerace newsletters Mark had strongly reiterated the very high physical and technical demands of this event, and urged that unsuitably experienced individuals should seriously reconsider their entry. Fortunately, he appears not to have bowed to the loudest voices by setting easy courses, and the onus is therefore on the weaker teams to gain the necessary fitness and wilderness experience if they are to compete again. At least this ensures that the Eco-Challenge will remain an adventure race, rather than just a race, for the (increasing number of) teams and individuals who already have adequate capabilities.

Anyway, back to the race. It's after midnight when we start paddling, and we've been ferried down to the lake on account of the paddling time lost with the rescue. Despite this decision having worked in our favor (an opportunity for one hour of sleep), there's no desire to gain an advantage by bending the rules. After all, what is the satisfaction of having covered 300 miles under your own power if you're aware that you cheated so much as 100 yards of it?

We paddle through the calm night seeing only the faint outline of the hilltops against the sky and two green glow sticks waving gently at the bow and stern of our other canoe. Despite our already close friendship before this event and the openness that comes from implicitly relying on one another, we're now so tired that nonrace conversation is spasmodic. Everyone goes through their own ups and downs, due to both energy levels and sleepiness. Generally, sleepiness seems to become worse at normal bedtime, and reemerges with vengeance during the three to four hours before dawn. The low-energy (blood glucose) periods, sometimes referred to as "hitting the wall," are more frequent and unpredictable, though also more easily prevented or abated. Usually at least one person is feeling OK, and their enthusiasm is generally a bonus rather than a pain in the arse.

At one point we drift the canoes together for a few minutes of rest and sustenance. After resuming paddling for some minutes,

Eric glances at the skyline long enough to realize that we're paddling in the opposite direction, back up the lake. It's times like this when the finish line seems a world away! Just after daylight we arrive at a dam and must portage the canoes and other gear[2] down to a river, which shortly gives way to the final twenty-six miles of lake. Though not shortly enough. Monty, Kristina and Bill get swamped in a rapid and take an unscheduled, early morning swim. It clearly amuses a passing motorist, but our bedraggled, shivering trio don't see the funny side of it just yet. We set off on the second lake, paddling hard as a means of warming up. The ridgelines of the protruding hills become endless, and Eric succumbs to short sleeps in the boat. I can't get comfortable with the idea of surrendering to sleep while so close to water, so I blindly paddle on. That's a reflection on my instinct for survival rather than my level of trust in Eric's balance. After all, if you inadvertently tip a boat over and tiredness keeps you asleep until you hit the water, will you instinctively breathe in? I'd guess no, but it's not worth finding out. Now the hallucinations begin to set in. For literally hours there is a huge concrete bridge in my peripheral vision, spanning the lake above our heads. But every time I look up it's not there. Probably the most frustrating aspect of hallucinations is that when they become severe (especially at night), you become preoccupied with exploring whether they're real or not, despite common sense dictating they can't be. Unfortunately, common sense is a little scarce when central nervous fatigue reaches that level!

After an eternity we reach the end of this wretched lake, only to glimpse the enormous hill that marks the onset of the mountain bike section. Afternoon becomes night as our bike route undulates along an electricity maintenance road. Having had just thirty minutes sleep in the sixty hours since waking on day two, I begin to suffer my worst-ever fatigue and become a bit of a liability. For instance, I twice crash due to falling asleep while riding (where's the survival instinct now?), and after later breaking my bike chain, am ever so slow in coordinating the necessary fingers and equipment to repair it. While Monty sets about fixing it in his torchlight (c. 2 AM), I turn my attention to watching the luminous mailboxes running around in the forest adjacent to the road. Who knows why the brain digs up these particular images, but they're sufficiently unnatural that I don't get confused by them.

We're all pretty low by now, and the simplest navigation problems take a ridiculous time to solve. However, if we can make it to the next Passport Control (PC), and then just seven miles farther to the transition area, we can sleep for a few hours while our support members take charge of our bodies (for example, applying blister dressings) and our gear (changing equipment and resupplying food). I finally regain a handle on reality and resume my usual role as navigator. Eventually we arrive at the PC (5.15 AM) and unanimously agree to a fifteen-minute emergency sleep. Despite being shaken from this slumber into a standing position and starting to walk up the road, I obviously don't wake up, because my first memory is of feeling very nauseated, with Monty standing directly in front of me on a forested road, explaining that this isn't a trekking section. When I go back for my bike, Kristina hasn't even woken up, and Eric looks as bad as I feel. Bill, who's been fairly amiable until now, gets us together and points out just how pathetic we are and that we haven't traveled 6,000 miles to behave like zombies. That is the single period of tension within the team, and it hits the mark, especially coming from the most easy-going member. It still takes forever to reach the transition because we're confused over permitted routes of travel and must also detour to get water, but at least we've now got our attitude back on track.

As we set off on the next stage, a fifty-three-mile mountaineering/glacial traverse over part of the Pemberton icecap, we form an unspoken and temporary alliance with two other teams who've caught us during our long transition. We've finally settled into the rhythm of relative sleeplessness, and once clear of the valleys and slide alder early on the following (sixth) morning, we make excellent progress through rugged but beautiful country—alpine meadows, tarns, snowfields, and isolated glaciers. The highlight of the whole event is our great sense of achievement in reaching the first time-restricted Passport Control (PC No. 20) with just a few minutes to spare, after keeping up a fast but necessary pace throughout this day. Because it allows us to start the 1,100-foot roped climb up an icefall before the 7 PM curfew, we immediately create an eleven-hour buffer on the teams who were close behind. In our haste to put someone on the rope before the safety officials decide to hold us here, the main navigator (me) goes up first, whereas our map goes up with the last person. So what? Upon reaching the top, I'm not even sure which direction we're headed as all our attention today has gone into reaching this icefall. It's another needless inefficiency because, if I had the map, it would be easy to use the one-and-a-half-hour wait, and the last remaining light, to plan our route through the snowfields ahead. It's another of the many lessons that, despite being painfully obvious in retrospect, get learned the hard way—through experience.

With the buffer of the ice wall below us, we retreat to the luxury of our sleeping bags in a rocky outcrop and catch up on some sleep. We're rudely woken one hour later (12.15 AM, day 7) by heavy raindrops, and there's a mad dash to get our down bags back into the packs, then don wet weather gear. There's little point staying here, so we set off for the distant Longspur peak and our next PC, located just a few hundred feet before the summit. The sense of real isolation and adventure becomes tarnished by having to sidestep four skidoos parked against some rocks. After abseiling down to the snowfield that forms a saddle against Longspur, we each tie into our main rope and set off, twelve meters apart. The solitary, methodical progress and absence of color force us into our individual inner worlds, broken only by the occasional shout of "Slot" as we pass over a crack in the snow.[3] Nobody clicks to the fact that this saddle is a good place to accurately reset the altimeters. The clouds descend on the mountains as we begin ascending toward the PC. On this section, when we need our altimeters most, their accuracy becomes suspect due to the simultaneous effects of our change in altitude and the deteriorating weather.

We climb to within what is later revealed as literally a stone's throw of the PC, but can't locate it in this gathering storm—a task made more difficult by the fact that it's 3 AM and the snowpack has become steep and has some wide slots. At least it's easy to locate one another to consider our options, since the leader need only stop and begin coiling the rope, a procedure that is repeated in turn until the fifth person emerges from the night. Even in our brain-dead state it's clear that the only real choice is to hole up somewhere until daylight and the storm eases enough to gather our bearings and again search for PC No. 21. We sidle the 200 or so meters across to the leeward ridge and search for a likely shelter in the scattered rocks. Despite such complete fatigue, there's still that deep satisfaction in finding a good campsite, even if in this case the best of them is just a couple of overlapping rocks jutting from the snow. We crawl in and spread out the nylon tent. Yet no one sleeps, probably thanks to the combination of a thunderstorm that seems to have an affinity for this hill, a barrage of hail sneaking into our shelter, the cold wind, and the cramponed boots and broken rock which poke into ribs and weary muscles.

Eric fires up our cooker, and we share a saucepan of hot cordial. That 35-cent sachet tastes better than any $35 meal I can remember. Snack and energy bars are passed around, but as we've eaten little else during the race, they are eaten mainly as a necessity. At least we've been in this game long enough to know that the longer the race, the more important it is to carry food that you like and will therefore eat voluntarily.

The dawn slowly brightens into a whiteout, and the storm seems to be worsening. The compulsory team equipment includes a two-way radio, for use in emergencies, but since we're merely delayed in a less-than-optimal location, we haven't considered using it. Monty checks the rule book and confirms that we're allowed to use the radio in a whiteout. The rules don't precisely state that the radio is to be used only if a team is *lost* in a whiteout, which we're not (not yet, anyway). Therefore, if Mark Burnett should decide to disqualify us for using the radio, we've got him on a technicality, and we set about reporting our situation in case officials are concerned about our whereabouts or safety. This might sound pedantic, but it illustrates a significant facet of such events: that officials are repeatedly confronted with unforeseen decisions, questions, and accusations generated by participants or support members. Predictably, the responses are not always to the team's liking, or well received.

The storm eases in mid morning, and we rendezvous with officials who've come over (200–300 yards) from the PC. After sharing stories and their hot food at the PC, we move on, across expansive snowfields. It's late afternoon when we reach a spectacular, massively crevassed icefall (PC No. 22). Crossing the bottomless, blue chasms by ladder, rope, or Tyrolean traverse, depending on their width, leaves us on a high. It's temporary. This night is similar to the last. Above bushline and craving sleep, we bed down for less than an hour before it begins hailing so heavily that we're forced to move on toward lower ground. The following day we reach the transition to rafts, and are rewarded by a product of the storm: high river flows have made for fast and exciting rafting down the Elaho and Squamish rivers. The final stage, at night, is mountain biking up to the finish at Whistler. Our collective mood of expectant euphoria is dampened a trifle when we lose our way. The irony is that after several days of navigating through untracked terrain, we're now lost on a road, made more embarrassing by being in the spotlight of a trailing film crew. Shortly afterward, as we begin a major hill climb on a rocky path, I suffer a disturbing mix of hallucinations and déjà-vu, convinced that we're the famous five, biking down an English country lane. The famous five maybe, but I've never been to England. Fortunately, reality again takes hold as we reach a sealed road at the top, because we're suddenly forced into fast bunch riding to stave off three other teams who've come up from behind, relatively fresh after being airlifted over the icecap (because of the storm).

Finally the finish banner looms; we're through it—we've done it. Then a blur: laughing, hugs, stories, celebration drink, bright lights, photos, greasy food—a total contrast to the last week (seven days, twenty hours). The two teams whom we shared some of the mountain stages with cross the line shortly afterward, and it's more congratulations all round. As we move away and the initial euphoria subsides, there's an odd feeling of realization, borne of having been on the go since before we can remember, that we're no longer racing. Back in the hotel we're still buzzing, recounting stories to ourselves as much as our support members. Eric, who's in the bath, hasn't said much for a while. Little wonder; he's asleep. It's nearly dawn—time for a bath, then into clean sheets for a well-earned rest. Physically, it takes little time to come back up, but emotionally it takes far longer to come back down.

Sitting now on a tram in downtown Melbourne, recalling this week from two years ago, the scenery, experiences and friendship are so strong. How many weeks of your life are so rewarding? In fact, how many weeks can you even remember? Modern, city-based living, by its very nature, seems to preclude that essential ingredient of personal growth: adventure. For this reason alone it seems that adventure racing is here to stay. If the Eco-challenge, as one such race, continues to be arduous and traverses interesting landscapes, yet doesn't treat the participants as ego junkies or pawns for media consumption, then I hope it remains. Once the comfort zone is exceeded, the event provides a rarely encountered, sustained medium for both the pretense and mediocrity of day-to-day life to be whittled away. Some previously unconfronted truths of your physical, emotional, and spiritual self then become evident to your or your teammates.

The unfortunate commercial reality of Eco-Challenge is that if the participants weren't parading on the media stage, they wouldn't be parading at all. Nonetheless, adventure and challenge are personal things, so it's not possible to fully identify or appreciate those of others. In this respect, I felt detached from the television coverage of this event, because it portrayed images and experiences much different from my own. It's easy to describe the physical course and how contestants progress along it, but that doesn't reveal what the event means to the contestants. You can't interpret it unless you perform it, and even then, the challenge and the experiences are unique to the adventure that unfolds for each participant.

As they say, I guess you had to be there.

Notes

1. Since 1997, teams have consisted of only four members (still including the opposite gender) and no support members. This adds to the expedition aspect, but removes some of the incentive and camaraderie connected with reaching transitions. Additionally, the event provided support members their own adventures and friendships.

2. We must carry all mountain bike gear, minus the bike, for the ensuing biking stage. Similarly, in that stage we must carry all canoeing gear, minus the canoe but including paddles. We use split-shaft kayak paddles and strap them to our bikes. The Australian team is somewhat more economical than us and saws its kayak paddles in half with Swiss Army knives.

3. Unless trekking under bush canopy, we rarely use our torches at night. This widens the field of view from that in the torch beam to the entire surroundings, albeit leaving it fainter and monochromatic. A side effect is relative visual separation from teammates, which leads to the internalization of our thoughts.

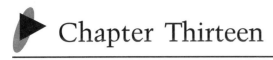

Chapter Thirteen

"Another Kind of Life"

Adventure Racing and Epic Expeditions

Martha Bell

While triathletes have seen new forms of the classic long-distance endurance race over the past decade, so, too, have adventurers seen new elaborations on outdoor pursuits. For example, twenty years ago road cycling produced mountain biking, which may now appear alongside a road cycle section or even displace it in triathlon events. Mountain biking has its own World Championships and was included as a sport for the first time in the 1996 Atlanta Olympic Games, and a professional race circuit serves as a training ground for world-level athletes and a means of attracting international sponsorship. For their part, early mountain biking enthusiasts originated the activity as a recreational pursuit. They could reach higher vistas off road more quickly in the backcountry than by more conventional means, backpacking (or tramping).[1] The sport

Martha Bell is currently completing her doctoral dissertation in sociology and women's studies at Massey University, Palmerston North, New Zealand, titled "Becoming Women Outdoor Leaders: Power and the Pursuit of Strong Bodies." She was previously a lecturer in outdoor experiential education and co-coordinator of the Outdoor Programme at the University of Otago, Dunedin, New Zealand. She is a former Outward Bound instructor and women's expedition guide. Her publications include journal articles and a number of book chapters.

The author thanks Christine Worsfold, Andy Thompson, John Guthrie, Marg Cosgriff, and Simon Hart for loaning and locating research materials, Pat Duffy for her help with French translation, and Pippa Guthrie for providing childcare.

219

of orienteering is another example. It has spawned rogaine, a 24-hour navigational race in the mountains. From Australia, this new sport also has its own World Championships, first held in New Zealand in 2000.[2] A unique offshoot of this is mountain bike orienteering in which riders strategize to reach control flags located at remote destinations over two days carrying everything they need on their mountain bikes.[3] When combined in an elaborate mixture of terrain, travel, and time, mountain biking, back-country running and twenty-four-hour navigation together form the backbone of adventure racing.

Triathlons, or 'multisport' endurance races, have expanded to take on such new combinations of adventure challenges, becoming multipursuit, multiterrain, multiday expedition epics. Adventure-based endurance races have thus emerged as a new form of cultural use of the outdoors. Distinguished from recreational outdoor pursuits, such as rock climbing or ski mountaineering, and competitive outdoor sports, such as sport climbing or ski racing, outdoor adventure races have married the two into a strangely paradoxical activity: a wilderness journey with a deadline.

Outdoor pursuits are most often treated as ends in themselves for personal challenge, self-development, and recreation.[4] The main objective is to acquire skill and competence. For some their display also becomes a performance, an art form. Rock climbing, for example, has aesthetic and rhythmic qualities which liken its careful execution to vertical dance. Climbing partners and spectators become the audience to outdoor ballet. Extended expeditions into wilderness areas, however, integrate the skill and art of outdoor pursuits with collective abilities, knowledge, history, and experience. Rock climbing may be as necessary as ice climbing to reach a pass or peak, abseiling is a means of retreat which often makes use of fixed ropes left by other climbers, local area knowledge helps in negotiating weather patterns, and experienced leadership unites an expedition in overcoming risks and unexpected obstacles. Individual outdoor pursuits are the means; the end is the whole journey.

Adventurers also have a long history of journeys into wilderness for *its* own sake, for spiritual experiences found only in the rawness of nature. The archetypal quest for the triumph of exploration and survival is deeply etched in human mythologies.[5] But quests for 'wild' places untamed—even untouched—by 'man,' for the edge of known feats, and for new depths to the human spirit inevitably require new sites for adventurers. As more and more remote locations are 'discovered' and documented, adventure sites are disconnected from tracts of land and resituated in a particular cultural formation: the first ascent by a British party, an all-women's expedition, the Cameron Descent, the Extreme Whitewater Kayak Race Series and so on. Competition for new human endeavours yields new mixtures of action, place, time and technology assembled for every contest. Innovation demands hybrids of what were once the newest crazes: heli-skiing, heli-bungee jumping (or adventure flying), ash skiing, snow rafting, night rafting, canyoneering and coasteering. Where it once 'made' history to be 'the first,' each now claims to be 'the ultimate.' Adventure racing is one such unlikely hybrid which emerged in the "action culture"[6] of the 1990s. In this context, it invites closer examination.

This chapter sketches the origins of multisport endurance races in New Zealand and then points to differences in race culture emerging from within the genre of endurance sport by outlining three related international adventure races. The Raid Gauloises, "the toughest and most dangerous adventure race in the world," was launched in New Zealand in 1989. A French corporate group brought the "original" adventure race to a country already historically constructed on traditions of outdoor hardship, physical prowess, and teamwork.[7] New Zealand teams won first, second, and third-place finishes in the inaugural race.[8] The race is held in a different country each year, and New Zealanders continue to be on winning teams. The Southern Traverse, New Zealand's "acclaimed"[9] adventure race, was started in 1991 by a water safety expert who had worked for the first Raid Gauloises two years earlier. A competitor himself, the founder of the Southern Traverse has also since raced in four Eco-Challenge races.[10] The Eco-Challenge, "the world's toughest endurance event,"[11] was first held in 1995 and won by the same New Zealand team in 1996 and 1997.[12] That team, Eco-Internet, also won the 1996 Southern Traverse and the 1998 Raid Gauloises[13] and placed second in the 1998 Southern Traverse.[14]

Descriptions of adventure races inevitably involve results. Race literature, however, insists that winning is not what adventure races are about. They are, according to one race director, "about challenging the competitors, not beating them."[15] Part of the concept is that "many participants aren't in the [race] 'just to win.' Personal growth is far more important to them than competition . . . . Victory is more than winning—it is success in completing an exceptional task, an extraordinary experience."[16] As little empirical research has been conducted into the experience or the nature of adventure racing, my exploratory analysis is based on popular media and electronic Web site files, as well as race newsletters, race reports, personal communication, and telephone interviews in New Zealand. As the founder of one race credits New Zealand with inventing "highly successful multisport endurance competitions" in the early 1980s,[17] this chapter focuses on races from the perspective of this country. New Zealand's consistently high profile in extreme wilderness ventures is also of particular interest in light of explicit connections made in media accounts between New Zealand's national identity and Kiwi competitors' stamina, grit, and grace.[18]

Multisport from Coast to Coast

> 90 kilometers across the Auckland isthmus from the Tasman Sea to the Pacific Ocean. It's a race, it's an adventure, it's a journey of discovery through Auckland's surprisingly wild places.[19]

In New Zealand, multisport events are generally held over one to two days in a local venue and comprise some variation on the 'original' triathlon's swim, cycle, and run segments.[20] The terrain may vary depending on whether the cycle or run is around the city or through downtown. While some courses are designed to follow natural areas such as steep hills, open water, or a forest track, increasingly, urban courses are designed for spectator vantage points and media coverage within "the contours of the city."[21]

The first triathlon in New Zealand was held in 1978 in Auckland as the Les Mills Ironman Championship race (an 800-meter swim, 12-kilometer run and 30-kilometer cycle). Based on surf championships, the ironman concept capitalized on the strong tradition of voluntary surf lifesaving training in New Zealand. The Les Mills event "was seen as the ultimate in adventure and endurance."[22] Twenty-two years later, at the 2000 Summer Games in Sydney, the triathlon was included in the Olympics for the first time. But multisport competitor and commentator John Hellemans calls it the "New Age triathlon," following a formula that is "purely performance with little real adventure." Not a real contest, this is instead "a slick moving operation where television and commercial interests dictate and where athletes are the superbly fit actors." In contrast, he sees the traditional triathlon as "an honest physical and mental challenge between yourself and the course, but never with too many risks" or any competitor "out of control."

"Real adventure," claims Hellemans, may still be found "through multisport events like New Zealand's Coast to Coast and similar races, also offsprings of the original triathlon," but which have resisted the new formula. As they emerged in the early 1980s, these alternative races moved competitions out of the cities, extended their duration, and altered some of the disciplines, usually substituting kayaking for swimming. Once in the hills or on the water, distance is not the only test. For example, the Speight's Coast to Coast, New Zealand's best-known endurance race, is a traverse of the Southern Alps in which the severity of New Zealand's alpine terrain also tests the endurance of the participants, "always with the mighty landscape as an impressive backdrop."[23]

Coast to Coast participants start at dawn with one foot in the Tasman Sea on the west coast and finish the race at the Pacific Ocean on the east coast. They cover 240 kilometers cycling, running, and paddling across the South Island. Designed to take two days, the race involves an overnight camp in native beech forest on the eastern side of the Main Divide. To reach the end of day one requires a beach run, a road cycle and a run up and then down the boulder beds of the Deception and Mingha rivers, crossing the Alps at 1,068 meters above sea level. Participants replenish themselves with food, rest, first aid, clean clothes, technical advice, and moral support overnight. Day two comprises a road cycle, a downriver paddle through the Waimakariri River gorges, and a second cycle into the now "legendary" easterly headwind across the Canterbury Plain and through the city of Christchurch to the beach.[24] Over the two race days the *longest* "record time" is twenty-four hours and thirty-seven minutes.[25]

Within the Coast to Coast, another race has evolved in the challenge to tackle the whole distance at once. The Longest Day race is for "those looking for the ultimate endurance challenge," once a description of the Coast to Coast itself. The Longest Day intensifies for the real "contenders" when they attempt to beat the time of twelve hours. The original two-day challenge has now become "the event of the masses" to which competitors return year after year.[26]

The mass appeal of the event is indeed evident in numbers. According to race director Robin Judkins, the race became very popular in 1986, its fourth year, and by 1989 applications for entry exceeded the limit. Whereas entries had previously been accepted on a 'first come, first served' basis, they had to be chosen by lottery (literally "out of a hat") after that year.[27] By the fifteenth year of the race, 1997, there were 2,220 applicants for 775 places.[28] The Department of Conservation, which manages the land estate on which 28 percent of the race takes place, agreed to increase the number of competitors allowed in 1998 as long as environmental impact was not significantly increased.[29] The decision also reportedly required changes "to make the transition area safer for spectators and crew."[30]

Supporters, spectators, and media teams contribute to the noted summer phenomenon, "Coast to Coast fever."[31] "Just about everyone in New Zealand knows of the Speight's Coast to Coast," enthuses one competitor.[32] Evening news television coverage developed in recent years with the inevitable stories of winners and nonfinishers may account for this. In bizarre circumstances at the race's start, cameras record their own contest with racers for the road. Lights glare and reflectors glow in the dawn darkness as the starting line of cyclists snakes by vehicles trying to match their speed in order to convey individual faces.[33]

With growth in numbers, the race has also had to accommodate increased support for competitors. No longer the generosity of a friend who comes along to drop off the equipment, now support means having a crew of helpers to set up camp, transport enough gear for a choice on the day (of boats or running shoes,[34] for example), and advise on navigation and tactics.[35] With cyclists, organizers, media vehicles, support crews, and spectators all traveling the one, steep, single-lane, sharply curving alpine road between coasts, Coast to Coast fever also produces an infamous "driving marathon."[36]

In the 1980s the Coast to Coast was not in a circuit of multisport races, rather it was just one of "about 35" summer races.[37] And to New Zealanders it was special and unrivaled. It was "not merely a race, [but] a concept," one commentator notes, "a two hundred and forty kilometer adventure from one side of godzone to the other."[38] Even today, competitors recommend, "enter it as an event, rather than a race."[39] They echo Hellemans' reflections on "those early days of triathlon" when, he says, participants aimed to "go the distance" rather than to compete.[40]

The modest " 'can do' mentality"[41] of popular culture may explain the motivation for ordinary people to 'have a go' at extremely difficult physical activities for recreation. A Canadian competitor openly speculates that entering the race just "for the experience" is an attitude typical of the New Zealand character.[42]

Even in magazines, experts share race tips and training schedules next to the best of a competition for readers' personal vignettes;[43] everyone can compete and be a winner. A first-time Coast to Coast competitor advises, "I am testimony to the fact that you don't have to be an athlete to compete in the Speight's Coast to Coast . . . be well prepared, have an understanding partner, a generous budget, a sense of adventure and a good sense of humor." She summarizes her involvement with unself-conscious understatement (despite being a novice): "the whole event was pure enjoyment—filled with some neat people and beautiful scenery."[44]

Personifying the 'have a go' attitude, race director Robin Judkins is perhaps the best-known spokesperson for the event. His enthusiastic involvement may contribute to its continued popularity. Just two years after the first Les Mills Ironman Championship in Auckland, Judkins organized the Alpine Ironman in Wanaka, where he had founded an adventure center.[45] And after a number of alpine-to-sea expeditions, Judkins tackled a coast-to-coast transalpine trip in 1982. Taking twenty-two and a half hours, it was reportedly "a saga"; the next year he invited other New Zealanders to try it.[46] Fifteen years later, he is said to embody the spirit of the Coast to Coast, still welcoming each of the competitors personally as they arrive at Klondyke Corner, the same overnight camp site on the same route, and at the race's finish.[47] And in 1990, he also organized the Cape Reinga to Bluff Xerox Challenge, a twenty-one-day, north-south race covering 2,500 kilometers. It is the longest coast-to-coast event that he knows of in the world. Participating himself in 47 adventure races since 1980, Judkins has been called one of the "characters" created through the history of adventure racing in this country.[48]

Within New Zealand, others have tried to capitalize on the concept by designing races that cross the country. The Express, a two-day multisport event between the cites of Napier, on the Pacific, and Wanganui, on the Tasman, was "billed as the North Island's Coast to Coast" for its launch in March 1997. Competitors later conceded that it was "a fair description." The men's individual winner had won the two-day Coast to Coast the previous month, but found the Express "even more demanding."[49] Such comments, and the position of the Express following the Coast to Coast on the multisport 'event calendar,' may perhaps shift the Coast to Coast from its ascribed place as the ultimate endurance race to that of a mere training event for harder challenges.

Internationally, Judkins' concept is credited with generating another Coast to Coast in Scotland, where the harsh, glacial terrain is much like that of New Zealand. The inaugural race held in 1995 attracted few competitors, but improvements the following year saw entries double to 130.[50] A loose affiliation appears to have developed: the prize for winners of the 1997 Longest Day was an entry in the Scottish Coast to Coast later the same year, and competitors in the Scottish event have traveled to New Zealand to experience the southern version.[51]

Scottish entrants in the New Zealand Coast to Coast are more than simply visiting 'offspring,' but are part of a trend in which athletes travel to compete outside their own countries. Following the February 1997 race, the Longest Day women's race winner told a journalist that she was preparing to participate later that year in the X Games in the United States, the Eco-Challenge in Australia, the Scottish Coast to Coast, and the Swiss Mountain Race.[52] It had been her first Coast to Coast.

The growing trend of competitors following an emergent endurance race circuit is constitutive of an increasingly professionalized cohort of racers.[53] This group in turn creates the need for a year-round calendar of races, an administrative infrastructure, and a definition of terms.[54] In 1997, the Coast to Coast, for example, had fifty-five overseas entrants—a "record number of internationals."[55] International competitors are important to race organizers, not for their particular national identity or diversity of competitive experience, but rather, argues one journalist, for the media coverage they attract. They are a key to "internationalizing" an event. An English participant, for example, who saw the Coast to Coast on Sky Television in Britain, entered the race while working in New Zealand as a university research fellow, a fact noted in the New Zealand media. A record of international interest is deemed the best way to encourage and retain what has, in the past, been hard-to-come-by media coverage for multisport events.

The 1997 Coast to Coast also recorded its highest level of women entrants, doubling their numbers to comprise 25 percent of competitors. "The emergence of the female presence this Longest Day" was also noted, as nineteen women entered that race.[56] Unfortunately, few details are reported by the media, as insights into the experiences of the women racers would make the phenomenon socially meaningful. For example, Andrea Murray, women's race winner of the Longest Day, was greeted by her twelve-month-old son at the finish line.[57] What might such an accomplishment mean for a woman who had, most likely, recently given birth, could have been breastfeeding, and would presumably have had to organize child care with or without the help of her husband (himself a competitor—men's race winner of the Longest Day the same year— and a doctor) while training and competing?[58] Interestingly, Judkins explains that "for the first time we've attracted substantial numbers of women not so much as contenders as for personal reasons."[59] This is possibly a reference to the fact that no women have yet broken "the magical 12 hour barrier" in the Longest Day, though twelve male competitors ("contenders") did complete the 1997 one-day race in under twelve hours.[60]

The Raid Gauloises assured the presence of women from the start by requiring that "the five-person teams must have at least one woman."[61] The practice was adopted in turn by the Eco-Challenge and the Southern Traverse. The race director for the latter, Geoff Hunt, believes that the rule has served the purpose of encouraging women to become involved, as evident in the all-women teams and women's divisions in many adventure races. He too notes that the numbers are increasing in the Coast to Coast and that "there are more women in the outdoors generally now."[62]

Adventure Racing

> The successful formula? A start and finish line containing 500km of non-stop racing in teams of five, with at least one woman—a race in complete autonomy with nature, with no use of motorized means.[63]

The Raid Gauloises, Eco-Challenge, and Southern Traverse, however, are quite different races from the Coast to Coast and other multisport events in New Zealand. While the shorter, triathlon-inspired races involve individual competitors using sealed roads for cycling sections, adventure-based races may be better defined by team competition, longer duration, and non-reliance on roads.[64] For example, in the ECNZ Tuatapere Wild Challenge on the southern coast, "very little of the 100km circuit can be reached by road—not even the start point" situated on a lakeshore. Competitors, race officials, and supporters are ferried by boat, but "getting kayaks out or teams in and out of the change-over point is more difficult and has to be done by helicopter." It has been dubbed "not your average multisport event" because this race takes racers through remote, dense and "primeval" wilderness: a "deep dark lake, steep hills covered in thick native bush and a backdrop of mountain peaks with a fresh sprinkling of snow."[65] However, team members actually race individually, each in different sections, the race follows established tracks, and the race is only two days in duration. This race sits just between "your average" multisport race and what are now characterized as the "off-road adventure races."[66]

In reality, adventure races often use roads. Geoff Hunt's more pragmatic account for the difference is that New Zealanders tend to use the term 'multisport,' while Americans use the term 'adventure racing.'[67] In the United States, Eco-Challenge race director Mark Burnett claims that "the adventure race" was *his* concept, registered in 1992, "following which adventure racing was born."[68] Although himself not American, he explains that he sought to create and bring "a new type of outdoor race to North America,"[69] apparently distancing himself from established multisport races and race culture in New Zealand.

> My intent was that adventure racing would be a defining term to better explain what Eco-Challenge was, essentially an expedition with a stopwatch. However, I failed to control a definition and since then adventure racing has grown to become a murky and undefined name used by all who are involved in outdoor competitions. While not intending to attempt to restrict other groups from using "adventure racing" as they wish, I have decided to redefine Eco-Challenge and have chosen "Expedition Racing" as the category and "The Expedition Race" as the tagline for Eco-Challenge. I will soon be announcing, along with other race organizers, the Federation of Expedition Racing Organizers (FERO) which will oversee and manage expedition racing.[70]

Robin Judkins would also question any real distinction between multisport races, adventure racing, and expedition racing. Clearly, the proliferation of terms indicates differences in the ways that race culture articulates itself, but may also represent a contest for what could be called brand identification. The Raid Gauloises Internet home page claims that each year's race is another edition of "the original outdoor adventure sport competition."[71] Judkins is scathing of French and American attempts to capture the space of "the original," insisting that New Zealanders were adventuring long before the advent of and further than the 'big' international races and New Zealanders continue to demonstrate their abilities by winning them. To his mind, they are all adventure races.[72]

Adventure introduces a new quality to the endurance race experience: isolated, field-based decision-making for 'safe' encounters with risk.[73] In the risk recreation literature, adventure is defined as any activity with an uncertain outcome, influenced by individual experience, perception, and skill, among other uncontrollable factors, such as weather conditions. Risk is commonly defined as the potential for danger and loss.[74] High-risk adventures require high levels of planning, preparation, and competence, including skill, strength, fitness, and training. Adventure racing, however, is a high-risk pursuit for which there can never be adequate planning; a team commits itself to reach a goal set by somebody else. Participants are confronted with constant choices in negotiating their route, pace, use of equipment, bodily needs, and, indeed, group goals. They cannot know the length of their trip in days, the length of time they will spend in various environments, or the food they must carry for those environments. They cannot know if their training will prepare them adequately for the terrain, weather, or other "nature dangers"[75] of the race course. Teams are under intense pressure to make safe judgments, for speed, time, and their stamina, but also to bond, that is to communicate and 'journey' well, as all members must finish the race together. Finally, team members are racing in remote (though not always foreign), unpredictable, and hazardous environments, for which neither they nor race organizers can ever be completely prepared, pages of prerace briefings notwithstanding.

Whereas risk recreation has been characterized as about private achievement, intrinsic motivation, and cooperative relationships,[76] adventure races are more public, commercialized displays, with extrinsic rewards, including sponsors' products and prize money, and are, despite some promotional materials, entirely competitive in nature. Notably, as the race circuit has become more established and athletes use one race to train for the next, race experiences were less likely to be 'adventurous,' that is, unpredictable in outcome. For example, the electronic team information posted by the 1998 Raid Gauloises for Team Salomon Presidio, made up of former Team Eco-Internet members, predicted that "this team of competitive athletes has come to win the race," and the official press release concluded, "they said they had come to win; mission accomplished." Each athlete had competed in previous Raids and four of the five had been on more than one winning team in past Eco-Challenges, Southern Traverses, or Raids.[77] Risk in this context becomes less an unpredicted hazard and more a magnification of known threats with deliberately contrived pressures simply intensified by the presence of "Mother Earth."[78] In at least one international race, when teams present their passport at field checkpoints, they are instantly ranked and often informed of other teams' progress. Consequently, the news of their own gain or loss since the last checkpoint becomes a new pressure on the team through the next leg and almost negates the notion that these races are wilderness expeditions with their own rhythm that happen to have a finite time limit.[79]

And yet, there exists a clear conception of adventure racing as recreational, even an enjoyable lifestyle, contributing to an enhanced quality of life. Successful adventure racers are often those who have disconnected their group performance from media and race officials' interest in ranking winners and shifted the terms of their commitment to a more interpersonal level. Ironically, as "the winners," they must then protest that winning was not their goal.[80] Race management often promotes this very paradox. Especially in the Eco-Challenge, teams are highlighted for their compassion for members and for their cooperative efforts to keep other teams in the race.[81] Teams that compete year after year are portrayed as part of the community and history of the whole event: "the veterans" reportedly return to compete "fueled by memories a continent away" of the previous race.[82] Individual competitors do return to compete, sometimes reconstituting teams of the same name in various ways.[83] Lifelong friendships are claimed beyond team boundaries, even when previous teammates resurface as rivals.[84] Yet, while claiming that they race "for fun," participants have admitted to taking painkillers to survive and even deer velvet, for "strength and endurance," on the Southern Traverse and Eco-Challenge races.[85] Brief descriptions of the 'established' international races may help to illustrate how contradictions such as these in the nature of racing experiences are constructing a new cultural form of sport in the wilderness.

"The Raid Gauloises: A State of Mind"[86]

When the Raid Gauloises was introduced in New Zealand in 1989, dramatic photographs of runners, riders, and horses galloping through alpine valleys symbolized the arrival of a new breed of hard and fast adventurers covering fantastic territory at superhuman speeds. It was reported that "the ultimate in adventure sport" was "being brought to New Zealand . . . by a band of French thrillseekers."[87]

Called The Grand Traverse, the inaugural race attracted twenty-six five-person teams, mainly from Europe, each paying NZ$13,000 in entry fees.[88] The 400-kilometer course traversed the Main Divide in the spectacular heart of the Southern Alps (just south of the Coast to Coast route) to finish amidst the glacially sculpted Southern Lakes. The planning took almost three years, and the secret route design was contracted to a New Zealand consultancy. It was the project of "Gerard Fusil, a French reporter who specializes in adventure sport," who had turned to New Zealand in search of "unspoilt countryside."[89] Race information now promotes the race as "the international leader in the field of adventure racing"[90] and "the 'Grand daddy' of sport and adventure events," claiming that with its New Zealand-based race almost ten years before it was "the first to enter the world of adventure racing."[91]

Translated, the name *Raid* literally means trek, expedition, or a raid on territory, although the latter is considered a military meaning; Gauloises is a cigarette producer, although sponsorship links are not explicit. The conviction of race organizers is that it makes the highest demands possible on the modern day 'rugged individual,' in every moral, political, and physical sense of that term. "The true innovation of the Raid Gauloises was to appeal to Man, to his untapped resources, and to his energy. In the Raid Gauloises, with no mechanical mean [sic] and in complete autonomy, Man must face himself and Nature." Emphasis in the Raid Gauloises is placed on the race's "simplicity": "this is absolute self-sufficiency, total immersion in a natural environment; the discovery of others, oneself, and another kind of life far removed from the everyday existence of modern society."[92]

For such a kind of life, competitors must train and discipline their bodies to maintain incredible strength for six to ten days on end. Race distances have stretched from 400 kilometers to 600 kilometers over the nine years of the Raid. Participants must be prepared to trek or run-walk for at least 30 percent of the race; as race information describes it, "you can go anywhere on foot."[93] Reaching various check-points involves navigation and route choice. Additional techniques are used to manage changes in terrain from desert, canyons, caves, rock faces, mountains, and volcanoes to glaciers, snow fields, forest, or jungle. Then there are canals, rivers, large lakes, or seas for which, when swimming is not possible, nonmotorized transport has included rafts, canoes, dugout canoes, and sea kayaks. Additionally, mountain bikes are de rigueur, while horses, camels, parachutes, and even gliders have been included at different times.

As any 'leg' of the course may take hours or days, participants must be technical experts in the use and repair of their equipment and also in the care of their animals. Horseback riding, for example, has enforced rest stops for the horses' sake. "Ride and run" was introduced so that horses would travel at the pace of the slowest runner; according to race organizers, "experience has shown that the competitors are often more resistant than the horses, which explains why teams have been seen dragging tired horses on foot at the end of the ride and run sections."[94] Many competitors arrive as recognized world champions in one particular discipline, that is, a sport such as mountain biking or kayaking, and aim to excel in the leg(s) of the race involving that discipline.[95] Teams may have two support persons to rendezvous with the team at checkpoints with food, first aid, and new equipment.[96]

Raid participants must be experienced in living in high-risk, backcountry environments, but must cope with any conditions in the country to which they travel for a race, generally with very little time in which to acclimatize to changes. After New Zealand, races were held in the diverse locations of Costa Rica, New Caledonia, Oman, Madagascar, Malaysia, Argentina, South Africa/ Lesotho, and Ecuador. According to organizers, the design of a race is based on the landscape: "competitors follow the course by exclusive use of natural means appropriate to the terrain being covered and the traditions of the host country. The mountains, forests, and rivers themselves are the determining factors."[97] Experienced racers know that the elements can transform the terrain in hours; teams that are struggling may even race a completely separate race as they endure a change in microclimatic conditions.[98] And, as each year organizers search out locations featuring new extremes of wilderness terrain, it could be argued that race directors design races to test new extremes of endurance within new elements.

The Raid Gauloises is distinct from other races in stressing that teams must approach the race with respect for indigenous people and their customs. The implication is that the race contributes to local life. The starting leg of the 1991 race, for example, incorporated traditional craft "handmade by the Kunie tribesmen"[99] of New Caledonia. "The 37 dugout canoes built for the event are now being used for fishing" by the families who recovered traditional knowledge in order to build them. They had been using motorboats.[100]

Paradoxically, though, the Raid Gauloises hopes overall to capture a transcendent "spirit of adventure" in what it claims is a "unique" though "universal"[101] way:

The Raid Gauloises brings world class athletes, endurant [sic] sportsmen and women, and nature lovers together in a marvellous human challenge: to finish in a complete team of five within the time limit. The Raid Gauloises goes beyond the discovery of a country, of the sometimes anachronistic lifestyles of the natives; it transcends values often forgotten and lost in our daily lives: solidarity, team spirit, the ability to adapt, serenity, the pleasure and pride we find in our accomplishments.[102]

Overwhelming interest in the event, argue the organizers, demonstrates "that outdoor-adventure-sports are becoming increasingly popular internationally and participation is no longer reserved for elite sports people, they appeal to a new brand of adventure-sports-athletes."[103] The offer of "a huge [NZ]$104,000 prize purse" in the inaugural Raid must have had some impact on the production of this new brand of highly mobile, high-achieving racers. In addition, "international media coverage is guaranteed because of its extravagant nature,"[104] noted one report wryly.

Southern Traverse: A "Race Against Nature and Each Other"[105]

The Southern Traverse was first raced in New Zealand in 1991, explicitly modeled on The Grand Traverse.[106] Up to and including 1998, the course traveled much the same geographical area as the first Raid, "over 400 kms through some of the most spectacular scenery of the magnificent Southern Alps of the South Island, with serrated mountain ridges, glacial formed [sic] valleys, bush-fringed lakes, clear pulsating rivers and pure crystal alpine air." In contrast to organizers offering the 'discovery' of a different country every year, the Southern Traverse is held in the same country every year on different routes.[107] The deep, dense, and rarely traveled southwestern valleys of New Zealand have provided substantial scope for challenging route design. Indeed, race director Geoff Hunt said of the 1998 race, "The most difficult part of this year's race is going to be the navigation."[108]

Promoters claim that "the Southern Traverse is now clearly recognized as a leader in the adventure racing world, not only in New Zealand but overseas."[109] In New Zealand, press coverage rarely mentioned one of the established three races without comparing it to, or listing racers' previous participation in, the others.[110] As with the Raid Gauloises and the Eco-Challenge, on-line reports of the

race are posted daily while the race is under way; "cybercast" journalists have in the past called the Southern Traverse "the queen
mother of all multisport races" and "the biggest little adventure
race in the world."[111]

Following "race tradition," neither the route nor the starting
point is revealed to the media or racers until just days before the
race.[112] For the first four years this event was a two- and then a
three-day race. It was estimated that the course would take four to
five days of non-stop racing in 1998, "the longest there's been,"
according to Hunt.[113] The different 'sections' have estimated times,
also given to teams at the prerace briefing. As in other races, teams
must decide when to stop and for how long they will sleep; in 1998
the winning team slept just three hours in 91.5 hours of racing.
Racers meet their support crews (of two or more persons) at check-
points for a change of food, equipment, and first aid.[114] Teams are
comprised of three or five men and women. Until 1996, when a
five-member Team Eco-Internet finished first, no five-person teams
had won the race. In 1998 there were three divisions for the three-
person teams: men, women and mixed; five-person teams are mixed
only. (Interestingly, the first all-women team to finish the race did
so in 1995,[115] the year that the first all-women team competed in
the Raid Gauloises in Argentina.[116])

The Southern Traverse is distinct from other races in that
participants are specifically called upon to use their skills and knowledge in an extremely isolated alpine environment, while mountain
running, mountain biking, and alpine kayaking.[117] In some ways,
this is the closest international adventure race to a backcountry
triathlon in that it uses the same three unglamorous disciplines in
various combinations year after year and unapologetically pits competitors against "the elements, terrain, and pain barriers."[118] In New
Zealand, all participants use their own equipment, including their
choice of boats (a choice not provided in the Eco-Challenge, where
race organizers supply the rafts, canoes, and sea kayaks to be used
on the different sections). In a telling comparison, one participant
says, "Geoff's very safety conscious, but there's just not the back-
stops that are there in the big Eco Challenges. You're on your own
in the Southern Traverse, there's no two ways about that."[119]

In other ways, the Southern Traverse is as extravagant and
ambitious as "the two established biggies."[120] After acquiring a
contract for a National Geographic documentary of the 1998 race,
race director Geoff Hunt was quoted as saying, "I can now attract
a serious sponsor."[121] The announcement of the media coup em-

phasized that National Geographic Television would "beam" the race "into hundreds of millions of homes around the world," giving the race the "exposure [needed to] put it on an equal footing with the Discovery [Channel] Eco-Challenge and the Raid Gauloises."[122]

In fact, the Southern Traverse had already attracted a media presence. One participant in the 1997 race reported that soon after the 10 AM start on Day 1, "it was actually a beautiful sunny day and we got interviewed by Sky TV"; later, when her team completed "a 1000m climb straight up a scrub-covered slope onto the Jumbo ridge ... we also got buzzed by the not-very-helpful Sky helicopter which seemed determined to blow me off the lip I was scrambling over and did do [so] for Scott's hat."[123] Reporters and photographers also use the transitions (changeover points between disciplines) and accessible shelters, such as a snow cave or ski lodge, to wait for teams, soliciting a quick word when they arrive for some sleep.[124] Increased media attendance gives race directors an additional organizational task: planning "where [documentary] shots will be most effective ... where the crews need to be and when they should be there."[125]

The traveling cohort of international competitors also gives the Southern Traverse exposure in an increasingly personality-focused media. Newspaper reports give the names of competitors who are winners of other races and highlight the countries from which teams enter; the list for 1997, billed then as the "biggest field ever," included Brazil, Japan, Australia, Canada, the United States, England, France, Germany, and New Zealand.[126] Focus is on the escapades of foreign competitors unused to the New Zealand high country. In 1996, the Japanese team East Wind GIII slept as it snowed and was woken when another team stumbled over the bodies of team members buried in fresh snow.[127] In 1997, the lost Brazilians burned their socks and underwear in order to keep warm in terrifying high winds and rain; they were rescued before reaching even the first check-point.[128] An American who slipped in the rain on exposed rock above a 100-meter drop to a swollen creek was prevented from falling by a Queenstown mountain guide who reached out his hand; "He saved my life," she was reported as gasping afterwards.[129] Tales of near tragedy and heroism are as valuable to the waiting media as a sound bite to construct stories of 'universal' human striving and endurance.

The better-known the competitors, the greater the benefit for the (after all, commercial) race organization. More competitors register each year as stories of extraordinary experiences circulate.

Not surprisingly, media corporations are now major partners in the three 'big' races (Fun Radio for the Raid Gauloises, Discovery Channel for the Eco-Challenge, and now National Geographic Television for the Southern Traverse).[130] However, the representation of adventure racers as more than elite athletes who happen to do well in wilderness conditions, but as a cohort of personalities who regularly compete in the same races, who do it because they love the outdoors, and who are even friends, also creates what could be called a renewable resource for race organizers.

Race director Geoff Hunt lists the names of world champion endurance athletes who have participated in the Southern Traverse on its Web site: Steve Gurney, John Howard, Robert Nagle, Ian Adamson, Keith Murray, Jenny Rose, Grant Dalton and John Jacoby; the same names appear in stories of struggle and victory in the Raid Gauloises and the Eco-Challenge.[131] A tribute from round-the-world New Zealand yachtsman Grant Dalton, on Team Chiquita in 1994,[132] is also posted on the site. It suggests that even superhuman athletes find themselves merely mortal when deep in the bush and in need of a strong dose of confidence-building. Emphasis on achievable ("I tackled the hardest event in the country and survived") feats democratizes the event's elitist gloss.[133] The image is so strong that a news story previewing the 1998 event carried a photo of the 1994 team, still capitalizing on Dalton's fame.[134] In contrast, the news story itself profiles a different kind of competitor, "a wild man adventurer in his spare time." Bill Godsall has raced every Southern Traverse held, "three times stepping onto the winner's podium." He is portrayed as a "mild-mannered" father who actually enjoys off-road wilderness bushwalking—the rugged Kiwi man in the backblocks.[135] According to a fellow competitor, he pays little attention to race glamor and hype.[136] Undoubtedly, for all adventure races, media reporters who focus on the already famous, the local characters, and the 'hot' teams increasingly contribute to 'making'[137] the history and culture of adventure racing.

Eco-Challenge: "An Ecologically
Aware Wilderness Expedition Competition"[138]

Media descriptions of the "fantastic terrain"[139] through which adventurers run yield little in the way of information about the wilderness itself, the indigenous species, their relationships, or their habitat. The Eco-Challenge was established specifically to highlight the environments through which it is possible to travel with minimum impact and to produce a new appreciation of global ecosystems and their diversity. Mark Burnett initiated a broad scheme three years before the first adventure race was held; he founded Eco-Challenge Lifestyles, Inc. in 1992 to promote "a positive environmental message." He then partnered with the United States-based Discovery Channel to finance his vision: to bring the best out of people when teamwork and problem-solving are put into the service of Discovery Channel's philosophy of "exploration and adventure in the pursuit of scientific knowledge."[140] The first race was held in Utah in 1995, a youth adventure camp was hosted in California in 1995, a year-round adventure training school for aspirant racers was started in California in 1996, and then Eco-Challenge Adventure Travel was formed for interested tourists to spectate at race venues in 1997.[141]

The Eco-Challenge race itself is named for more than just attitudes. Race rules dictate strict environmental practices: "In travelling the remote back country areas, one needs to be both skilled in the outdoors and aware that one cannot conquer the land but merely hope to pass through peacefully. All competitions follow responsible back country rules: pack it in, pack it out; no camp fires; camp and travel only where permitted."[142] The explicit focus on these values makes the Eco-Challenge distinct from other races, and they are reinforced by the inclusion of an environmental service project at the location of every race.[143] A philosophy of service underpins the expectation of responsible action, and this endorsement is carried through race literature emphasizing a spirit of compassion.[144]

In the media, however, this expedition race is presented much like the other races with no greater eco-consciousness than what is already practiced by experienced backcountry travellers, and perhaps less. In fact, there is no evidence of the environmental service project in newspaper, magazine, or electronic coverage of the 1996, 1997, or 1998 races, nor is it covered or even alluded to by the televised Discovery Channel video documentary.[145] (Indeed, the 1997 documentary shows that when race organizers themselves provided a meal at Kirrama Camp, it was served on disposable plastic plates and utensils.)[146] Furthermore, no details of an environmental project were given to participants of the 1998 Morocco race in prerace newsletters.[147] One racer later described the 1998 project, cleaning up a local beach with village children, as a token gesture, saying that it did not appear to be mandatory and not all racers took part. She said that litter was found on the race course by her team and that solid human waste was not packed out and was sometimes found lying exposed on the trail.[148] The official press release announcing the 1999 race host, Argentina, makes no mention of a service project or environmental activities before the race.[149] Environmental values were not highlighted in the hourlong promotional concert by Argentineans given for 1998 racers after the Morocco race.[150]

Through the 1997 Discovery Channel video documentary, viewers actually see the environments in which racers trek, paddle, swim, climb, abseil, and cycle, from the rocky gorges of the Herbert River to the misty rainforest of Mount Bartle Frere and then the rough seas south of Cairns, yet an opportunity to learn about the actual ecosystems is lost. Ecologists have found that there are "tens of thousands of local systems . . . [grouped into] perhaps thirty major kinds . . . such as the tropical rain forest, coral reef and grassland,"[151] but the narration of the documentary says nothing about the complexity of these life-support systems. Crocodiles, leeches, and stinging tree are made into "exotic and sometimes hostile"[152] threats to human life, but viewers do not learn why they live in that habitat. 'Nature' is instead represented as the spiritual master of human destiny and "chaotic, dangerously powerful and to be feared or challenged."[153] Ecologists would find this a limited, "prescientific" cultural perception in which nature is thought to preexist human influence (that is, "minimum impact" race protocols will leave nature undisturbed as humans "pass through peacefully").[154]

Ecologically aware or not, "Eco-Challengers" attempt to complete a course of over 500 kilometers and cross the finish line with all four team members, always including one of the opposite sex, within ninety-one meters of one another. Failing to check in at a checkpoint or abide by race rules may result in a time loss penalty or disqualification.[155] Credit is sometimes given if a team stops to help other racers in distress, as happened in 1998 when Team New Zealand swept past Passport Control 2 while sea kayaking after loaning its radio to Team Just Do It France, which had swamped its boats.[156] Since 1996 no support crews have been allowed to assist racers, and huge plastic gear crates are transported by race management to various check-points for equipment, food and clothing changes.[157] All cooking, strategizing, and responsibility for team morale is shared by team members.

In this race, as much as in the others, teams must weigh up individual needs for food, drink, bodily care, rest, navigation decisions, and, most of all, sleep during the race and at camps at the end of each leg (which could comprise, for example, two or three different disciplines). Sleep deprivation is perhaps the single most devastating factor for racers to overcome—reports of all adventure races make reference to sometimes quite severe hallucinations.[158] Similar to other races, this race has included trekking or run-walking, rafting, canoeing, sea kayaking, mountain biking, horse-back riding, climbing, abseiling, canyoning, coasteering,[159] and, in 1998, camel riding. Timing must incorporate not only team members' stamina but also the hours of daylight, so that, for example, the team does not arrive at a river section, particularly for rafting, after dark, when a "dark zone" curfew restricts movement until dawn (unless a rest is planned).[160]

While racers must prepare for any disciplines, race director Mark Burnett clearly makes some choices of discipline for spectator effect. The start of the 1997 race, for example, filmed by camouflaged cameras at dusk, was "pure Hollywood," according to one reporter. Burnett swooped in by helicopter to shake the hands of the nearly 200 competitors before they launched off into the night over treacherously uneven ground.[161] Said another reporter, "The setting sun might look good on television, but it cloaked a brutal introduction to adventure racing."[162] In 1998, the mid-day race start featured a spectacular camel caravan lurching along "wind-whipped sand dunes . . . like something out of *Lawrence of Arabia*, just as race director Mark Burnett had hoped."[163] Competitors were told to expect a restart for the 'real' race farther down the beach.

Burnett is undoubtedly the most prominent force in the success of this race and indeed in the construction of the entertainment extravaganza the Eco-Challenge is becoming. Not only does his personality drive the Web site, but his almost paternalistic presence at races is recorded in media reports and the Discovery Channel documentary series. Burnett relates to racers as familiar friends when they arrive at check-points; he says of a subdued Team Eco-Internet arriving with an injury, "Just knowing them for so many years, I could tell that something was up with them."[164] Later, he enthuses to the camera about the "big extended family" created before and after the race each year. He radios the instruction for rescue crews to intervene when Team East Wind of Japan fails to cope with the coastal storm off Cairns, and he is there to debrief Team Dalriada of Northern Ireland when they must pull out of the race at the same stage.[165] His excitement and charisma seem to generate motivation—according to one participant in Morocco in 1998, "People just want to work with the guy."[166]

Working with the Discovery Channel Eco-Challenge means joining a corporate office in Beverly Hills in the business of 'packaging' exploration and discovery. Burnett is not only the "race architect,"[167] but also produces television specials about the races, dating from his experience as the leader of the first American team to enter the Raid Gauloises. He produced the 1995 Utah Eco-Challenge for MTV and the 1995 New England Eco-Challenge for ESPN. He then produced the 1996 Canada Eco-Challenge, the 1997 Australia Eco-Challenge, and the 1998 Morocco Eco-Challenge, all for Discovery Channel.[168] He explains in 'real audio' on the Web site that he wanted to "put together a package that would be something that people would just never ever forget . . . to do something typically Arabic . . . to include all the best of Morocco."[169] The television channel carries the slogan "Discover Your World" when introducing the Discovery Channel Eco-Challenge series; Eco-Challenge Lifestyles, Inc. packages the world's "best" for discovery and rediscovery.

Adventure racers, with their hopes and disappointments, help to sell the product. Andrea Murray, a member of Team Eco-Internet interviewed after its win in Australia, tells the camera, "We like adventure. And we used to like to go out into the bush at home in New Zealand and just explore. And we look at ourselves as sort of modern-day explorers, if you will, because everything *has* been explored, but *we* haven't been there."[170] The program then cuts away to a Discovery Channel advertisement for a contest aimed at viewers: "You View It, You Do It!!"[171] Extreme experiences are available to anyone who wants to 'give it a go,' to 'do' a modern day discovery, rather like sampling ethnicity through foods at a delicatessen.

Constructing Competition

Although they [sic] have a small population of 3.5 million, New Zealand has a reputation of producing great sportsmen. The team members of the All Blacks and Peter Blake (winner of the America Cup) are only two cases in point. In the first Raid Gauloises, the New Zealanders claimed the first three places. Undoubtedly, the country incites its people to adventure, to go further and to push themselves to their limits.[172]

Although there's a lot of commonality between Canada and New Zealand in terms of our treatment of open space, the Coast to Coast is a truly Kiwi thing. Your unique ability to sit down and think of the most outrageous course for an outdoor event is reflected in how well New Zealanders do in multisport endurance events offshore—the Eco-Challenge, for example.[173]

Race promoters for the Raid Gauloises and the Eco-Challenge have emphasized that participants in adventure races are just ordinary people, from many countries, "from all walks of life."[174] Together in teams, racers may express some aspect of collective motive or spirit when selecting a team name. In some races they are named for their sponsors, though Eco-Challenge race rules specifically prohibit teams wearing a corporate logo or being named for any kind of "for-profit business."[175] Teams are most frequently named by country. The concept of constructing local or national identities as the basis for competition seems antithetical to the new globalization of cultural forms and, in this case, the democratization of access to global wilderness, that is, the new adventure sites. And yet, teams are differentiated by and competition constructed through a national identity to the extent that at least one race, the Eco-Challenge, will now require all team members to be of the same country in 1999 and race under its name.[176] Already, the prerace and postrace ceremonies at the Eco-Challenge closely resemble the parade of countries preceding major international sporting contests such as the Olympic Games.[177] Racers are also given race jerseys, to be worn at all times, with a patch sewn on the sleeve simulating the flag of the country the team 'represents,' irrespective of its members' (often mixed) nationalities.[178]

The increasingly internationalized construction of competition benefits both adventure racing and New Zealand in a specific way, as both become more active cultural players in the global economy. Adventure racing is adopting more and more of the signifiers of sport as a commodity in the entertainment industry. Award-winning film and television broadcasts have been produced of every Raid Gauloises and Eco-Challenge, while the 1997 and 1998 Southern Traverse races were also filmed. Adventure racer John Howard was given the instant status of a sport icon when he was called "the Michael Jordan of adventure racing."[179] And adventure race officials now receive competitive bids to "secure" the opportunity to host the annual "event"; for example, the Australian Tourist Commission justified their successful bid by predicting (even before the 1997 Eco-Challenge race was held) that it would "generate more than AUS$80 million worth of publicity for Australia's tourism industry," while showcasing some of the "natural assets" that would attract adventure tourists, in particular "in the lead up to the Sydney 2000 Olympic Games."[180]

When the Southern Traverse acquired the contract with National Geographic Television to broadcast the 1998 race, director Geoff Hunt told a newspaper reporter that "It's not just good for the race, it's good for New Zealand."[181] The internationalization of adventure sports in wilderness extremes is also good for the local economy and national identity. It has been argued that "the origin of residence of sportsmen or women is no longer relevant in international competition, whether they be European skiers representing New Zealand, Pacific Island rugby players in England or Welshmen at the Coast to Coast."[182] But for New Zealanders, nation, sport, and (masculine) identity have been melded by the media since Sir Edmund Hillary stood on the summit of Mount Everest.[183] The cultural positioning of New Zealanders as heroic explorers is still available: one journalist observed of the 1996 Eco-Challenge, in which only four teams of seventy finished the original course, that "the presence of New Zealand multisporters in most of the front-running teams . . . was as much a source of comment as the ability of slide alder to break the spirit of teams made up of mere mortals." To be known as New Zealanders has benefited racers from this country in gaining television footage and race sponsorship, as much as the wilderness itself has served race organizers in captivating international interest (for "the country incites its people to adventure"). The ensuing success of the fourteen New Zealanders in the top seven teams in 1996 was thought to suggest that "a (relatively) long tradition of multisport racing, a familiarity with the outdoors and a 'can do' mentality is the ideal background for successful adventure racing."[184] As racers compete annually and races become more similar, experience becomes as important as stamina. It was said that the 1996 winning Team "Eco-Internet's Kiwi connection provided an experience base that was the envy of most other teams." Individual ability and experience is still tied to national history and character stereotypes; New Zealander John Howard, whose Team Eco-Internet won again in 1997, is described in the 1997 Discovery Channel Eco-Challenge documentary as a window washer who lives simply, reminiscent of Hillary's modest beekeeping career, *and* as "perhaps the best adventure racer in the world."[185] As if proving the connection between Kiwi stoicism and individual stamina over time, Howard had already won the Coast to Coast twice in the early 1980s and several Alpine Ironman races at the same time—according to one journalist, "long before Gerard Fuseil [*sic*] thought up the Raid Gauloises concept and brought it to New Zealand for its world premiere."[186]

Conclusion

The language of popular culture has devolved the meaning of adventure.[187]

Adventure racing, expedition epics and even the urban "enduros" are all aspects of a new consciousness which may or may not warrant the term *alternative,* but which pervades, as much as it is informed by, popular culture. It is a competitive style produced by global capitalism and the advent of electronic reproduction and simulation, enacted at the local level of bodies and communities. The style is constructed through a certain identifiable physicality and encounters with risk, linked by discourses of human achievement and a moral imagination. And yet, in many ways adventure racing is simply another personal indulgence for those privileged to pursue their physical fantasies on a global scale. Net-surfing eco-athletes snack at the adventure deli, work out in nature's gym and star in the made-for-television movie. While extreme endurance adventures are becoming "the established athletic achievement of the masses,"[188] adventure sites shift relative to who is having the adventure: "everything has been explored, but *we* haven't discovered it yet."

While many issues conspicuously lack attention in this short analytical foray, there is plainly much scope for future inquiry. Of most interest to me, along with the power of discourses of identity and physicality in continuing to shape how adventure races are constructed, and deconstructed, in the future, is the emergence of further action hybrids within the context of extreme experiences in 'nature's' wilderness. Could adventure racers ever complete such excruciating endurance feats without a secret course, painkillers, and a stopwatch? Are the cultural needs for extreme sport different from those for extreme adventure? In what ways is the Western world already complicit in a risk culture[189] such that the pursuit of bodily danger, that is, explicitly 'doing risk,' is the only 'real,' or available, response to living with risk (such as pollution, nuclear waste, and increased climatic damage)?

It is interesting to conclude by considering the imperative behind Gerard Fusil's project, Authentic Adventure, which debuted in 1999 as a new adventure race for teams of seven members, at least two of whom must be women, designed in two parts "to challenge both mind and body."[190] The first part is a 'classic' adventure race, and it is followed by a cooperative project with a host country which must encompass an artistic, humanitarian, scientific, cultural, or industrial initiative. Perhaps Fusil has returned to a humanistic ethic: risk experiences are still meaningful only when they build community.

Notes

1. Audrey S. Keller, "The World Mountain Bike Championships," *Hemispheres*, Sep 1994, p. 97.

2. Jill Dalton, rogaine competitor, personal communication, Auckland, New Zealand, 7 Sep 1998.

3. Rob Greenaway, "From the sublime to the ridiculous," *New Zealand Adventure*, No. 80 (Dec 96–Jan 97), p. 61.

4. Alan Ewert, *Outdoor Adventure: Foundations, Models, Pursuits and Theories* (Columbus: Publishing Horizons, 1989).

5. Joseph Campbell, *The Hero with a Thousand Faces* (Princeton: Princeton University Press, 1949); Maureen Murdock, *The Heroine's Journey* (Boston: Shambhala, 1990).

6. "Bungy company stretches into new adventure territory," *Otago Daily Times*, 21 Feb 1994, p. 20.

7. Jock Phillips, *A Man's Country?* (rev. ed.) (Auckland: Penguin Books, 1996), pp. 2–42, 264, and 272.

8. "Raid Gauloises: History," http://www.raid-gauloises.com/web_anglais/esprit-histoire/histoire/histoire1989.html.

9. David Williams, "National Geographic to broadcast race," *Otago Daily Times*, 28 Sep 1998, p. 1.

10. Geoff Hunt, Southern Traverse race director, personal communication, Queenstown, New Zealand, 14 June 1998.

11. Andrew Sanders, "True grit hardly for show," *Sunday Star-Times*, 17 Aug 1997, Sec. B, p. 10.

12. Alan Nelson, "Damn Kiwis and Slide Alder," *New Zealand Adventure*, No. 79 (Oct–Nov 1996), pp. 52–55; Nelson, "Head and Shoulders Above the Rest: The 1997 Eco-Challenge," *New Zealand Adventure*, No. 85 (Oct–Nov 1997), pp. 55–56; Sanders, "Defending champ leads," *Sunday Star-Times*, 17 Aug 1997, Sec. B, p. 10.

13. "Team Success," *Otago Daily Times*, 29 Sep 1998, p. 11.

14. Marc Hinton, "Beastly test of mind and body," *Sunday Star-Times*, 6 Dec 1998, Sec. B, p. 9.

15. Sanders, "True grit," p. 10.

16. "Raid Gauloises: A Sports-Nature-Adventure Concept," http://www.raid-gauloises.com/web_anglais/esprit-histoire/concept.html.

17. "About Eco-Challenge," http://www.ecochallenge.com/aboutEco.html.

18. Tony di Zinno & Derek Paterson, "The Biggest Little Adventure Race in the World," http://www.southerntraverse.com/html/race96.html.

19. Head 2 Head, ad, *New Zealand Adventure*, No. 90 (Aug–Sep 1998), p. 54.

20. John Hellemans, "Auckland World Cup—Wet & Wild," *New Zealand Multisport*, April–May 1997, p. 25.

21. "The Capital Quad," *New Zealand Adventure*, No. 87 (Feb–March 1998), p. 61.

22. All quotations in this paragraph from Hellemans, "Auckland World Cup," 1997, p. 25.

23. Ibid.

24. Bruce Ansley, *Coast to Coast* (Lyttelton: Icon Publishers, 1984); Margie Baker, *Coast to Coast* (Lyttelton: Icon Publishers, 1986).

25. David and Margot Burton, "The Flying Scott," *New Zealand Adventure*, No. 88 (April–May 1998), p. 54.

26. Michael Jacques, "Fifteen years from Kumara to Sumner: The Speight's Coast to Coast," *New Zealand Multisport*, April–May 1997, p. 21.

27. Robin Judkins, Coast to Coast race director, personal communication, Christchurch, New Zealand, 22 Sep 1998.

28. Jacques, "Fifteen years," p. 17.

29. An Environmental Impact Assessment is submitted to the Department of Conservation annually. (Judkins, personal communication, 1998).

30. Terry Moore, "Longest Day Grows," *New Zealand Adventure*, No. 86 (Dec 1997–Jan 1998), p. 66.

31. Jacques, "Fifteen years," p. 18.

32. Ingrid Taylor, "Be Prepared," *New Zealand Adventure*, No. 88 (April–May 1998), p. 53.

33. Jacques, "Fifteen years," p. 18.

34. Ibid., 19.

35. Dave Smith, "Support crews have their own obstacles to overcome," *Otago Daily Times*, 13 Nov 1997, p. 34.

36. Tourism Industry Association New Zealand, ad, *The Quarterly* (New Zealand Outdoor Instructors Association), No. 5 (March 1998).

37. Judkins, personal communication, 1998.

38. Jacques, "Fifteen years," p. 17.

39. Burton, "Flying Scott," p. 54.

40. Hellemans, "Auckland World Cup," p. 25.

41. For use of the phrase, Nelson, "Damn Kiwis," p. 52. For modesty and the national (male) identity, Phillips, *Man's Country*, pp. 264–265 and 277.

42. Greenaway, "The two-day, 238.8 kilometre pasta paradise," *New Zealand Adventure*, No. 82 (April–May 1997), p. 58.

43. Burton, "Flying Scott," p. 54; Chris Coll, "Coast to Coast '98 Saved My Life," *New Zealand Adventure*, No. 88 (April–May 1998), pp. 52–53; Taylor, "Be Prepared," p. 53.

44. Taylor, "Be Prepared," p. 53.

45. Judkins, personal communication, 1998; Ansley, *Coast*, 1984; Baker, *Coast*, 1986.

46. Jacques, "Fifteen years," p. 17.

47. Ansley, *Coast*, 1984; Baker, *Coast*, 1986; Jacques, "Fifteen years," p. 17.

48. Judkins, personal communication, 1998; Jacques, "Fifteen years," p. 17.

49. Daniel O'Regan, "Express Tougher than Expected," *New Zealand Adventure*, No. 83 (June–July 1997), p. 56.

50. Greenaway, "The two-day," pp. 57–58.

51. Burton, "Flying Scott," p. 54; Greenaway, "The two-day," pp. 57–58.

52. Mary Kirk-Anderson, "Andrea gets going," *New Zealand Adventure*, No. 82 (April–May 1997), p. 59.

53. Judkins (personal communication, 1998) says endurance athletes have been professional in New Zealand since 1990, although they tend to have regular jobs because there is not yet enough prize or endorsement money to live on.

54. Marc Hinton, "Exhausted Gurney's got a gripe," *Sunday Star-Times*, 29 Nov 1998, Sec. B, p. 5; Alan Nelson, "The Clash of the Dates," *New Zealand Adventure*, No. 90 (Aug–Sep 1998), p. 51.

55. Quotations and information in this paragraph from Greenaway, "The two-day," pp. 82 and 58.

56. Jacques, "Fifteen years," p. 18.

57. Jacques, "Fifteen years," pp. 17–20; Kirk-Anderson, "Andrea," p. 59.

58. The Discovery Channel documentary on the 1997 Eco-Challenge actually features a close-up shot of the then eighteen-month-old son reunited with his mother when she finishes in the winning team. ("Agony & Ecstasy" (Part 5), "Discovery Channel Eco-Challenge Australia '97," [Discovery Channel Cable Television Network] video documentary broadcast in New Zealand 30 May 1998.)

59. Jacques, "Fifteen years," p. 18.

60. Jacques, "Fifteen years," p. 20; Judkins, personal communication, 1998.

61. "The Southern Traverse: The Concept," http://www.southerntraverse.com/html/concept.html.

62. Hunt, personal communication, 1998.

63. "Raid Gauloises: Press Release No. 2 May 1998," http://www.raid-gauloises.com/web_anglais/actualites/presse2.htm.

64. The existence of roads has long been a basis to American conceptualizations of the 'wilderness' necessary for adventure: an area is most natural if roadless and hence "could not be traversed without mechanical means in a single day." Roderick Nash, *Wilderness and the American Mind*, Third Ed. (New Haven: Yale University Press, 1982), pp. 4–5.

65. David Wall, "Wild Place, Wild Race," *New Zealand Adventure*, No. 88 (April–May 1998), p. 57.

66. Nelson, "The Clash," 1998, 51.

67. Hunt, personal communication, 1998. Indeed, *New Zealand Adventure* magazine informed readers in mid-1996 that race reports, training and multisport events were to be covered as "core to every issue," and by Dec 1997, Multisport was a regular feature for *Adventure* readers alongside Tramping, Mountain Biking, Rockclimbing, and Adventure Travel. ("Despatches—From the Field: New Adventure Icons," *New Zealand Adventure*, No. 86 [Dec 1997–Jan 1998], p. 12).

68. "Eco-Challenge: What's New. Founder's Letter," http://www.eco challenge.com/founders.html.

69. "About Eco-Challenge," http://www.ecochallenge.com/aboutEco. html.

70. "Eco-Challenge: What's New," http://www.ecochallenge.com/ founders.html.

71. "Raid Gauloises: Homepage," http://www.raid-gauloises.com/ web_anglais/princi.htm.

72. Judkins, personal communication, 1998.

73. Isolated risk management, though, is perhaps diminishing as races get bigger and go farther; for example, the 1998 Eco-Challenge allowed teams two radio call-ins while at altitude to medical specialists, free from race penalties. ("Eco-Challenge: The Latest," http://www.discovery.com/ indep/ecomorocco/reports/latest.html, 13 Oct 1998.)

74. Simon Priest and Rusty Baillie, "Justifying the Risk to Others: The Real Razor's Edge, *Journal of Experiential Education*, 19(1) (1987), pp. 16–22; David W. Robinson, "The Risk Recreation Experience: Subjective State Dimensions and Transferability of Benefits," *Journal of Applied Recreation Research*, 17(1) (1992), pp. 12–36.

75. Andrew Sanders, "Hard yakka," *Sunday Star-Times*, 10 Aug 1997, Sec. B, p. 16.

76. Robinson, "Risk Recreation," p. 13.

77. "Raid Gauloises," http://www.raid-gauloises.com/web_anglais/ equateur/course/classement/f_classe.htm.

78. For use of the term by race director Mark Burnett: "Agony & Ecstasy" documentary.

79. "Kiwis Feature in Raid Gauloises," *Otago Daily Times*, 26 Sep 1998, p. 24; "The Razor's Edge" (Part 3), "Twist of Fate" (Part 4), "Agony & Ecstasy" (Part 5), "Discovery Channel Eco-Challenge Australia '97," video documentary broadcast in New Zealand 30 May 1998.

80. Team Eco-Internet was featured by Discovery Channel's 30 May 1998 documentary, and team members explain (Parts 3 and 5) how they handle this conflict. See also comments by Team Endeavour after the 1997 South Africa/Lesotho Raid Gauloises in Anne Woodley, "NZ/USA Team Second in Raid," *New Zealand Adventure*, No. 82 (April–May 1997), p. 60.

81. One team in the 1990 Raid Gauloises was noted for inflating the canoe of another team ("Raid Gauloises: History 1990 Costa Rica," http://www.raid-gauloises.com/html/history1990.html). Team East Wind carried an injured member of the team for the entire second half of the 1997 Eco-Challenge ("Twist of Fate," "Agony & Ecstasy"). In the 1998 Eco-Challenge, Team Idaho gave extra food to Team Finland after the latter miscalculated how much food it would need to carry (Trisha Smith, "The Discovery Channel Eco-Challenge Morocco: Live Coverage of the World's Toughest Expedition Race," http://www.discovery.com/indep/ecomorocco/reports/report14.html, 16 Oct 1998, p. 2.

82. Smith, "The Discovery Channel Eco-Challenge Morocco," http://www.discovery.com/indep/ecomorocco/reports/report1.html, 28 Sep 1998, p. 1.

83. The most notable example is Team Eco-Internet, which has retained the name through constant shuffles of team members. See Smith, "The Discovery Channel Eco-Challenge Morocco," http://www.discovery.com/indep/ecomorocco/reports/report8.html, 10 Oct 1998, p. 3.

84. Team Eco-Internet 1997 captain Robert Nagle tells the documentary film crew: "The people that I've raced with in the past—and it's not just the four of us that are here today, but there are others that are sort of really close to us who are racing today on other teams, um, and—we sort of form a corps and a cadre and I hope that we can continue to race. And if we can't continue to race then we will always, *always* be the greatest of friends." ("Agony & Ecstasy")

85. David Williams, "And they reckon it's fun . . . ," *Otago Daily Times*, 5 Dec 1998, Sec. C, p. 23; Murdoch Dryden, "Southern Traverse Diary," *New Zealand Adventure*, No. 90 (Aug–Sep 1998), p. 53.

86. "Raid Gauloises: Press Release No. 3 Aug 1998," http://www.raid-gauloises.com/web_anglais/actualites/presse3.htm.

87. "The Grand Traverse," *New Zealand Adventure*, No. 34–35 (May/June 1989), pp. cover and 26–27. It is interesting to consider the context of the event, that is, the aftermath of the bombing of the Greenpeace ship Rainbow Warrior in Auckland Harbor in 1986 and intense anti-French sentiment. The French reconnaissance team, pictured in dark glasses and low hats with some faces partly in shadow, not surprisingly resembles a group of secret agents.

88. "Grand Traverse," pp. 26–27; "Raid Gauloises: History," http://www.raid-gauloises.com/html/history1989.html.

89. "The Grand Traverse," p. 27.

90. "Raid Gauloises: Press Release No. 2 May 1998," http://www.raid-gauloises.com/web_anglais/actualites/presse2.htm.

91. "Raid Gauloises: Press Release No. 1 Oct 1997," http://www.raid-gauloises.com/web_anglais/actualites/presse1.htm.

92. "Raid Gauloises: Concept," http://www.raid-gauloises.com/web_anglais/esprit-histoire/concept.htm.

93. "Raid Gauloises: Disciplines," http://www.raid-gauloises.com/web_anglais/esprit-histoire/discipli.htm.

94. Ibid.

95. "Raid Gauloises: History—1995 Argentina," http://www.raid-gauloises.com/web_anglais/esprit-histoire/histoire.htm.

96. "Raid Gauloises: Concept."

97. "Raid Gauloises: Disciplines."

98. As happened in Oman: "Raid Gauloises: History 1992 Oman," http://www.raid-gauloises.com/web_anglais/esprit-histoire/histoire1992.htm; for a similar situation, see Fiona Woodham, "A Tale of Two Races—The Southern Traverse," *New Zealand Adventure*, No. 81 (Feb–March 1997), pp. 56–58.

99. "Raid Gauloises: Disciplines."

100. "Raid Gauloises: History 1991 New Caledonia," http://www.raid-gauloises.com/html/history1991.html.

101. "Raid Gauloises: Press Release No. 3 Aug 1998."

102. "Raid Gauloises: Press Release No. 1 Oct 1997."

103. "Raid Gauloises: Press Release No. 2 May 1998."

104. "The Grand Traverse," *NZ Adventure*, No. 34–35 (May/June 1989), p. 26.

105. "The Southern Traverse: The Concept."

106. Ibid.; Hunt, personal communication, 1998.

107. "The Southern Traverse: The Race," http://www.southerntraverse.com/html/race.html.

108. Marc Hinton, "Climb every mountain," *Sunday Star-Times*, 22 Nov 1998, Sec. B, p. 20.

109. "The Southern Traverse: Past Events," http://www.southerntraverse.com/html/past.

110. Hinton, "Climb," p. 20; Nelson, "The Clash," 1998, p. 51; Andrew Sanders, "Getting over the hump," *Sunday Star-Times*, 4 Oct 1998, Sec. B, p. 16; Williams, "National Geographic," p. 1.

111. "The Southern Traverse: The 1996 Race," http://www.southerntraverse.com/html/race96.

112. Dave Smith, "Clear statement of intention has been issued," *Otago Daily Times*, 10 Nov 1994; Woodham, "A Tale of Two Races"; "Southern Traverse," *Women Outdoors New Zealand (Otago) Newsletter*, Dec 1997, p. 1; "The Southern Traverse: Registration Information," http://www.southerntraverse.com/html/registration.html.

113. Hinton, "Climb," p. 20.

114. "The Southern Traverse: Support Crews," http://www.southern traverse.com/html/crew.html; Smith, "Support crews," p. 34.

115. One of the two all-women's teams dropped out and the other became the first all-women team to finish the race, placing within the top ten teams. (John Fridd, "Women upset race efforts unheralded," *Otago Daily Times*, 15 Nov 1995, p. 30.) Interestingly, before 1995 teams with four women and the obligatory member of the opposite sex had considered themselves all-women. (Hunt, personal communication, 1998)

116. "Raid Gauloises: History," http://www.raid-gauloises.com/web_anglais/esprit-histoire/histoire.htm.

117. In 1997, abseiling was introduced to the race (although rope skills would be considered part of any mountain running or mountaineering expedition), and in 1998, caving also required rope skills, among other specific techniques. These were to become permanent activities in future races. (Hinton, "Beastly test," p. 9; David Williams, "Winners with hours to spare," *Otago Daily Times*, 5 Dec 1998, Sec. C, p. 23.)

118. Dave Smith, "International field for today's Southern Traverse start," *Otago Daily Times*, 10 Nov 1997, p. 22.

119. Bill Godsall, returning with the 1997 winners, Team Cromwell, compared the two races in a prerace interview. (Hinton, "Climb," p. 20).

120. Nelson, "The Clash," 1998, 51.

121. Williams, "National Geographic," p. 1. When Hunt was asked about sponsors in 1998, he said that that year he and co-director Pascal Lorre were essentially the sponsors, although they had support from Macpac/Goretex, Air New Zealand, Canon, and Skyline Gondola. (Hunt, personal communication, 1998).

122. Williams, "National Geographic," p. 1.

123. "Southern Traverse," p. 2.

124. Derek Paterson, "X-Rated Traverse" *New Zealand Adventure*, No. 87 (Feb–March 1998), p. 58.

125. Williams, "National Geographic," p. 1.

126. Smith, "International field," p. 22.

127. Di Zinno and Paterson, "The Biggest Little," http://www.southern traverse.com/html/race96.html.

128. Paterson, "X-Rated Traverse," p. 59; "Southern Traverse," *Women Outdoors New Zealand (Otago) Newsletter*, Feb 1998, p. 2.

129. Paterson, "X-Rated Traverse," p. 59.

130. For Fun Radio's involvement: "Raid Gauloises: Press Release No. 2 May 1998;" for Discovery Channel's involvement: "Argentina selected as host nation for Discovery Channel Eco-Challenge," http://www.discovery.com/indep/ecomorocco/mediacenter/980904releasea.html; for National Geographic's involvement: Williams, "National Geographic," p. 1.

131. "The Southern Traverse," http://www.southerntraverse.com/html/concept.html.

132. Dave Smith, "From high waves to mountaintop," *Otago Daily Times*, 10 Nov 1994.

133. Grant Dalton inspirational tribute; "The Southern Traverse: Support Crews."

134. Hinton, "Climb," p. 20.

135. Hinton, "Climb," p. 20. For the man in the backblocks mythical character, see Phillips, *Man's Country*, pp. 283 and 288–289.

136. Christine Worsfold, Eco-Challenge competitor, personal communication, Dunedin, New Zealand, 28 Sep 1998 and 18 Nov 1998.

137. Ian Heywood, "Culture made, found and lost: The cases of climbing and art," in *Cultural Reproduction* (Chris Jenks, ed.), (New York: Routledge, 1993), pp. 104–119.

138. "About Eco-Challenge," http://www.ecochallenge.com/about Eco.html.

139. Hinton, "Exhausted," p. 5.

140. "Eco-Challenge: What's New," http://www.ecochallenge.com/race/morocco/whatsnew.html.

141. "About Eco-Challenge" "Mark Burnett," http://www.ecochallenge.com/race/burnBio.html; "The Razor's Edge," "Twist of Fate," and "Agony & Ecstasy."

142. "About Eco-Challenge."

143. "Eco-Challenge: Rules of The Race," http://www.ecochallenge.com/race/raceRules.html.

144. The Raid Gauloises, in contrast, emphasises team solidarity, loyalty, and intelligence. ("Raid Gauloises: Concept.")

145. See, for example, Nelson, "Damn Kiwis," p. 52; Sanders, "Hard yakka," p. 16; Sanders, "Defending champ," p. 10; Sanders, "True grit," p. 10; Alan Nelson, "Look Ma, No Support Crew—The 1997 Eco-Challenge," *New Zealand Adventure*, No. 84 (Aug–Sep 1997), pp. 57–58; Nelson, "Head and Shoulders," pp. 55–56; Nelson, "The Clash," 1998, 51; Jenny Duggan, "Camels, climbing, all part of challenge," *Otago Daily Times*, 9 Sep 1998, p. 15; Sanders, "Getting over," p. 16.

146. "The Razor's Edge."

147. Newsletters 1, 2, and 3. Worsfold, personal communication, 1998.

148. Worsfold, personal communication, 1998.

149. "Argentina selected as host nation for Discovery Channel Eco-Challenge," http://www.discovery.com/indep/ecomorocco/mediacenter/980904releasea.html.

150. Worsfold, personal communication, 1998.

151. Daniel Botkin, *Discordant Harmonies: A New Ecology for the Twenty-first Century* (Oxford: Oxford University Press, 1990), p. 8.

152. "The Razor's Edge."

153. Botkin, *Discordant Harmonies*, p. 24; Nash, *Wilderness*, p. 4. As one of many examples, Mark Burnett reportedly warns the 200 racers

in Morocco that "You are not in control of your own destinies—nature is." (Smith, "The Discovery Channel Eco-Challenge Morocco," http://www.discovery.com/indep/ecomorocco/reports/report3.html, 1998, p. 3.)

154. Botkin, *Discordant Harmonies*, p. 24.

155. "Eco-Challenge: Rules of the Race," http://www.ecochallenge.com/race/raceRules.html.

156. Smith, "Discovery Channel Eco-Challenge Morocco," pp. 2–3.

157. Nelson, "Look Ma," pp. 57–58; "Discovery Channel Eco-Challenge Australia '97" documentary.

158. New Zealand competitor Keri Barnett says sleep deprivation is one of her biggest fears. (Duggan, "Camels," p. 15) New Zealand competitor Andrea Murray says, "you can neglect yourself . . . can't be bothered opening up your pack to get out the sunscreen." (Sanders, "Hard yakka," p. 16) See also Williams, "And they reckon," p. 23.

159. Coasteering involves jumping into the surf and scrambling out again to walk a coastline under cliffs and around headlands.

160. Sanders, "True grit," p. 10; "Eco-Challenge: Rules of the Race."

161. Sanders, "True grit," p. 10.

162. Nelson, "Head and Shoulders," p. 55.

163. Smith, "Discovery Channel Eco-Challenge Morocco," p. 2.

164. "Twist of Fate."

165. Sanders, "True grit," p. 10; "The Razor's Edge," "Twist of Fate," and "Agony & Ecstasy."

166. Worsfold, personal communication, 1998.

167. Sanders, "True grit," p. 10.

168. "Mark Burnett," http://www.ecochallenge.com/race/burnBio.html.

169. "Mark Burnett tells why he chose Morocco," http://www.discovery.com/indep/ecomorroco/burrnetl.ra.

170. "The Razor's Edge."

171. The lucky viewers chosen will travel to the site of the next Eco-Challenge and may then participate in one of the disciplines of the race. ("Twist of Fate")

172. "Raid Gauloises: History."

173. Greenaway, "The two-day," p. 58.

174. "Discovery Channel Eco-Challenge Australia '97" documentary.

175. "Eco-Challenge: Rules of the Race."

176. Hinton, "Kiwi seeks," p. 5.

177. Worsfold, personal communication, 1998.

178. "Discovery Channel Eco-Challenge Australia '97" documentary; Worsfold, personal communication, 1998.

179. Sanders, "True grit," p. 10.

180. "Press Release: Eco-Challenge Wins Australia International Attention," http://www.atc.net.au/news/media/070897.htm.

181. Williams, "National Geographic," p. 1.

182. Greenaway, "The two-day," pp. 82 and 57; see also similar arguments by Andrew Blake in *The Body Language: The Meaning of Modern Sport* (London: Lawrence & Wishart, 1996).

183. Phillips, *Man's Country*, pp. 264 and 277.

184. Nelson, "Damn Kiwis," p. 52.

185. "The Razor's Edge;" see also Hinton, "Kiwi seeks," p. 5.

186. Nelson, "Damn Kiwis," p. 54; Ansley, *Coast*, p. 92.

187. Peter Shelton, "The Lost World: Has Modern Skiing Sucked All the True Adventure out of the Sport?" *SKI*, Jan 1998, p. 41.

188. Jacques, "Fifteen years, p. 17.

189. Ulrich Beck, *Risk Society: Towards a New Modernity* (London: Sage, 1992).

190. "New International Multisport Event," *New Zealand Adventure*, No. 85, (Oct–Nov 1997), p. 58.

Kayaking/Whitewater Sports

Chapter Fourteen

The Wrong Side of the Thin Edge

Ron Watters

I was tired and spent as I rose up over another big wave. Appearing out of white foam like an apparition was the end of a paddle. The paddle, an arm's length away, was that of one of the kayakers in front of me. I knew instantly what had happened to him. He was caught, midstream, in a backwash of water known as a hole. I had one fraction of a second . . . and then our boats crashed together.

Somehow, I had managed to pivot sideways to avoid ramming his body with the nose of my boat, but as soon as our boats collided, I was thrown upside down. I rolled quickly back up. Confused momentarily, I wasn't sure where I was or what had happened, but the other boat was gone. Apparently, I had knocked him loose, but

Ron Watters is an adjunct faculty member of the Department of Sports Science, Physical Education and Dance at Idaho State University. He is the author of seven books on outdoor topics, twenty-five professional papers, and a variety of book reviews, essays, and non-technical articles for general readership. He is one of the founders of the Association of Outdoor Recreation and Education and the founder and chairman of the National Outdoor Book Awards. For twenty-five years, he was the director of the Idaho State University Outdoor Program. Caring deeply for America's untrammeled wild lands, he served on the board of directors of the River of No Return Wilderness Council and worked for the protection of the Middle Fork of the Salmon River, Main Salmon River, and the wild lands of central Idaho. The Council's work resulted in The Central Idaho Wilderness Act, which created the Frank Church River of No Return Wilderness, the largest congressionally designated wilderness in the forty-eight contiguous states.

I had also succeeded in planting myself squarely in the hole, and I found myself holding on for dear life in the violently surging water.

It is moments like these when the metaphor *on the thin edge* seems particularly apt. Teetering on an edge or walking a fine line are visual images that give shape and form to that abstract quality of sports in which the element of risk of bodily harm separates it from other endeavors: a climber delicately perching on the edge of the cliff with the abyss looming below, a circus performer balancing on a high wire without a protective safety net—and, yes, a kayaker caught precariously in a vicious hole in the midst of a raging rapid.

It is that balancing act on the edge that makes high-risk activities so powerful in their appeal. The potential benefits to participants in high-risk sports are many and profound. One of the most powerful is the intense personal feelings of arousal and excitement, the 'adrenaline rush,' if you will.

Everyone needs excitement: a baby exploring beyond the confines of its crib, a college student challenging a professor's facts during a lecture, a young man and woman initiating intimacies. But some people need more than the normal forms of life's excitement and take it one step further, participating in high-risk activities, sports played on the edge, where the consequences are far greater—where, as the great American mountaineer and outdoor philosopher Willi Unsoeld once said, "it has to be real enough to kill you."[1]

Isn't all this talk about the possibility of dying—about the wrong side of the fine edge—a little bit fatalistic? Certainly, unnerving thoughts of my own mortality flashed through my mind while I was being flung about in that violent mid-river hole.

I stayed up for a moment, then the powerful currents of the hole slapped me upside again. Under the water, I was tossed from side to side like a rag doll clamped between the jaws of a dog. It was everything I could do to hang on to my paddle.

Though weak, I managed to roll up and caught a quick glance downriver. It didn't look good. I was midway down a long rapids. The river below me strained through a maze of large boulders and slammed up against a cliff. Already tired from the long stretch of rapids above the hole, my energy was ebbing quickly.

I knew that by now my companions were far down the river. If I swam, I'd be on my own. It would be a terrible and frightening swim through those unplacable boulders. Instinct told me that my chances of surviving the swim were close to nil.

The German philosopher Fredrich Nietzsche once wrote: "When you look long into an abyss, the abyss also looks into you." Indeed, I found my eyes locked on the cold, icy stare of the abyss.

I don't recall how many times my boat had been knocked over end for end, but during one of the endos, the bow dove deeply, catching a downstream current. Suddenly I was out of the hole, the boat listing heavily to one side and spinning out of control toward the boulders below. With my remaining strength, I made feeble strokes towards shore. Two last pulls on my paddle jammed the boat onto a pebbly beach a few feet above the boulder death trap. I was safe.

Although shaken, I got back in my kayak and finishing running the rapid without any further mishaps. Now more than 20 years later, I still enjoy kayaking, and I still feel just as firmly as ever that high-risk sports are essential, that we must do everything that we can to protect the right of people to participate in such activities. But I also look back at this experience as the beginning of a perceptible change in me. Once you've seen those red eyes glowing from deep in the dark void, you're never really quite the same.

The world has become far too safe, and heretofore unknown lands are mapped in far too much detail. As a consequence, we need as many outlets as possible for people to participate in challenging outdoor activities. We need wilderness lands; we need rock climbing areas; we need wild rivers; we need outdoor schools; and given proper environmental safeguards, we need free and unfettered access to outdoor areas. The right to risk is unalienable. It makes our society healthier and more vibrant.

Yet, at the same time, we need to relook at what has happened to high-risk activities over the last quarter of the twentieth century. In our efforts to provide programs, create new markets, and promote high-risk sports, we have gradually come to a point where we have overglamorized them and created an image for general consumption that is far different from what these activities really are. We have diverted people's attention from the not-so-glamorous possibility that one can get killed, concentrating attention only on the fun and safe side of the dangerous edge. It is a mendacious, one-sided view that has pervaded nearly every corner of our society: magazines, television programs, commercials, movies, outdoor education programs, and guided and outfitted trips. The effect has been to make the high-risk experience into something akin to a visit to Disneyland or the carnival. There's a big difference. At Disneyland everything is safe. Not so in the outdoors.

We were far better off when climbers, kayakers, backcountry skiers and the like were considered a part of the lunatic fringe. To illustrate the dramatic changes that have occurred, it is helpful to look at whitewater rafting. Twenty-five years ago, it was considered fairly adventurous to take a trip down the Middle Fork of the Salmon, a river consisting mostly of Class III rapids. Now, glossy, colorful brochures invite the public to take trips down wild Class V rivers—no experience necessary. Indeed, with proper equipment and well-trained guides, Class V whitewater is possible and is run all the time. But what if something goes wrong? What if one of the clients is thrown out of the boat above a rapids? Then what?

If rafting passengers fall into Class III water, they can usually be pulled back into the boat without much trouble, but all bets are off when it's Class V water. Charlie Walbridge, who for years has been collecting data on river accidents, has observed a troubling trend. He reports more fatal accidents occurring because boaters are unprepared—or simply overwhelmed—by the severity of the water they are running. "For years the physical ability, experience, and fitness of rafting guests have been declining," says Walbridge. "Better equipment and improved guiding skills make it possible to run more difficult rivers, but the guest who ends up in the water may overwhelmed and helpless."[2] The margin of safety on Class V water is extremely thin. Competent and safe kayakers and rafters who run such water do so only after slowly developing their skills and working up to it.

Yet, more and more commercial-guided operations are offering Class V trips to people who essentially walk in off the street. What is alarming is that such trips can create unreal expectations on the part of the paying passengers. They go on the trip. They have an exciting time, and some of them leave with the feeling that now they can run such water on their own. The same thing can happen to those who watch movies and videos of high-risk sports. Caught up in the thrill of it and seduced by the nonchalant attitude of many of these films, they say, "Hey, I can do that too."

This false sense of security, according to psychologist Michael Apter, comes from an unrealistic assessment of their ability.[3] Using the metaphor of a cliff's edge, Apter theorizes that every activity in life has three zones: a safe zone where one is far away from the cliff's edge, the danger zone where one walks on the edge, and the trauma zone where one has fallen off the edge and has been hurt or killed. Apter believes that when people seek excitement, they put themselves in what he calls a protective frame built through skill, proper equipment, and preparation. The protective frame allows them to come close to the edge, but not to fall into the trauma zone.

What can happen, according to Apter, is that people can be tricked into thinking they are operating within a protective frame when in reality they are not. Their illusions reinforced by what they hear and see on the media and combined with lack of knowledge and skill, the boundaries of the protective frame are completely obscured. Apter says: "One seems simply to be playing an exciting game with no repercussions."[4]

That is exactly what the overglamorization of high-risk sports can do. It blurs the distinction between what is real and unreal. It happens to the paying passenger on a guided trip—or the impressionable viewer of an 'action video'—who then goes out and jumps in a Class V river on his own and drowns.

There is no protective frame for those lured by Madison Avenue ad campaigns. High-risk sports are dangerous games of brinkmanship—not with a human foe, but with passive forces of nature. Thus, it is incumbent upon participants that, even though they may sometimes balance precariously, they stay at all costs on the living side of the edge. One misstep and the game is over.

Sometime after my close call on a river, I began thinking more about the limits of high-risk sports. How far do we dare take them? At what point do we cross the line in our eagerness to interest others and lead people on an uncertain path? Those questions haunted me for a number of years as I worked on the biography of kayaking's most famous personality, Dr. Walter Blackadar.[5] If there was any life in which the hard questions of high-risk sports were asked, it was in Blackadar's. His story and experiences are worth a closer look.

Blackadar is one of those giants who come along every so often, who envision great possibilities, make a great leap, and forever change the nature of a sport. For anyone who loves the outdoors, his life story reads almost like a fairy tale. He was a well-liked and respected physician in a small town in Idaho. Originally from the East, he moved west in 1949 so he could be near fishing, hunting, and river running. He took up kayaking in the 1960s—long before it became fashionable to drive around with a kayak strapped to the top of a car. In fact, at the time the number of kayaks in the state of Idaho—one of the West's most profligate states for whitewater rivers—could be counted on one hand.

His early kayaking days were carefree and hedonistic. He was famous for serving up a potent mixture of vodka and lemonade from his water bottle. He had quickly adopted the West—and its mythology—as his own, and around the campfire at night, he regaled trip companions with wild stories and demonstrated his prowess with a .44 magnum pistol. On a hot afternoon, he would shed his clothes, *salvo pudore*, and frolic on the beach with his young kayaking friends. The difficulty of the rivers he ran increased each year. He approached rivers cautiously, but there was always a light, carefree attitude to his trips—until a fateful day on the West Fork of the Bruneau River.

The Bruneau River lies in the remote, basaltic desert of southwest Idaho. It is an undulating land, draped in a grayish-green shroud of sage. Slicing through the desert like a bolt and branches of lightening is the Bruneau River with its several tributaries and forks. In April of 1974, Blackadar put together a party of five kayakers to run the West Fork of the Bruneau. Blackadar, who had run the river before, did not consider the West Fork to be a particularly difficult river as long as the two or three unrunnable rapids were located and portaged.

As they worked their way down the river, they employed a cautious approach: Blackadar was first. Julie Wilson, a young admirer of Blackadar visiting from the Southeast, was in the second position behind Blackadar. Wilson replicated his moves, stopping when he did and not passing him. The other three kayakers on the trip fell in behind Wilson. Unless the water was obviously easy, no one was to go beyond Blackadar.

Midway through the second day of the trip, they approached a falls that consisted of four drops through a maze of boulders. The falls was one of the unrunnable rapids that had to be portaged. But when river runners first approach a rapids, it is sometimes difficult to ascertain its difficulty until moving up closer to the edge. Blackadar found himself in that position.

He couldn't see the coming falls. A juniper tree had fallen and blocked three-fourths of the river, hindering his view of what lay downstream. To get to a better position, he paddled around the tree and slipped into an eddy, the last remaining stopping point just above the falls.

Looking below him, he now knew that the falls was unrunnable and would have to be carried. According to kayaking protocol, the other kayakers should have stopped in eddies above Blackadar and waited for a signal, but the Juniper tree complicated the situation.

Julie Wilson paddled around the tree, but the eddy that Blackadar occupied was too small for her to get into. She drifted towards the edge of the falls. Blackadar, now realizing her danger, yelled. It was too late.

Reacting quickly, Blackadar sprinted out in front of Wilson. He knew she was heading into a dangerous falls, and he wanted to be in front of her to guide her along the best path he could pick. They both plunged into the falls. On the first drop, Blackadar capsized and tried desperately to roll.

When Blackadar came up, he had lost track of Wilson. He plunged down through the next drop, and the next, and somehow ran the rest of the treacherous falls. Not finding her at the bottom, he hoped that she might have been washed downstream. Leaving the others, who had managed to get out at different points midway down the falls, Blackadar paddled off trying to find her.

He never found her. After searching for several hours, an agonized Blackadar realized that Julie Wilson had drowned, her body caught somewhere under the water in the falls. It wasn't until three weeks later, while Blackadar was attending Julie's memorial service in Atlanta, that her body was found by friends near the falls. She was buried overlooking the river and the rapids that now bears her name.

I interviewed many of Blackadar's friends and acquaintances when I was working on his biography. It was obvious that Julie Wilson's death devastated him. He had danced with danger on rivers, playing the odds, but had always managed to come out the winner. He delighted in balancing on the fine edge separating life from death, staying an arm's length away. He had thought carefully about his own death and, writing about it, he had said that it would willingly but grudgingly be accepted. But in the end, when death came on the river, it was not his own. It was somebody young and hopeful, just starting her life.

There are a number of parallels between Walt Blackadar and a contemporary of his in the mountaineering world, Willi Unsoeld. Willi Unsoeld had named his daughter, Devi, after what he felt was one of the most beautiful mountains in the world, the 25,645-foot Indian peak, Nanda Devi. In 1976, Devi, who had been well schooled in art of mountaineering by her father, attempted to climb her namesake. On the climb, she was stricken with a blood clot and died. It was impossible to remove her, and like the desert where Julie Wilson lies by the Bruneau River, the remote Himalayan mountain became her resting place.

Unsoeld could never look at death quite the same way. "How does one handle the death of a surpassing human being?" he asked:

"You don't. It handles you. It rubs your nose in the reality of your mortality."[6] Both Unsoeld and Blackadar learned the despair of losing someone and the dark emptiness of the other side of the edge.

Walt Blackadar never recovered. He returned to kayaking and continued to push back the barriers of the sport. His last great problem was Devils Canyon of the Susitna River, which drains the southern half of the Alaska Range, the roof of North America. Although he ran all of Devils Canyon's rapids, he never quite ran them cleanly without a swim, the way he wanted. His third attempt at the Susitna, when he almost lost his life during a horrifying swim through some of the canyon's largest rapids, seemed nihilistic.

Yet, he was conservative and protective when it came to other members in his party. Once, while ABC was filming him and several other outstanding kayakers on the Colorado for a nationally televised program, Blackadar asked one of the kayakers, Lynn Ashton, to wear a larger life jacket. He had long felt that more buoyant life jackets increased one's chances of survival in big-water rapids such as those found on the Colorado. She agreed. Blackadar turned away with tears in his eyes. It was a moving, poignant moment, and there was little doubt that his tears were for Julie Wilson.

What happened to Julie Wilson and Devi Unsoeld can happen to anyone involved in high-risk activities. We must never forget them. Their stories remind us that our companions, friends, and loved ones on high-risk forays can also slip and tumble over the wrong side of the edge as easily as we can. Indeed, if Blackadar's haunted life after Julie Wilson's accident is any indication, there is a wrong side of the edge for the survivors as well.

No matter how eloquently we wax, death on a river or on a mountain cannot be easily explained away. Listen to what John Krakauer has to say in *Into the Wild*, a book about a young man by the name of Chris Johnson, who, in April of 1992, traveled to Alaska and attempted to live off the land. Tragically, Johnson's attempt to survive in the Alaskan wilderness failed, and he essentially starved to death. Krakauer describes where he meets with the parents of Johnson for an interview. Johnson's mother sits at the dining room table, looking through pictures of her son, and breaks into tears. She was "weeping as only a mother who has outlived a child can weep," Krakauer writes, "betraying a loss so huge and irreparable that the mind balks at taking its measure. Such bereavement, witnessed at close range, makes even the most eloquent apologia for high-risk activities ring fatuous and hollow."[7]

Walt Blackadar broke into tears often in the years following Julie Wilson's death, and though haunted by her death and plagued by injuries, he doggedly continued to kayak. In 1978, in an attempt to ready himself for another film project with ABC American Sportsman, he joined with several friends to run the South Fork of the Payette, a river not far from his home in Salmon.

Part way down the river, two lead kayakers spotted a log just barely showing above the surface of the water and extending nearly all the way across the river. They quickly caught an eddy on the far right. Blackadar was immediately behind them.

To the two kayakers pulled off to the side, it look as though Blackadar did not see the log. It might have been hidden under a surge of water when he looked downstream. To their horror, Blackadar nonchalantly drifted toward the log. They had no time to warn him.

He was suddenly jarred when his kayak hit the submerged tree. The bow immediately dove under, and the onrushing water slammed his body against the log. Blackadar reached over the log, laying on his paddle in a technique known to kayakers as a high brace. The high brace might have helped him get around one side of the log, but the log slanted toward deeper water. As the current bounced the boat, he was pulled deeper and deeper into the water. He held bravely onto the high brace, even as his head slowly disappeared under the water. The back end of the boat rose up, stood vertically and collapsed against his body. The boat and Blackadar were completely trapped and immersed.

There was nothing the shocked kayakers could do—no way of reaching him, no possible way of getting a throw rope to him. To have someone swim out and try to get a rope to him would have been impossible—and foolish, since it could have risked entrapping two people. And so, Walt Blackadar died on the river. His body was recovered the next day and he was buried in the Pioneer Cemetery overlooking the South Fork of the Payette River.

Julie Wilson, Devi Unsoeld, Walt Blackadar. What is there to learn from them? Certainly none of them would have would have discouraged us from taking up kayaking and climbing and other adventurous activities. They all talked of how important such sports were to them. On the other hand, I'm sure that all three of them would have also agreed that risk in outdoor activities must be carefully evaluated. How is that done? Very simply, one must start slowly, learn the skills of the sport, and put in an apprenticeship. With such a foundation, one then has the knowledge to make informed decisions about how much risk is personally acceptable and about the steps that can be taken to minimize it. We all have our own thresholds of acceptable risk, and we must never let bravado or marketing hype or pressure from others influence that.

Accidents such as I have described here are warning shots across the bow. They are reminders that we have moved ever closer to the fine edge. Once all the fanfare is stripped away, these activities are real—real enough to kill people. Outdoor educators, guides, writers, outdoor companies, and filmmakers must do everything possible to make potential participants as fully aware of the risks as they do of the fun and excitement of sport. Not to do so does irreparable harm to high-risk activities and ultimately to those eager to try them.

Notes

1. Laurence Leamer, *Ascent: the Spiritual and Physical Quest of Willi Unsoeld* (New York: Simon and Schuster, 1982), p. ???.

2. Charles Walbridge, "River accident overview 1995," *American Whitewater*, Sep/Oct 1995, pp. 29–37.

3. Michael J. Apter, *The Dangerous Edge: the Psychology of Excitement* (New York: The Free Press, 1992).

4. Ibid.

5. Ron Watters, *Never turn back: the life of whitewater pioneer, Walt Blackadar* (Pocatello, Idaho: Great Rift Press, 1994). (Available from the author at 1-800-585-6857).

6. Leamer, p. 328.

7. Jon Krakauer, *Into the Wild* (New York: Anchor Books, 1996).

Chapter Fifteen

Whitewater Sports

From Extreme to Standardization

Jean-Pierre Mounet and Pierre Chifflet
Genevieve Rail, translator

Whitewater sports have the image of extreme sports; they are perceived as adventurous and dangerous—adventurous, since they presuppose that those who practice them set off in search of the unknown in off-limit spaces; dangerous, since they presuppose that bodily risks, including those of fatal accidents, are omnipresent for the participants. Such an image is fostered by the media. For instance, in 1989, a French television program featured "audacious" kayak enthusiasts attempting to cross a "torrent spiked with rocks" (the upstream part of the Isère river in Savoie, France). The coverage dated back to the early 1960s and the sportsmen were described by the commentator as "merry cracked pots." Interestingly, in 1989, part of the same path was open to the public and could be covered

Jean-Pierre Mounet is a professor of sociology of sport sciences at the Joseph Fourier University in Grenoble, France, where he is Director of the university's "Loisir, Environnement, Sport, Tourisme" Institute. He has published internationally in leisure and sports studies, particularly on outdoor recreation and the use of rivers in action sports.

Pierre Chifflet, professor at Université Grenoble, France, was director of EROS researchers Group between 1986 and 2000 and director of the sport sciences faculty at the University of Grenoble 1 from 1977 to 1982 and from 1990 to 1996, after which he assumed the direction of STAPS *International Revue* from 1988 to 1998. He is the author of papers concerning sports organizations, sports politics, sport's actors, logics of action and relationships between competition and leisure in sports.

either by rafting or whitewater swimming by inexperienced but supervised tourists. In a matter of a few years, a river that had once seemed inaccessible to the general public had become a venue for commercial activities offered to beginners.

Whitewater sports that carry the image of extreme sports have thus become, in the commercial domain, safe sports. Technological progress may in part explain the shift of this sporting space toward banality, but this explanation remains insufficient. The issue is rather to comprehend how an extreme sport may become a marketed 'sporting commodity.' An analysis of the social context and the modalities of practice allows us to answer this question and to understand the dynamics of these sporting activities.

Supply and Demand in Whitewater Sports

Until the 1970s, French sport practices were controlled solely by national federations. Because of this history, each sport federation has developed the same model: a high-performance sport model. At the national level, the ministry responsible for sport still controls the federations, supports high-performance sport, and regulates the supervision of sport. At the local level, the sport clubs are helped by districts or communes. Hence, a national system of associations still exists, and it accommodates a substantial number of participants. This national system has been used as a model to establish legal rules concerning safety in sport and its marketing. A specialized diploma for sports instructors (B.E.E.S.) is necessary to professionally supervise a group of sport participants.

Next to this associative federal model, other sport practices have developed since the 1970s: winter sport tourism in mountain resorts (ski), summer sport tourism in sea resorts (swimming, sailing, waterskiing, etc.), and leisure activities closer to home (outdoor camps, health clubs, bike paths, etc.). More in-depth analyses show multiple differences among all these leisure sport activities. However, a contrast can be observed between sports practiced in normalized spaces and sports practiced in 'uncertain' spaces. Outdoor sports belong to the second category. They attract sport participants requiring less regulation, more improvisation, direct contact with nature, and a spirit of adventure. In general, participants in this alternative model had not found what they were looking for in the federal associative model.

It is thus in the context of leisure and tourism that the practice of outdoor sports has developed. In the domain of whitewater sports, kayaking is the oldest. Imported from the United States, rafting has been the first alternative to kayaking. Then came whitewater swimming, which is of French origin. Finally, there are various inflatable rafts such as the canoe-raft, the kayak-raft, and the raft-tube.

As all outdoor sport activities, whitewater sports have become extremely popular. The public demands contact with nature in an unconstrained atmosphere. The need for companionship within groups and a refusal of complicated instruction and specialization in sporting activities[1] have fostered the development of commercial activity in this domain. The clientele freely buys and consumes a service designed by sports supervision professionals and accessible to the general public.

The significance of this commercial sector, in comparison to the federal associative sector, may be assessed if we take as an example the Durance river—a river known across Europe and located in the High Alps, in France. In 1992, almost 90,000 commercial passages were registered on the stretch of the Durance most frequently visited (seventeen kilometers). The same year, the French Kayaking Federation counted only 25,000 members among its affiliated clubs.[2]

Currently, a whitewater sport activity is offered in over half of the French sport touristic proposals.[3] In 1993, the number of boarding days went up to 2.5 million. With a turnover of 280 million French francs and the direct creation of more than 4,000 jobs,[4] the economic weight of this business sector is not trivial. Within the context of such development, the economic actors are whitewater companies. There were 600 companies in 1993. Depending on the specific case, the legal status may be different. Approximately half of these companies have the status of a sport association, which prohibits the distribution of profits. The other half have the status of a commercial firm. However, in both cases, instructors are supervising 'clients.' Instructors all have the same training, which is provided by clubs affiliated to the French Kayaking Federation. It is these experts specializing in 'sport accompaniment' who are structuring the sport supply, that is, the manner in which each sport is practiced.

Yet, to propose whitewater sport activities in a commercial form to a clientele lacking whitewater experience presents a safety problem. How can instructors ensure the safety of their clients while maintaining the extreme sport image? Indeed, company clients are numerous since whitewater sports have an 'extreme' image fostered through social representations: danger associated with the unknown, whitewater hazards, etc. Companies must use this representation and uphold the image of an extreme sport to sustain the flux of sport tourists and ensure their safety. Many types of difficulties emerge from this, and they must be resolved.

Rivers present natural physical configurations that are locally varied. The supply of water through successive affluents, the speed of current, the clutter of the bed with rocks, the tightening up or spreading out of the wave, and the inclination are among the many factors that determine the zones of variable difficulty for whitewater practice. However, this sport practice varies according to specialties. Everyone agrees that the newer whitewater activities are technically less difficult than kayaking. But it is impossible, a priori, to classify them according to technical difficulty. Each craft allows for a slightly different exploitation of the river, according to its potentialities and limitations; it is thus necessary to take such factors into account.

To guarantee the safety of the clients in a whitewater river presents two additional problems. On the one hand and contrary to other sport activities, one cannot stop anywhere since the river constitutes a variable milieu in perpetual movement. Risk is always present since a trajectory error or an interruption in the action of the participant may lead to an important drift in the torrent. On the other hand, there may be submerged obstacles or objects that are invisible from the surface and that represent a real danger in navigation. At all times, the moving water threatens to bring this type of danger to a new location on the course.

A Study of Courses in Whitewater Sports

Our hypothesis is that instructors adopt strategies that allow them to preserve the extreme image while managing safety. Our definition of the concept of strategy is not that of a conscious decision on the part of those responsible.[5] Rather, the concept of strategy is used here to mean that each instructor is considered a rational actor in light of his or her economic and moral interests. Behaviors may be the outcome of a limited rationality[6] that takes into account only a portion of the strategic possibilities, but they are nevertheless rational. Hence, the modalities of operation of whitewater sports in the commercial sector are not random. To verify this hypothesis, the courses of a number of whitewater sports associated with one French river, the Guisane (on the west side of the French Alps), have been analyzed. Furthermore, semi-structured interviews have been conducted with each instructor to obtain information or explanations on the choice of trajectories and courses previously observed.[7]

Choosing the Proposed Activities and Courses

Choice of Courses

The distribution of courses according to the difficulty of the river stretch is shown in Figure 1. An analysis of the spatial layout of the 'products' all along the river highlights important discontinuity in the use of the milieu. The navigable part of the Guisane is seventeen kilometers long and, depending on the course, corresponds to levels 2, 3 and 4 of the classification adopted by the International Federation. A closer analysis of the difficulty levels is necessary to understand the link that may exist between the local natural configurations and the courses utilized. Figure 1 shows the parallel between the difficulty levels of the different stretches of the river[8] and a synthesis of courses used in 1992 by whitewater companies.

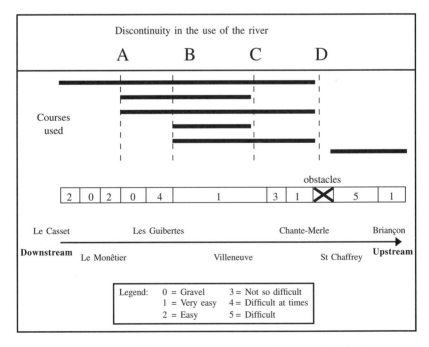

Figure 1. Difficulties and Courses Associated with the River

The first limit (A), located at Monêtier, corresponds to the first launching area. Since upstream there are gravel and very shallow waters, only the raft-tube—with its small draft—may access the uphill part of the limit. The second limit (B), located at Guibertes, marks the other launching area. Its location allows one to avoid a difficulty immediately upstream: level 4 rapids for a few hundred meters. The third limit (C), in the village of Villeneuve, coincides with a landing site. It is the last site where one can land if level 3 rapids located downstream are to be eluded. The last limit (D) corresponds both to the presence of dangerous obstacles in the river (that is, an iron post, then the nonsecured threshold of a micro power station) and to the beginning of level 4 Basse Guisane rapids.

As shown in the figure, the segmentation of the river allows one to limit the difficulties in the courses proposed to the public. The choice of launching and landing sites delimits the stretches of river of different difficulty levels. However, the proposed courses are not the same for the various whitewater activities.

Correspondence Between Courses and Whitewater Activities

Information on the courses' technical difficulty levels are presented in Figure 2. This information is inferred from the terms used by whitewater companies. The commercial terminology reflects, for the clientele, the need to have a certain technical progression so that increasingly difficult courses may be reached. But such learning remains strictly limited to basic maneuvers ensuring that the participant will not stay completely passive in the river. This minimal technical progression of a novice clientele—or a clientele that has experienced only a few whitewater descents—has two complementary origins. On the one hand, it is indeed necessary, in independent craft, to know how to steer in the river. On the other hand, it represents an opportunity to develop customer loyalty by leading clients to consume again. This is particularly true for rafting since the coxswain may ensure a correct trajectory without the help of his or her clients.

The 'products' are classified into four categories from the easiest to the most difficult: (0) learning, (1) initiation, (2) progression, and (3) exceedingly difficult. It is useful to note that the global distribution of these categories is not done solely on the basis of the river stretch's difficulty level: certain activities are limited to zones for beginners whereas others may develop in more

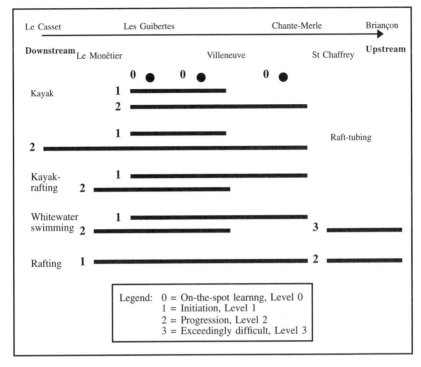

Figure 2. Commercial Terminology for Technical Difficulty Levels
(adapted from Mounet & Chifflet, 1996)

difficult zones. There is overlapping due to each specialty's sporting technology; initiation for certain specialties may correspond to
more demanding courses for others. Such technological overlapping is synthesized in Figure 3. For instance, kayaking can start
only with learning activities, and initiation takes place on the easiest
part of the river, as is the case with raft-tubing. The course used for
initiation in kayak-rafting and whitewater swimming corresponds
to the one used for progression in the case of kayaking; the latter
having reached, in this course, the upper limit of difficulty that
may be proposed to the clientele. Raft-tubing, kayak-rafting, and
whitewater swimming have a common course for the progression
category, and the course used for initiation in rafting is the same
as the course used for initiation and progression in kayak-rafting
and whitewater swimming. Finally, the only exceedingly difficult
course offered to the public (a few clients only) is associated with

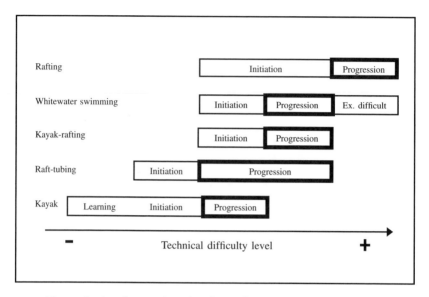

Figure 3. Synthesis of Technologically-Induced Overlapping

whitewater swimming in the Basse Guisane rapids, which also welcomes progression for rafting; on this course, neither raft-tubing nor kayak-rafting is proposed because of the high risk involved. Therefore, the courses proposed to the public are chosen according to the technological potential of the different types of craft. It is no longer an extreme sport practice that is proposed to clients, but a commodified sport product. For a novice public, we can classify these whitewater products according to the following increasing order of accessibility: kayaking, raft-tubing, kayak-rafting, whitewater swimming, and rafting.

By operating a selection of courses proposed on the basis of the type of craft used, companies give themselves the means to exploit the difficult milieu of whitewater. On the basis of the interviews conducted with professional instructors, we can conclude that trajectories are proposed following an empirical approach. On adequate river stretches, the trajectories must present some difficulties—some foam, some sensations—to preserve the attraction for extreme sports while maintaining a maximum level of safety. However, the problem related to the permanent instability of such an environment and the presence of eventual obstacles is not resolved. Its solution is found in the 'shaping' of trajectories in the river.

Normalization of Technique

Whitewater instructors are unanimous: they assess that it is in the middle of the river, in the vein (that is, the place where water is the deepest and most rapid), that safety for them and their clients is maximal. Clients do not necessarily share the same certitude. Some of them would prefer to sail along the bank and not feel swept away in high speed. Systematic observation of commercial groups involved in raft-tubing showed, indeed, the tendency to get closer to the bank. It is the repetitive orders of the instructors that force clients to use the middle of the river.

To guarantee the safety of their clients, whitewater instructors bring their craft or their group in the vein and endeavor to stay there. This systematic behavior corresponds to a veritable normalization of activities. Instructors respond not only to safety criteria, but to training criteria. They have all been trained similarly and been taught to navigate in the vein to limit the risks inherent to the practice of whitewater sports. Their social-spatial representation of the river forces them to focus on this zone and on the natural configurations induced by it, to the point where they practically do not see the environment near the banks. When there are few rocks, the physical choice of being in the vein does not impose itself inevitably; however, focusing on the recommended trajectory forbids them to think of any modification. The major safety criterion thus induces a normalization of the navigation technique.

Standardization of Courses

When interrogating instructors about their activity in the river, we come to understand that their courses are repetitive. Each instructor always uses the same access routes and the same stopping points, except if there is a particular problem. The exceedingly difficult course, for instance, is common to all the managers of a given whitewater company, to the extent that a specific stopping point may be labeled by everyone with the name of the company that uses it regularly (for example, "UCPA beach"). The craft and the whitewater groups of one company will thus always enter the river at the same place, navigate along the same trajectories (in the vein), stop at the same sites, and land in the same way. This very strict "shaping" of whitewater commercial products may be considered as a veritable standardization of the activity. However, this spatial restriction in the activities of the instructors does not come from ignorance of what the river has to offer: asked about the opportunities to stop in the river, each instructor is able to cite almost all of the stopping points used by the other companies.

If this standardization is systematically operated, it is because it offers many advantages. It allows for the anticipation of technical difficulties and a sufficient amount of time for the necessary maneuvers to be completed by inexperienced clients. It always uses the same locations that are recognized permanently, which is important in a milieu where diverse submerged objects, regularly transported by the river, may be dangerous in navigation. It also tacitly distributes the clients and prevents the overcrowding of certain stopping points.

Conclusion

The safety afforded by staying in the vein has a corollary: the use of a trajectory perceived by novices as the most dangerous. This is the paradox of whitewater sports: technical safety is found in the most impressive part of the river. On the one hand, instructors may offer an extreme sport activity without major risks. On the other hand, clients are persuaded that they have conquered the unknown and vanquished danger by navigating in the foaming and rapid zone.

Confronted by a difficult milieu, whitewater companies have thus created original products that allow their clients lacking specific technical training to access a whitewater experience. Through standardization of their clients' spatial behavior, instructors actively render the activity secure. A mental layout of the milieu—which remains totally unknown to the clientele—is favored over a physical layout. Clients thus benefit from an illusion of freedom and 'extreme,' and may practice activities even when given minimal technical training. As for instructors, they uphold their position as irreplaceable guides, which is commercially advantageous for them.

Extreme sports have become a commercial product for a significant proportion of the public. And the practice of a whitewater sport in a commercial framework is indeed an extreme practice: clients often reach their physiological and psychological limits. They have powerful emotions and envisage their sport practice as a personal exploit. However, we must note that this notion of 'extreme' corresponds only to the possibilities of each individual. It must be distinguished from the notion of 'extreme' corresponding to the values of global society. Indeed, other sports enthusiasts accomplish exploits which are extreme if we take into account physical, physiological, social, and psychological criteria associated with the world population. For them, extreme sport has another value since, in this case, maximal security is not ensured and the exploit is accomplished at serious corporeal risk.

Notes

1. COFREMCA, *Pour un repositionnement de l'offre tourisme-loisir dans les Alpes françaises* [For a repositioning of the tourism-leisure supply in the French Alps], (Savoie, France: Mission Développement Prospective, 1993); C. Pociello, "Espaces sportifs, innovations et prospectives [Sports spaces, innovations and perspectives]," in B. Michon and C. Faber (eds.), *Corps, espaces et pratiques sportives*, (Strasbourg, France: UFR STAPS, University of Social Sciences of Strasbourg, 1992).

2. J-P. Mounet, "Les activités commerciales d'eau vive: facteurs symboliques et investissement physique de la rivière [Commercial whitewater activities: Symbolic factors and physical investment of the river]," *Revue de Géographie Alpine*, 82(1) 1994.

3. J-P. Mounet, 1997, "Les activités physiques et sportives dans l'offre touristique [Physical activities and sports in tourism supply]," *Les Cahiers Espaces*, 52 (1997), pp. 102–110.

4. J-M. Darolles, L. Greffeuille, & J-P. Mounet, *Canoë, eau vive et tourisme* [Canoeing, whitewater and tourism] (Paris: AFIT, 1997).

5. M. Crozier and E. Friedberg, *L'acteur et le système* [Actors and systems] (Paris: Seuil, 1977).

6. H. A. Simon. (ed.) *Administrative behavior* (New York: Macmillan, 1957).

7. See J-P. Mounet and P. Chifflet, 1996, "Commercial supply for river water sports," *International Review for the Sociology of Sport*, 31(3) (1996), pp. 233–254.

8. According to a classification system born of ichtyology; see P. Chaveroche, "Recherche sur les préférences d'habitat de la truite fario" [Research on the habitat preferences of the fario trout] (unpublished doctoral thesis, University of Provence, France,1990).

CLIMBING

Chapter Sixteen

Xtreem

David Dornian

A couple of the competitors swipe each other's hats while we cool our heels in isolation, waiting for our call. They wave the shapeless punk chapeaux over their shaven heads like comic toreadors and bounce around on the crashmats, running on wobbly knees to escape each other's mock wrath. They are being largely ignored. Others in the room are trading CDs for their discMen, or trying to persuade the volunteer monitor guarding the door to take favorite music out to the emcee and his PA system, to play when their turn comes to climb. An intense few are quietly trying to stretch and center themselves. They gaze four feet into the floor in front of their stockinged toes, floating on the waters of performance anxiety that surround them, kept dry by the prophylaxis of personal audio. It's 8:30 AM on a winter Saturday. There's rain sweeping the logo-plastered vehicles jamming the parking lot outside.

Plugged in like this to their own private hopes (or at least some reasonable pop alternative), these athletes might be waiting to compete in any individual sport, anywhere in the Western world. They display all the classic symptoms, radiating across the spectrum of pre-performance anxiety. Some are psyching up. Others are

David Dornian lives in Calgary, Canada, and has been climbing in the Rockies and around the world for thirty-two years. He is a past competitor and currently manager of the Canadian National Competition Climbing Team and chairman of the Alpine Club of Canada's Competition Climbing Committee. He writes about climbing and skiing culture for outdoor periodicals and is the sometimes editor of the notorious *Calgary Mountain Club World News*.

trying to calm themselves down—it's hard to decide what will bring out your best when your heart rate's rising but your sweat's cold, and you have no idea whether what comes next will require finesse or fury.

When their allotted moment arrives, they will each be granted one opportunity on a climb they've seen only for the first time half an hour ago, during competitors' previewing. Right now it's each climber's job to translate to muscle memory what they saw and heard over that couple of hectic minutes, and commit to heart what they were told by the jury president about boundaries and rules. That done, all that remains is for each to wait patiently for the isolation monitor's call to come show their stuff in front of the restless audience that waits out the door and down the hall.

There's a computer printout taped on the wall of the storage/classroom that is serving as the isolation area this day, announcing the running order for the next heat. This roll is usually an inversion of the current position of the competitors relative to one another to this point in the competition. The current leaders will now climb last—to better the optics for the spectators, and to generate a little dramatic tension in what is essentially a one-shot sport. It's easy to wander across the room to count the names ahead of your own, guess at the time each might take for their attempt on the route, and estimate the minimum duration of your incarceration. At a well-attended competition—and they're almost always well-attended, climbers are incredibly competitive—this might translate into hours. Right now, a confident group whose names don't appear till the bottom of the page are doing what they've trained for most of their suburban adolescence—they're slumping in couches and lotusing on the carpet, watching Saturday morning cartoons on the gym's video monitor.

———

As spectacle, competition climbing is supposed to have gut-grabbing gravity, risk, and respect. You're led to expect nods across the dinner table the night before the event: "You wouldn't get me up there on that wall in a million years, Son." Molar-cracking tension: "Oh, no! He's off at the sixth clip, and there's four still to climb." Or at least that's the impression created by the pre-event advertising. I'm not so sure about the dental hazards for the spectators, but I do know about the chiropractic ones I face as a competitor—the gig definitely has its share of knuckle-cracking boredom. The name of this game was originally "sport climbing." That was before old-guard mountaineers appropriated the term a couple of years ago to disparage certain routes and climbing tactics in the out-of-doors. Now the activity is identified internationally as "indoor competition climbing" and is meekly tugging at the skirts of the International Olympic Committee. Welcome to Extreme Sport *Lite*: Emotional pressure cooker—Not.

Simply put, the trouble with watching any kind of climbing, when you're not a climber yourself, is that once you've been exposed to the novel environment a couple of times and the initial surge of sympathetic fear and vertigo wears off, there's little about the activity that's obviously impressive. It's slow-moving—a careful trapeze act presented by each competitor with varying levels of proficiency, repeated all day, for sometimes three or four days in a row. Competitors never face one another on the course. At the end of their turn, they simply untie from the rope and join their fellows at the edge of the crowd, the better to compare notes with those who have gone before—"How high did you get?"—commiserate with those who come after—"Tough one, dude. You were just a slap from the bucket"—and put away their gear while they watch and hope that the next guy out doesn't get as high on the wall as they did. Worse, the good performers are usually less exciting than the bad ones—the true standouts at the sport demonstrate greater economy of movement. They spend less time and energy figuring out the route. They don't have to fight for it. When they fall, they're as surprised as the audience. A large part of their success can be attributed to the fact that they are better able to remain calm and centered, which to the untutored observer makes them appear curiously nonchalant. Counter-intuitively, they're often smaller, and appear weaker, than their opponents.

The physical emphasis in competition climbing is on strength/weight advantages: just a few pounds of bodyweight can make a crucial difference when a participant is required to do pull-ups on the pads of two fingers. So the better performers in the game tend to be shorter, and slight to the point of actually appearing skinny. As with the more familiar athleticism of amateur wrestlers, female gymnasts, and ballet choruses, the ideal body image for the indoor competition climber encourages a fanatic level of both devotion and denial. Aspirants often flirt at the dark edge of overtraining, injury, and eating disorder. This is a comparatively nouveau aesthetic, even for the cross-trained, multimarket, alternative-sports-minded new millenium and it is not easily assimilated by audiences bred through television to hulking designated hitters, rookie full-backs the size and price of office buildings, and towering second-string centers ransomed from agrarian societies in the Third World. As a climber, my capacity for wooden body tension and elfin movement are the two major components of success in the over-hanging world (think *Peter Pan*, but turn up the bass on the soundtrack). When there are no opponents to dominate on the field of honor, there is no immediate way to demonstrate your superiority, there is no one to "take it out on." The climber is against the course, and gravity is relentless and always the eventual winner. At climbing comps *everyone* falls, even the winner has to let go and sag onto the rope—it's the only way back to the ground. Although it's not unusual for athletes in more popular sports to compete as individuals—that is, against the environment and themselves—this problem is aggravated for the presentation and acceptance of competition climbing. The environment here—the field of play—is totally unfamiliar to a layperson. Just about anyone can identify with running out on a grassy pitch, or remember what it's like to step onto a hardwood court. And if they're not too far into their beer, they feel a surge of excitement and a jolt of inner fantasy realized when they watch another athlete do the same. But your typical viewer has no sympathetic recall whatsoever for gripping molded resin edges bolted to an overhanging wall till their knuckles turn blue while pawing for foot purchase in overtight rubber slippers. The climbers may be swimming against a universal current, spawning toward the distant ceiling, absolutely elemental in their efforts, but the guy in the crowd with the inline skates and the Starbuck's latté is telling his girlfriend, "It doesn't look that bad, you know? I bet I could do it." Well, he couldn't, really, but that's not the way it looks to the spectators. When the guy gestures with his cardboard cup and says, "Look at that scrawny kid. He isn't even breathing hard. And he gets those clip things to catch him all the way to the top," he may not be saying much, but they're nodding to themselves. That is if they're not already yawning.

That's another problem. Given the overhanging geometry of the artificial climbing surface, the better seats aren't—the action is best watched lying down. As spectacle, the sport puts you to sleep.

———

In indoor competition climbing, as each participant is led to the front of the wall, a judge repeats the instructions he gives to every

competitor. If the forerunners have done their jobs during the previous week and the course is set well, each successive climber
manages to puzzle and struggle a little higher than the person
before, the routes difficulty confirming their reverse seeding based
on the outcome of the qualifying rounds. Each climber's turn ends
either at the anchors atop the route, or more often, with a slip and
a sag onto the end of the rope. Winning can mean simply hanging
from the same hold for a few more seconds than your opponent
did. But until the entire field has climbed, enabling comparative
heights attained on the route to be assessed, there is no ready way
of positively identifying that winning performance at the time it is
given. From a position in the paying seats in front of the wall, apart
from not furnishing any cue about how hard to clap, the image
presented can often be one of defeat, even in victory.

Sure, there's competition in competition climbing, but half
the time happens out of sight of the spectators—for instance, back
in isolation this Saturday morning, while the public part of the
proceedings is grinding through the gears in front of the spectators,
a much more exciting event is already taking place. A bunch of the
hopefuls who've been warming up on the bouldering wall have
become distracted and are blowing all their energy and ego trying
to burn one another off problems that no one but their peers will
ever see or acknowledge. They're crowding forward to spot one
another, putting dots of chalk on the wall, pointing to holds and
daring the others to try the problem they have just created. Later,
when the main event is done and prizes awarded, the audience
dispersed, winners and losers alike will press to the foot of the wall
they so recently failed on, describing moves, exchanging advice,
pleading to be allowed back on the course. They won't do this out
of regret, nor in the vain hope of a second chance, and it isn't like
the prizes will even go as far as to defer their expenses. It happens
this way at every event just because winning and losing have little
to do with the overall experience of climbing. Opponents will go
their separate ways later and will likely meet at future events
down the road, but this particular playing field will never be repeated. The competitors truly didn't come here to test anyone but
themselves. Terrain is the truest adversary of all, and at the end of
everything it's the terrain that's still standing, unbeaten. For the
moment at least.

It is ever thus: At the Canadian National Sport Climbing
Championships in Edmonton in 1992, a kind of a theme was introduced when Jordan Mills became bored in isolation and constructed

a football pool-style lottery on the outcome of the competition. When the kitty was done circulating, you could have won almost as much on this inside wager as you could by winning the event outside in front of the judges. The inside game continued long after we had awarded the final prizes and begun to break down the folding chairs and stack the tables for another year—everyone figured they could climb the finals route on their second attempt, and begged for a chance to try. So we locked the doors and held a self-judged red point contest for informal second prizes—giving away all the ropes and gear that manufacturers had provided for the event, augmented by the official winners' unwanted equipment prizes from competing sponsors. It was every bit as exciting, and a lot more vocal, than anything that had happened during the 'real' national championships.

——

All of the foregoing can be taken as an informal, but informed, summary of why indoor competition climbing will never fulfill its ambitions to become widespread, lucrative, and popular with non-participant audiences. Now, here are:

Ten Reasons Why Indoor Competition Climbing is the Best Sport in the World:

1. *It has the common touch.* It doesn't favor one particular age, sex, physiotype, language, or culture over any other. Although the demographics in competition climbing are presently weighted toward the traditional mountain sport communities and educated middle-classes, cheap and easy access to indoor climbing walls and outdoor crags is rapidly broadening and expanding the participant base of the sport. At the same time, climbing is nerd nirvana—it's different enough that it doesn't particularly favor the athletically experienced or the aggressively inclined. For example, reaction time isn't critical—losing that 'half a step' isn't going to sideline you to the old-timers' league for the rest of your life at the ripe old age of thirty—and skinny guys with wire-rimmed glasses and mothers with kids can not only compete, they can be favorites. There's even prize equity between the sexes. The first-place female at officially sanctioned competitions wins what the first-place male does, second-place female wins the same size prize as the second-

place male, etc. These prizes often amount to damn-all for either sex, of course, which makes it easy, but hey, when you have them, they have to be equal.

2. *It is essentially self-coached.* You can prepare and compete on your own, even at international levels of competition. This is great because when success comes, it is yours individually and thus doubly rewarding. The setting of goals, the arc of training, planning, and strategizing, mental preparation, competition readiness, rest, recovery—they're all idiosyncratic and vary greatly from climber to climber. Advice helps, sure, as it does with any activity—you can always benefit from the experience and objective viewpoint of others. But the sport is still new enough that it lacks both the science and the recorded history of results that cause coaches to force particular regimens on players, as they do in more established disciplines. So it's one of the last refuges of the self-trained athlete—which I suppose puts it right up there with ferret-legging and championship chili cook-offs, but at least we're not racehorses yet, to be selected for our sport early because of our physiques and bloodlines, forced into programs, taught to not ask questions but simply obey our coaches and managers. We come to the sport ourselves, because of its own virtues and rewards. It's not like you earn dates with your high school's cheerleaders by onsighting the route set for the difficulty final down at the climbing gym. In my experience, you tend not to play the hero and win the girl in this game. In fact, the larger worry is often not to play the goat and get beaten *by* the girl.

3. *It isn't expensive.* Even for an individual who wishes to commit full-time to the sport, its practice can come ahead of self-promotion, saving, and the solicitation of patronage. Starting out, focus can be kept on training and competition without the worry of taking time and attention away from athletic concerns to accumulate resources. All the way to international levels, champions can still get good enough for World Cups climbing in their basements and garages, sharing space, time, and encouragement with a couple of friends.

4. *It's geography-independent.* No mountains required. No season to be observed. Nor does it have a national 'seat' or native culture, although the French seem to be working on that.

5. *No one gets "beaten."* There are winners, but no losers. Competition climbing works like sailing or ski racing. It's great to win an event outright, but it's great simply to perform and place well, also. It's your overall ranking over the course of a competition *series* that really counts. In the past, various prizefight and winner-takes-all formats have been applied to competition climbing by promoters attempting to generate some good, old-fashioned, rock-'em-sock-'em sports excitement, but to no avail. Even the longer-established speed climbing formats developed by the Russians in the 'sixties, where climbers race head to head on easier identical routes to generate a single winner and a clear loser for each heat, get less attention from the crowds and competitors than the on-sight difficulty events when the two are held in conjunction. As a result, rather than barricaded locker rooms on opposite sides of the stadium, there is more of a community or even a 'circus' feel to climbing events. The intimidation and uncertainty stimulated by the event itself tends to foster support groups in isolation and mutual comfort after the climbs. You make friends—not enemies—when you compete. As mentioned before, it's nerd nirvana. Don't tell the all-attitude, T-shirt and sunglasses, Xtreem sport marketing cartels that, though, or they'll cut off the supply of rear-window stickers for our camper vans, and end the PowerBar giveaways at climbing events.

6. *The playing field is different every time.* The challenge is in the climbers' physical and mental capacity to respond to new geometry. As a competitor, you're never bored. Well, never bored until you're actually waiting to get on the route . . .

7. *The scoring is simple and easy to understand.* There are few subjective calls required of the judges, usually rendering straightforward winners and nicely segregated placings. Results are largely indisputable. There is seldom reason to argue with officials.

8. *Your performance is yours alone.* It's a familial sport that supports a team approach, but those teammates aren't in a position to let you down. And while any glory may reflect brightly on that team, it is credited directly to the individual and the performance that earned it.

9. *It's fun.* There's no body contact. No one throws things at you. There are no whistles. There's no mud. You don't have to get wet or be cold. The locker rooms, such as they are, are co-ed. What more could you ask for?
10. *It's honest.* It still, as yet, has nothing to do with sports utility vehicles, beer after the game, golden oldie radio stations, organ music, ticket scalpers, Orlon stadium mascots, guys in gray with whistles, "making the team," going to the Olympics, collector trading cards, tobacco sponsorship controversies, flying the school colors, salary strikes, haircuts, headbands, newspaper sports columnists, titanium anything, or climbing in the real mountains.

I think it's great.

Chapter Seventeen

The Great Divide
Sport Climbing vs. Adventure Climbing[1]
Peter Donnelly

Introduction

While climbing may be one of the oldest of the so-called 'extreme' sports,[2] recent events, such as the 1996 Mount Everest tragedy, have made it one of the best known, and images of climbing are now everywhere. Many products have begun to use climbing themes in their advertising, but business services have taken to the symbolism of the sport in a big way—an interesting contradiction for many older climbers because it flies in the face of a more traditional anarchic and anti-materialist approach to the sport. Everything from mutual funds to temporary employment agencies, banks,

Peter Donnelly is director of the Centre for Sport Policy Studies, and a professor in the Faculty of Physical Education and Health at the University of Toronto. His research interests include sports politics and policy issues, sports subcultures, and mountaineering (history). He has published numerous scholarly articles on those and other topics. Recent books include: *Taking Sport Seriously: Social Issues in Canadian Sport* (1997; second edition, 2000), and *Inside Sports* (with Jay Coakley, 1999). His current sporting interests include rock climbing/mountaineering (continually proving the inverse relationship between age and risk taking), hiking, and skiing.

An earlier version of this paper was presented at the annual meeting of the North American Society for Sport History, Springfield, Mass., 23–26 May 1997.

and real estate companies have used climbing images. The city where I live uses a photograph of a female rock climber on a nearby cliff as an image to attract business development. And climbing forms the basis of a recent popular motivational self-help book—*Adversity Quotient* divides the population into 'quitters,' 'campers' and, at the top of the heap (of course), 'climbers.'[3]

But the growing popularity of climbing in the last 15 years coincides with the most serious rift in the history of the sport—a rift between two forms of climbing that could result in a fundamental change in the nature of the sport. Since the techniques and styles of climbing are basic to this account of the division between sport climbing and adventure climbing in the climbing community, I begin with a brief, and very simplified, description of rock climbing technique.[4]

The basic method of using the rope for safety in climbing is known as *belaying*, of which there are two types: the *fixed belay* and the *running belay*. Although there are numerous variations on this, a normal roped climb (on rock or ice) occurs with two climbers, one attached to each end of a rope, moving one at a time. The first climber sets off, reaches a point where he/she is able to fix him/her self to the rock or ice (a fixed belay), and takes in the slack rope (i.e., keeping the rope relatively tight) between them as the second person climbs. The safety of the second is assured in the case of a fall because the first climber is able to hold him/her without being pulled off, and before the second falls any distance. If a climb is longer than the length of a rope (normally about 50 meters) the process continues as the second climber then takes a *fixed belay* and pays out the rope to the first climber as s/he climbs the next 'pitch.' While the second climber is moving, s/he is continually belayed by the leader, and a slip will be stopped by the rope in a very short distance. However, a fall by the lead climber is much more serious—on the first 'pitch' the leader could hit the ground; on subsequent pitches s/he is likely to fall at least as far below the second as s/he has climbed above. To prevent this, the leading climber may be protected from a long fall by a series of *running belays* or 'protection'—snap links or 'karabiners' are attached to the rock or ice by a variety of means, and the moving rope runs through them. Proper belaying techniques by the second climber will ensure that a leader will fall only as far below a *running belay* as s/he has climbed above it. If protection does not alter or damage the rock (as do pitons or expansion bolts) and is used only for safety, the technique is known as 'free' or 'clean' climbing.

When protection is actually used by the climber to assist in his/her progress, the technique is known as 'aid' or 'artificial' climbing.

Between these two extremes there are numerous microvariations and various meanings associated with particular styles of climbing. The main areas of dispute between the two major factions in climbing, now commonly referred to as 'adventure' climbing and 'sport' climbing, concern:

- how protection is attached to the rock
  In general, adventure climbing favors using natural rock features such as cracks and spikes as the environmentally sound (that, do-no-damage, leave-no-traces-of-your-passing) means to attach running belays. Sport climbing usually uses expansion bolts inserted into holes drilled in the rock as a relatively permanent means of attaching karabiners. Pitons—spikes hammered into cracks in the rock and (usually) subsequently removed for reuse—may be employed by both styles of climbing, but are used less in modern climbing because of the ongoing damage caused to rock features.
- when protection is attached to the rock
  Adventure climbing 'ethics'[4] favor attaching protection to the rock during the course of an ascent—often a tricky matter, depending on the vulnerability of one's position and how far one is above the previous running belay. In sport climbing, protection is often preplaced—for example, by drilling bolt holes and inserting the expansion bolts while 'rappelling' (descending the cliff using a rope attached at the top)—before an ascent is attempted.
- how the 'protection' is used
  Ethics in adventure climbing generally favor protection *only* as a means of safety should a fall occur; it is not for resting or assisting the ascent. In sport climbing, particularly when a first ascent is being 'worked,' protection may be used for resting ('hangdogging'), for sometimes deliberate short falls ('yo-yoing,' another form of resting), or as a hand- or foothold while a move is being studied.
- how the ascent is accomplished
  The term *on sight* may be used by both adventure and sport climbing to describe an ascent made from bottom to top, not 'weighting' the protection (using it for a rest, or for a controlled fall for a short distance), and usually the first time one sees the route. One difference between the two is

that on an adventure climb, the leader usually places all of the protection, while on a sport climb, the leader may just have to clip snap links into preplaced bolts. Within sport climbing, there are various recognized styles of ascent other than 'on sight,' including 'redpoint' and 'pinkpoint' ascents (different degrees of rehearsal and amount of equipment in place), and a 'flash' ascent (similar to 'on sight').

There are two fundamental characteristics of climbing that have characterized much of its history as a sport. The first is the noninstitutionalized, self-governing nature of the activity; the second is the maintenance of a tension balance between difficulty and risk.

The emergence of sport climbing represents such a fundamental rift in the sport because it violates both of these characteristics. In fact, the rift is so fundamental that it might be compared to the split between rugby union and rugby league at the end of the last century over the issue of amateurism. In the following, I provide a brief description of the development of these two fundamental characteristics, examine the emergence of sport climbing and competitions, and consider the way in which the sport as a whole is dealing with the issue.

The Development of Climbing

Climbing emerged as a sport in the European Alps in the second half of the nineteenth century. It resulted from the presence in the Alps of tourists seeking adventure and natural scientists seeking data—many of these individuals were imbued with the new spirit of athleticism. The sport eventually developed into a series of climbing 'games,'[5] and met all of the criteria for being considered as a legitimate sport except that there was no institutionalized competitive structure (the situation in the former Societ Union was somewhat different). In other words, notwithstanding the fact that climbing had no governing bodies, no formal competitions, no written rules, and no means of enforcing rules, it adopted the prevailing sport culture of the late nineteenth century and resembled most other sports.

The system of rules and conventions that exist in climbing (termed "ethics" by climbers) is socially constructed and socially sanctioned.[6] That is, the rules are created by a form of consensus among climbers—both verbally and through climbing journals—transmitted by the same means of communication, and enforced by self-discipline and social pressure. Ethics are based on the premise that, given enough time and enough resources (human, financial, technical), anything can be climbed. Therefore, some guidelines are needed to give a mountain or cliff a 'sporting chance'—ethics introduce an element of uncertainty to the outcome because, in order for sport to exist, the chance of failure must also exist. Failure may imply a safe retreat from a position considered too difficult or dangerous, or it may mean a fall, injury, and even death. Ethics also permit an informal level of competition by ensuring that climbers attempting similar types of ascent employ similar means.

Ethics usually take the form of a series of proscriptions based on the difficulty and the danger of the ascent being attempted.[7] In the "bouldering game," ascents of small cliffs and boulders up to 7–8 meters in height, everything is proscribed. (Rock shoes and, more frequently these days if the base of the climb is hazardous, a landing mat are the exceptions.) As climbers proceed through the hierarchy of climbing games—rock climbing, big-wall climbing, alpine climbing—more and more equipment and techniques are allowed until the ultimate "expedition game." Because the chances of reaching a Himalayan summit are extremely limited, almost any resources that climbers can muster are permitted. Such ethics help to maintain the tension balance between difficulty and risk. In the bouldering game, usually the only danger is a potential broken ankle if one has a bad landing after a fall—therefore climbers may undertake enormously difficult ascents with little fear of the consequences of failure. In the expedition game, the objective dangers of altitude and weather are so great, and the chance of failure so likely, that climbers use, within certain limits, almost any means available in order to make the ascent and descent safely. However, in this constantly changing and self-limiting sport, the expedition style of ascent has now become largely the province of guided tours (cf., the 1996 Everest disaster[8]) and nationally supported teams of climbers attempting to bring their country into the 'Everest club' of nations that have successfully climbed the mountain. Leading climbers tend to favor a modified form of alpine climbing—fast, lightweight ascents rather than the heavyweight sieges of expedition climbing.

Because there are no referees or formal sanctions to ensure compliance with ethics, the only sanctions are derision, public denouncements, and refusal to publicly record a claimed ascent.[9] The type of competition facilitated by the ethics depends on record keeping, either in the climbing literature or in the oral history of a particular locale. Record keeping makes it possible to engage in direct competition for first ascents (of a mountain, a new route on a mountain, or a new route up a cliff), which may also include first solo, first female, and first winter ascents. Record keeping also makes indirect competition possible—competition for the style or quality of an ascent—which may refer to the speed of an ascent but is usually considered in terms of how closely an ascent conforms to prevailing ethical standards. For example, if a first ascent has been accomplished using two points of 'aid' (for example, pitons or expansion bolts), and a climber on a subsequent ascent manages to ascend the route with only one, or no points of aid, that becomes the new best standard for the route, and is often 'recorded.' Special praise is reserved for those individuals who bring the ethics of a game lower in the hierarchy to a new level (for example, solo climbing a rock climb or a big-wall climb means that bouldering ethics have been brought to a more dangerous game), and this is precisely the case in alpine ethics superseding the expedition game, noted above.

However, climbers are not 'compulsive' in enforcing ethics, or best ethical standards for a route. They recognize that climbing occurs at both a recreational level and an informally competitive level. Strict enforcement is not only impossible, but unreasonable. It would mean that climbers ascending the classic peaks of the Alps or the Rockies would have to wear tweed jackets and use hemp ropes—as did those who first ascended the peaks in the nineteenth century— or employ even less equipment. It would mean that once a route has been solo climbed, all subsequent ascents would have to be solo. On many rock climbs and mountain routes it is quite permissible to use more equipment than may have been employed on the first or subsequent ascents, because those making the ascent are engaged in recreational activity and are not involved in competition. (However, cheating often involves appearing to be competitive by claiming to use less equipment than one actually has.)

Also, the tension balance between difficulty and risk would be violated by obliging subsequent and less talented (usually recreational) climbers to conform to the best standards for the route— particularly a solo standard that involves the highest levels of risk. Because there are no written rules, this remains a subtle and controversial aspect of ethics that is constantly in flux.

All of the major controversies in climbing have been concerned with maintaining this tension balance between risk and difficulty. On the one hand, risks that are too great, leading to a number of deaths, mean bad publicity for a sport that rarely attracts media attention—and climbers recognize that negative publicity may lead to controls and/or bans on their sport (cf., the aftermath of the 1996 Everest disaster, with a great deal of talk about imposing limits on guided tour expeditions).[10] Whenever there are a number of deaths in a particular type of climbing, there are attempts to achieve a new consensus among climbers that will reduce the risk. On the other hand, new forms of safety equipment and technique (for example, equipment that has not [yet] been proscribed and will reliably hold a climber in case of a fall, and equipment that may be used to limit the distance between running belays, thus ensuring that leaders do not take long, and therefore dangerous, falls) result in climbers being able to attempt high levels of difficulty with little risk.

The expression used by Anglo-Saxon climbers to describe the use of new safety equipment on established routes is "bringing the climb down to the level of [skill of] the climber." While ethics attempt to maintain uncertainty of outcome, they also attempt to maintain a relatively 'level playing field' for at least a certain period of time after a first ascent has been accomplished. For a new ascent that is rated as the most difficult in a particular locale, subsequent climbers are supposed to equal or better the style of those making the first ascent, at least until overall standards have improved to the point where that climb becomes accessible to more recreational climbers. Thus, it is not competitive (and it is an ethical violation) to claim that one is equal in ability to those making the first ascent if one has used more equipment.[11] The point at which one is no longer "bringing the climb down to one's level" (rather than bringing one's own skill and courage up to the level of the climb) is quite indeterminate, and may be used as a put-down long after climbers are no longer making competitive gestures by making the ascent.

The major problem with sport climbing for the climbing community is that it has violated the tension balance between difficulty and risk. The widespread use of expansion bolts for running belays, and the use of those bolts every two meters or so, ensuring that leaders will never fall far, has permitted climbers to pursue difficulty for the sake of difficulty. Climbers, as in the bouldering game, will attempt incredibly gymnastic and difficult moves when they are a short distance above the ground because the move can be attempted, and practiced in safety, with no risk. Also, the psychological element of 'exposure' is removed.[12] While sport climbing places climbers in spectacular situations, sometimes more than 100 meters. above the ground, the reliability of new equipment, and the confidence of climbers in that equipment and the belayer, do not completely remove the psychological element of 'exposure,' but they do tend to bring the ground a great deal closer in the knowledge that one is unlikely to fall more than two to four meters.

Sport climbing has also been associated with the introduction of formal, organized competitions into the sport, and those involve governing bodies, sponsors, written rules, and other aspects of institutionalization. This violates the anarchic and self-regulating nature of the sport and has been of concern to many climbers. The following section considers the emergence of sport climbing and competitions.

Sport and Competition Climbing

Present-day climbing competitions have two sources. First is the speed-climbing competitions that emerged in the already institutionalized Soviet system of mountaineering after the Second World War. The competitions spread to other Eastern bloc countries, and Western climbers gained a brief exposure to them during the few climbing exchanges that took place in the 1960s and 1970s. At the 1972 Olympics in Munich, the German Alpine Club held a meeting between delegates from a number of Western Alpine Clubs and Eastern bloc climbing representatives to discuss a Soviet application to have speed climbing considered as an Olympic sport (with a view to its introduction at the 1980 Moscow Olympics). The proposal was not popular with the representatives of the West, and speed climbing has not yet been approved as an Olympic sport. Second is the 'French' (and to a lesser extent, Italian) style of rock climbing that began to develop in the 1970s. This emerged from a French climbing culture where extreme difficulty was embraced in climbing on the Fontainbleu boulders outside Paris, and speed—regardless of ethical considerations about the amount of equipment, or 'weighting' that equipment—was of great importance for safety in Alpine ascents. These elements of difficulty and disregard for Anglo-Saxon concerns about 'ethics' and 'fair play' came together in the limestone gorge of Verdon, where extremely steep and high cliffs afforded little natural protection. Americans had been experimenting with expansion bolts in Yosemite in the 1960s, and these were adopted by the French climbers as the means of protection. Thus, the route and its difficulty became rather more significant than the means of achieving it in the French style, and throughout the 1970s a style of climbing that involved bolting, hangdogging, hold-chipping (using a hammer to trim a razor edge and unusable flake of rock into an edge broad enough to hold a climbing shoe), and other forms of route preparation began to develop.

The French style proved to be spectacularly photogenic. Clothing styles in the sport began to change from drab working and ex-military styles to brightly coloured spandex, and a number of superstar climbers began to emerge. As the sport grew in popularity in Europe and North America (for a variety of reasons including the publicity associated with the French style), it began to commercialize rapidly. This commercialization led to a number of young climbers being able to make a living from sponsorships. Also, for younger Anglo-Saxon climbers, the French style resolved the problems that they were experiencing with regard to making new ascents in locales that had apparently been 'climbed out' by their predecessors. When all that apparently remained was steep rock involving spectacularly difficult moves with very little natural protection, the risk—difficulty tension balance had swung too far in the direction of risk for these climbs to be made. But the French style permitted a swing in the other direction—towards difficulty with limited risk. A third piece in the puzzle leading to competitions in the West was a growing number of exchanges with the Soviet bloc, and younger Western climbers finding that competitions were fun.[13]

These elements came together in 1985 at Bardoneccia, Italy, where the first 'sport climbing' competition was held.[14] It offered prize money from sponsors and organizers, and was quickly followed by two events (one at Arco, Italy, the other at Bardoneccia again) which attracted 150 climbers (including British and Americans), and offered approximately US$40,000 in prize money, and a car. Rather than speed climbing, these events took place on natural rock and involved ascending a preset, preprotected route of increasing difficulty—the individual reaching the highest point was the winner.

The outcry, particularly from older established climbers, was enormous. While criticism was never fully articulated in terms of growing institutionalization and the upsetting of the risk-difficulty tension balance, those themes were evident in most of the statements against sport and competition climbing. National Alpine Clubs and the Union Internationale des Associations d'Alpinisme at first refused to countenance any involvement in the activity, but when sport climbers threatened to form their own organization, the clubs relented and established sport-climbing competition sections in an attempt to maintain some control of the direction of their sport. The first change that was instituted was to shift competitions to artificial rock walls, primarily for environmental reasons (to prevent damage to the rock, and from crowds of spectators in fragile mountain environments). But the change also facilitated the development of competitions—they could be held indoors, even in the evenings; they were more accessible to television; it was easier to charge admission costs; and route setting was more easily controlled.

Climbing-wall technology had begun to develop in the 1960s and improved in the 1970s as the outdoor education movement developed and as climbers began to see indoor walls as a ready means of winter training. But wall technology has improved by an order of magnitude in the last ten years—climbing walls have become a staple feature in most big cities for both climbing training and as a fitness alternative. And competition has thrived. While there have been problems at the top level—a World Cup circuit and national teams that are having some difficulties, failure to obtain a continuing television contract and stable sponsorship—the X Games on ESPN have injected some new life into the sport, and local and national-level competitions continue to grow.

Implications

In the Introduction I compared the emergence of sport climbing and formal competition with the legalization of broken-time payments by the Northern Rugby Union. The result was a rift over the issue of amateurism, and the emergence of two different sports— rugby union and rugby league. The entrepreneurs of the Northern Union were able to resist the strength of the Rugby Union by reflecting the reality of having working men as talented players, and develop an economic rationality as gate-taking clubs where competitive success was important. But the sport was able to split precisely because there were institutions in place to determine who could, and could not, play; the rules by which they played; and the competitive structure of the sport(s).

In climbing, there are no institutions with such powers. It is impossible to determine who can participate, or the way in which they might participate. Competitive structures are determined by consensus; sanctions are imposed by consensus, or by a refusal to record achievements; and the geographical reach and diversity of the sport ensures that local ethics frequently prevail over any national consensus.

Thus, the full consequences of the emergence of sport climbing are not yet apparent. On the one hand there are many climbers who are fearful that competition and the development of legislative bodies will lead to restrictions, certification, and testing throughout the sport—the full incorporation of climbing. On the other hand, there are many others who have accepted competition as an enjoyable and inevitable variation in the sport; they argue that this is just another climbing 'game' that will not have a detrimental impact on the sport as a whole; and that the two types of climbing (adventure and sport) will co-exist with (as is now evident) many individuals crossing over the two styles.

There are all kinds of evidence to suggest that co-existence, even the incorporation of sport climbing into the larger climbing culture, will be the final outcome. Local ethics, in many places, combine aspects of sport and adventure climbing; some of the most hardened initial critics of competition have been won over by the excitement of good competitions; climbing magazines—the major medium of communication among climbers—have, to a greater or lesser extent, all reported on climbing competitions and treat sport climbing as just another aspect of climbing; and local accommodations have been made with some cliffs being designated as sport-climbing cliffs while others are reserved for adventure climbing (similar local accommodations have been made for environmental protection—for example, voluntary climbing bans during bird nesting season). However, disputes are also still in evidence, and this major shift in climbing toward the dominant sport culture[15] has the potential to cause an even more major transformation in the sport replete with intended and unintended consequences. For example, apparently innocent links with government through minor sources of funding (such as the British government funding the British Mountaineering Council through the Sports Council, or the availability of European Community funding to climbing organizations—funding used for administration, and for educational, access, and conservation work) result in accountability and a certain amount of implicit control.

Climbing on publicly owned lands (for example, national parks) also has a controlling effect as government supervision of parks, concerns about environmental preservation, and costs such as those for mountain rescue continue to escalate. Climbers promoting and seeking careers in outdoor education and adventure tourism have also led, and are leading, to government and/or self-regulation (for example, certification and the imposition of safety standards).

But the sporting-goods industry has been the major force in incorporation, fueling and in turn being fueled by a rapidly growing number of climbers. The industry's presence is evident in a growing number of individual and expedition sponsorships, in the rapid development of equipment to make the sport 'safer and easier' (a sporting-goods industry imperative somewhat at odds with the traditions of climbing), and in its organization and funding of competitions. The need to make a living, when combined with the opportunity to be involved with climbing on a full-time basis (as a bureaucrat, in the marketing or manufacturing of equipment, in outdoor education or tourism, or as a professional), proves quite compelling for many young people.

When these are combined with the acceptance of organized competition, and continuing attempts to have sport climbing competitions recognized as an Olympic sport, they raise questions about the future of the activity. For much of its approximately 120-year history, climbing has remained outside of the dominant sport culture. To use Raymond Williams' typology in a rather simplistic manner, adventure climbing represents a cultural form that has been "residual-not-incorporated," not opposing the dominant sport culture but representing an alternative way of 'doing sport.'[17] Sport climbing represents an "emergent-incorporated" cultural form, with many practitioners who are anxious to become a part of the dominant sport culture of Olympic medals, record books, television contracts, and sponsorship. However, the ongoing richness of debate in the climbing community is an indication of the continuing strength of the anarchic and community-controlled subculture of the sport, one that will not easily be incorporated into the dominant sport culture.

Postscript

Climbing represents a fascinating laboratory for sociologists and historians of sport. The institutionalization of sport has been a major topic of research in both disciplines, and climbing serves as a fascinating case of the processes by which a sport might resist institutionalization. Also, the 19th century records of the institutionalization of sports are usually incomplete, and many other sports emerged in an institutionalized form following the model of the earlier sports. The current processes in climbing, apparently both resisting and embracing institutionalization, and maintaining some integrity as a single activity, provides rich insights into this process, with documents and first-hand accounts readily available.

Notes

1. P. Donnelly, "The invention of tradition and the (re)invention of mountaineering," in K. Wamsley (ed.), *Sport History and Social Theory* (Dubuque, Iowa: Brown & Benchmark, 1995), pp. 235–243; P. Donnelly, "Mountain climbing," in D. Levinson & K. Christensen (eds.), *Encyclopedia of World Sport* Vol. 2 (Santa Barbara: ABC-CLIO, 1996) pp. 657–663; P. Donnelly, "Rock climbing," in D. Levinson & K. Christensen (eds.), *Encyclopedia of World Sport* Vol. 2. (Santa Barbara: ABC-CLIO, 1996) pp. 803–808.

2. J. Stoltz, *Adversity Quotient: Turning Obstacles into Opportunities.* (New York: John Wiley & Sons, 1997).

3. The focus here is on rock climbing specifically; and while there are similarities with ice climbing, and many of the techniques are used in mountaineering, the primary concerns relate to rock climbing.

4. 'Ethics,' the informal rule structure of climbing, are detailed in the following section.

5. L. Tejada-Flores, "Games climbers play," *Ascent*, May 1967, pp. 23–25.

6. A complete history of the development of ethics is beyond the scope of this paper, but will be outlined in my forthcoming book on the origins and development of climbing (Manchester University Press).

7. Tejada-Flores, "Games climbers play."

8. J. Krakauer, *Into Thin Air* (New York: Villard, 1997).

9. Peter Donnelly, "Take my word for it: Trust in the context of birding and mountaineering," *Qualitative Sociology*, 17(3) (1994) pp. 215–241.

10. After a series of Alpine accidents in the 1860s and 1870s that killed a number of young upper- and upper-middle-class British men, the Alpine Club, the *Times*, and even Queen Victoria condemned the sport, and there were questions as to whether it could be regulated. The Alpine Club began to pay major attention to safety issues. In the 1930s, after a number of German and Austrian climbers died attempting serious north-face routes in the Alps, the British climbing establishment in the form of Colonel Strutt (then president of the Alpine Club) condemned the recklessness of the climbers and suggested that the climbs represented a blind devotion to Nazism and Hitler.

11. Other areas of debate have concerned the use of pitons, and gymnastic chalk—pitons because their insertion and removal scars the rock, and both because they leave visible evidence of the passage of humans. While both of these are environmental concerns, the latter is also

an ethical concern, because the scars and chalk marks trace a route, and mean that subsequent climbers do not need the same route-finding skills as those making the first ascent.

12. This may be likened to walking a gymnastics balance beam—on practice beams, just a few centimeters above the floor, little thought is given to walking across the beam; when the beam is at competitive height, especially if there are mats around, most normally healthy people will have little difficulty walking across the beam; if the beam is placed above a 100-meter drop, one knows that one has the ability to walk across the beam with little difficulty, but it becomes a great deal more problematic to do so.

13. Americans were perhaps a little more ready for competition than the British and northern Europeans because they had had a system of bouldering competitions in place since the 1960s, quite organized on a local basis with equipment stores offering their wares as prizes.

14. See K. Berkhout, "Competitive sport climbing: The social construction of a sport" (unpublished master's thesis, University of Western Ontario, London, Canada, 1991).

15. See, for example, P. Donnelly, "Subcultures in sport: Resilience and transformation," in Alan Ingham & John W. Loy (eds.), *Sport in Social Development: Traditions, Transitions and Transformations* (Champaign, Ill.: Human Kinetics, 1993), 119–145; and P. Donnelly, 'Prolympism': Sport monoculture as crisis and opportunity, *Quest*, 48(1) (1996) pp. 25–42 for a discussion of the dominant sport culture and alternative/resistant sport cultures.

16. Raymond Williams, *Marxism and Literature* (Oxford: Oxford University Press, 1977); Williams, *Problems in Materialism and Culture* (London: Verso, 1980).

SURFING

Chapter Eighteen

Vintage Days in the Big Waves of Life

Greg Page

I'll never forget my first wave. My Dad pried me up from my death grip to a tentative stand-up position on the front of his ten-foot board. I've been a surfer ever since chasing waves, being chased by sharks, and chasing the dollar so I can surf some more. I've seen lots of good days but only a handful of huge days. These took place during special winters of special years.

Winter of 1962–63

As far as I was concerned, when I was seven, my Dad was the best surfer in the world. That is, until we stood together on our second-story balcony to watch big-wave surfing pioneer Greg Noll ride giant waves at the Breakwater, a big-wave surf spot inadvertently created by the Army Corps of Engineers to protect King Harbor in Redondo Beach, California. My Dad told me that Noll had paddled about a mile through and around the outside of the harbor to surf those monsters that day. I still remember seeing him charging across a massive wall wearing his trademark black and white striped

---

Greg Page has been surfing and skateboarding since the early 1960s. His father, who is well into his seventies, still surfs as do his brothers Ty and Brant. In 1979, he paddled a surfboard 270 miles down the Grand Canyon rapids of the Colorado River. Greg has been a surf lifeguard since 1974. He currently resides on the surf-rich shores of Taranaki, New Zealand, with his wife and two children and has a tandem surfing business.

trunks. I wanted trunks just like Greg Noll's, and I wanted to surf big waves when I grew up.

Now that I am a grown-up surfer, I still want to ride big waves, but it takes a special breed of surfer with the desire, skill, and luck to ride the biggest waves on the planet. Going into the new millennium, surfing is setting new standards for itself, especially in the realm of big waves. The surfing competitions of the late nineties are pushing the big-wave envelope farther as professional surfers vie for big-money prizes and the respect that comes with them.

But you can't depend on big waves to always be there like a mountain, river, or rock wall. They are transitory, cyclical, and dependent on a huge variety of circumstances. They pay no heed to stressed-out contest organizers, egomaniacal surf stars, or soul surfers. The odds of scoring big waves are better now with the accumulated knowledge of the world's surfbreaks and weather patterns, but some years are always going to be better than others, and some will be vintage.

The Swell of the Century: The Breakwater, December 1969

In my 35 years of surfing, they are still the biggest waves I have ever seen. A gigantic storm in the Gulf of Alaska produced waves on a scale that hasn't been seen since. One after another they roared in from the Northwest, each with a magnificent plumage of windswept spray blown back by the South wind. They marched sternly toward shore like soldiers in long regimented lines, even and smooth until they bombarded the Breakwater.

I phoned my Dad at work, and he drove to our beachfront home for lunch with a couple of workmates to check these waves out. When they arrived, he said he had seen plenty of days this big, and he reckoned the waves were about fifteen feet. I told him these were only the small ones, in between sets. My dad plugged in the coffee percolator, but before the water had a chance to boil, the horizon went black as the next set of mackers brewed outside. The waves traveled over the deep submarine canyon losing little speed or power before the bottom quickly shallowed and they stood up to their full height about 500 yards offshore.

The first wave of a set would always be an impossibly long wall, closing out before blasting into the massive granite boulders with the newly formed eight-foot-high concrete seawall on top. The whitewater from that first wave would rebound off the Breakwater to form a smaller side wave that traveled almost parallel to the beach, unbroken at a great rate of speed until it met with the next wave. When these two combined, the wave would "bounce" and nearly double the size of the open ocean wave.

I imagined myself surfing these waves. My eyes followed the only logical path, which was directly below the rapidly moving ricochet bounce. The peak warbled as it shifted down the line until the lip unloaded, pitched out, and exploded on the flat water in front of the wave. The lip peeled evenly like a big zipper closing around a huge pipe. Sometimes the peel rate would slow and the wave would spit out a mass of spray that was choking the barrel, then speed up again. I had no problem "riding" the wave up to this point, but I could never figure out what to do next. After about 200 yards of a grinding left tube, the wall would stretch for two blocks and then topple over all at once in a mighty closeout. There was no chance of an exit, and all that whitewater would surely drown a man.

These waves were as high as the thirty-foot lampposts on top of the seawall. Huge rocks were shifted and waves broke over the breakwater, re-forming into yacht-wrecking waves in the inner harbor. A haze of sea spray filled the air. The crack and rumble of these mighty beasts shook the windows in our house. I don't know how many other surfers imagined riding these Jack and the Beanstalk waves, but certainly no one tried the real thing.

Two days earlier, that same swell closed out the whole North Shore of Oahu with estimated 60-foot-plus waves. Looking for somewhere that could handle the swell, Greg Noll drove around to the Westside, where the legendary point surf of Makaha was in full cry. He nearly drowned after taking off and riding one of the biggest waves ever attempted. Noll quit surfing after that wave, closed his surfboard manufacturing business, and moved to Northern California to fish.

The surf pumped that whole winter. I saw my Dad ride fifteen-foot waves, the biggest of his life. My eleven-year-old brother Ty and I surfed a couple of scary eight-foot days.

March 1974

There were several big days each winter but nothing anything like the swell of '69. Ty and I were getting near the top of the pecking order at the Breakwater and were usually the first guys out when it got big. Ty had won the US Champs at Huntington Beach in

1970 for his age group and was twice runner-up. I didn't do so well in contests and didn't really care. I was part of the anti-competition mood then prevalent in California.

The winter surf season of '73–'74 was another mediocre year until an intense storm in the Gulf of Alaska lit up the coast with a powerful swell in early March. I would almost drown and get the best wave of my life during that week of waves.

Nowadays, professional surf forecasters transmit up-to-the-minute reports via telephones, faxes, pagers, and live video feeds on the Internet. In 1974, a surfer needed to check the conditions daily and keep his ears tuned to the fiberglass telegraph. I surfed shoulder-high waves in the morning before attending classes at the local junior college. When I got home, the swell had jumped to triple overhead and still rising. The waves looked extremely powerful and consistent. A crew of about thirty dodged the biggest ones and tentatively rode between sets. I was out there.

Well, almost. There is no way to paddle out at the Breakwater or any of the other beaches in the area when the swell gets over eight feet. Unknowingly, the Army Corps of Engineers provided a simple yet dangerous path out beyond the impact zone. Anyone could do it. Surfers from up and down the coast would converge on the Breakwater because of the big, powerful waves and the ease of getting out the back. Just walk out along the seawall, clamber down the car-sized granite boulders and jump right in. Time it right and it's a piece of cake. Time it wrong . . .

There is a real party atmosphere when the surf comes up at the Breakwater. Hundreds of spectators sit up on the wall and you can hear them hooting when the big sets approach and screaming approval as riders hurl themselves over the ledge. As surfers take another walk out to the jump-off spot, the wall critics heckle the kooks, praise the last wave of their heroes, and commiserate about the bad wipe-outs.

I joined the queue of about fifty surfers waiting for their chance to get wet. The perfect-shaped waves crashed into the rocks relentlessly for about twenty minutes, and most of them were going through unridden. Nobody was too keen on jumping off while whitewater surged to the top of the wall. It would be suicide. But this was my spot and I couldn't wait any longer. I pushed my way to the front of the line and waited for slightest lull that would give me time to run down the rocks, jump as the next wave hit, and paddle to safety about twenty yards away.

I saw my chance and didn't hesitate. I hopped down two big boulders and launched myself just as a medium-sized wave surged up the rocks. Unfortunately, my fin got caught on the edge of the jump-off rock and I tumbled head over heels into water. As I sheepishly surfaced, I heard the gallery laugh and jeer at my predicament. I swam for my board—which was only a couple of yards away—when I heard the whistles and hoots signaling the next set. I could see the surfers farther out than me scratching for the horizon, and I knew if I didn't get away from the rocks, I would be dead meat.

I stroked as hard as I could, and as I saw the first wave lift, I thought I just might make it over the beast. When I was halfway up the wave, the lip pitched way out over me. I sank the nose of my board into its guts and started coming through the back when I felt myself slowly going up and backwards. I was locked in the lip and on my way over the falls. Down the mines. Shafted. Hanging on to my board upside down and going over faster now, I expected the worst, but when I hit, the lip drove me into deep, calm water and the wave passed me by. I swam safely to shore, collected my board and tried it again.

This time I made it out the back, and I took my place in the line-up and waited for the big one. It was only a matter of moments before the biggest wave I had ever come face to face with finally arrived. I wasn't going to let it go without me. I spun my board around, put my nose down, and paddled as hard as I could. I felt the wave lift behind me, and even though I was paddling like crazy, I was still being lifted up, almost going backwards. I was looking down an impossibly steep wave that was two stories tall when I felt the sudden acceleration and I stood up. I zoomed down the face of the wave faster than I had ever gone before but not fast enough.

I had taken the first wave of the set and I was about to pay the price for not choosing more carefully. I made it to the bottom just before it closed out. I straightened out in front of the mountain of whitewater following me and lay on my board, hoping to prone it out. The impact hit me like a truck. I went spinning and tumbling like a rag doll. I punched myself in the nose as I cartwheeled in the cauldron, and then I was pinned on the bottom in the cold darkness as the violence rumbled by me. I was craving air when I was finally able to push myself off the bottom and head for daylight.

The surface was thick with foam, and just before I got my head up for a breath, the next wave hit me. My lungs were aching as I was driven down and over and around and around. I was lost. Didn't know which way was up. Needed a breath. Seeing stars. Relax. Panic. No, relax. Getting dark. My feet found the bottom, and I gave one last push and broke the surface gulping air and foam.

The next morning Ty and I were the first out. The waves were bigger still but silky smooth and incredibly hollow. I chose my wave more carefully this time. As I made the drop, the peak shifted ahead of me, making the wave more concave, and a silvery blue lip pitched. I was flying along as I pulled up under the lip and watched it land way out in front of me. I saw my brother paddling up the face fifty yards away looking back at me in the biggest tube of my life. I tried to say something, but I could manage only a loud hum. The whole wave was humming and glistening and breathing and pounding, and then the lip slowed down and I found the open door and came flying out.

January 1983

The El Nino had a profound effect on the surf in 1983. The jet stream lowered and directed storm after storm across the Eastern Pacific, producing swell after swell. While I was enjoying the deep powder of Utah, my brother, Ty, rode some huge surf in Southern California.

One day he illegally paddled through and around King Harbor to reenact Greg Noll's feat of riding huge Breakwater. Unfortunately, the Harbor Patrol wasn't impressed and chased Ty for half a mile to the wave zone. Ty avoided arrest but risked his life by paddling close to the wave-swept rock jetty.

The next day, not wanting to repeat those exploits, Ty and his friends looked for somewhere else to surf and ended up checking out Indicators on the Palos Verdes Peninsula. The waves looked huge but perfect, so they suited up and made their way carefully down the 300-foot-high cliff. One slip on this muddy, narrow trail with loose rocks would mean certain death.

At the bottom of the cliff, they were confronted by some hostile local surfers. Palos Verdes is infamous for territorial zealots who resort to thuggery, violence, and vandalism to protect "their" waves.

Ty argued, "If this is your spot, why aren't you out there?" That logic sent them back into their shells.

The next obstacle was paddling out through the giant shorebreak over sharp rocks covered with spiny sea urchins. They timed it perfectly and somehow made it out the back. The waves themselves proved to be the ultimate danger. Ty's board was only seven-feet, five-inches while his friends were both on six-foot, ten-inchers. These were serious waves that required big-wave guns in the nine-foot to ten-foot range.

However, the waves were smooth and perfect, and Ty managed to bag several big ones. The waves kept on getting bigger, and Ty's friends almost drowned before getting washed in. Ty decided to stay out on his own, knowing he might never get a chance to ride waves this big again. Several huge waves came through that Ty estimated were forty to fifty feet high. They looked like they were moving in slow motion, making a thunderous noise. He made some weak attempts at catching some of these monsters, but backed out after looking over the edge.

Ty has strong Christian beliefs, so he paddled into deeper water and prayed for strength and power. He said that he felt like Jesus just took over and started surfing through him. He got wave after wave, witnessed by hundreds of spectators on the cliff. Finally, Ty got a wave he couldn't get out of and thirty feet of whitewater cascaded over him. He was on such a combination of adrenaline and religious high, he said he didn't even feel it.

In 1983, Ken Bradshaw won the prestigious Duke Kahanamoku contest in big waves at Sunset Beach, Hawaii. Most of the other contests in the growing professional circuit were held in small beach break conditions where organizers were more interested in crowds on the beach than in good big surf.

Winter 1998

El Nino once again caused huge waves in the winter of 1998. In January, Ken Bradshaw got towed by a jet ski into the largest wave ever ridden at Outside Log Cabins on the North Shore in Hawaii. Although scorned by surf purists, tow-in surfing looks set to break all previous big-wave barriers and more than a few bodies in the process. Tow-in surfing started early in the 1990s as big-wave riders explored breaks deemed unrideable by conventional methods. Now every big swell has more new participants eager to get towed in to the next realm.

In February, Taylor Knox earned $50,000 by successfully paddling into and surfing the biggest wave of the winter surf season.

His single ride at Todos Santos Island in Baja California defined the new attitude of surf contest promoters, who now realize the value of quality surf. More competitions in the future will be bound to this ethic, giving the big-wave riders their true place in the sport's hierarchy.

In October, I went for what I thought would be a pleasant small wave at an out-of-the-way spot near my home on the South Island of New Zealand. I chose to ride my new six-foot, seven-incher from my quiver of five boards designed for different conditions. My friend and I were the only ones on the beach except for several rare penguins on their way out for their daily feed. The waves looked considerably bigger than what we expected, but we decided to go out anyway. I had a bad feeling.

We jumped into the rip at the base of the cliff and were aided in the 300-yard paddle by the strong rip that pulls out along the headland. Out the back, the waves were solid in the five- to six-foot range, but breaking unpredictably. I took off on my first wave, rode it for a while and dove through the face as it closed out around me. I came up safely through the back, but my small-wave leg rope kept stretching until it finally snapped. My board popped out about forty feet away, but I couldn't get to it before the next wave took it away. That was the last I saw of my new board. During the twenty-minute swim in, I tried not to think about the Great Whites that are sometimes seen cruising these waters. Later, I borrowed my friend's board and paddled to the end of the headland, searching the rip and climbing up the rocks for a better vantage. Pulling myself up a ledge, I came face to face with a bull seal.

Back on the beach, I decided I don't need the biggest waves in the world to satisfy my lust for surf adventure. There is an adventure with every wave. Maybe that is why Dad is still surfing at 70. Give those striped trunks to Ken Bradshaw. And I change my mind back again: My Dad is the greatest surfer in the world because he gave me the gift of surfing.

Chapter Nineteen

Expression Sessions
Surfing, Style, and Prestige
Douglas Booth

I'm quite envious of surfers.
I haven't quite worked out what the attraction is,
but [surfing is] obviously fun and quite addictive
because people do it all year round.
It looks free and happy and exhilarating.
I'm curious to see what the addiction is.

—Sally Dawson, a nonsurfer

[The ocean is] the only place I could find true equality.
The wave comes, and it lands on you, me and the next guy.
It's bigger than human relations. We're all goin' under.
I loved that aspect. I gravitated toward it.
I wanted to be out there more than on land.
The ocean was the *only* place I wanted to be.

—Legendary surfer Laird Hamilton

Surfing, the act of standing upright on a board and guiding it across
the face of a breaking wave, is a form of dance in which the

Douglas Booth is a senior lecturer at the University of Otago, Dunedin,
New Zealand. He teaches sports history and sports policy in the School of
Physical Education. His primary research interests are the politics of sport
and national identity, and the politics of popular culture. He has written
extensively in these areas and serves on the editorial boards of *Journal of
Sport History* and *Sport History Review*.

boardrider, or surfer, "dances to and with a natural energy form."[1] Pierce Flynn defines dancing as "an organic unity between man and nature that is mediated by cultural processes."[2] At its most basic level, surf dancing is part of the culture of pleasure. Here, former American prosurfer Jamie Brisick speaks for millions of surfers worldwide when he says: "I surf for the same reason I perpetually flog myself to the heights of orgasmic pleasure—because it feels good."[3] Such is the euphoria that committed surfers, those who surf to live and live to surf, have turned their dances into distinctive lifestyles. But these lifestyles are not simple manifestations of a hedonistic culture. They are complex in both their internal dynamics, roles, rules, and symbolic meanings, and in the social and cultural interactions they initiate across society. Moreover, they are in a state of constant flux. This chapter analyzes surfers' lifestyles, the ways that surfers have historically differentiated and separated themselves from "outsiders," and the ways they distribute prestige and honor within their social group.

Surfing and Society

Since they revived the ancient Polynesian art of surfing early this century,[4] surfers have been pursuing, and developing, their own lifestyles. By definition, a lifestyle expresses an individual or group's need for social exclusiveness and distinction.[5] Logically, then, lifestyles reflect relationships at specific conjunctures as individuals and groups react to broader social, cultural, economic, and political circumstances. Surfers' lifestyles manifest in distinctive tastes, aesthetic and ethical dispositions, argot, dress, and humor, all of which separate surfers from non-surfers. But these lifestyles also reflect cultural and temporal variations. This section briefly explores the six primary styles adopted by surfers this century: the hedonism of Hawaiian beachboys; the highly structured and regimented sporting club lifestyle of Australian lifesavers; the carefree, fun lifestyle of California surfers; the subversive spirituality of soulsurfers; the clean-cut, health-driven lifestyle of professional surfer athletes; and the fast-paced, aggressive nihilism of the abrasive generation.

Hawaiian Beachboys

Surfing developed in Hawaii in a climate of moral latitude and, by the interwar years, Waikiki was the archetypal hedonistic paradise in the Anglo world. At Waikiki, indigenous Hawaiian beachboys and *wahines* (beachgirls) forged and maintained a breezy, relaxed, and casual culture, introducing visitors to *leis* (flower necklaces), the *hula* (a "licentious" dance) and surfing. In 1927, Charles Paterson, president of the Surf Lifesaving Association of Australia (SLSAA), described Waikiki as "a riot of color in costumes, dressing gowns and coolie coats." There were no restrictions on bathing costumes at Waikiki, unlike Australia and California, where barechested *men* faced prosecution. "People wear what they like" at Waikiki, an incredulous Paterson reported: "Some roll [their costumes] down to the waist—men and girls both." Surfing was an integral part of Waikiki hedonism. Paterson observed beachboys "giving exhibitions" and "taking out bathers" on boards.[6]

Australian Lifesavers

In Australia, surfing initially developed under the auspices of the SLSAA, a unique organization that assumed the mantle of guardian of public morality at the beach. The foundation members of the SLSAA were middle-class surfbathers who pursued health and hedonism at the beach. They formed surfbathing (later lifesaving) clubs with three objectives in mind: to provide facilities for changing clothes and social amenities at the beach, to legitimize public hedonism at a time when moralists frowned upon seabathing, and to patrol local beaches and provide a safety and rescue service for other beachgoers. Surfbathers quickly discovered the value of sport in fulfilling these objectives. Sports, such as beach sprinting, ocean swimming, surfcraft races and precision military-style marching, not only kept members fit for duty, they "proved" that they were highly disciplined athletes who would help preserve high moral standards at the beach. Within a decade of the SLSAA's formation, sport had become the *raison d'être* for most lifesavers and a more restrained hedonism had emerged.

SLSAA beach inspectors policed behavior, bathing costumes, and surfboards. As late as the Great Depression, the SLSAA recommended that men cover their chests at the beach. Surfboards were a particular concern. Heavy and cumbersome, they posed a danger to both their riders and the surfbathing public. Equally important, surfboards threatened to introduce an unacceptably alluring hedonism into the lifesaving clubs from which the SLSAA was eager to distance itself. In short, most early Australian surfers belonged to a lifesaving club and volunteered the bulk of their leisure time to patrol beaches and train for lifesaving competitions. Few had the opportunity to surf for pleasure and to develop their dancing.

California Surfers

Many California and Hawaiian surfers also patrolled beaches and performed rescues. But, unlike their Australian counterparts, they were employed as professional lifeguards, and they had free time to surf for pleasure. Unencumbered by the dictates of a regimental surf lifesaving association, California surfers were at liberty to create hedonistic, nonutilitarian lifestyles. However, it was only after the Second World War, through a combination of unique circumstances, that a distinct surfing lifestyle emerged in California.

Cheap air travel allowed many Californians to return to Hawaii, where they had observed idyllic beach conditions during wartime postings. When they returned to the mainland after their Hawaiian sojourns, these pioneer surfers took with them

> the symbols of the warm *aloha* of Hawaii. They wore the flowered print silk shirts of the islands, casual, colorful, loose and easy. And the thong slaps. And the classic surfer shorts, cut longer to just above the knee to protect the leg from rubbing on the waxed deck. At Windansea Beach and San Onofre grass shacks were built, not unlike the palapas on the beach at Waikiki.[7]

The laid-back Hawaiian beachboy lifestyle resonated with a youth culture undergoing liberalization in the wake of the Second World War, and it contributed to the further development of a distinct California surfing lifestyle with its own argot (for example, "like wow," "daddy-o," "strictly squaresville"), antics and pranks (hidden surfboards, disconnected distributor wires), dress (bleached blond hair and goatees, T-shirts and striped Pendleton shirts, narrow white Levi jeans and Ray-Ban sunglasses), and ethos (endless parties, "surfaris"—weekend and holiday jaunts in search of perfect waves). The surfari, in particular, became the essence of California surfers' lifestyle; it also quickly became synonymous with escapism, freedom, idealism, and fun in popular discourse.

The distinctive style and tastes of California surfers diffused worldwide with Hollywood and specialist surf films. In the wider society, however, there were many who felt that surfers transgressed accepted sartorial and behavioral norms. In Australia, for example, newspaper correspondents, local councilors and school principals denounced "long-haired" surfers who blocked footpaths, stairways, and promenades, turned public toilets into changing rooms, drank wine in public, passed loud, foul remarks at girls, and wore jeans, lumber jackets, "gaudy sweaters and socks and casual footwear."[8] Adding to these allegations of "antisocial" behavior were popular fears about surfer "itinerants," "nomads" and "wanderers" who never seemed to work but just travelled to far-off, exotic places. In the USA, Australia, New Zealand, and South Africa, "surfer" became a dirty word. A small number of local councils even banned surfboards from their beaches. In Australia, the California style engendered hostility between those surfers who, with their "free-and-easy attitudes," were simply "out for a good time," and those who remained loyal to "the indigenous beach movement"—the SLSAA.

Soul-surfers

In the mid-1960s a new zeitgeist changed the cultural meanings of surfing from a happy-go-lucky, fun activity into an opt-out lifestyle called soul-surfing. Andrew Milner describes the period as a form of "apocalyptic hedonism."[9] On the one hand, "the frantic economic urgency of producing fresh waves of ever more novel-seeming goods, at ever greater rates of turnover," combined with a "recurring apocalyptic motif" of nuclear war and environmental deterioration, produced intense feelings of normlessness among youth. On the other hand, "commodity cultures of affluence" produced a feverish lust for pleasure. However, it was the apocalyptic motif, with its debilitating and disorientating nihilism, that best explains the cultural shift in surfing.

Disciples of the prevailing counterculture, an amalgam of alternate, typically utopian, lifestyles and political activism, soul-surfers transformed the traditional work-leisure dichotomy into a work-is-play philosophy. They rejected high consumption, materialism, and competition, and they expounded a form of "fraternal" individualism that extolled creativity and self-expression, often on small communes and country farms. Soul-surfers danced to liberate their spirits. Prominent Australian surfer Ted Spencer, for example, claimed that he "danced for Krishna" when he surfed, while his peer, Robert Conneeley, described surfing as "the ultimate liberating factor on the planet."[10] Soul-surfers also considered surfing an oppositional cultural practice: "By simply surfing," bellowed surfing legend Nat Young, "we are supporting the revolution."[11]

It was an unsustainable zeitgeist. Establishment medias launched savage attacks on surfers, labeling them undisciplined, indulgent, and decadent; they were rotten, long-haired, unwashed drug addicts. But the demise came from within. Yippy leader Jerry Rubin's immortal words, "People should do whatever the fuck they want,"[12] could not reconcile alternative independence with an interdependent society. Drugs were the key to the soul-surfer's supposed enlightenment,[13] but while they may have given Ted Spencer and his ilk "an insight and an appreciation of the energy of . . . underlying things," as historian David Caute points out, "the claimed journeys to 'inner truth' degenerate, on inspection, into puddles of vomit."[14]

Professional Surfer Athletes

Competition was an integral part of the early surfing milieu. In Australia, Hawaii, and California, surfers competed in paddling races and compared dancing styles. In 1954, the Waikiki Surf Club organized the first international surfing championships at Makaha. Judges awarded points for length of ride, number of waves caught, skill, sportsmanship, grace, and deportment. Although the Makaha championships technically founded a new sport, the Makaha event remained a fraternal social gathering rather than a sporting competition.

Surfing really developed as a fully-fledged sport only in the 1960s. Ironically, the social backlash against surfers provided the initial impetus to organize regional and national surfing associations in the early 1960s, particularly in California and New South Wales. (Representatives of national associations formed the International Surfing Federation at the first world surfing championships at Manly, Australia, in 1964.) Surfers recognized that organized competition was essential for public acceptance. "Competition," Hoppy Swarts, the inaugural president of the United States Surfing Association noted, "helped develop a new image with the public—the public has come to respect our surfers in the same way as they respect other athletes."[15] Around the same time, one Sydney newspaper announced that surfers had "matured" since they had formed an official body and that they now had "the right to promote their sport."[16] Several years later, Fred Hemmings, the 1968 world surfing champion, made a passionate plea for surfers to support professional surfing: "*professionalism will make surfing legitimate.* Once the naive public, through the magic of television, sees a series of pro-contests, it will be easy for them to realise that surfing is a clean healthy S-P-O-R-T."[17]

The single greatest obstacle to the development of professional surfing was the anti-competition ethic of soul-surfing. But, paradoxically, the work-is-play philosophy of the counterculture provided a small group of perspicacious surfers with an awareness of the social and economic possibilities afforded by competition. In short, these surfers realized that professionalism had the potential to offer surfers an avenue to eternal hedonism. As Bill Hamilton, a professional surfer from Hawaii, laconically put it, "to live the way *you* want, that ol' green stuff makes the path a lot less cluttered."[18]

In 1976 surfers launched their own professional grand prix circuit. Professionalism forced surfers to radically change their style of public presentation. "Surfers will have to be clean and healthy athletes; there will be no room for drugs," warned Fred Hemmings.[19] Pioneer surfer manager Mike Hurst said that the success of professionalism would depend upon surfers' appearance and intellect, their ability to articulate, project, and be colorful and, he added, they must be photogenic.[20] Australian surfer and journalist Graham Cassidy, promoter of the 1974 Surfabout—one of Australia's first professional tournaments—insisted that surfers "put their old . . . ways aside and come up with a character . . . acceptable to the public."[21] The constitutions of successive professional surfers' associations have all included a "code of conduct" compelling members to "forward a good image" to sponsors and the public. Five-time world champion, American Kelly Slater, is the quintessential professional surfer athlete: "I always want to portray a good image, 'Don't do drugs, stay in school.' . . . it's really important for me to say that in every interview."[22]

The Abrasive Generation

When surfers dance, they translate a host of philosophies, cultural tastes, values, and perceptions into movement. For many younger surfers, their dancing reflects their interpretation of contemporary urban life. For example, instead of escaping into nature, they immerse themselves in greasy, foul-smelling waters that assault and jolt their senses. The ocean is a sewer for the built environment, and, like the ashen skies above and the pallid concrete ribbons and blocks that abut urban beaches, it is a constant reminder of human degradation and contamination. Crowds are a further reminder: at urban beaches surfers find no relief from aggressive competition and no space for reflection, contemplation, or relaxation. The result, as Dave Parmenter so eloquently puts it, is that

> the typical young surfer of today, affected more by MTV and street culture than our own heritage, no longer has any reverence for the wave. Surfing, for them, has become another "fuck you" sport like skateboarding, with the wave becoming just another piece of urban terrain to scrape up against and deface. Their surfing is base nihilism. Like their punk/thrash anthems, the key is to abrade: learn three notes, crank up the amps and disguise an utter lack of talent with sheer noise.[23]

For the abrasive generation of surfers, then, style means spontaneity, individualism, self-expression, competitiveness, profanity, nihilism, and general social dissatisfaction.

Surfing Culture

Lifestyles function to differentiate and separate groups from outsiders. But as the preceding discussion about surfers' lifestyles suggests, there is nothing in this definition "to imply that harmony is more than an optional extra" within a lifestyle group.[24] On the contrary, as Max Weber recognized, "*competitors* who continue to compete" are the building blocks of lifestyle groups.[25] So what do members of lifestyle groups compete for? In a nutshell, prestige, or the recognition of individual merit. Social theorists agree that "prestige is . . . a prime force in human society."[26] In his analysis of heroes, William Goode describes prestige as

> a system of social control that shapes much of social life. All people share the universal need to gain the respect and esteem of others, since without it they can not as easily elicit the help of others, and all individuals and groups give and withhold prestige and approval as a way of rewarding or punishing others. The foundations of social life rest in part on the universal need for respect, esteem, approval and honor.[27]

The remainder of this chapter examines the basic sources of prestige among surfers: dancing style, success in organized competition, and conquering big waves.

Dancing Style as a Prestige System

Historically, surfing has produced three distinct regional styles, each with its own cultural and technological components: Polynesian rhythm, California "hot dogging," and Australian shredding. These are discussed in turn.

Polynesian Rhythm

Indigenous Hawaiians based their style on flowing in rhythm with the breaking wave. Hawaiians emphasized "the wave and the performer as a coordinated unit; the surfer dances *with* the wave, letting it lead him along its natural direction."[28] Underpinning this dance was a casual and relaxed Polynesian philosophy which legendary Hawaiian surfer Gerry Lopez expressed in the words, "it's easier to ride the horse in the direction that it's going." According to Lopez, Hawaiians have benefited from "extended experience" of the ocean, and they are therefore "older and wiser (in terms of self-preservation)." Hawaiians have "traditionally exhibited an innate respect for the waves" and "instead of attempting to impose their order on the waves they seek to join forces."[29] No one has ever embodied this "unobtrusive" style better than Bill Hamilton: "Ever wonder what happened to Billy Hamilton?" Lopez once asked. Well, "he got *so* smooth in the water that sometimes a wave would go by and spectators wouldn't even register that it was being ridden, let alone by whom."[30] Hamilton explained his approach and style as follows:

> After about six years of concentrated effort, perfecting turns, cutbacks, noserides, etc., I became aware of the total correlation of man, surfboard and wave. This discovery had a profound effect on my surfing, and sent me one step further into a new dimension—the flow... I would surf with my mind open, reacting to the situation as it appeared, and utilizing whatever maneuvre it took to get to the next experience.[31]

Technology also had a major effect on Hawaiian dancing style. Early unrefined "planks" imposed severe limitations on surfers' movements. Few riders of planks ever mastered the art of turning and most simply danced in broken waves (white water) while travelling "dead ahead." Gently rolling waves allowed riders to angle their boards and travel across the face of the wave, but without fins and shaped rails, "sliding ass" was a constant hazard. Surfers wanting to change direction either dragged one foot in the water like a rudder or stepped to the back of the board and "tilt-danced" it from one track to another.[32]

This limited technology produced a rigid, statue-like style; proficient surfers demonstrated their superior balance rather than graceful movement. It was only after 1935, and the introduction of the fixed fin to the bottom of the tail, that surfers began tracking along the wall and changing direction by leaning and shifting their weight, and by bending their knees and pushing. Graceful poses—bent knees, arched backs, outstretched arms—coincided with finned longboards during the interwar years.

California Hot Dogging

California surfers developed the first highly maneuverable surfboard—the malibu. They dominated board technology for over a decade from the early 1950s and they ushered in "hot dog" dancing: maximum turns, climbing and dropping the board along the wall of the wave, stalling, walking to the nose of the board, dipping the head into the crest of the wave. Hot doggers displayed grace and elan and they attempted to transform Hawaiian rhythm style into what Dave Parmenter calls "an original American dance... a delightful mixture of ancient Polynesian sport, bullfighting, skiing and sailing." Bullfighting? According to Parmenter, Ernest Hemingway

> brought bullfighting into popularity in the Forties, and quite a bit of the toreador and his "grace under pressure" ethic was later absorbed into surfing: the Manolte arches, the clipped but elegant body english when duelling with the curl, and the graceful foot-pedalling up to the nose to taunt the wave.

Skiing? The telemark, in particular, influenced carving turns. Sailing? "Longboarding a perfect point wave," Parmenter suggests, "is a lot like sailing really; you trim through a fast section, cutback or 'come about' when it slows down, and then set up trim again on a new 'tack' as the wave lines up again."[33] Thus, unlike Hawaiians who flowed with waves under nature's guidance, California surfers tried "to enhance the beauty of a breaking wave."[34]

Australian Shredding

If Californian surfers attempted to enhance the aesthetic value of nature's waves, Australian surfers were the first to dominate the wave through sheer aggression. They adopted a style in which they "dance *on* the wave, attacking it from all angles and reducing it to shreds."[35] It is a philosophy which has its origins in the formative years of the militaristic SLSAA.

From a technological perspective, planks and malibus could not accommodate aggressive surfing. Australian shredding required short boards that would respond to the slightest thought and movement of the dancer, freeing him to move anywhere on the wave. Australian boardmaker Bob McTavish pinpoints 1967 as the year in which "three quarters of the development of the short board" occurred.[36] It was a major turning point in the transformation of surfing from a smooth, rhythmic style into a gymnastic dance in which the wave became the apparatus on which to perform every imaginable maneuver.

Organized Competition as a Prestige System

The advent of organized international competition forced surfers to codify their dancing styles. That the process took over 20 years reflected both cultural variations and surfers' and sponsors' political interests. In the early years rules varied between contests, and judging appeared inconsistent and biased. The Hawaiians initially resisted all efforts to modify their style. It took nearly ten years before an outsider—Australian Midget Farrelly—won at Makaha on New Year's Day 1963. Farrelly, who caustically described Hawaiian surfing style as "stand on the centre of your board and look like a man, if possible against the setting sun,"[37] danced hot-dog-style to win the final. Coincidentally, the judging panel that year included, for the first time, two Californians (Dick Brewer and Buzzy Trent). The Waikiki Surf Club resolved the "problem" of style the following year: it simply returned to an all-Hawaiian judging panel![38]

But the most bitter debates over style were between Australians and Californians. In mid-1966 the Australian magazine *Surfing World* published a conversation with Bob McTavish and Nat Young in which the pair boldly announced a "new era." According to Young, new-era surfers went for "blatant changes of direction [and] radical manoeuvres," looked for the "most intense areas of the wave" and "chas[ed] the curl without too much thought for aesthetics."[39] In the same edition, staff writer John Witzig wrote that the aesthetic grace and poise of postwar surfing had been swept away by "the onslaught of impetuous youth" and replaced with aggression, power, and radical (creative) maneuvers on short boards.[40] Several months later Young won the third world surfing championships at San Diego.

American surfers ignored Australian pronouncements. Instead they hailed the emergence of California "high performers." The entire sport, Bill Cleary wrote in *Surfer* magazine, is following (Hawaiian-born and California resident) David Nuuhiwa's "relaxed creativity."[41] "Rubbish," retorted Witzig:

> [O]ur Nat Young completely dominated competition at the World Surfing Championships in San Diego. Has everyone forgotten that David was beaten? Thrashed? . . . everything the pedestal of California surfing is being built upon [outdated board designs, restricted wave contests, limited manoeuvres] means—nothing! The direction . . . is towards dynamic and controlled aggression in surfing. Nat . . . is part of this "power" school of surfing: he has crushed the "pansy" surfers of California . . . . We're on top and will continue to dominate world surfing.[42]

Little wonder that Hawaiians and Californians considered Australians intensely arrogant.

Professional surfing competitions finally resolved the style issue—in favor of Australian shredding. For the first two decades of prosurfing, Australians dominated. Between 1970 and 1975, four Australians won the Smirnoff [Vodka] Pro event in Hawaii, then regarded as the men's world championship.[43] Between 1976 and 1992 six Australians won eleven of the seventeen world titles based on accumulated points over a set number of contests.[44] In addition to winning world titles, Australians finished in the top two every year between 1976 and 1992 (except in 1989), and they filled at least eight of the top sixteen places in all but three years in that period (1976, 1978, and 1991). In 1992 Australians secured a remarkable ten places in the top sixteen.[45]

While the best professional surfers undoubtedly earn the respect of their peers, many surfers still remain ambivalent about dancing for points. Renowned Australian big-wave surfer Bob Pike was among the first to express this concern as early as the 1950s:

> I don't like to compete and I don't think any of the top board riders do. It takes too much of the pleasure out of

the sport and creates too many jealousies. Competitions are all against the spirit of surfing which is supposed to be a communion with nature rather than a hectic chase for points.[46]

Even Graham Cassidy expressed doubts: "Deep in my subconscious I have this reluctance to be part of competitive surfing. I'm racked with these fears . . . that what I'm doing is going to take away from surfing the virtues that first attracted me . . ."[47]

However, it did not take long before the rewards of professionalism became apparent even to the most skeptical soul-surfers. Reflecting on *Tracks* magazine's initial position, former editor Phil Jarratt said that

recent graduates of country soul, the cool school and drug consciousness, we of the editorial team were determinedly low key about pro surfing. . . . In our corporate view pro surfing was to be encouraged because it gave us something to write about, but sucking up to sponsors didn't fit in with our image of the surfer as outlaw.[48]

But the hedonistic content of pro-surfing quickly converted Jarratt.

I have one lasting memory of those formulative years of pro surfing: we are sitting on the balcony of a Burleigh Heads [Queensland] high-rise unit during the first remarkable week of the Stubbies [contest] in 1977. We are sunned and surfed out but the fridge is full of beer, we have binoculars and a clear view of several thousand beautiful women and MR [Mark Richards] and [Michael] Peterson shredding six foot barrels. By turning our heads 90 degrees we can watch the Centenary [cricket] Test on the large television. David Hookes is hitting Tony Greig all over the [Melbourne Cricket Ground]. Hookes slashes, MR rips, beer slurps, tits jiggle, sun beats down. This is as near to a religious experience as I've been in my life.[49]

Surfing's Ultimate Prestige System—Big Wave Dancing

Irrespective of the era, "national" style, and performance in organized competitions, surfers reserve the most prestige for those who prove themselves dancing on "violent masses of water which rise up suddenly and break with ferocious intent," often into shallow

water overlying coral heads and lava rocks that smash bones and
rip open surfers' flesh.[50] Honors, however, go to those surfers who
successfully perform on 25–30-foot waves at the shrine of big-wave
dancing—Waimea Bay.[51]

Robert Morford and Stanley Clarke define personal prowess as
"a quality that entail[s] skill, muscular strength, and endurance
combined with an appreciation of strategy, or what Homer called
cunning," and ambition as "the will to excel and to assert oneself
in the pursuit of personal glory and fame." But as they note, neither is enough for recognition and honor. This requires "great courage."[52] Greg Noll's graphic account of his attempt to dance on a
25-foot wave at Makaha Point in 1969 is testimony to the courage
needed in big surf:

> Finally a set came thundering down . . . I caught a glimpse
> of my wave. I turned and began paddling, hard. I felt a
> rush of adrenalin as the wave approached, lifted me and
> my board began to accelerate. Then I was on my feet,
> committed. You could have stacked two eighteen-wheel
> semis on top of each other against the face of that wave
> and still have had room left over to ride it. . . . my board
> began to howl like a goddamn jet . . . I flew down the
> face, past the lip of the wave, and when I got to the
> bottom . . . I looked ahead and saw the sonofabitch start-
> ing to break in a section that stretched a block and a half
> in front of me. The wave threw out a sheet of water over
> my head and engulfed me. My board flew out from under
> me. I hit the water going so fast that it was like hitting
> concrete. . . . tons of whitewater exploded over me. It
> pounded me under. It thrashed and rolled me beneath
> the surface until my lungs burned and there was so much
> pressure that I felt my eardrums were going to burst . . .
> the white water finally began to dissipate and the turbu-
> lence released me. I made it to the surface, gulped for air
> and quickly looked outside. There was another monster
> heading my way.[53]

Prestige is a paradoxical form of power: "It gives coherence to
the community even while it expresses social differentiation; it
gives purpose and direction to individual lives even while it is a
matter conferred by the community; it is one and the same time
divisive and unifying."[54] Those who tackle big waves confront the

problem of confining their activity to a small, exclusive group that can control access (that is, "locals only") and prevent challengers from usurping their status, while simultaneously exposing their activities to everyone. But if exposure invites challengers and ignites disputes over prowess, skill, style, and courage, why is it necessary in the first instance? Exposure is essential because a courageous act must be seen before it can be judged.

Oceanographer and big-wave dancer Ricky Grigg and champion surfer Jeff Hackman illustrate this point. Grigg first:

> [In the '50s] we all started riding really big waves and it became competitive. You got damn scared at times. You got so scared you needed each other to do what you were doing. I've been real scared at Waimea . . . I've taken off on waves at Waimea that I probably wouldn't have, had Greg Noll not been watching.[55]

Hackman describes "the single most electrifying thing" that he saw during his competitive career as occurring in 1974, just prior to a semifinal of the Smirnoff event. The contest was held in 25–30-foot waves at Waimea Bay, and Hackman and a number of others were in the water waiting for the start of the heat. The biggest wave of a set approached, and a young local, "T-Bone," started paddling:

> The wave just jacked up and it was huge. It started to suck him up the face and he was at the moment of commitment. We were all so close we could see the expression on his face. He . . . faltered his paddling rhythm for a split second and I could tell he was wondering. Suddenly we're yelling . . . at him to go, go! . . . what's he gonna do? Every surfer in the world that he respects and admires is watching him. Suddenly he's hanging there in space . . . he just plunged, fell out of the sky, landed on his board and the both of them got sucked back over the falls again. There was a split second where he knew he wasn't going to make that wave and where he could have pulled back, but he didn't. He pushed it too far, but he knew he had to or it wasn't worth a damn thing.[56]

More recently, a small band of big-wave devotees have been redefining surfing. Using finely tuned (and regularly tested and flushed!) jet skis, they are towed, like water skiers, into massive 40- and 50-foot waves that break on Hawaii's outer reefs. As well as narrow surfboards and cushioned straps for their feet, tow-in equipment includes "a battery of safety equipment from neck braces to hospital grade oxygen."[57] In the quest for prestige and honor, tow-in surfing has sparked intense debate. Critics call tow-in surfers "phonies" and label the practice "cheating." They charge that without a "take-off and drop" the tow-in crew evade the most dangerous part of surfing. One critic, Dave Parmenter, elaborates:

> Did you ever see the movie *Hatari*? They're hunting rhinos in Kenya and they have this special truck with a seat on the hood, and as they go alongside the rhino at 50mph, the guy in front drags him with a noose. To me surfing is having the rhino charge *you*, and you're there by yourself in a pair of trunks. It's Greg Noll, a solitary guy facing his ultimate fear, and here comes a big black one around the point. You have to choke back that fear, turn around, match the speed of the wave and choke over that ledge. These tow-in guys have the truck, and they're chasing right along with the rhino, at its speed. They're going faster than the wave right off the bat. Plus it's motors and noise, the smell of octane—that doesn't appeal to me at all. And this extreme surfing, you've got to have a partnership, your gear, your walkie-talkies. I've never thought of surfing as teamwork.[58]

Laird Hamilton, the undisputed king of tow-in surfing, rejects these arguments. The real issue, he says, is "high performance and efficiency." Being towed in allows the surfer to get deeper into the tube, while footstraps mean that "you can do a bunch of slick stuff." Moreover, towing means that surfers can "ride the wave twice as far *and* be back to catch another wave" quickly. Thus, it is "totally superior" with respect to both physical exertion and the actual time spent dancing. In Hamilton's words, "I'm here to surf, OK? I've done enough wiping out. I want to make the wave now. Most guys think tow-in surfing is weak, or it's not manly or something, which is great. Killer. They'll just be that much farther behind when they see the light."[59]

The debates surrounding tow-in surfing confirm that the concept of lifestyle always involves an element of the extreme—whether it be of fashion, language, or behavior—and that in a "sporting" lifestyle, the extreme involves physical risk.

Notes

1. Pierce Julius Flynn, "Waves of Semiosis: Surfing's Iconic Progression," *The American Journal of Semiotics*, 5, 3/4 (1987), p. 400.

2. Flynn, "Waves of Semiosis," p. 400.

3. "Surfers on why they surf," *Tracks*, Oct 1991, 80.

4. In the nineteenth century, Calvinist missionaries "banned" surfing in Hawaii, and it went into rapid decline. By the end of the nineteenth century fewer than a few dozen Hawaiians surfed. The tourist industry in Hawaii helped revive surfing, which then diffused worldwide. Leonard Lueras, *Surfing: The Ultimate Pleasure* (New York: Workman Publishing, 1984), pp. 68–100.

5. Barry Barnes, *The Elements of Social Theory* (London: UCL Press, 1995), p. 141.

6. SLSAA, *Twentieth Annual Report 1927–28*, 1928, p. 12.

7. Lueras, *Surfing*, p. 117.

8. For example: "Observer," letter, *Manly Daily* (Sydney), 15 Oct 1965; R. McKinnon, letter, *Daily Telegraph* (Sydney), 13 Feb 1964; " 'Hoodlum packs' sleep on beach: Council plans action," *Manly Daily*, 7 Oct 1965; T. Monoghan, "Balgowlah Boys' High School ended a year of scholastic achievement," *Manly Daily*, 18 Dec 1962.

9. Andrew Milner, "On the Beach: Apocalyptic Hedonism and the Origins of Postmodernism," in Ian Craven, *Australian Popular Culture* (Cambridge: Cambridge University Press, 1994), pp. 190–204.

10. Robert Conneeley interview, *Tracks*, April 1978, p. 18; Ted Spencer interview, *Tracks*, Aug 1974, p. 10.

11. Nat Young, Letter, *Tracks*, Oct 1970, 7.

12. Quoted in Irwin Silber, *The Cultural Revolution: A Marxist Analysis* (New York: Times Change Press, 1970), p. 58.

13. Nat Young, *History of Surfing* (Sydney: Palm Beach Press, 1994), p. 110; Phil Jarratt, *Mr Sunset: The Jeff Hakman Story* (London: Gen X Publishing, 1997).

14. David Caute, *Sixty-Eight: The Year of Barricades* (London: Hamish Hamilton, 1988), p. 40.

15. Editorial, "The competition scene," *Surfer*, 9, 2 (May 1968), 27.

16. "Early problems," *Manly Daily*, 15 May 1964.

17. Fred Hemmings, "Professionalism is white!" *Surfer*, 10 (5) (Nov 1969), pp. 64–5.

18. "1971 Smirnoff pro-am," *Surfer*, 13(1) (April/May 1972), p. 53.

19. Hemmings, "Professionalism is white," pp. 64–5.

20. Interview, *Tracks*, April 1977, p. 13.

21. "A profile of Graham Cassidy," *Tracks*, Dec 1977, p. 17.

22. Interview, *The Surfer's Journal*, 1(2) (1992), p. 90.

23. Dave Parmenter, "Epoch-alypse Now: Postmodern Surfing in the Age of Reason," *The Surfer's Journal*, 4(4) (1995), p. 117.

24. Barnes, *Social Theory*, p. 147.

25. Ibid.

26. Quote by Walter Goldschmidt, *The Human Career* (Cambridge, Blackwell, 1992), p. 48. See also Jerome Barkow, "Prestige and Culture: A Biosocial Interpretation," *Current Anthropology*, 16(4) (1975), and William Goode, *The Celebration of Heroes* (Berkeley, University of California Press, 1978).

27. Goode, *Celebration of Heroes*, vii.

28. Gerry Lopez, "Attitude dancing," *Surfer*, 17(2) (1976), p. 104.

29. Ibid.

30. Ibid., p. 101.

31. Parmenter, "Epoch-alypse Now," p. 112.

32. Lueras, *Surfing*, p. 107.

33. Parmenter, "Epoch-alypse Now," p. 118.

34. Ibid., p. 117.

35. Lopez, "Attitude dancing," p. 103.

36. Bob McTavish, "So how come no one asked sooner?" *The Surfer's Journal*, 4(3) (1995), p. 48.

37. Craig McGregor, *Profile of Australia* (Chicago: Henry Regnery, 1968), 287.

38. Young, *History of Surfing*, p. 94.

39. Ibid., p. 101.

40. John Witzig, "An end to an era," *Surfing World*, 8(1) (1966), pp. 37–41.

41. Bill Cleary, "The high performers," *Surfer*, 8(1) (1967), pp. 38–49.

42. John Witzig, " 'We're tops now,' " *Surfer*, 8(2) (1967), pp. 46–52.

43. Nat Young (1970), Paul Neilsen (1972), Ian Cairns (1973), and Mark Richards (1975).

44. Peter Townend (1976), Wayne Bartholomew (1978), Mark Richards (1979–82), Tom Carroll (1983–84), Damien Hardman (1987 and 1991), and Barton Lynch (1988).

45. Australian domination of professional surfing began to wane in 1993. This followed the introduction of the World Qualifying System. Only the top sixteen of the forty-four surfers on the 1992 World Championship Tour were invited to compete in 1993. The other twenty-eight graduated from contests which made up the World Qualifying System. Brazil and California invested heavily in World Qualifying contests between 1992 and 1994. The result was a massive shedding of Australian surfers from the World Championship Tour. Californians and Brazilians took their places. They qualified without surfing outside their home countries. In 1993 only one Australian qualified for the 1994 circuit. In 1995 the final three contenders for the world title were Americans and twenty-one of the top forty-four were from the United States, including Hawaii.

46. "Australia's fifty most influential surfers," *Australia's Surfing Life*, 50 (1992), p. 88.

47. Phil Jarratt, "A profile of Graham Cassidy," *Tracks* (Dec 1977), pp. 16–17.

48. Phil Jarratt, "Pro surfing in the olden days," *Tracks* (May 1985), p. 12.

49. Ibid.

50. Rod Kirsop, "Sunset Beach," in Nick Carroll (ed.), *The Next Wave: A Survey of World Surfing* (Angus and Robertson, Sydney, 1991), p. 130; Greg Noll and Andrea Gabbard, *Da Bull: Life Over The Edge* (Berkeley: North Atlantic Books, 1989), p. 136.

51. An honor roll would include: Eddie Aikau, Jose Angel, Ross Clarke-Jones, Peter Cole, Darrick Doerner, George Downing, Ricky Grigg, Laird Hamilton, Brock Little, Mark Foo, Greg Noll, Buzzy Trent, and Fred Van Dyke. Aikau and Angel drowned in nonsurfing accidents, and Foo died in December 1994 while surfing 20-foot waves at Mavericks, central California. No one has ever paddled into a wave over 30 feet; surfers call these dimensions the "unridden realm." Mark Foo, "Waimea Bay," in Carroll, *The Next Wave*, pp. 144; Noll and Gabbard, *Da Bull*, pp. 143–148. It appears that the laws of physics preclude such a feat. At thirty feet "the water moving up the face of the wave is moving faster than the surfer's ability to paddle into the wave. The surfer gets sucked to the top of the wave until it becomes so steep that he falls down the face." Fred Hemmings in Noll and Gabbard, *Da Bull*, pp. 189–190. Then again, as waterman Brian Keaulana notes, when the big swells come, "funny things happen—dentist appointments, gotta pick up the kids, absences unexplained." Jenkins, "Laird Hamilton," p. 120.

52. Robert Morford and Stanley Clarke, "The Agon Motif," in J. Keogh and R. S. Hutton (eds.), *Exercise and Sports Sciences Reviews*, 4 (1976), pp. 167–168.

53. Noll and Gabbard, *Da Bull*, pp. 7–8.

54. Goldschmidt, *The Human Career*, p. 31.

55. Noll and Gabbard, *Da Bull*, p. 146.

56. Jarratt, *Mr Sunset*, p. 125.

57. Jenkins, "Laird Hamilton," p. 110.

58. Ibid., p. 111.

59. Ibid., p. 114–115.

SKATEBOARDING

Chapter Twenty

Authenticity in the Skateboarding World

Becky Beal and Lisa Weidman

The purpose of this chapter is to illustrate the values and norms that constitute legitimacy, or authenticity, in the skateboarding world. Both authors spent a considerable amount of time with the skateboarding world in the late 1980s and early 1990s. Lisa Weidman worked at a skateboarding magazine for several years, and Becky Beal did an extensive ethnographic study of skateboarders. Using our experiences and research, we describe the characteristics that skateboarders and the industry use to identify an authentic skateboarder. The first section, on the skaters' perspective, is based primarily on Beal's interactions with skateboarders; the second section, on the industry's perspective, is based on Weidman's

Becky Beal is an associate professor in the Department of Sport Sciences at the University of the Pacific (Stockton, Calif.). She teaches courses in the sociology and philosophy of sport. Her research interests include "alternative" or emerging sports as well as gender relations and sports. She continues to investigate the skateboarding scene, including the interplay of media and skaters' identities.

Lisa Weidman is an assistant professor in the Grady College of Journalism and Mass Communication at the University of Georgia, where she teaches courses in magazine writing, editing, design, and production. She holds a doctoral degree in mass communications from the Newhouse School of Public Communication at Syracuse University. From 1986 through 1992 Dr. Weidman was the advertising manager at *Thrasher*, one of the most popular and long-lived skateboarding magazines in the United States. Her primary research interests involve sports media, alternative media for adolescents, and various other aspects of popular communications.

337

experiences and interpretations of advertisements placed in the skateboarding magazines by companies selling skateboards and related products and services.

Context of the Skateboarder Identity: The Skateboarding Community

It is an anthropological notion that one's identity is bound by one's culture. Before we discuss what constitutes an authentic skateboarding identity, an overview of common values and norms of the skateboarding community will be presented. My previous research[1] has addressed how skateboarding differs from mainstream sport in two significant ways. Unlike traditional youth sport, skateboarding is not organized and run by adults. Secondly, skateboarding does not rely on competition. This contrast to adult-organized leagues is very important for the identity of skateboarders. Skaters have an identity of "other" which is represented in the following letter to a newspaper editor. "Skaters have a completely different culture from the norms of the world's society. We dress differently, we have our own language, use our own slang, and live by our own rules."[2] The following discussion relies on the interviews with and observations of skateboarders that I conducted over a two-year period (1990–1992), with follow-ups during 1997–1998.[3] From that research, two central values of the skateboarding culture were identified: participant control and the devaluing of competition.

Participant Control

Many skaters commented on their attraction to a sport in which they were the ones who made the decisions about the activity. This was mainly represented by their statements about the absence of authority as an important aspect of the sport. For example, Paul claimed that to skateboard "[you] don't need uniforms, no coach to tell you what to do and how to do it," and Kathleen noted that skateboarding has "no referees, no penalties, no set plays. You can do it anywhere and there is not a lot of training." Craig contrasted skateboarding with other sports and noted that it, "is not as military-minded" and "you're not part of a machine; [you] go at your own pace." The skaters asserted that this lack of formality allowed them more freedom to explore and express themselves. For example, Jeff described the skating context as "a lot less confined [than organized sport]. People are open to a lot of new things when you skate. . . . Baseball, basketball, soccer, and swimming, I did them all pretty well, but didn't really pursue them that much. Skating is so fun because it's so progressive, there's so many things, like in baseball there's not much else you can do once you can hit the ball. . . . That's what I like about skating: it's abstract, it's not your average hit-the-ball-and-run sport."

De-emphasizing Competition

The skaters often described their sport as something different from competition. Jeff stated: "I don't know if I would classify it [skateboarding] as a sport. I suppose I just define sport as competition. Unless you are on the pro or amateur circuit, you're not really competing against anybody." Pamela, an 18-year-old skater, made this comparison:

> Soccer is a lot of pressure. . . . You have to be as good if not better than everybody else. You have to be; otherwise, you don't play at all. Skating, you can't do that, you just push yourself harder and harder. . . . Swimming is just sort of there, you get timed—now, for me—you go against the clock—now, when you skate, you *don't go against anything*, you just skate, that's what it is.

While discussing the issue of competition, Doug suggested:

> Most skaters don't, you know, I don't hear, I don't hear skaters whining about, you know, other people being better than them or striving to be, or bumming out because they're not mastering something, whereas in other athletics you do. There's a pressure to succeed where there isn't in skateboarding because there's not huge goals to attain. How do people measure success in skateboarding if you're not skating in contests, which most people don't? Skaters, even in contests, it's more an attitude of having your best run, making all your tricks, as opposed to beating somebody. . . . It's not "I got to beat this guy, this is the guy I'm going to beat."

Not only was competition devalued, but competitive attitudes were seen as a negative attribute. As noted by Charles, "Skaters who are assholes are people who brag or skate to compete." This was echoed almost universally, as Jeff noted:

> Nobody really seemed to like competitive natures. For instance, me, Philip, and one of our friends all found that to be a really big turn-off. This guy would pull a really good trick and rub it in their faces. And then there's Hugh, who can do stuff and doesn't go, "Oh, wow, bet you can't," but he's fun to be with . . . and he encourages you, so that's pretty cool.

Skateboarding and Individualism

The skateboarding structure that developed from the values discussed above encouraged each individual to create a personalized form of skateboarding. Each participant identified his or her own criteria regarding training procedures, goals, and style. The internalization and personalization of these core values were central to being accepted as a legitimate member. The participants expressed this by noting that skateboarding was a lifestyle as opposed to a separate realm of one's life. This finding is similar to Fox's (1987) analysis of punk subculture, where the central members were those who lived the punk ideology throughout all aspects of their lives, and not just on Saturday nights.[4] This consistent commitment to subcultural norms, identified as a specific lifestyle, was also an indication of authenticity for skateboarders. Their commitment was demonstrated by the daily practice of sport and by the regular display of core subcultural values (for example, anti-establishment behaviors). The skateboarders' lack of interest in competition is partially explained by its formal environment and partially by the fact that legitimacy is constituted by their daily engagement as opposed to the outcome of an isolated event.

Another indication that individualism was central to the skateboarding identity was the status bestowed upon newcomers. Often those who just entered the sport had not yet cultivated a personal style. Instead, they displayed a prefabricated version of a skateboarder. In my research, these newcomers were often referred to as "rats." They were often younger and proved their interest in skateboarding by conspicuously displaying name-brand clothing and equipment. The older skateboarders saw this as an initial stage and were quick to point out that these were not true skateboarders. For example, one long-established skater poked fun at the rats: "He wears the clothes, he is a skater. I wear; therefore, I skate." This flaunting of subcultural markers often occurs in the initial stages of developing a subcultural identity. Donnelly and Young described a similar situation with novice rock climbers who bought all the right equipment but did not know how to use it.[5] The unsuspecting rookies' knowledge was often tested by the longstanding members. This testing helped to identify and demarcate authority and status within that subculture.

Having individualized criteria also provided frequent opportunities for self-fulfillment because each skateboarder had many chances to successfully meet his or her own criteria. This differs greatly from adult-run "little leagues," where an outside authority sets the goals for all participants and success is distributed only to those who win. The following describes the value the skateboarders Beal interviewed placed on individualistic standards.

Nonconformity

As noted above, skateboarders defined their sport, at least partially, by claiming that it was significantly different from mainstream sport. In particular, skateboarders saw themselves as nonconformists. The average age of the skateboarders Beal interviewed was 16 years. One common topic of conversation was their experiences of school. An experience that was often described was being an outsider, and not wanting to fit into a world of conformers. For example, Pamela described the different social groups in her school and remarked about how the most popular girls were the "trendies," girls who "end up being like everyone else. . . . Trendies are really superficial." I asked her what "trendies" thought of skateboarders. She replied, "I don't know. I really don't pay much attention to what they thought. If I listened to what everybody else thought, I would be a trendy. No, I do what I want, and if they don't like it, too bad." Philip described the students in his high school and claimed that those who conformed or had money had the most prestige. The group to which he belonged had the least prestige:

> After that comes the group I'm in. We're the alternatives and that—basically we're, we're individuals. That's what they say we are: "You're an individual" [stated ironically]. I hang out with George, and he and I make up the alternative group.

During my two and a half years with the skateboarders, I frequently had them give me feedback on my interpretation of their subculture. One of the most significant comments they gave me was that even though they shared certain basic values (for example, participant control and de-emphasis on competition), it did not mean that they shared all values or were a homogenous group. I did encounter a wide variety of skateboarders. Those interviewed identified themselves as high school honor students, committed Christians, skinheads, feminists, high school teachers, or high school drop-outs.

An apparent contradiction occurred. I wondered how skateboarders could be identified as such if there was not a standard with which to conform. The skaters claimed that their type of conformity was considerably different from that of traditional groups because they consciously chose to conform to a certain set of values, whereas others simply accepted the status quo. The conversation of two skaters illustrates this.

Philip: We're not saying that skating doesn't have any conformity, but it's more by your own choice.

Jeff: It's not conformist conformity. . . . I think skaters are more aware of conformity than jocks. I think jocks just seem to deal with it and say, "Okay, well, that's just the way it is." But skaters go, "Jeese, why do I have to do that, man? I don't want to buy these shoes. I don't want to have to buy 100-dollar shoes just to fit in."

Skaters valued most nonconformist behavior. I found that skaters distinguished types of nonconformity. They valued it more if it was seen as a creative means of self-expression, and valued it less if it was simply an unreflective rebellious act. Those who thought that skateboarding had an essential nonconformist meaning were seen as not grasping the individualized and personalized core of skateboarding. Jeff and Philip explained that as these people became involved in skateboarding and realized there was no inherent meaning to the activity, they dropped out of skateboarding. Jeff and Philip claimed that those who quit skateboarding were the ones who were looking for a predetermined rebellious meaning.

Creativity and Self-expression as the Valued Means of Nonconformity

Warning: Surgeon General states that skateboarding may be hazardous to the health of our society because it promotes creativity and individuality at a young age. Could promote devastating amounts of enjoyment. (Statement on a T-shirt of a skateboarder)

One of the most frequent comments addressing why people liked to skate was that it provided an outlet for creativity and individual expression. Doug, a 25-year-old skater and public school teacher, commented,

A lot of them [skaters] are really involved with artistic endeavors, are very artistic. You can see the parallel; it's a kind of freedom of expression that skating is. How do you express yourself playing football, playing basketball? When you're skating it's—basically skating reflects your mood at the time and how you're skating, what you're doing. You know, it's definitely, you know, a way to express yourself.

Many athletes, as well as sport sociologists, would claim that one can express oneself through organized sport, but the point is that these skateboarders felt they had more opportunity to be creative in skateboarding than in traditional organized sport. The opportunity to set one's own standards was essential to feelings of self-fulfillment, as illustrated by Grace's comment: "For who's to say what trick is better? I like to do stuff that feels cool, that gives me butterflies in my stomach." Alan, a fifth-grade student and skater, wrote a school essay about the ability to express himself without judgment: "The reason I love to skate is because its [sic] a chalenging [sic] sport. It's the way I express myself. It's something I can do by myself and nobody's there to judge me." The skaters were quite aware that there were no formal or outside standards by which they needed to judge themselves; as Craig noted, "There's no such thing as a perfect '10' for a trick."

Not only did skateboarders appreciate the lack of authority that enabled them to freely create, they also creatively challenged authority. In fact several skateboarders felt that the essential values of skateboarding—participant control and lack of concern for competition—directly defied the status quo. One 15-year-old participant claimed that people thought skateboarding was "dumb" because there was no outcome. In other words, skateboarding was worthless because skaters did not rely on competitions to judge the outcome. Another way to judge the worth of an activity is whether one gains physical health benefits. Philip commented, "What I kind of figured out is that Rollerblades are the socially acceptable skate tool. . . . Here's their big excuse: 'It's aerobic exercise.' " An older skateboarder explained that people don't like spontaneous sport, such as skateboarding, in which unstructured and expressive human interaction is demanded. He claimed that people prefer sport that is organized and where the goal—to compete and to win—is concrete.

Another sign of a skater was the ability to challenge social standards. Kathleen and Mark frequently mocked the dominant standards of conformity. One story they told was of an "inspirational" speech about personal control given by the high school football coach at a pep rally. The coach held up a weed and a corn stalk and explained that each individual could choose to be a weed or a plant. Mark commented that dandelions used to be considered plants. Mark and Kathleen noted the irony of the message. According to the coach, taking control of your life meant conforming to what the dominant group labels as good.

Authenticity

It appeared that embracing the central values of the subculture—participant control, self-expression, and a de-emphasis on competition—was essential to the authenticity of a skateboarder. As noted previously, these values implicitly challenged those associated with traditional sport and, therefore, nonconformity to mainstream standards was also an indication of authenticity. This must be qualified, because not accepting the rules and regulations of adult authority was the outermost layer of legitimacy. What gave a skateboarder more status was whether his or her style of nonconformity was a creative form of self-expression. From this point, authenticity becomes more fluid; it is the individual expression of self (as long as it challenges some aspect of traditional values and norms of organized sport or society at large). Yet, authenticity seemed to have one other component that was not directly identified by the participants, and that was masculinity.

Gender

Through my interactions with the skateboarders, it became apparent that females were not taken as seriously as males. Females who skated were often perceived as groupies and were often referred to as "skate Bettys." Doug explained "skate Bettys" in this way:

> They do it because they want to meet cute guys, or their boyfriends do it. It's the alternative crowd; it's like the girls that are kind of into alternative music and that stuff, and kind of skating goes along with it, not as much punk, but not mainstream, and, um, they like the clothes. It's a cool look. I think it's a cool look.

Obviously, this comment marginalizes the role females have—it's not that of a skater, but of someone who wants to associate with real skaters, who are assumed to be male. Not only did the male skaters assume that females were looking for cool guys, but they also assumed that females were less physically capable. One example is Brian's comment: "Oh, sometimes there are girls that like skaters, like they hang out, but they don't really, they aren't like, they just try to balance on the board." Eric claimed that "it takes too much coordination for a girl, and it's too aggressive."

The four females I interviewed were quite aware of this attitude. Grace, a 21-year-old skater, believed "males feel threatened by her," and thus treat her differently. Specifically, she felt patronized and overprotected by her male friends. For example, they were more concerned when she fell, and more enthusiastic when she learned tricks for the first time. Pamela claimed that she had to be better than the males to be accepted by them. To negotiate being part of the group, all of the females stated that they had to become "one of the guys." This indicated that masculinity was assumed to be the norm on which authenticity was evaluated. Females are not accepted as legitimate participants until they become guys (that is, like males).

Authenticity from the Perspective of the Skateboard Industry

The Nature of the Skateboard Industry

The companies that manufacture and sell skateboard parts, accessories, and clothing in the United States and Canada (collectively known as the skateboard industry) are also concerned with authenticity, particularly their own. The owners and managers of these companies work very hard to maintain an authentic image in the eyes of their clientele. Some of the strategies they employ in order

to be seen as authentic are self-selection, sponsorship of professional and amateur skateboarders, and appealing to skateboarders'
values through the advertisements they place in skateboard magazines. Each of these strategies is described below.

Self-selection

Certain people are more likely to be successful as skateboard entrepreneurs than others. Arguably the most important factor affecting a company's success is whether or not the owner understands
the skateboard culture. If the owner demonstrates a good understanding of skateboard culture, skaters will deem the company to
be authentic. Thus, skateboarders themselves, particularly well-
known, professional skateboarders, have the best chance for success (if they have sufficient funds to get a company going), as they
tend to have the best understanding of skateboarders. People who
do not understand skateboard culture tend not to get involved in
the skateboard industry, and those outsiders who do attempt it are
usually unsuccessful.

Sponsorships

The skateboard industry maintains close contact with its consumer
base by sponsoring professional and amateur skateboarders. Sponsorship involves an exchange of goods and services: the manufacturer or retailer supplies a select group of skaters with free
equipment, clothing, stickers, etc., in exchange for feedback and
creative input with regard to product design, distribution, advertising, and overall company image. For example, sponsored professional skateboarders are generally involved in the creation of the
graphics that appear on the bottom of their signature boards. Some
pros even draw the images themselves. Thus, board graphics generally reflect the personality, sense of humor, or interests of the
sponsored pro. This gives the board an authentic, skater-created
look, which reflects positively on the manufacturer that has allowed the sponsored pro to express him- or herself creatively on
the signature board.

Advertising

The skateboard industry advertises in skateboarding magazines—and
almost nowhere else. Since the late 1980s, the industry has had four

or five nationally-distributed skateboarding magazines from which to choose, but two magazines have dominated the market in terms of ad sales, circulation, and influence. These are *Thrasher*, which has been published since 1981, and *Transworld Skateboarding*, which has been published since 1982. Most viable members of the skateboard industry advertise regularly in one or both of these magazines.

Skateboard industry manufacturers and retailers use the feedback and creative ideas they solicit from sponsored skaters to create a company image that is authentic in the eyes of skateboarders. The authentic skateboarder identity is not always depicted explicitly in ads for skateboard products, but the ads usually appeal to some aspect of what is considered authentic by skaters. In other words, the core values described earlier in this chapter are often played to in skateboard industry ads. Below are descriptions of some of the ways that those core values are employed.

Participant control

Many ads use the core value of participant control to appeal to skateboarders. One aspect of this strategy is that manufacturers are rarely pictured in ads. The few who are shown are skater-owners, and they are almost always shown skating. Most often, sponsored skaters and the products they use are depicted in ads, giving the appearance that skaters are in control and are of primary importance.

De-emphasizing competition

Like the skateboard culture in general, ads for skateboard products de-emphasize competition. As mentioned above, most ads feature pictures of sponsored skaters in action, but these photos are rarely taken from contests. Far more often, the pictures are derived from impromptu skate sessions or from planned photo shoots that take place at a favorite skate spot, such as a schoolyard or a backyard ramp. Taken in these "natural" surroundings, the photos are not flashy or professional looking. They belie their commercial purpose. They depict regular guys (mostly) having fun and skating on their own terms, thus sending the message that the pictured skater has a total commitment to skateboarding, not for the sake of winning competitions or making money, but for the pure enjoyment of skating.

Individualism and nonconformity

Another value to which the skate industry appeals through its advertising is non-conformity. Ads sometimes contain images of skateboarders breaking the law, taking great risks in their skating, or behaving in an otherwise unconventional way. For example, an ad for Anti-hero Skateboards depicts one of its team riders smoking a joint and another holding a pistol while sitting in the driver's seat of a car.

The appeal to individualism is accomplished through the display of individualized board graphics and individualized ad campaigns for signature products. As mentioned above, it is customary for pro skaters to design their own board graphics. It is also quite common for skateboard companies to hire skateboarders as ad designers. Self-expression and individualism are valued just as much in this arena as they are in skateboarding itself. Thus, the authenticity of the skaters themselves comes through in the advertising and becomes a part of the company image. An example of this, where individualism takes the form of quirky humor, is an ad for the Ed Templeton signature skate shoe (run in the November 1997 issue of *Thrasher*). The ad features a full-page photo of two older women, conservatively dressed in matching blouses and skirts, walking next to a large, pebbly beach. Each lady's head is obscured by a black circle in which appears an illustration of a sheep's head. Next to one sheep head is a handwritten statement: "have you seen the new sheep ed templeton skate shoe?" Next to the other head is this reply: "f—k that fool! i'll knock him upside the head with my handbag!" The only other writing on the page is a telephone number and a tiny "S" logo.

Insider mentality

The Ed Templeton skate shoe ad also represents an appeal to an in-group mentality, another common strategy for convincing skaters of a company's authenticity. Usually, such ads contain little or no information so that those in the know (the insiders) will "get" the ad and feel validated for having gotten it; outsiders will be left out (and will strive to become insiders). Nike's recent campaign ("What if we treated all athletes the way we treat skateboarders?"), which has been run in the skateboard magazines as well as on television, demonstrates an attempt by an outsider company to appear to be an insider. This effort has been largely unsuccessful, however, as sales of Nike skate shoes have been slow. Skaters know that Nike is a huge sportswear corporation, not a member of the skateboard industry, and certainly not an insider.

Masculinity

Many ads appeal to skateboarders through the core value of masculinity. Some of these ads appeal specifically to male, heterosexual desires, while others appeal to skaters' admiration of toughness and risk-taking. Of those that appeal to skaters' desires, some depict masculine (hetero)sexuality and sexual prowess through the use of female models who possess a number of feminine characteristics, such as long hair, classically beautiful faces, bronze skin, curvaceous but slender bodies, and little in the way of clothing. The models sometimes function as trophies or adornments for fully-clothed (and usually recognizable) male skateboarders. In other cases, the female models appear only with the products being advertised (or even without the products) and function as sexual enticements to the young male readers. For example, Fresh Jive clothing company ran an ad in the May 1997 issue of *Thrasher* featuring a full-page picture of a young woman sitting in a seductive pose and wearing only a see-through baby-doll-pajama top and a g-string.

An appeal to masculine toughness, or the ability to tolerate unpleasant experiences, can be found in ads that depict scary, morbid, or creepy images, such as skulls, skeletons, blood, spiders, and monsters. One example is an ad that Blind Skateboards ran in the November 1997 issue of *Thrasher*. The company logo features a cartoon image of the Grim Reaper, complete with scythe. The ad promotes a "Safe Death team board" which features an illustration of a man lying on the sidewalk beneath a giant metal safe which appears to have fallen from a window where the Grim Reaper character now stands, smiling. The dead man is lying in a pool of blood. The image of the board and its graphics is contained within a photo of a skateboarder holding the board and reenacting the scene in the board graphics (his head appears to be crushed beneath a safe). Most readers would quickly realize that this photo is staged (the blood looks very fake), but the image is sufficiently gory to appeal to skaters' appreciation of a masculine toughness in which mortality is mocked. Yet another ad that appeals to the value of toughness is for Slimeball skateboard wheels (run in *Thrasher*, June 1998). This ad features a profile image of a professional skateboarder leaning over and vomiting; the former contents of his stomach, vegetable-rice soup and two Slimeball wheels, are suspended in air.

Ads that appeal to masculine risk-taking and the teenage sense of immortality often depict death-defying skateboard stunts. For example, an ad for Stereo brand skateboards, run in *Thrasher*, June 1998, features a full-page photo of a well-known pro skater, riding his skateboard in a crouched position, with the front wheels of his board in the air and his back wheels resting atop a wall that appears to be about four inches wide and ten feet high. The skater is just about to drop down to the sloping cement below the wall—a very risky move, to say the least. As mentioned above, this kind of picture could also represent individualism.

Commitment to the sport/lifestyle

Skaters have a keen appreciation for skateboarding history. They honor legendary skaters from the past and admire longevity in the industry. A deep and long-term commitment to the sport and lifestyle is another form of authenticity. Companies that are well established in the industry often demonstrate their authenticity by emphasizing in their advertising that they have a long history in skateboarding and a long-term commitment to the sport. For example, when Santa Cruz Skateboards reached its twenty-fifth anniversary, it publicized the fact in its ads. New companies owned by prominent skateboarders or other respected members of the skate community demonstrate their authenticity by emphasizing the long-term involvement of the owner.

A final note on skateboard industry advertising

Skate industry ads do not authenticate skateboarders. In fact, the reverse is true; the skaters who read the magazines and see the ads are critical judges who evaluate ads for their authenticity. If an ad is deemed authentic, the advertiser will be respected. If not, the advertiser will lack credibility in the eyes of skateboarders and will have to work very hard to overcome this reputation.

Epilogue

Several researchers of popular culture have relied on Goffman's[6] dramaturgical concept of the self and social processes to help illuminate the concept of authenticity.[7] Goffman suggested that people had different styles and intentions regarding self-presentation, depending on whether they are in the front or back region of the stage. The front region is where people are consciously performing for a specific audience. The back region is the area in which one is performing for no audience and, therefore, is seen as a place where people can be themselves, candid and authentic.[8] Donnelly and Young[9] claimed that a significant indicator of authenticity is when the participant is no longer worried about the *general* audience, while Fox[10] claimed that no longer consciously performing for *any* audience was a sign of authenticity.

Skateboarders use what is conventionally considered a front region—public settings such as parks and city streets—to display their backstage style and values. As Goffman noted, "By invoking a backstage style, individuals can transform any region into the backstage."[11] Authenticity for skateboarders is not determined by a successful front-region performance for a general audience, whereby the general audience grants authenticity to the skaters. Rather, authenticity is proven in the back region through an internalization and public display of the norms and values of the skateboard culture, which are really recognizable only to other experienced skateboarders. Thus, authentic style is developed in the back region, with and for other skateboarders, which may explain why the "rats" were not seen as authentic. They used the front region to develop their style.

Goffman argued that the behavior in the back region may constitute offensive or anti-social behavior in the eyes of the general audience, whereas the front region is a place of polite decorum. "In general, then, backstage conduct is one which allows minor acts which might easily be taken as symbolic of intimacy and disrespect for others present and for the region, while front region conduct is one which disallows such potentially offensive behavior."[12]

One sign of commitment to the skateboard subculture (and thus a sign of authenticity) is to willingly forgo any benefits that may come with conforming to general norms and values. Thus, skateboarders' public display of nonconformist (backstage) behavior has a cost: the general audience does not accept them as legitimate citizens of the larger culture. Skateboarders are willing to forfeit such public acceptance because being perceived as authentic by other skaters is so important. In fact, authenticity is arguably the single most important factor determining admittance into the subculture.

Notes

    1. Becky Beal, "Disqualifying the official: An exploration of social resistance through the subculture of skateboarding," *Sociology of Sport Journal* 12 (1995), pp. 252–267. Becky Beal, "Alternative Masculinity and its Effects on Gender Relations in the Subculture of Skateboarding," *Journal of Sport Behavior* 19(3) (1996), pp. 204–220.

2. K. Maeda, "Rights for Skateboarders," letter to the editor, *Windsor Beacon*, Oct 1991, p. 17.

3. I write as a witness and as a participant in the skateboarding subculture. In sociological terms I was a participant observer, though I didn't know it at the time. Yet like any participant observer, I was both involved and removed. I was not a skateboarder when I became involved in the subculture, and though I learned how to skate a little and became accepted as a legitimate member of the skateboard community because of my affiliation with the magazine, I was never considered, nor did I consider myself, a legitimate skateboarder.

4. Kathryn Joan Fox, "Real Punks and Pretenders: The Social Organization of a Counterculture," *Journal of Contemporary Ethnography* 16(3) (1987), pp. 344–370.

5. Peter Donnelly and Kevin Young, "The construction and confirmation of identity in sport subcultures," *Sociology of Sport Journal* 5 (1988), pp. 223–240.

6. Erving Goffman, *The presentation of self in everyday life.* (Garden City, N.Y.: Doubleday Anchor Books, 1959).

7. Donnelly and Young, "Construction and confirmation"; Gianna M. Moscardo and Philip L. Pearce, "Historic Theme Parks: An Australian Experience in Authenticity." *Annals of Tourism Research* 13 (1986), pp. 467–479; Pirkko Markula, "As a Tourist in Tahiti: An Analysis of Personal Experience," *Journal of Contemporary Ethnography* 26(2) (1997), pp. 202–224.

8. Goffman, *The presentation of self*; R. Wallace and A. Wolf, *Contemporary Sociological Theory: Continuing the Classical Tradition* (Englewood Cliffs, NJ: Prentice-Hall, Inc., 1986).

9. Donnelly and Young, "Construction and confirmation."

10. Fox, "Real Punks and Pretenders."

11. Goffman, *The presentation of self*, pp. 128–129.

12. Ibid., p. 128.

Chapter Twenty-One

Drawing Lines

A Report from the Extreme World (*sic*)

Jeff Howe

"Yes. Wait, no. I don't know."
—Professional skateboarder Mark Gonzales responding
to the question, "Is skateboarding a sport?"

Life is funny. In 1966 Paul Van Doren was part-owner of a small but profitable company making niche footwear that featured rubber, nonslip soles. They were for sailors, and sailors liked them. One year later, an unanticipated element of the beach community began patronizing Van Doren's store. It turned out the shoe also fit the particular needs of surfers. It was a happy accident, and Van Doren prospered.

For years Vans, as the shoes were called, remained a cult item. One could spot their signature waffle print on beaches from San Diego to Santa Cruz, but rarely on inland surfaces. As a matter of course, surfers and sailors spend little time in Pittsburgh or Peoria. Then another happy accident. The movie "Fast Times at Ridgemont High" became the sleeper hit of 1982. In the movie, a skateboarding Jeff Spicoli (played by a young Sean Penn) beats himself over the head with a readily identifiable Vans shoe to test the potency of his marijuana. Both are righteous, and Spicoli—the incidental rebel, the

Jeff Howe lives and writes about culture, law, and technology from his Brooklyn loft space. His writing appears regularly in the *Village Voice, Yahoo Internet Life,* and the *Industry Standard.* He plans on skating well into his eighties.

unassuming libertine who has a double cheese and sausage pizza delivered to his US history class—became, however briefly, a paragon of cool. So did his shoes; Vans tracks blossomed throughout the land, becoming *de rigeur* footwear for anyone else channeling Spicoli's particular brand of rebellion through indifference.

Steve Van Doren, Paul's son and current vice-president of promotions, no longer waits for happy accidents. He doesn't have to; in 1988 Vans was acquired by McCown De Leeuw & Co. in one of Michael Milken's final deals before he was busted for junk bonds and sent up the river. Now they're loaded. In November of 1998 they built and completed the world's largest skatepark and over the past four years their revenue has more than doubled. An improbable hybrid of grassroots ideals, prodigious capital, and marketing savvy, Vans has attained the paradoxical status of a grassroots corporate institution. Having nurtured its stubbornly loyal market of surfers, skaters, snowboarders and BMX riders for over thirty years, Vans possesses the street cred and the market leverage to create as well as exploit a trend.

To this end, the company produces "The Vans Warped Tour," a roving festival of extreme sports, extreme music, and extreme marketing. On last year's tour some thirty bands on four stages represented pretty much all the post-punk genres, from ska (Mighty Mighty Bosstones) to thrash (The Offspring) to swing (Cherry Poppin' Daddies). An impressive array of promotional booths for X-friendly companies like Mountain Dew and G-Shock watches lined the grounds. A nearby "independent film tent" offered the "newest in underground cinema." Throughout the day, pro skateboarders, BMX riders, and in-line skaters performed demos on half-pipes and street courses.

The overall effect is a Wagnerian opera for all things Kapital X. If you're a member of the target market, it's all-encompassing and exhilarating and empowering. And because it's all this, it's also faintly unsettling, like the feeling you get when a TV commercial makes more sense of your life than the show you're watching. Warped is a timely conflation of counter-cultural signifiers conveniently swept clean of the messy by-products of more authentic underground events. It's Altamont without the stabbings, a Sex Pistols show without all the unsanitary gobs of spit. Finally, it's a lot of fun and, I believe, the purest expression to date of the skatepunk subculture as commodity.

It's such a good sell it draws into question whether *skatepunk* and *subculture* can still appear in the same sentence. Warped sells out at every stop, and last year they were voted the number one summer festival by readers of *Alternative Press* magazine. For most of its brief history, skateboarding provided disaffected youth with an outlet for their anomie, it articulated what Greil Marcus, music critic and punk rock historian, characterized as "the voice of teeth ground down to points." At Warped, skateboarding is one more consumer fetish in the larger economy of pop culture.

In the summer of 1998, Vans warped four cities, the last of which was the already sadly warped Asbury Park, N.J., a beachfront ghost town of abandoned fun houses, broken glass, and condom-strewn boardwalks. I covered the event for the Village Voice, but I had another agenda as well.

As both a skater and a journalist I've watched the "extreme sports" juggernaut with skeptical interest. Before the mainstream media entered the scene, it had never occurred to me that skate-boarding—or snowboarding or surfing for that matter—could be construed as a sport. Sports involved balls and points and uniforms. But over the past several years the boundaries around "sport" have blurred, and this is a not-altogether unfortunate development. But it is, for me, a confusing one. Is skateboarding a sport? If so, and clearly many powerful people believe it is, then why? I spent my weekend in Asbury Park asking that question of a broad range of people. "Is skateboarding a sport? If not, then what is it?"

Some, like the ESPN producers who were filming the skate-boarding contest, expressed little uncertainty. "Yup," one said. A bored-looking security guard figured it was, like, a new sport. Other attendees ventured farther afield. Matt Pinfield, the program director of MTV's alt.rock program "120 Minutes," equated skating with, natch, rock'n'roll, pointing out the common affinities with danger and speed.

The most provocative response came from a 12-year-old boy, a local whose father had dropped him off at the contest site earlier in the day. Squinting thoughtfully, he gave the question some consideration before responding. He decided that skating is like drawing, which he also enjoys, because "you make lines in both of them." It's an insightful comparison. A skater's line encompasses the path a skater takes through a given terrain and the tricks he or she performs along the way. It's a more-or-less improvised composition taking place in time—a dance whose choreography emerges with its execution.

But by far the most common response I received was a mixture of uncertainty and indifference. "Sure" was a frequent reply, as was "Who cares." This ambivalence has a time-honored history among skateboarders. It's skating as tautology: Skateboarding is skateboarding is skateboarding.

Part of the difficulty in classifying a comparatively 'new' social behavior like skating—or the other board 'sports,' surfing and snowboarding—stems from why people practice them in the first place. Skateboarding's initial, glittering appeal lies in its negation, what it's not. Skating is not football, not piano lessons, not church or sit-com reruns and it's certainly not homework. It's not safe, or even advisable. It's displeasing to pedestrians, and so in many cities it's not even legal. For many young skaters, it feels exactly like something they're not supposed to be doing, thus satisfying a crucial adolescent need to defy the pack and express the nascent self.

For several decades, this anti-anything stance served the overlapping communities of skateboarding, snowboarding, and surfboarding well. After all, contemporary cultural history has drilled them in the formula that as soon as anything interesting emerges, it will be labeled, categorized, canned, packaged, and sold back to us at a markup. From the beats ("Jack Kerouac Wore Khakis!") to the hippies ("K-Tel's Groovy Sounds of the '60s!") to grunge ("1991: The Year Punk Broke!"), as soon as it can be named, it can be sold. Is it any wonder board practitioners would rather not 'be' anything at all?

But by defining itself through opposition, by offering itself as a kinetic voice of protest, skateboarding also necessarily indicates what it is. It can't escape the dialectic of action and reaction. By not being dance as taught in school, it becomes street dance. By not being political, it becomes political. By not being religion as experienced in temples and mosques and gray-stoned cathedrals, it becomes its own religion. And, as I've finally begun to accept, by so forcefully not being any of these things, skateboarding becomes sport.

Every morning I wake up a skateboarder. It's not my primary identity. I am also a man. I am white. I am a Midwesterner, transplanted to New York, so I'm also a New Yorker. I am a writer, a twentysomething, my girlfriend's boyfriend. Every day I am all these things in different amounts as my unconscious continues the daily construction of self. But every day I am also a skater. It's not just a thing I do, but something I am. An attitude and outlook enforced by experience and memory and the track history of scars that cross my knees. No ball sport could ever provide such an identity. Skateboarding—as Mark Gonzales later observed after his initial indecision—is a lifestyle. So as I investigate what skateboarding means to the culture at large, what it has to offer that culture and how that culture receives it, I must first examine how I became a skateboarder.

My dad grew up in Camas, Washington, a mill town on the bank of the turbulent Columbia River. He was the descendent of intrepid homesteaders, and the stories of his youth tend to alternate between the hardships of the Depression and the sacrifices made to the war effort. As it does for many, adversity proved fertile ground for achievement: in high school he played first French horn in the band, guard on the basketball team and sat on student council. In 1948 he graduated valedictorian of his class. He worked his way through some nine years of college, spending his summers shoveling salt cakes in the mill, or later, firing artillery in the Army Reserves. In 1963 he accepted a teaching post at Ohio State University in Columbus, Ohio, and moved our family back in that most inexplicable of directions: East.

Seven years later his lawyer called to ask if he and my mom were still looking to adopt. According to rumor (truth, in these instances, being spare) my biological father, a prominent professional in Phoenix, had sired an illegitimate child—me. Details get fuzzy beyond this point, but at any rate a quiet, out-of-town birth was considered favorable to a local delivery. Two days after the call, my parents picked me up at the hospital.

I was raised in Worthington, an affluent suburb to the north of Columbus. My parents had mortgaged heavily against my father's somewhat meager professor's salary to buy a house in a promising school district. Columbus was booming, one of the only diamond studs in the rust belt, and Worthington fulfilled the city's rising demand for good schools, spacious lawns, country clubs, and well-patrolled streets. Most of all, it provided an idyllic atmosphere in which to raise children, with plentiful creeks, playgrounds, and trees to climb. It was the *Adventures of Huckleberry Finn* as an after-school special. Like many fathers, mine strove to give his children a more comfortable environment than he had enjoyed. In Worthington, he succeeded. I did not know want, in my home or any other. The world of current events played out on our small, kitchen television set—hardship was contained within its diminutive frame.

But comfort stultifies, and Worthington was the epicenter—geographically and metaphorically—of comfort. My second decade coincided with that most stultified of eras, the '80s. Worthington embodied perfectly the Reagan-cum-Eisenhower value system. Lily white, staunchly conservative, and predominantly Protestant, its mores were articulated on multiple levels, be it through zoning or public referendum or the required "town history" curriculum taught in grade school. Dogs were to be chained, yards were to be strictly maintained, and Jews were to stay off the golf course. The big political battle of my youth was to stop Columbus from sending their kids to our schools. Worthington avoided strife by eluding heterogeneity. There is little dissent in a town without dissenters.

It was a perfect petri dish for teen rebellion.

At least one thing is certain: Surfing begat skateboarding begat snowboarding. In the years following their respective births, they have wandered away from one another, then returned to influence the others. All three are distinct, all three are practiced on radically dissimilar terrain, and all three have cultivated their own systems of logic. Yet the essential movement in each may be reduced to a single divine instant of conception. On a day whose date is gratefully lost to history, a Polynesian climbed atop a wave and moved forward by standing sideways.

So unnerved and awestruck were the Polynesian royalty by the spectacle of men walking on water that they passed a law decreeing that only members of the royal family could stand upright on the board. Several hundred years later, in 1820, a Western missionary in Hawaii would again try to ban surfing, considering it a sin. In our century, beaches have prohibited surfing, mountains have forbidden snowboarding, and cities have outlawed skateboarding. What is it about riding over the earth's surface on a board that pisses people off?

In my case, skateboarding was not basketball. Due less to native ability than to the genetic accident of height, I was a pretty good player. It's my Dad's favorite sport, so he encouraged me to play, and since everyone needed to play something, I played basketball. To be fair, I also loved the game—the perpetual motion of the ball, the scramble beneath the rim, the natural grace of athletes other than myself. But by freshman year they'd taken everything thrilling and spontaneous about basketball and boiled it down to a drill. I didn't relate to the other players, and the coach turned out to be a smarmy bastard named Buddy Baker with a German field general's sense of discipline and destiny. I didn't quit basketball to skate, really. I quit because it became boring and annoying—the essence of school in the guise of athletic conquest.

This wasn't cool. As I said, everyone had to play something, and now I was playing nothing. The upper classes determined cool.

Sex, beer, snuff, Jeep Wranglers with fake bullhorns on the hood, cutting class, button-down shirts, fighting, high school football games, and loads and loads of Led Zeppelin were all very cool. Hierarchies were forming; lines were being drawn; some of my friends fit the mold; others didn't—I stood astride a gap in coolness. There was a choice to make, and by the end of the year I'd made it. In a town where you were either with us or against us, a jock or a nerd, a Caucasian or an Other, a Buckeye or a Wolverine, I chose the only viable escape route: I skated. It's definitely not cool, but it wasn't exactly uncool. It was more like none-of-the-above.

Most of my old friends played soccer or wrestled. They did cool things and went to the places where other cool people went. A few, like me, kept skating. The rift between us and them widened. In a high school that tirelessly promoted the Greek ideal of the student-athlete, we'd simply opted out, being neither. We gravitated toward unwanted spaces. Smoking was not cool; we hung out in the smoking grounds. After school we skated behind parking lots, in drainage ditches, and on halfpipes built in abandoned lots. This brought us into contact with skaters from around the city, and we slowly entered a community woven from disparate strands around a common pattern of dysfunction and dissent. We formed a band that played simple songs badly, loud, and fast. We were called the Suburban Morons, and we performed on backyard ramps and at a seedy downtown nightclub called Neely B's. High school became a building. It's where I went before I went somewhere else, anywhere else.

Codes were significant. I shaved off half my hair, bought old man shirts at thrift stores, and painted atomic explosions on torn leather jackets. I branded Lincoln's profile into the back of my hand with a molten penny. Identities were forming. I shocked and mystified teachers and old friends. I was vilified in return, to my deep satisfaction. I cultivated an adolescent ideology, and began to comprehend the structures I was trying to escape. It worked. We were pariahs, untouchable, exempt from the ruthless social caste system of high school. As conspicuous as I'd become—a florid expression of teen-angst cliché—I was also invisible. I was a skaterat, and subject to another community's norms and values.

Subcultures, by definition, are built through the creation of exclusive, esoteric meanings. These meanings are often articulated, refined, and rearticulated through cultural products, be they music or 'zines or, in the case of skateboarding, kinetic expression. If these products offer the promise of broad aesthetic appeal, the media co-opts them and sells them to the culture at large. But because of the diverse demographics in a mainstream audience, the product must be made to conform to a cross-cultural Esperanto—the language of advertising. This act of translation—the explication of these meanings to a mainstream audience—requires the violent distortion of condensation. Consequently, the media manufactures subcultural meaning as much as it translates it, with varying degrees of commercial success. With extreme sports, it succeeded. With electronica, however, it failed.

In the summer of 1997 electronica descended on America. Not the form of music it referred to—which had been present in one form or another since 1974, when Kool DJ Herc first rocked the Bronx barrio blocks—but the *name*. "Electronica" originally meant a loungy form of British techno, aka "armchair techno." But facing lagging sales and the dearth of any genuine musical movements to promote, the recording industry attempted to manufacture its own under the term *electronica*. Eager to replicate dance music's popularity in Europe, major labels like Maverick began signing acts, MTV introduced a show devoted to dance music, *Amp* (now canceled), and a full-scale marketing blitz was initiated. It was to be, as *Time* noted in June of that year, the "summer of electronica."

American consumers have a tendency to buy what they're told to buy, yet somehow the electronica campaign failed. Beyond the success of crossover bands like The Prodigy, even the most vaunted electronica acts failed to catch on. If the music industry was left scratching its head, however, critics and musicians were not. Critic Frank Owen called it "the most idiotic and irritating name change since Prince became the Artist Formerly Known As . . ." Moby, an American pioneer of dance music, said it had been like declaring a punk rock revolution in 1985. The problem was that outside music industry marketing departments, electronica didn't exist. It was an attempt to construct a genre from a disparate group of musical styles related only by an incidental reliance on prerecorded music.

Dance music—like the various activities that have come to be called extreme sports—is made up of various, distinctly separate subcultures. There's techno and house and jungle and ambient and probably a few hundred other varieties of electronic-based music emerging from the bedrooms of teenage DJs around the world. While these subcultures share overlapping influences and histories, they maintain an autonomy engendered by the cultivation of individualized sensibilities, styles, and audiences. In the years following the failure of the music industry to sell electronica to a mainstream audience, these subcultures have flourished, producing ever more innovative sorties into the outer regions of beat and sampled sound.

"A rave kid who goes to a party does not call house music electronica, he calls it house," says Ed Brough, a DJ and writer who produces electronic "happenings" throughout the Midwest. "The genres are called what they are for a reason. Techno is called techno for its affinity to machinery and technology. Drum'n'Bass, on the other hand, is more about miscegenation, a collision of sampling with all the various aesthetic approaches to sampling, which in turn forms a template of its own. There are genres out there that don't even have names yet."

The comparison between electronica and extreme sports is apt. If anything, the different extreme sports share even less in common than do the different genres of dance music. Before ESPN introduced the Extreme Games in 1995, the only contact rock climbers had with skateboarders was when they passed each other on the freeway. So how did sports broadcasting succeed where the music industry failed? The answer, I believe, is that they were simply selling a more enticing product.

A 1994 *USA Today* interview with Steve Bornstein, president/CEO of ESPN, divulged that "according to expert market research, the extreme world is inhabited by bungee jumpers, in-line skaters, sky surfers, mountain bikers, skateboarders, endurance marathoners, sport climbers, windsurfers and street lugers." Bornstein told them that ESPN had seen "a need in the extreme world for [the Extreme Games]."

"We saw a need in the 'extreme' world for this," Bornstein told *USA Today*. I'm not sure where in our solar system the "extreme world" is located, but it sure sounds exciting. I believe it's the world depicted in Mountain Dew's long-running "Do the Dew" ad campaign, where teen-age rugged individuals perform all manner of death-defying stunts in testament to the deep frisson their sponsor provides. The stunts themselves are meaningless; the image of the "extreme" is all that counts. The "skateboarding world," by comparison, sounds far less alluring.

What the skateboarding community lost on its inclusion into the extreme world—and what techno or any other genre of dance music retained following electronica's dismissal—is the power to call

itself itself, its power of naming. Naming, as literary critic Kimberly
Benston has written, functions as "the means by which the mind
takes possession of the named." Within this logic, America doesn't
buy skateboarding, it buys the whole, chimerical "extreme world,"
and skateboarding, an indistinct element within that world, loses its
meaning, at least within the reality imposed by the mass media.

Skating stands at a crossroads, its meanings—and thus its future—ambiguous. A thesis of sorts: To resist this act of naming, or
at least propose alternative names—dance, performance, kinetic
grafitti, or just simply skateboarding. Even the name of this book/
essay, and consequently its central premise, conspire against me.
Skateboarding: one of twelve extreme sports. The truth is that board
culture couldn't possibly share less in common with kayaking and
rock climbing. Skateboarding is skateboarding is skateboarding.

The house was still dark as I tumbled down the stairs and threw
my backpack over my shoulder. My mom was still sleeping; my
Dad was awake in the family room, sitting in his seat on one side
of the couch and working on papers. The TV and the radio were
both tuned to the news.

"Off to school already?" he asked.

"Yeah," I answered. "I've got detention." He sort of nodded,
then returned his attention to the sprawl of pen-scrawled disserta-
tions in his lap. I slammed the door as I left, and took the cut-
throughs to Riley Road. A gray Chevette was parked in the street,
its windows steamed in the crisp morning air. I pounded my fist on
the hatch and a set of keys flew out the driver's side window and
over my head. Grabbing the keys off the pavement, I opened the
hatch, threw my board on top of the others, then climbed into the
back seat.

"Wake'n'Bake, dude," said Sean, shoving a pipe in my face.
From the driver's seat, the back of Scott's head bobbed and giggled.
I pulled hard on the pipe as Sean reached back to hold the lighter
over the bowl. Scott started the car, still giggling, and we drove
away. In twenty minutes we'd pulled off the interstate, bounced
down an uneven dirt road and parked in a bed of shoulder-high
weeds. We grabbed our boards and tools and walked the rest of the
way to The Ditch. It was still early enough to play music, so we
sat the jam box up on a concrete wall and cranked the Circle Jerks.
The Ditch, a concrete culvert about fifty feet long by twenty feet
wide, lay just beneath the freeway, and during rush hour we had to
scream in one another's ears to talk.

It was late spring, and our first trip of the year. From October through April The Ditch was full of sewage from the nearby developments. This seven-month shit river left an inch of stinking waste in its wake, but we didn't care. It was a ritual, cleaning the Ditch, an honor. We'd brought shovels and industrial brooms, as well as wood, nails, and hammers to repair the roll-in ramps.

It was just a meaningless piece of utilitarian architecture, completely invisible from the freeway. People who didn't know it was there never would. But among Ohio skaters it was famous. No one was sure when skaters first discovered The Ditch, but by the time we'd started hitting it, it'd been fully renovated. The lip was slick and shiny with years of metal residue from trucks. Besides the roll-in ramps, well-ground concrete curbs had been brought in, one on each side. The angle of the banks was just steep enough to pull airs, and the flat was exactly proportional to the walls, so you could build plenty of speed between tricks. A skater couldn't have designed it better. Up to fifty people hung out here on a summer day, sessioning, fighting, partying, talking shit, playing music, snaking each other, and otherwise creating a disturbance that no one capable of being disturbed ever noticed.

We spent all morning sweeping and shoveling out the crud. After a quick trip to Wendy's, we ceremoniously took our first runs. Seven months out of practice, we each unceremoniously slammed in the flat. It didn't matter; we'd been dreaming about this day all winter, and within a couple of hours we were ripping all our old tricks. Sean started pulling his tweaked-out backside airs off the curb. He pulled airs twice as high as anyone else who skated here, and he went twice as fast. He got angry when he skated, his face contorting as he grunted and cursed. He was totally rad, absolutely fearless. But it was all tech, no style.

I was all lip tricks, disasters and boardslides and frontside rock'n'rolls. But mostly I just carved back and forth, picking up speed and hitting 5-0 grinds the length of the lip. I was silent as I skated, everything outside my movement and moment faded away. I was the smoothest, the cleanest, the poet-geek-king drawing my lyrics in speed and shaven concrete.

Scott sucked, and didn't do much of anything besides axle stalls, but so what? We smiled all day long.

"The body seems unaware of its surroundings," Paul Valéry told his audience. "It seems to be concerned only with itself and one other object, a very important one, from which it breaks free, to which it returns, but only to gather the wherewithal for another flight." The "other object" on which Valéry's body is so narrowly focused is the Earth. The body is pulling airs.

Valéry, the esteemed French essayist and poet, the first skate critic, was describing the mobius strip of the halfpipe, and the skateboarder using it to fly, return to Earth and fly again. It will be two decades before a bunch of bored surfers invent the skateboard, but like Da Vinci before him, Valéry foresaw the age of flight.

The intent of Valéry's lecture, given preceding a dance performance in 1936, was to describe the philosopher's relationship to dance. But what does intent matter? I call Valéry the first skate critic. If you believe me, I'm telling the truth. If you don't, then I've told a lie.

In the end it's moot. Meaning isn't fixed in place. It's tricky and unreliable, and in this media-saturated age, relies more on the interpretive properties of the medium through which the message is received. Which is responsible for meaning, the painter or the painting, the dancer or the dance? Photographer Cindy Sherman's "Untitled Film Stills," begun while she was still a student at SUNY Buffalo, were credited with initiating a new practice of feminist art-making. The photos appropriate the style, composition, and narrative content from classic fifties Hollywood movies, but 'star' Sherman herself as the protagonist. By isolating and recontextualizing traditional female cinematic roles—the ingenue, the siren—Sherman brilliantly exposes the subterfuged moral content of these movies. The art world hasn't been the same since. Why did she make the photographs? At first, she has admitted in interviews, because she loved old movies. Her photographs were devotional paeans to which the critics ascribed teeth.

Again, the closed dynamic of the dialectic: Skateboarding's not dance, and so it's also dance. It's dance to me. If a skateboarder decides his movements are essentially aesthetic, considers the halfpipe a stage, his friends the audience, and himself a performer, then is it so? Likewise, if a top-dollar pro considers himself a jock, an uber-X-athlete pushing the limits of the sport, is that so? It depends on their relative power to name, in other words, the reach of their voice.

Now what if ESPN decides skateboarding is a sport, that it can be judged and quantified and described within a ball sport sensibility? In many of the 730,000 households that watched the 1998 summer X Games, it probably carried the ring of truth.

It would be obvious to point out that we were searching for family. It would be less obvious to record that we found it, at least for a while. Skateboarding was our house. It provided our days with structure, and framed our priorities. Skating became an end, rather than something to do along the way. Everyone I knew skated. I would leave early in the morning, while the curbs were still slick with dew. I stopped coming home after school, and went days on end without seeing my parents. Skateboarding consumed me, as it did my friends.

Skating is violent, and so were we. One frozen Ohio winter, when snow and ice had made skating outdoors impossible, we entertained ourselves driving through rural areas playing mailbox baseball at high speeds as one of us hung out the window and swung the bat with the combined propulsion of car and muscle. By the time we were arrested we'd smashed half the mailboxes in the county.

We also smashed each other, slamdancing our way through countless punk shows, breaking our noses, wrists, and arms on the beer-slick floor. We were bonded by the mutual need to punch, cut, lash out in words and actions and skating. The vernacular of skateboarding was invented for us. We shredded, ripped, and tore with our boards. We tweaked our airs and slammed our bodies. Skating, a highly charged form of destruction, wasn't entertainment. It was catharsis.

If skateboarding was our house, it was furnished with our anger, a shared rage of mutual isolation and a fury bred of futility. These emotions seemed to generate from our families. Mine was perhaps the least unhappy—it was nothing. I was an odd, emotional child from a stranger's womb. The prevalent emotion in my house was incomprehension. I couldn't understand my parents, who watched Lawrence Welk and had never been drunk, and God knows they couldn't understand me. I probably had the least cause for my anger, though.

Jim wouldn't talk about his mom, whose death he'd witnessed, a mysterious event marked by his gray hair. His dad was perpetually on the road, leaving Jim to raise his little brother. Zach lived up the street from Jim. He was older than the rest of us, a part-time student at Ohio State, but his attendance was spotty. Like his mom, he was an alcoholic, occasionally recovering. Sean's parents were still together. They were also big drinkers, which worked out in our favor, not only for the free booze but because of the atmosphere of lenience and oblivion that pervaded Sean's house. We did our drugs at Sean's. It was fucked up for us, though we didn't know that. And hell, it could have been worse.

Worse was Stu's parents. They divorced when Stu was a baby, and both neglected him. His father was a playboy, his mother a disaster. At one point she bought a golden retriever puppy. Refusing to house-train it, she kept it locked up in a bathroom the size of a closet, which reeked so badly we stopped using it. Even then, in relative ignorance, I realized some parents didn't deserve children. We disgusted them. So did Stu. Stu was always picking fights, usually with me. Later he became a cop.

We built from the materials around us, but somehow our house stood, shakily, while those we slept in were falling apart. Skating offered unconditional affirmation. It didn't matter if we were good or not, so long as we kept doing it. We had to love skateboarding; skateboarding loved us.

If there was ever any doubt concerning just how meaningless the term *extreme* could get, the ESPN broadcast of the Ralston Purina "extreme games for dogs" laid it to rest. Canines, consumers discovered, also inhabit this increasingly bizarre extreme world. But if *extreme sports* means nothing, and skateboarding means something, what does it mean?

This is an impossible question to answer. It's not so much that skateboarding means different things to different people, though that's certainly true as well, but that skateboarding 'means' in several different ways. First of all, skateboarding means something to the culture at large—it has an iconic significance. Once it meant Jan and Dean. Ten years later it meant wispy boymen hanging ten on skinny, fiber-flex boards. In my day it meant skatepunks, if it meant anything at all, and at the turn of the millenium, it means baggy pants, The Gap, and Mountain Dew. This is a woefully incomplete list, but as I said, it's an impossible question. But that doesn't mean we should stop trying.

But skateboarding's iconic meaning is simple, a sound bite. It's a function of an external logic, that of mainstream culture. The meanings inside the skateboarding community are vastly more complex, as well as veiled from outside interpretation. Where an outsider sees a "skater," someone within the subculture sees an array of signifiers, each one contributing to a highly sophisticated expression of allegiances, affinities, and individual identity. From the board (Girl or Chocolate, longboard or short?) to the pants (JNCO or Fresh Jive?) to the hat to the backpack to the hair to the wheels to the shoes to the tape in the Walkman, the subculture of skateboarding means far more to itself than it ever means to anyone else. The aggregate of these individual styles creates a sensibility that informs every aspect of the subculture, from its graphic art to its fashion to its highly specialized argot.

But beyond any of this, the act of skating itself is capable of signification. When a skater skates, he or she is performing tricks or "moves." This is the formal language of skateboarding, and since skating's emergence it has grown exponentially. Though it's probably the most fixed and stable of skateboarding's ways of meaning, it's also the most abstract. Because it's so abstract, before we understand what skateboarding is saying we have to understand how it's saying it.

Dance, to return to that, speaks in a language codified through centuries of usage. The conventions of this language have seeped into our culture to such a degree that we can't help but register its voice, even if the components of its speech are nonverbal. Like dance, skating is a form of nonverbal expression, but unlike dance, skateboarding has very little of the history helpful for building an agreed-upon vocabulary—a set of meanings. Also unlike dance, no attempt is made to 'read' its language. Yet I don't believe this means a skater can't express the range of ideas and emotions that a dancer can. Skating can be mournful, or playful, or as with my friend Sean, ferociously angry. Or like much dance, it can simply express the sheer exuberance of living in three dimensions, a celebration of the physical body in play.

A skater must be communicating something. Why else follow an invert with a layback grind? Or a sugarcane with a caballerial? Or a 540 with a 540 with a long, drawn-out stale fish? Only a skateboarder would know. But I doubt he or she would be able to explain it. Skaters understand this language intuitively—no translation necessary. And perhaps this is as it should be. Since the act is spontaneous in nature, any attempt at scripting a performance would distort the act.

When skating is received as a sport, it diminishes the potential meanings embedded within this language. Every contest that takes place reduces each trick to a point value. It requires a codification of the most brutal sort. It's skating as athletic arithmetic, drained of all cultural and aesthetic significance, a meticulously quantified system of kinetic motions. Skateboarding is skateboarding is figure skating.

How do you write a book in the form of a question? Is skateboarding a sport? "Yes. Wait no. I don't know." And I *don't* know. Because there isn't an answer. Is skateboarding dance? It is to me. Is skateboarding an act of Refusal? Does it articulate for other people, as it did for me, the "voice of teeth ground down to points"? Or is it just skateboarding?

Questions are frustrating; they lead you in circles. But answers are worse. They're boring, and end before they start. Then again, maybe I'm asking the wrong questions. Maybe the media can't kill skateboarding. Is there really an intrinsic element of deviance to skating that can never be sold off?

"You can't spoil skateboarding," says Kevin Thatcher, co-publisher of *Thrasher* magazine, the TK-year-old house organ of skateboarding. "ESPN may think of it as something they can sell to their advertisers, but it can't be ruined that way, because you can always turn off the television, drop in off your front porch and skate down the street."

Maybe he's right. Skateboarding doesn't need us. Unlike pop singers, politicians and ball sport superstars, skating doesn't need our adoration—or even our recognition—in order to survive. Neither our money nor our interest is appreciated or even noticed by a subculture that, frankly speaking, doesn't give a damn. What we fail to understand is that we need board culture, as we once needed rock'n'roll, as the hippies needed LBJ, as the mainstream will always need rebellion, and the revolution will always need the oppressors.

Skateboarding offers a way out, a path of opposition. A board is more than a slab of wood; it is a lifestyle of abdication, a silent vote for freedom without fame, glory without glamour, entertainment without consumption. Even if skateboarding doesn't need us, we need skateboarding because we need to know what we aren't in order to understand what we are.

We all draw lines, and in order to 'get' skating, in order to take possession of skateboarding, we need to draw our lines with subtlety, in a way that accounts for skateboarding in all its complexity. Skateboarding may indeed be a sport. Hell, maybe it's even an extreme one. But it's a simplistic, and in the end, unfortunate vision of it. We must also draw the lines in our portrait to account for skating as a subculture, a cultural response, as a dance and a political act and a religion. If we don't, skating doesn't lose, we do.

"What the fuck? Yeah, that's great. Skateboarding's an art form. That's so stupid. Skateboarding is something that's fun to do; that's it. Why do all these shitheads out there have to try and evaluate it? Just leave it the fuck alone." I should probably heed his advice, but I can't. For me, skateboarding is writing.

EXTREME SKIING

Chapter Twenty-Two

May 27, 1998

Kirsten Kremer

"It's for me?" Who could be calling me here, I wonder? I'm in New Zealand at Nick Grant's, owner of G-Force paragliding in Queenstown. Usually, I like to climb in the fall, but due to a finger injury on the Six Mile Creek in Alaska I'm taking a break from climbing. Queenstown is a great location for paragliding and I'm working on the Shotover River to make a little more money. My main profession so far is guiding for Class V Whitewater in Alaska.

"Who was that?" Nick asks.

"Someone who wants me to write about extreme skiing," I reply and ponder. I'm flattered, but why me when there are people who have taken skiing to an extreme level that even I can't imagine? I agree to take the project on, even though I don't consider myself at the highest end of extreme skiing, attempting to paint a picture from a practitioner's point of view.

Skiing is one of the oldest sports in the existence of humankind. Snow has always been a part of certain cultures, and throughout modernity we have developed the equipment and knowledge of numerous glissading tools, including the snowboard, telemark and alpine skis. The snowboard is excellent for surfing in the powder, telemark skis are great for backcountry, and downhill skis offer dual edges with rigid support for various terrain. All three prove to be awesome devices for glissading and should be included in the topic of extreme skiing.

Kirsten Kremer earned a B.A. in religious studies at University of California at Santa Barbara. She now lives a simple life in a small cabin in Alaska. She guides seasonally for Class V Whitewater, Valdez Heli Ski Guides, and Alaska Mountaineering School. She engages in climbing, skiing, and flying with appreciation and gratitude for the lifestyle.

Still, a differentiation must be made clear between extreme skiing and free skiing. Perhaps a look at the driving forces may help to understand why some humans find it necessary to express themselves in these ways.

It seems to be the prevailing thought amongst my friends that extreme skiing is a category in which a fall will most likely result in death. Numerous descents of this sort occur daily in the Alps. Snowboarders are descending terrain at high speeds successfully. A snowboarder named Johan nailed a line on the N. Face of the Aiguille du Midi that I'd only think about climbing. Valla MacDonald skied an 8,000 meter peak after she won the World Extreme Skiing Championships in Alaska, saying her aspirations in skiing were for mountains, not competing. Skiing in places where there is exposure to death from the terrain is what I associate with extreme skiing. Cliffs, steep terrain avalanches, rockfall, seracs, cornices, and crevasses are examples of some of the hazards.

Free-skiing, or free riding, is any individual's expression of glissading. As there are many individuals, there are many expressions ranging from extremely fast skiing, jumping, flying, or whatever you can imagine. Free riders are creative and everyday we learn another possibility or new expression. Ski resorts offer an arena where a rider can practice in a relatively controlled area. Free-skiing can be very dangerous, can involve exposure, and could cause death, but there is generally a little more room for error. Johnny Mosely displayed this perfectly in the '98 Olympics, winning the freestyle gold with a 360° with a grab, a new trick with lots of personality.

Skiing, both extreme and free, has common driving forces. In our lives, we aspire to be successful. This universal thought is definitely true for the extreme skier. Success is magnified to its truest meaning. If the extreme line is skied without error, the skier in that moment has found success. Some people find success in their lives, and some people use their lives to find success. Freedom is a driving force for all snow riders. Certainly, if you've glissaded, you have felt the wind in your face and freedom of the mountains. Ernst Forest, an avid 40 yr. old thrill seeker from Jackson Hole, says that skiing is his life because of the freedom. "It's me being free and being myself skiing." You can find Ernie with his telemarking buddy, Rutter, punching lines like S & S Couldir in Jackson Hole daily because they want to be free. We all want to express ourselves in some way or another. Skiing presents an excellent and unique opportunity for this. "Actions speak better than words." Intertwined with the landscape and weather, skiing offers this freedom and forum for self expression in existence with nature.

With every step, I can hear my heart beating and my breath echo in these walls of freedom. I'm poor, without a job at this point, homeless and happy. I've escaped these material things. Looking up at the huge granite walls and overhanging seracs, down at the maze of crevasses below, I know I'm lucky. I haven't been to church in awhile, but I am in God's kingdom now. Breathtaking beauty and absolute freedom to roam, explore, live, and die as I please. I'm more afraid of being stifled, bored, and trapped in the cages they call buildings than I am afraid of dying. I want to live, really live.

It's almost 6:00 AM and the dawn is upon us. We've been walking in the dark with headlamps since 4:00 AM, negotiating crevasses and listening to the glacier awaken in the first light. Our . crampons pierce the Styrofoam snow, our breaths take shape in the cold air, and our eyes look forward to the next summit.

Success will be measured in the here and now, by the return of our tomorrow. We took the last Aiguille du Midi Telepherique up yesterday and spent the night in the Simond hutt last night. No one slept well because we were anxious for the climb, lightly packed, and disturbed by a sea level Spaniard retching with altitude sickness. We awoke at 2:30 to have tea and prepare our gear for the day ahead, taking care not to slip in the frozen vomit. We didn't bring sleeping bags because we knew the hut had blankets. Last week we were forced to take refuge here as we missed the last tram down after a climb on Mount Tacul, France. We wanted to keep our gear to a minimum so we could reach the summit of Mont Blanc and ski down before dark. We started with a party of four on two separate rope teams. Thor, a bold 21 year-old from Taos with visionary drive, and I teamed together. Isoc, a snowboarder and Freddy, a telemarker, teamed together on another rope for the crevasse field on Tacul.

As we reached the summit of Tacul, the sun put orange light on our path. Mt. Maudit was the next stepping stone to our goal. With the break of dawn, a cold wake of air flushed over our bodies. The immediate dangers of the crevasses were behind us, but the cold was frightful. Thor and I stayed roped as we were moving smoothly together and a slightly exposed traverse waited ahead. I looked back, but could not see the others. Freddy had said his toes were numb, but I thought we all were numb. Bundled and breathing into my neck gator, my feet as stiff as my Rossi Course K's, we pressed on. As I looked back, I was surprised to see Isoc walking alone, especially when Freddy had been the first in our group a week ago to reach the summit of the N. Face of the Aiguille du Midi. Isoc said Freddy decided to turn back with cold feet.

Only a third of the way so far, but we hoped we would have time to warm up on such a beautiful day. We found a slot to traverse around Mt. Maudit near its summit and the Mont Blanc stood like a giant dome just before us. We coiled the ropes and continued the walk to the summit at our own pace. It was crisp clear blue skies with a wind to chill any flesh exposed. Although the mountain appeared to be relatively close, it wasn't . The snow was perfect for walking, changing foot angles to avoid the calves from cramping, and still the summit didn't appear any closer. At this point the climbing is the same step after step—up this massive white dome.

Many thoughts, invited and not, fill my mind. An endless myriad of possibilities taking shape . . . where will I go next, what do I want from life, what do I want to give back? "Why am I here" questions, with "nature" as my only true answer. Deep in the mountains and deep in my thoughts: listening to the silence of flowing frozen snow crystals, the piercing of the crampons, the beckoning summit. In the silence, I can hear my soul cry out in pleasure, connecting with the ultimate energy.

The summit is incredible. The view is 360 degrees of amazing Alps. We duck behind the windy summit to have a snack in the sun. Soon we will be glissading down the mountain. We walk down the thin icy ridge before putting our boards on. There are tracks indicating someone has side-slipped this ridge line . . . very exposed . . . definitely extreme skiing. I contemplate the idea; I wait for a safer spot. I'm psyched to have reached the summit and anticipate returning safely. After some firm snow, we ski into a glorious powder field with the looming danger of the monstrous hanging seracs above. Isoc rails beautiful layouts on his board while Thor flows huge fat ski turns. The descent goes by quickly and I am glad I have the ability to go to extreme places with my skis.

SHIT!!!! I've overslept . . . boots, skis, poles, pads . . . where's my other knee pad? Rolling over the sleeping mummies, I finally find my stuff. These apartments in Chamonix Sud aren't exactly made for six. No time for breakfast today, not even coffee. The competitors have a meeting at the Brevent before the contest starts. It will be faster to walk than wait for the bus . . . the walk will be good for my head. These contests always make me nervous. The crisp air on this bluebird day is refreshing, but my body still feels the anxiety of a powder day. It snowed the last two days. The hotel faces (the contest site) will be awesome if they didn't slide. Powder days in controlled places almost make me noxious because it's an open invitation to go faster and jump bigger.

I didn't really plan on competing when I came to France this year. I just wanted to ski and climb. I thought I might if I could afford it, but as the contest drew near, I realized I needed that money for rent. Last week while I was having a Guinness at the Irish Pub, the owner of the Bar Du Moulin asked me if I was going to compete in the Red Bull Extreme Thrill. I told him I couldn't afford it. He said he would pay if I wore his jacket with "Bar Du Moulin" printed on the back. That was an easy deal. "Sure." I was stoked! Plus the coat was all black: perfect, a perfect match to my spray-painted black skis. My former ski sponsor cut my sponsorship before I left for France, saying "We don't sponsor women in free-skiing." I said I'd cover the labels (since I didn't have enough money for new skis) and the new marketing dweeb offered me black paint. What a good idea, I thought.

As I'm riding the gondola up to the tram, I can see a few skiers picking their way through the contest site. It bums me out a bit, as I was hoping for an untracked course. Now I need to hurry so I can have the same advantage as the other skiers. I pick a line that follows a ramp above a cliff with a lot of exposure. The skiing is not difficult here, but a fall could be deadly. It cliffs out at the bottom, but the jump is less than 25 feet. I show Wendy Fischer the line as well. She's super cool, and has won the World Championships in Alaska two years in a row. The women are competitive, but more friendly and helpful overall than the men in these contests. There's so few of us pushing these limits, we seem to bond together quite well.

The day is amazing, finally bluebird, it's a shame this is the only contest day left. Only two runs, winner takes all. That's cool I guess, only one day of anxiety, and then I can hang out on some steep granite wall tomorrow with my partner, Thor. Chamonix is awesome. Skiing, rock and ice climbing, and paragliding all just out your front door with tram access. The French are so adventurous, the lines that have been skied here are unbelievable.

The officials just decided we can't ski the half of the mountain I scoped out for our first run. Bummer. Now I have to wing it on some other line. Hurry up and wait: I'm finally in the gate.

Now, turn it on until the finish line. I hit a small jump at the top, then GS turns through the powder and avalanche debris towards the bottom. Not great, but I'm in 4th place so far with a small point spread. I know the second run will be the deciding factor. Who will go to the exposed cliff area? All the other girls, except Wendy, avoid the cliff area.

This time I run before Wendy. Two years ago, we stood in the gate together at the Squaw Valley Extremes on the deciding run. She went first while I listened to the crowd cheering and waited up top wondering what her line was like and how I could beat it. I jumped the ice falls at the bottom and crashed . . . Wendy won. She wishes me luck. This time I'm stoked in the gate. I know exactly where I'm going. Nervous, but everything is good. I drop a 10-foot cliff at the top and ski down towards the big cliff area, riding the ramp above the 100+ ft. cliff and swooshing snow over its edge. At the end of the rib, a few turns around some trees and off over the edge of the last cliff. Stick . . . I ski out and to the finish. Sweet. I can take my helmet off and relax in the snow with my friends. It's a good life.

Wendy comes into the course hot, flashes the top, but has problems on the last cliff drop. Not clean enough to keep the lead. The scores are tight, but I manage to take it. Sweet, the reality sets in at the awards party with a thousand bucks stuffed in my jog bra. The music pumps, the lights flash, the skiers rage all night and I surprisingly make it home with all the money, but the other prizes somehow evade me. Somebody else was psyched, too.

When my head clears in the morning, I start thinking about how I should spend the money. I think about just paying all my rent so I won't have to scrape for food, but that isn't exciting enough. Instead, I go on a search for a used paraglider.

I'd been watching the paragliders all season and dreamed of doing it myself. In a couple of days, I had my hands on a sweet, new (to me) beginner wing. Thor pitched in so he could learn, too, and that way we had enough to buy a book. The ABC's of paragliding, luckily in English since our understanding of the French climbing guide wasn't so great. So we read, and practiced on the ground for a month, everyday in the morning and evening. I caught a couple tandem rides with Alex Fandel off the Brevent and the N. Face of the Aiguille Du Midi.

At 9:00 AM, I meet Alex at the Aiguille Du Midi tram with my own wing. No wind. I lay my wing out on the N. Face, buckle my lightweight harness, take a breath of courage and run forward to inflate the wing. The wing doesn't come up straight and I stop, gather up the glider and lay it out again for another try. This time it's good, I hear Alex yell. "Clear . . . keep running." Now I'm flying. A 30-minute sled ride to the valley floor from 13,000 ft. I don't want to die, but in the meantime, I'm sure glad I'm living.

The phone at Tsaina lodge on Thompson Pass, Alaska rings. I'm having coffee with some of the best skiers in the world. The World Extreme Skiing Contest is quickly approaching and the skiers are pilgrimaging to the Chugach. "It's for you, Kremer." I feel guilty about putting this piece on the backburner and explain that I've been living in a tent, snow camping and working for Valdez Heli Ski Guides. I'm surprised at the persistence of the *To the Extreme* book editors, tracking me down in such odd places and promise to make another attempt at writing. I came up here early in March hoping to score a job guiding for Doug and Emily Coombs. I planned to compete as well since I'm already here. The growing excitement reminds me of the Red Bull Extreme Thrill in Chamonix last year.

SHIT!!!!

The contest didn't work out, and I've been guiding for Valdez Heli Ski guides ever since. Moved up from the tent and into a white schoolbus called Cloud 9.

Chapter Twenty-Three

Oh Say Can You Ski?

Imperialistic Construction of Freedom
in Warren Miller's *Freeriders*

Joanne Kay and Suzanne Laberge

In the past three decades, extreme sport has been infused with a marketing strategy, an ethic, a vocabulary, an attitude, and a style. It inspires personal introspection and public allure. It has been associated with co-optation by the commercial, the marginal, the countercultural, and the postmodern. Performance is paradoxical—imbued with individualism and collectivism, the ludic and the prosaic, aesthetics and kitsch. What emerge are tenets that contradict

Joanne Kay is a doctoral candidate and lecturer in sport sociology at the University of Montreal. She is an elite-level triathlete and a member of Canada's national team. She is also a freelance journalist whose features appear in *The National Post, The Montreal Gazette* and *The Ottawa Citizen.* Her areas of research include gender, new sports culture, extreme sports, media and corporatization of sports. Her dissertation bears on the social signification of adventure sports in light of Bourdieu's concepts of habitus, field and symbolic power. She received her master's degree in communication studies from McGill University in Montreal.

Suzanne Laberge is a professor in the Department of Kinesiology at the University of Montreal, where she teaches sociology of sport and physical activity. She has published in a variety of journals, notably in *Men and Masculinities, Sociologie et Sociétés, Sociology of Sport Journal,* and *Society and Leisure* on issues associated with gender relations, bodily culture, doping in sports, extreme sports, and theoretical discussion. She is mainly known for her neo-Bourdieusian and feminist analyses of gender, class, and health practices.

381

and co-exist: participation and competition, amateurism and professionalism, urban play and wilderness adventure, the 'authentic' and
the constructed, the youthful and the nostalgic, the self-determined
and the regulated, the resistant and the complicit. But with all its
inherent ambiguity, one staked value of extreme sport perdures—in
combination with or despite any others—and that value is freedom.

As a concept, 'extreme' flexes and expands to accommodate a
plethora of sport practices, allowing for the seemingly incongruous
to flourish under one ensign. Accordingly, chapters on activities as
disparate as adventure racing and skateboarding can be linked in a
book's common thematic, and a multitude of sport forms can fall
under one appellation. Extreme skiing, then, like its other extreme
counterparts, is not limited to a single practice or a single context,
neither to the competitive circuit, nor the trail-less and the steep
beyond the spectator's gaze.

In this chapter, we will analyze Warren Miller Entertainment's
1998 film *Freeriders* to demonstrate how a tenet of the extreme
subculture, in this case *freedom*, can be co-opted and commodified
to suggest and/or reify a sport's 'extreme' status. In *Freeriders*,
Warren Miller uses the implied promise of freedom as a marketing
strategy underlying extreme skiing's image as an avant-garde commodity in the extreme sport market. We will examine three 'devices of connotation'[1] through which Miller's film contributes to
what we describe as an imperialistic construction of freedom. The
first, *commoditization*[2] of freedom, refers to Miller's positioning of
extreme skiing within freeriding[3] culture, constructing an inextri-
cable relationship between skiing and (American) freedom. Through
the second device, *exportation* of freedom, Miller ships abroad self-
branded freedom—with a freeriding 'world tour'—constituting a
form of symbolic violence towards anyone not American. Finally,
a third device, *(post)modernization* of freedom, combines
postmodern filmmaking techniques with modernist (American revisionist) historical (re)construction to naturalize the existence of
extreme skiing in contemporary extreme sport culture.

'Total Freedom' and the Tourist Infomercial: Commoditization of Freedom

As the word *extreme* takes up permanent residence in mainstream
(categorical) conceptions of sport, it has become a neologism for
those comprehended in its meaning. 'Free skiers' want to distance
themselves both from the European extreme ski movement—which

incorporates freeclimbing and higher levels of risk-taking—and from the "crazy X Game participants"[4] who they feel diminish social recognition of their status as professional athletes.[5] 'Free-skiers' have aligned themselves with the standards and structure of institutionalized practice, rejecting the mainstream conception of marginal sport. Yet they maintain their alternative status through the sport's social correlation to freedom. The term *freeriding* betrays neither the mainstream classification that determines it to be 'extreme' nor the participant opposition to its reductionist connotation. To the mainstream, 'freeriders' are extreme, to the freeriders, 'extreme' is mainstream, but to all, freeriding is the paragon of freedom.

Warren Miller, capitalizing on the 'extreme' controversy, insists on the specificity of 'freeriding' and the freedom that this name implies. Miller sells skiing—and freedom through analogous association—as one would sell a product in a TV infomercial. Miller has mastered the hard-sell consumer hook: freedom is playfulness, mobility, American (and can be seen at a theatre near you . . .). Our host tells us that we are embarking on a "search for total freedom" which can be found at a Miller-endorsed mountain resort (probably not so very near you . . . Order now!), and if the images of thrills and spills in the opening montage haven't hooked you, perhaps the pressure of a limited offer will: "because if you don't do it this year, you'll be one year older when you do . . ." (But wait, there's more . . .)

Playfulness and the Culture of Innocence

Presently in his seventies, and after a fifty-year filmmaking career that has produced almost the same number of films all bearing his signature, the now-retired movie mogul—the "originator of extreme sports filmmaking"[6]—has shifted control of Miller Entertainment to his son Kurt.[7] True to the Warren Miller ski film formula, however, Miller still narrates, waxing poetic about the innocence and purity of skiing. His tongue-in-cheek statement that "after a lifetime of following my heart on a pair of skis, I still don't know what I'm going to be when I grow up" denotes the unconstrained freedom of childhood with all of youth's boundless possibilities. Set to the adolescent tunes of Toad the Wet Sprocket, Cake, Counting Crows, the Dave Matthews Band, Presidents of the United States and Semisonic,[8] montaged footage features crews of (predominantly young white male[9]) skiers and snowboarders launching themselves off cliffs and out of helicopters into the sea of powder below. Landings range from the ridiculous to the sublime, blended so that the consummate and the calamitous appear equally worthwhile to their performers. The apparent pleasure that the plummeting freerider takes in the explosion of powder that awaits him or (rarely) her on landing is a nostalgic reminder of the childish insouciance one once found puddle-hopping or jumping into a pile of leaves. Miller's high-intensity sequences present freedom in the fearless, adrenaline-seeking 'play' of the freeriders, where skiing is spontaneously prelapsarian, childlike, and thrilling. When Miller introduces a 13-year-old nordic jumper in Park City, Utah, he praises those abilities in her that are the result of youthful freedom and ignorance: "that's when they don't know enough to be afraid."[10] The implied corollary is that maturity is bound up with the anticipation of consequence, and thus with fear: "to know—that is to have knowledge—is to instinctively understand the relationship between what you know and what you do."[11] Miller presents the adult consumer with a paradoxical invitation: to seek the bliss of youthful ignorance, denying the normative (adult) accommodation to the threat of mortality.[12]

The Myth of Mobility

One of Miller's recurring themes is that freedom can be found in mobility—upward and westward. His vision of mobility implies an accessibility and freedom of choice that lies, in truth, in stark contrast to the limited access available only to the privileged and wealthy. As such, Miller's connection of freedom to mobility constitutes a form of what Pierre Bourdieu calls symbolic violence towards anyone without financial means.[13]

> Don't forget that it's always snowing somewhere in the world, and all you need is a good snow report of where it is falling to pack your stuff. . . . So quit your job and rent a U-Haul trailer now so next winter this can be you, not just you sitting there watching this wishing this was you. . . . If you try another poor excuse to take the day off and you come back to work with a sunburned face, and you get fired, it'll be worth it because for the day, you'll be a freerider.[14]

Traveling to resort towns, however, is not your only option, according to Miller. He suggests that one can choose to *move* to a resort town as well:

Many of the people who live around this modern city [Salt Lake City] live here because they can get up early and drive just a few miles east to the nearby mountains and find their own freedom by getting first tracks.[15]

As the median household income in Park City, Utah, was $58,000 as of 1998 and the average home price $457,000,[16] residence in this town is prohibitively expensive for most Americans and non-Americans alike.

Heli-skiing in Chile, Norway, Switzerland, France, Greece, and especially America, according to Miller, is not a matter of means but rather of choice. If leaving your job, your family, and all your responsibilities is not something you are willing to do, then freedom cannot be yours, no fault but your own.

The assault of elite access is further manifested in the valorization of 'freeloading.' One of Miller's young stars, Jason Patnode, describes his appreciation for his job:

> . . . this gig totally rules. The cars, free food, hot tubs, free condos, and the women—oh. Free pathfinders. We got it all, man![17]

As a Warren Miller rider, Patnode has everything money can buy, but apparently doesn't need any actual money. The assumption once again is that if you do not have the means to procure freedom (often camouflaged as a Nissan Pathfinder or a bikini-clad woman), and you are not one of "the smart ones [who] live in a ski resort," you have made the decision to opt out of the freedom package made available to you.

One scene in the film blatantly exemplifies the symbolic violence which usually only flows as an undercurrent. When a French Canadian skier is asked to show his knowledge of 'American English,' he first explains that he has learned his American accent from television. He then jettisons all traces of his Quebec heritage in the phrase, "my trailer has a propane heater." One needn't know that this is a direct quotation from the animated series "King of the Hill"[18]—a parody of "white trash" America that takes place in Arlen, Texas ("Small Town, USA")—to read the mockery in the text. References to "trailer trash" appear regularly in American parody and social classifications, referring to a largely uneducated, low-income segment of the American population. Although the gap between the haves and have-nots is widening, the hoax of equal opportunity and equitable prosperity still condones ridicule of low economic classes. Miller's inclusion of such a seemingly innocuous but ultimately derisive comment reinforces the lie of accessibility. Miller constructs his audience through association with negative identity. From the mouth of a Canadian (whose national identity is most often associated with being 'not American'[19]), the viewer understands that those who achieve freedom are 'not poor.'

Land of Opportunity

For Miller, extreme skiing constitutes an objective correlative to American hedonism. Although this theme will come up in the descriptions of American exportation and American revisionism, here we are exploring its position in the construction of freedom as a commodity. Skiing in this sense is linked to all that is quintessentially America—'life, liberty and the pursuit of happiness.' For Miller, extreme skiing appears not to be a constitutional right to individual freedom, but an individual freedom from collective responsibility as well.[20] As freeriders surf the powder snow of a distant mountain accessible only by helicopter, we learn that it is the Fourth of July. Miller asks "What are you doing on the Fourth of July?" The anniversary of the American Declaration of Independence is thus marked by what Miller deems to be the ultimate homage to freedom—freeriding.

As Miller travels from one North American ski refuge to another (in between stints at international vacation resorts), we learn that American snow delivers supreme freedom:

> When the snow is like this in the canyons of Utah, your most basic instinct, your instinctive search for freedom, is finally being satisfied.[21]

As such, Miller reveals, the history of skiing *is* the history of America.

> Almost 200 years ago, the real pioneers, the trappers and fur traders exploring this part of America found it so abundant in everything they wanted out of life, the two of them got together and started a trading post. It later became Jackson Hole, Wyoming—and today, they're trading information on ski conditions.[22]

Miller's revisionist approach to the American pioneering spirit is again presented through what *Skiing* magazine has dubbed "patented Miller silliness."[23] We watch beginners tumbling, chair lift screwups, shovel races, and a Dummy Big Air contest in which unmanned, hand-crafted contraptions of all shapes and sizes launch off a jump site. He also includes the latest updates to freeriding, such as powder kayaks and double-tip skis. On the American slopes, Miller presents a sporting arena marked by an anything-goes attitude—an attitude that is becoming increasingly linked in mainstream consciousness to America's pioneering and innovative spirit.

> The proliferation of new sports stems not so much from a lunatic fringe but from the center of a soul that cherishes the pursuit of happiness. The sports inventor's mantra, 'been there, done that,' is an update of 'Go West, Young Man.' "[24]

Pioneering, which once implied hard work and exploration of unknown terrain, is here linked to hedonistic pursuits and exploration of the 'disneyfied' unknown. Individual indulgence and immediacy of gratification rather than collective responsibility and prospects for the future inspire Miller's pioneering spirit. The 'unknown' no longer enkindles the cautious courage of selfless exploration, but rather the casual thrill of capturing one's 'big air' on film.

Soldiers of Fortune: American Exportation of Freedom

Warren Miller invites us to join him on his "search for total freedom, which can only be found on the side of snow-covered mountains . . ." We learn that he is going to take us "all over the world to the meet the people [he] calls freeriders." However, as we move from continent to continent, traveling thousands of miles to foreign lands, we meet the people who probably live within a day's drive of our homes. When we leave North American soil, most often the 'locals' are seen not riding down their steep slopes over jagged mountain edges, bursting through light, fluffy powder under crystal blue skies. It is primarily the American skiers that Miller has flown in (of the 74 ski talents represented, more come from Colorado alone than all the international skiers combined), along with *his* cameras, *his* crews, *his* drivers, *his* pilots, *his* gofers, and *his* continuity experts, that we see. The locals bustle around in their markets and gape idiotically at the cameras while the fearless and free Americans claim 'first tracks' on *their* mountains.

This is the second instance of symbolic violence: Through cultural appropriation and the exportation of the American brand of freedom, the mockery previously aimed at the poor, in this case, turns itself on any culture or lifestyle which is 'not American.'

Following the Miller formula, a foreign resort town is introduced with panoramic grandeur. Through sweeping helicopter-mounted camera shots, we see their landscapes, their temples, their schools, and their farms. We see their (mostly American) tourists purchasing postcards, eating in their restaurants, and buying their produce. We then witness the arrival of our 'freedom fighters'—the Warren Miller skiers, who stride confidently through exotic cultures, unaffected by what after several stops on the world tour become nebulous surroundings. It is clear that for Miller—who once chose to film a snowboarder grinding down the sacred steps of a Japanese temple[25]—imperialistic cultural mockery is funny. His ethnocentric narrative bent can be witnessed in his send-up of local customs and industry. For example, he finds the road linking Chile to Argentina so steep that "unless they are going downhill, the 18-wheeler drivers can't go faster than their IQ."[26] Assuming that an 18-wheeler rarely travels faster than 70 miles an hour on the flat and slows to speeds of 30 miles an hour or less on long, steep climbs, logic would dictate that these local drivers range from mentally retarded to brain-dead.

Miller's flippant commentary is too often tinged with facile racism, indicating his apparent freedom from the evolving cultural and political superego of the last fifty years. Miller's juvenile world vision is again present in his need to preserve organic uniformity: foreign countries become denaturalized theme parks where pain, poverty, and prejudice do not exist. As a filmmaker both fixated on childish fantasy and fixed in adolescent narcissism in search of egocentric gratification, Miller's freedom from responsibility and political consciousness constitutes freedom to deride and insult.

In Norway, for example, Miller flouts local ecological and liability protection:

> With unbelievable bureaucratic foresight, the Norwegians wrote a law against helicopter skiing just two years after the helicopter was invented.[27]

Listening to Miller's self-congratulatory narration, we see imported American skiers climbing into a Warren Miller logo-plastered helicopter (this another trademark of Miller-films, where Nissan Pathfinders and American Airlines jets cruise through the film "with the subtlety of a buffalo stampede"[28]) to ride the Norwegian slopes above the Arctic Circle. This segment implies that Americans are freer than their local counterparts—they can rise above the regional constitution and still be true to their own. Throughout their stay in Norway, Miller's skiers nurture a growing disgust for the country's industrial lifeblood. After an apparently invariable diet of fish (and assuming they would otherwise have 'freedom of choice,' it is clear that there is nothing else to eat in Norway), the American skiers condescendingly quip at its ubiquity: "It's not Norwegian toothpaste—it's caviar in a tube."

In London, we learn, there are no ski mountains. Miller's primary intent in including London in his tour is obvious: "It only snows here once every seven and a half years. But there are a lot of ski shops . . . and a lot of Brits who just wander around in their ski gear looking for birds."[29] After filming a local man-made hill ("Plastic on the Palisades") and filming his skiers in the requisite 'Beatles in London' pose, we are whisked off to Zermatt, the town that time apparently forgot. It is significant, then, that in this town that bans combustion engines and is described by Miller as a place that "even change can't change," the camera fixes (seemingly) interminably on one of Miller's export talents skateboarding through its streets. Locals react with Milleresque predictability, with confusion or indifference, with blank stares or bemusement. We follow their gaze to witness urban youth sport and all that it suggests clashing violently with rural 'old world charm,' but as in all the overseas sequences, it is the locals who appear as foreigners in their own land.

American Revisionism and Self-Reflexive Cinema: (Post)modernization of Freedom

By linking freedom to nostalgia but not to the past, to the American dream but not to American life, to youth but not to the margins, Miller normalizes the existence of extreme skiing in avant-garde culture while targeting an expansive mainstream audience. For fifty years Miller's films have defied the laws of marketing. An aging sport presented to a youthful audience should logically have slid into the category of 'so ten minutes ago.' Yet in *Freeriders*, this formula contributes to an association with contemporary extreme sport culture. With the consumption of his films the ultimate objective, the sale of freedom is a loss leader[30] in Miller's marketing strategy.

That Miller began his filmmaking career in the fifties is significant. Postwar America was marked by rampant consumerism—what was to become the longest cycle of capitalist expansion in history, spreading to Europe in the 1950s and later to Japan and the Pacific.[31] Simplistic 'apple pie' concepts were etched into the American psyche, inspiring citizens' faith in the country's formula for prosperity and the American Dream. Individually and collectively, Americans began to expect and demand world recognition as the flagship of prosperity and democratic freedom, and national pride became the country's chief export.

In *Freeriders*, Miller nostalgically clings to concepts of wealth distribution, democracy, and freedom that echo the ideals of the fifties, even though the American Dream can no longer be substantiated by present-day social realities. While the optimism of the fifties has been replaced by widespread uncertainty, Miller's modernist messianic faith, that technical innovation and purity of form can assure social progress, is left undisturbed in his films.

Nostalgia and the American Dream

Miller's narration is strewn with nostalgic references and historical allusions documenting the freedom bequeathed by the pioneers of the past to the present. We learn how a hill and a T-bar grew into the mountain enterprises we visit today—how gondolas, high-speed quad-chair lifts, helicopters (Pathfinders and American Airlines) have increased access to many more acres of freeriding terrain. And we appreciate how "expensive, exotic, space-age fabrics . . . and high-tech aerodynamic devices" have helped in "the search for ultimate freedom."

Miller traces the history of freedom/skiing through a nostalgic historical revision in which he poses as a key actor in the transhistorical development of the (American) sport. After viewing some vintage Warren Miller film footage, we learn through his narration that Miller was instrumental in the development of Alpental resort in Washington State:

> [Bob Nicholson] asked me to make a movie of Blue Whitaker Alpental to publicize the resort . . . With that movie, he built a ski resort he named Alpental.[32]

Through his narration, Miller reestablishes a historical and nostalgic tie to his origination myth of skiing/freedom as presented by his skiers:

When I was in Alaska, I was dropping in on this first descent . . . Powder so deep, it was blowing my mind. I couldn't believe it. I was ripping down a huge face! This filming dude was hanging out of a helicopter, watching me rip down the mountain and boom. Avalanche. The filming was epic, and that was the start of my career.[33]

Miller then claims responsibility for introducing skiers to the industry and products too: in the sequence demonstrating the powder kayak, Miller explains:

And if a kayak looks strange to you, think back to when I first started filming snowboards 20 years ago and what you thought of them then.[34]

As Miller writes himself into the history of snowboarding's rising popularity, he claims a particular brand of skiing immortality, suggesting that he is indispensable to innovation in contemporary extreme sport culture.

What's Old is New Again

In Steamboat, Colorado, at the Nissan Freeriders Exhibition, we are witness to big-air competition and a lesson in 'new school technique.' Jon Mosely, an Olympic gold medalist in moguls (and later, in 1999, an X Game medalist in 'big air') explains:

Old school is more of the straight jumps. In new school, we're starting to do more awkward takeoffs, more snowboard style.[35]

Moseley, who represents the sport's avant-garde, exclaims that his next feat will be to "ski for Warren Miller." Miller's film, then, most possibly represents the cutting edge of the avant-garde. Moseley's youth is juxtaposed with Klaus Obermeyer, who at the age of 78, skis with young freeriding companions in another protracted sequence. We learn (but realistically doubt) that Obermeyer, the inventor of quilted ski parkas, inflatable ski boots and the snow kayak, is still so competent on skis that "he can stay ahead of most of the young freeriders who live in Aspen."[36]

For Miller, extreme skiing is no longer 'skiing'; rather, it is 'freeriding.' The term 'freeriding' links skiing, a sport that has been traced back in (American) history to the 1850's,[37] to the relatively new sport practices of snowboarding, powder kayaking and big air contests.[38] With his continual blending of old and new sport practice, Miller ensures that what was old is new again.

Closing in on the final montage and leading into Semisonic's rendition of "Closing Time," we witness a Freerider tribute to honor fallen skiers who "will always be remembered by the members of the 'freerider's club':"

> We miss all of those fallen freeriders and what they stood for and what they accomplished. Their adventures have inspired a lot of other skiers to try and go for even more freedom with even steeper descents.[39]

There is mordant humor in the notion that increased risk will avenge the death of those who died at the hands of risk. In this rendition, dead skiers are 'fallen heroes'—martyrs of the sport. Death, as in war, pioneering or religion, is seen here—not as tragic—but as the paradigm of public virtue, as dutiful self-sacrifice for country, mankind and comrades.[40] (Dulce et Decorum est pro Patria Mori[41] . . .) In an age when the idealism of 'pure' causes, 'just wars' and nobility is challenged and supplanted by moral ambiguity, Miller offers steeper descents—the promise of gratification and an homage to fallen companions. (Greater Love Hath No Man Than This, That He Lay Down His Life For His Friends[42] . . .)

This homage takes place in Whistler Blackcomb, a place where a locally sold bumper sticker honors Trevor Peterson, "professional ski hero," extreme ski movie star (indeed a stone engraved with his name is the subject of a momentary pause by one of Miller's cameras in the 'fallen Freerider' sequence) and father of two, who died ('in action') on the slopes of Chamonix. The sticker—which reads "Trevor would do it" (an update, perhaps, of "They died that we might live"[43]?)—can be seen plastered on signs warning of a dangerous slope.[44] Miller captures the Blackcomb spirit, according to which fallen skiers who pushed the limits of danger, leaving children fatherless and spouses widowed, are hailed as freedom fighters who died for a worthy cause. It apparently gives solace to those left alive that death is noble in the name of freedom . . . or a steeper descent.

The nature of Miller's trivialization of the sacrificial theology of war memorials—to suggest that fallen freeriders, like fallen soldiers, have not died in vain—is captured in President Lincoln's famous words at Gettysburg:

From those honored dead we take increased devotion to that cause for which they gave the last full measure of devotion, that we here highly resolve that these dead shall not have died in vain, that this nation, under God, shall have a new birth of freedom.[45]

Media Blur and the Dissolution of Polarities

The final mode adopted by Miller to commodify freedom is evident in the filmmaking process itself. Miller's film, in one respect, is symptomatic of a new trend in filmmaking and sport-media productions which incorporates the self-reflexive, self-promoting, omnipresent filmmaker. In another respect, although Miller is still a modernist in vision, his film exemplifies the interpolation of 'real' history and fiction writing so that neither is autonomous or closed to the other. *Freeriders* is both a fictional history and a historical fiction. It is a docufable, infomercial, and personal history of the social. It blurs distinctions between media and sport, creator and creation, production and product. As such it constitutes a fictional (re)construction of freedom.

Robert Rinehart distinguishes contemporary sport by performers' new awareness of their performance.[46] In Warren Miller's films, this no doubt can be seen in skiers' sudden abundance of 'Kodak Courage,'[47] whereby the promise of cinematic immortalization inspires the hubris to perform otherwise impossible feats. This distinction of contemporary sport is analogous to a distinction in contemporary filmmaking where the producer, too, has a new awareness of performance. Warren Miller's presence is manifested in narration, on Pathfinders, cameras, and helicopters bearing his name—and most importantly, through his tendency to turn the cameras on themselves—to document the filming process with self-conscious irony. The self-conscious performances in Miller's film also exemplifies quintessential capitalist kitsch, offering the viewer only a commodified tracery of the spontaneous gesture—a derivative excitement that comes from reflection—or what Milan Kundera, in *The Unbearable Lightness of Being*, called the "meta-tear."[48]

Robert Alter has described the self-conscious genre as one that systematically flaunts its own condition of artifice, privileging equally the ostentatious nature of the artifice and the systematic operation of the flaunting.[49] This postmodern style, culturally pervasive in literature, art, music, and theater, is further tinged by American nostalgia, finding eloquent expression, for example, in the great American novel *Huckleberry Finn,* which begins famously with the words:

> You don't know about me without you have read a book
> by the name of The Adventures of Tom Sawyer; but that
> ain't no matter. That book was made by Mr. Twain and
> he told the truth, mainly.

This century-old self-reflexive novel marked a critical shift in the narrative tradition. The narrator, the protagonist, speaks directly, in his own voice—what Erving Goffman designated 'breaking the frame' and the Russian formalists called 'exposing the device'— playfully inverting convention. Warren Miller echoes this style, which can be described as 'metafiction,'[50] thus naturalizing his own presence in extreme ski/freedom culture.

The closing credits of Warren Miller's *Freeriders* are set against "never-before-seen vintage shots of Warren Miller . . . and a rare glimpse of the Warren Miller cameramen, hard at work on location across the globe."[51] Miller's inclusion of the production process in the final product illuminates a trend that places equal importance on the 'final edit' and the accompanying 'making of' sequel.[52] Again, Miller blurs the conventional distinctions between claimed function and fiction,[53] and (re)constructs his own (rhetorical) historical presence in our postmodern imagination.

Conclusion (Slippery Slopes?)

The purpose of this paper has not been to raise a discussion of American cultural imperialism,[54] though it must, nor to disillusion those for whom extreme sport proclaims freedom, though it might. By examining one film from the Warren Miller series on winter sports, our goal was to highlight the constructed character of 'extreme' sport and its tenets, through semiotic theorizing as constructed and arbitrary as the terms themselves. Freedom, as we have tried to illustrate, can be marketed and sold. It is analogous to extreme sport in our collective imagination, a false consciousness perhaps, shared among practitioners, producers, consumers, and scholars alike; what is private for the practitioner can be profit to the producer. What denotes the mainstream to the scholar denotes the margins to the consumer. But for all, freedom is a loaded abstraction that touches the individual and the collective; it is authentic to the person and authenticated by the social; it is a personal right and a cultural privilege; it is the progress of modernity and a paean to nostalgia. Freedom is American, it is 'extreme' and it sells.

The last four hundred years of philosophy, politics and art [have been spent] praising autonomy—the free are those who can spontaneously direct their desire, follow their heart, and not be swayed by public opinion, by fear of the crowd or by what the wheel of fashion decides is in or out. The denunciation follows that of the world as a theatre, the teatrum mundi with 'all the men and women merely players.' The desires of the world's players are socially based and hence somehow fraudulent. An actor whispering fine words will only be echoing sentiments originating in a figure off-stage.[55]

Notes

1. David Lodge, *After Bakhtin: Essays on Fiction and Criticism* (London: Routledge, 1992), p. 122.

2. We use this term in the sense used by Robert Rinehart (*Players All: Performance in Contemporary Sport* [Bloomington: Indiana University Press, 1998], p. 2), referring to a 'been there, done that' mentality that values the *collection* of experience (in this case the experience of freedom) as an individual commodity.

3. The term *freeriding* is displacing *extreme skiing* in participant discourse. While in its designation by the mainstream, the phrase *extreme skiing* poses no conflict, alternative sport participants often resist the 'extreme' label, suggesting that its mainstream connotations contradict a desired image. This opposition has been reflected in the extreme ski world by the title given to one of the sport's governing bodies: The International Free-Skiers Association, a member-run organization started in 1996 by skier Shane McConkey to standardize events. The association is seen as a more democratic and less bureaucratic alternative to other regulating bodies such as the FIS (Federation Internationale de Ski), and it currently sanctions free-skiing competition, slope-style, half-pipe and big-air events.

4. Extreme skiing is linked to youth and subcultural participation in magazines such as *Freeze*, touting "new ski culture" and modeling layout and content design on skateboard and snowboard revues with similar male adolescent markets.

5. Phone interview with IFSA vice president, 18 Feb 1999.

6. Warren Miller Entertainment, www.mountainzone.com

7. Michael Finkel, "Miller Highlight" *Skiing*, Oct 1995, p. 36.

8. "Warren Miller's *Freeriders* Production Notes," Warren Miller Entertainment, www.Mountainzone.com.

9. See Kyle Kutz, "BMX, Extreme Sports, and the White Male Backlash," this volume.

10. *Freeriders*, Warren Miller Entertainment, 1998.

11. John Ralston Saul, *The Unconscious Civilization* (Ontario, Canada: Anansi Press [CBC Massey Lecture Series], 1995), p. 5.

12. Patrick Baudry explores extreme sport as a paradoxical practice through which practitioners attempt to deny their mortality in what ironically becomes a planned suicide. In this sense, the more one attempts to deny mortality, the more its certainty is highlighted. See Baudry, *Le Corps Extreme: Approche sociologique des conduits a risque (The Extreme Body: Sociological approach to risk practice)* (Paris: Editions LHarmattan, 1991).

13. Pierre Bourdieu, "La Domination Masculine" ("Masculine Domination"), *Actes de la Recherche en Sciences Sociales*, 84 (1990), 2–31; Pierre Bourdieu, *Sur la television; suivi de l'emprise du journalism (On Television)* (Paris: Editions Liber, 1996).

14. Miller, "Freeriders."

15. Ibid.

16. Hal Clifford, Peggy McKay Shinn, and Norbert Turek, "The Ten Best Mountain Towns," *Mountain Sports & Living*, Jan/Feb 1999, p. 63.

17. Miller, "Freeriders."

18. Fox debuted this series on Jan 12, 1997. The title character, Hank Hill, sells propane and propane accessories for a living.

19. By identifying oneself as 'not American,' it is the American identity that is reified and privileged by establishing oneself as the 'other.'

20. This is perhaps more obvious to the Canadian authors, for whom contrasting doctrines of accountability and conformity, 'peace, order and good government,' are linked to national identity.

21. Miller, "Freeriders."

22. Ibid.

23. Daniel Green, "Warren Miller's New Reality" *Skiing*, Oct 1994, p. 28.

24. Roger Thurlow, *The Wall Street Journal*, 18 Dec 1996, p. A1.

25. "Vertical Reality," Warren Miller Entertainment, 1994.

26. Miller, "Freeriders."

27. Ibid.

28. Green, "Warren Miller's," p. 28.

29. Miller, "Freeriders."

30. The loss leader in a marketing strategy is a product that does not accrue individual profit but contributes to profit on other products by its association.

31. Paul Johnson, *Modern Times: The World from the 1920's to the 1990's* (New York: Harper, 1991), p. 147.

32. Miller, "Freeriders."

33. Ibid.

34. Ibid.

35. Ibid.

36. Ibid.

37. E. John Allen and John B. Allen, *From skisport to skiing: One hundred years of American sport, 1840–1940* (Amherst: University of Massachusetts Press, 1993).

38. Big Air contests are an updated version of aerial competition including 'new school' tricks co-opted from snowboarding.

39. Warren Miller's *Freeriders* Production Notes.

40. Jon Davies, "Duty and self-sacrifice for country: The new disparagement of public ideals," in Digby Anderson (ed.), *The Loss of Virtue: Moral Confusion and Social Disorder in Britain and America* (New York: National Review, 1992) pp. 69–82.

41. Epitaph of Horace.

42. Ubiquitous.

43. The memorial at Kilmartin, Argyllshire (cited in Davies, "Duty and self-sacrifice," p. 79).

44. Kristen Ulmer, "Trevor Peterson, Ski Hero," *Skiing*, Sep 1996, p. 42.

45. Davies, "Duty and self-sacrifice," p. 80.

46. Rinehart, *Player's All*, p. 8.

47. Kathleen Gasperini, "Kodak Courage," *Mountain Sport and Living*, Jan.Feb 1999, p. 43.

48. According to Kundera's distinction between the first and second tear (see Avishai Margalit, "The Kitsch of Israel," *The New York Review*, 24 Nov 1988, pp. 20–24), the second tear is the "meta-tear" (p. 20), the tear we shed from solidarity with the collective feelings of the group we belong to at the sight of the first tear. It is a manifestation of a vicarious sentiment: it does not come out of the person's direct involvement with the object of feeling but rather out of a derivative excitement that comes from reflection. Margalit extends Kundera's distinction to define kitsch in its purest form: when the second tear comes without the first one's ever occurring.

49. Robert Alter, *Partial magic: The novel as a self-conscious genre* (Berkeley: University of California Press, 1975), pp. x and xi.

50. David Lodge (*After Bakhtin*, p. 43) refers to 'metafiction' as a new phenomenon in the history of fiction whereby the exposure foregrounds the existence of the author, the source of the novel's *diegisis*, in a way that runs counter to the modernist pursuit of impersonality and mimesis of consciousness.

51. *Freeriders Production Notes*

52. Imax film crews, for example, simultaneously shot footage for the 1999 release of *Extreme* and *The Making of Extreme*, a made-for-TV documentary.

53. The more nakedly the author appears to reveal himself, the more inescapable it becomes, paradoxically, that the author as a voice is only a

function of his own fiction, not a privileged authority but an object of interpretation. (Lodge, after *Bakhtin*, p. 43)

54. Discussion of Americanization and cultural imperialism in sport has increased recently. For an exploration of these concepts, see Peter Donnelly, "The local and the global: Globalization in the sociology of sport," *Journal of Sport and Social Issues*, 23: (1996), pp. 239–257; Barrie Houlihan, "Homogenization, Americanization and Creolization of sport: Varieties of globalization," *Sport Sociology Journal*, 11 (1994), pp. 356–375.

55. Alain de Botton, *The romantic movement: Sex, shopping and the novel*. (London: Picador, 1995), p. 69.

SNOWBOARDING

Chapter Twenty-Four

Snowboarding

The Essence Is Fun

Jake Burton

Every October I throw a party for the extended Burton family. It has always been an occasion to have a great time before getting down to the hard work of the winter. About a thousand people come over to my place in Moscow, Vermont, for food, drink, music, and merriment. And football. In the afternoon, we mark off a few gridirons on the front lawn and go at it until it is too dark to see the ball. Old and new friends, both men and women, come together for some serious fun—smiles are common and the competitive fire escalates through the dusk, reaching something of a frenzied pitch in the final game. It might just be touch football, but winning matters. This is one of my favorite aspects of the event.

Jake Burton is president and founder of Burton Snowboards. Jake began Burton Snowboards in Londonderry, Vt., in 1977—an event that is generally recognized as the birth of modern day snowboarding. From a Vermont barn, Jake created a sport, an industry, and a lifestyle. Jake's motivation continues to be his commitment to preserving the sport of snowboarding, and making the world's best snowboarding equipment. Despite the fact the ski industry is on the decline, snowboarding is recognized as the world's fastest growing sport, and Burton Snowboards remains the industry leader in virtually every market in the world. With headquarters in Burlington, Vt.; Innsbruck, Austria; and Saitama, Japan; and over 600 employees, Burton equipment is sold in more than 30 countries by approximately 6,500 specialty retail shops worldwide. Jake's focus has always been on the athletes' interests and the sport's progression as a whole. Jake has generously contributed his knowledge and experience in the snowboarding industry. His input has kept the sport moving forward as the wave of the future.

Snowboarding, at its core, is no different from these annual football sessions. Both the sport and the business of Burton are firmly rooted in a passionate blend of fun and poker-faced seriousness. Snowboarders are dead serious about having fun, and we have always had a helluva lot of fun busting our asses to create a sport and successful company.

The influences and inspirations that created snowboarding are varied. The granddaddy of it all would have to be the ancient Hawaiian god-king who had the bravado and balls to harness the power of a Pacific wave while standing on a hewn plank of mahogany. In this act of unprecedented audacity, the ancient Hawaiian brought to mankind a sublime sensation that seems to resonate particularly well with the inherent motions of the human body—the dynamics of surf-inspired board sports. Skateboarding has had and continues to have its impact as well. Snowboarders compete in half-pipes, and a good bit of freestyle riding is transposed directly from what is learned on ramps and city landscapes with four wheels underfoot. And, of course, skiing yielded basic technology (which we've surpassed) and the concept and technique of riding on packed resort snow. At a deeper cultural level, however, sledding is the seminal influence.

The sledding hill, and its culture of youthful play, was where it all started. The original Snurfers, primitive snowboards developed by a guy named Sherman Poppen in the mid-sixties, were used on sledding hills, not ski runs. Kids, myself included, left the Flexible Flyer at home, dragged our Snurfers up the hill all day and hung on as best we could during the descents. It wasn't too serious, and it sure the hell wasn't elitist. It was all about fun and doing it with friends. These days, when a bunch of guys hike the pipe all day or go off into the backcountry, it's not that much different. Also, this impact of sledding on the sport is evident in the distinct attitude snowboarders have toward ski areas: rather than seeing them as country-club-like places with recreation and fireside socializing, snowboarders view ski areas simply as big sledding hills with one major improvement—lifts. The ski resort, where the influences of surfing, skateboarding, and skiing meet, is still just a place to have a good time going downhill. In snowboarding, fun is still paramount and elitism is still absent.

My own motivations for starting a snowboard company back in 1977 were grounded in both the fun and seriousness of snowboarding—both a passion for the sensations of snowboarding and a powerful entrepreneurial drive. As a kid growing up in Long

Island in the 1960s with a background in skiing and a little surfing, I enthusiastically took to the local sledding hills with a Snurfer under my arm. I developed some decent skills, and given the lack of widespread participation, came to see Snurfing as "my thing." It became part of my identity. In time, I got older, went off to college, and jumped on the corporate career track in downtown Manhattan. A year into life as a suit, however, I was shocked that no one had taken Sherman Poppen's Snurfer concept to the next level. Though I initially didn't see the ski area thing that has revolutionized the business of winter sports, I did see more than a toy or a fad—I saw a backcountry sport that people would take very seriously. Seeing this business opportunity to develop a sport, I turned my back on the mainstream Fortune 500 life and headed up to Londonderry in southern Vermont to start making boards. With a real personal interest in surfing down a mountain, I was primarily driven by the chance to create a successful business.

In the early years, snowboarding and building the company were the entirety of my life and of that of anyone who came to work at Burton. They might have been crazy times, but we managed to have a great time along the way. I would wake up in the morning, start working right away, and then go to sleep when the work was done. One year when I was on my own, work included everything: designing the product, making the boards, manning the customer service line (which rang in my bedroom at all hours), repairing machinery, doing the taxes. Trying to figure out the best way to make boards was a constant learning process of making do with available resources. Unaware of bandsaw technology, I initially shaped the boards with a pin router—an incredibly powerful version of the more common tool. A couple of times the router grabbed the grain of the wood at the wrong angle, tore the board out of my hands, and fired it across the room. Luckily, I was alone at the time.

We certainly rolled up our sleeves on a daily basis, but work wasn't everything. After a year or two, a real passion for the joy of making turns became a powerful part of my life. What began as a business opportunity in something that I enjoyed a great deal became not only a company that I was building, but a sport that I would rather be doing more than anything else. During this time, people from various parts of mainstream society repeatedly doubted what I was doing and questioned the integrity of snowboarding. The more I was confronted with this skepticism, the more I believed in the virtues and strengths of the sport and the more I became something of an evangelist. Not simply because I wanted to make a living, but more so because I knew the value that it added to life—a shitload of fun! At every opportunity, we got out on the surrounding hills to ride our latest innovations. Almost every night after work, we would load up the Volare wagon and take turns driving to make shuttle runs after the lifts closed on the lower part of Bromley Mountain. They might not have allowed us on the lifts, but we were starting to ride the ski slopes, and soon we would be banging on their doors to show them the future.

In the early eighties, with our edgeless wooden boards in tow, ski area managers certainly didn't see us as the future—more like a ragtag band of bored skateboarders and surfers with some simple winter fad which was sure to quickly disappear. We were convinced otherwise. Our drive to open American ski resorts to snowboarders was guided by our passion for the sport (massive amounts of vertical feet in a day meant a whole lot more fun) and the understanding that significantly growing the sport and the company depended on lift access. In 1983, Mark Heingartner (who was working for Burton at the time) and I heard that Stratton allowed snowboarders, so we went up to check it out. They didn't. But we did get a chance to talk to Paul Johnston, the mountain manager. He told us to come up in the middle of the week and take some runs with him and his ski patrol so that he could learn more about the sport and our equipment. Afterward, riding with us, he met with his board of directors, all of whom opposed the granting of access. But since none had a good reason, he decided against them and made the executive decision to give snowboarding a trial period. For doing so, he deserves a great deal of credit for promoting the sport and giving birth to the outstanding relationship snowboarding and Stratton have developed over the years. Once they opened the door, Mark took charge of establishing a professional program of instruction and certification at the mountain to make sure snowboarding was successful and we didn't blow what could have been our only chance.

Success at Stratton marked the beginning of a long campaign to gain acceptance of snowboarding at resorts in the States and around the world. Through the eighties, we opened more and more lifts: Breckenridge, Boreal, Vail, Stowe. Overcoming the ignorance and prejudice—epitomized in such humorous words as "knuckledragger"—was a process that required solid education, professionalism, and persistence. Just as we poured every bit of energy into making the best possible boards, boots, and bindings, we tirelessly worked to enjoy that which we were denied: the opportunity to drop into Corbet's Couloir or pick a line down Squaw Valley's famed Pallisades. It was probably during this time of dealing with mainstream resistance in order to further the interests of snow-boarding that I developed a professional role that I often play now—that of advocate for the sport's interests. Meanwhile, the struggle with ski areas continues to this day; ironically, the resort that hosted the snowboarding event at the 1998 Olympics in Nagano, Japan, doesn't allow snowboarding—neither do American resorts such as Aspen Mountain, Taos, Alta, and Mad River Glen.

Many observers, especially those outside the sport, viewed the recent Olympic debut as the pinnacle of acceptance, a passage into alpine athletic manhood of sorts. It was certainly a significant event and with all the attendant controversies, probably good for the sport. But the competition itself was disconnected from the tradition and spirit of competitive snowboarding—run by skiers, it was nationalistic, formalistic, and conducted in the pouring rain. From the early Nationals held at Suicide Six in the beginning of the 1980s to the most recent U.S. Open held at Stratton, competi-tive snowboarding has always been a gathering of riders simulta-neously having a lot of fun as a community and competing like hell as individuals. The Olympics lacked this combination. Con-versely, when Doug Bouton hung on his edgeless wooden board as he hit 63 mph at the Nationals in 1981, the people whom he beat were his friends. At the time, though we took it incredibly seri-ously, it was little more than a bunch of buddies on a sledding hill trying to see who could go the fastest. In many ways, it is still that way today. In the modern era, when an uber-competitor like Terje Haakonsen throws down to rise above the hundreds of riders at the Open, he too is defeating many of his friends. Whereas the com-petitors are world-class athletes on the one hand and average Joes on the other, the spirit of competition is essentially the same at international snowboarding events like the U.S. Open as it is dur-ing the football battles on my front yard each October.

Entry into the Olympics also brought an intense political battle to snowboarding—a battle that had major implications for the cul-tural integrity and future of the sport. To amend a long and convo-luted story, the aging bureaucrats of international skiing, the FIS, were given sanctioning power over Olympic snowboarding and in turn attempted to use this opportunity to control all of competitive snowboarding for the other three years and eleven months out of each four-year cycle. They tried to remake competitive snowboarding in the tired, boring image of international skiing: FIS events only, national teams, national coaches, national uniforms, big corporate donors. When an outside influence with a history of antagonism to the sport began to take steps that would have destroyed the diverse, laissez-faire nature of competitive snowboarding, sucked out the athletes' trademark individualism, and converted the fun of competition into a perpetual nationalistic circus, I instinctively got involved to defend the sport. It took absolutely no conscious effort—I was naturally motivated to do whatever it took. When the fun that lies at the heart of snowboarding was at stake, I got serious about making sure that the sport didn't go down a path that would have killed its soul. Winning the battle mattered enormously. After lengthy negotiations and necessary political maneuvers, we won.

As snowboarding and Burton look toward the future, growth and movement into the mainstream is inevitable. Large companies with no tradition in or ownership of snowboarding are getting into the market as both manufacturers and sponsors. Let to run free, these people, like the FIS, could negatively impact snowboarding. Through it all, our goal as a company and as leaders in the industry will be to temper and minimize the destructive influences of the mainstream that threaten the sport's traditions and cultural integrity. Above all, snowboarding has to remain fun, innovative, and driven by young people with a natural passion and energy for the sport. As a community, we have to resist the urge to make a quick buck. The success that we are so serious about pursuing must come within the context of respect for traditions and history. Our development of a step-in binding system—one that allows people to engage the boot to the board without using their hands—is a clear example of this stewardship. While others rushed ahead to give riders systems that utilized bicycle technology to deliver convenience at the expense of authentic snowboard performance, we held out until we could develop a system that maintained the unique feeling and dynamics that have made snowboarding so much fun and so successful. This will continue to be our innovation philosophy: drive technology forward within the context of snowboarding.

Personally, I'll continue to approach the sport with an equal passion for the fun of riding and the seriousness of the business. I'll continue to get up in the predawn a hundred or so days a year and make my way to Stowe for some early-morning powder runs with good friends. I'll continue to enjoy the sport with my family and take any opportunity to teach someone the basics—one of the best parts of snowboarding is just being around the enthusiasm and stoke of a beginner. And I'll continue to fight important battles on behalf of snowboarders. I'll do my best to make sure the sport remains true to the spirit of sledding and the energy of pickup football.

Chapter Twenty-Five

Selling Out Snowboarding

The Alternative Response to Commercial Co-optation

Duncan Humphreys

Of all the 'extreme' sports, snowboarding has made what seems to be the most spectacular, and sudden, entrance into the public eye and popularity. The snowboard industry predicts that by the year 2005, half of all ski field patrons will be snowboarders.[1] Already 45 percent of first-time visitors to ski fields in the US are snowboarders.[2] Yet, just fifteen years ago most ski fields banned snowboards.

But participants in extreme sports have not welcomed commercial popularity. The majority of snowboarders, like participants in related activities, such as tow-in surfing and skateboarding, and in music-based subcultures, such as punk, reject widespread commercial co-optation. The basis of this rejection resides in an artistic philosophy that values freedom and self-expression, but which, ironically, is responsible for increasing the popularity of snowboarding. Initially, however, this philosophy led to managers banning snowboarding from the ski fields.

This general ban came about for two main reasons. In the late 1960s and early 1970s snowboarders symbolized 'snow surfers.' Like

---

Duncan Humphreys finished his Masters degree at the School of Physical Education at the University of Otago, New Zealand, and decided to fully pursue the lifestyle he wrote about. He presently instructs kayaking and guides rafts in the summer, leaving the winter to snowboard.

soul-surfers who chased waves, 'snow surfers' embodied the counterculture and came to be seen by the public as misfits, subversive nomads, "rotten, long haired, unwashed drug addicts"[3] and disciples of obscure Eastern religions. Secondly, negative images of skateboarding also contributed to the general dislike of snowboarding. As journalist Charles Gant explains, "America views skaters as social pariahs. Castigated as profane, degenerate, dangerous and criminal, skaters are the most pervasive manifestation of the nation's outlaw culture."[4] Fearful of such unsavoury characters ranging over middle-class, family ski resorts, ski field managers banned snowboarders.

The first major field to open its doors to snowboarders was Stratton Mountain (Vermont) in 1983. Other fields quickly followed. By the end of the decade the majority of ski fields allowed snowboarders. But there was an ulterior motive. Skiing had reached a growth plateau and snowboarding offered ski fields a new youth market and ongoing economic prosperity. *Ski* magazine summed up the importance of snowboarding when it described it as one of the 100 greatest things that had ever happened to skiing: "it attracted a whole new generation of young riders to the ski resorts, giving the ski world a much needed shot in the arm."[5]

'The New Sensation': Exploitation and Opposition

A major turning point in the acceptance of snowboarding was the decision by the governing body of skiing, the Federation Internationale du Ski (FIS), in 1993 to include snowboarding in the 1998 Winter Olympic Games in Nagano, Japan. While the decision was an attempt to control snowboarding, it also played a major role in its 'legitimation.' The editor of *Transworld Snowboarding*, Billy Miller, argued that "there's a lot of money in [the Olympics], enough to change snowboarding's public status from fad to legitimate sport forever."[6] In 1997, Park City (Utah) and several other large fields announced that they would repeal their bans on snowboarding. Previously they had justified the ban on the grounds that customers were "overwhelmingly opposed" to riders,[7] and liked the field because "there are no snowboarders."[8] Five years later, Park City was the location for the 2002 Winter Olympic snowboarding events.

Ten years after snowboarding gained access to the slopes, the skiing community recognized it as "the new sensation."[9] Ste'en Webster, editor of *NZ Snowboarder*, argues that snowboarding has followed surfing in its development:

Ten or twenty years ago surfers were seen as ratbags, but now you have surfers as models for clothing. You can buy surfing product three thousand miles from the ocean. In the seventies it was underground, now it is accepted . . . Snowboarding is mirroring that growth.[10]

However, like surfers, snowboarders debated these developments. The International Snowboarding Federation (ISF), the original snowboard governing body formed in 1991 from individual national administrative organizations dating back to 1987, believes that the FIS usurped power to exploit snowboarding for short-term profit. The ISF charges the FIS with having no long-term interest in snowboarding, and accuses it of stepping in to control snowboarding only after the activity started to show commercial profits. Mark Fawcett, an ISF negotiator and boarder, argues that the "FIS's focus is obvious, they want to make money from this . . . they want to rob it."[11] John Bache, president of the New Zealand Snowboard Association, remembered the resistance early snowboarders faced from the skiing establishment. For him it is

hard to deal with organisations that told you to piss off because they 'knew' snowboarding was a passing fad . . . Now that they've seen the continuing decline in skier numbers, and the continued growth of snowboarding, FIS wants in. They are being driven by greed.[12]

Others fear for snowboarding under FIS mismanagement which, for example, was largely responsible for the cancellation of the 1995 FIS World Skiing Championships.[13] ISF coach Rob Roy wants "to make sure that those who take over the sport don't kill it because they don't know any better."[14] Victoria Jealouse, an ISF rider, argues that "the ski industry will bend over backwards for snowboarders right now. Eventually they'll go back to their past, to what they know. No matter what the FIS says, they're going to fuck up competition and the industry."[15] Moves by the FIS to use nonsnowboarding fields like Park City, which rejected snowboarding for so long, and those surrounding Nagano, which still banned snowboarders, and to use non-snowboarding manufacturers like Phenix (a popular Japanese ski wear manufacturer) to clothe the FIS US Snowboard team, give credence to the ISF view. As one commentator put it,

while the world watches snowboarding make its official debut [at Nagano] as a socially acceptable and mainstream

sport, what they won't see are giant-slalom competitors
getting escorted off the mountain after their race is done,
and halfpipe competitors looking up from their contest
playpen at all the mountains they're still not allowed to
ride.[16]

These moves also anger those snowboarders who don't care
about sporting competitions, much less the Olympics. In an article
entitled 'Getting FISted,' the authors of *Flakezine*, an on-line commentary of the snowboarding industry, spat,

> The bottom line is FIS doesn't give a lump of feces for
> snowboarding, snowboarders, or snowboarding culture.
> They simply see snowboarding as another way to sell
> sponsorships, gain power, and control another winter
> sport. Anything they say to the contrary is a bald-faced
> lie. They are a bunch of unethical, evil cretins set on
> destroying snowboarding as we know it.[17]

Although representatives from the FIS claim they want to
help snowboarding develop and grow, it is not hard to see that
behind their justifications lie the healthy profits snowboarding offers.
Hanno Trendl, head of FIS Snowboarding, sees the FIS as putting
snowboarding on the "next level": "everyone respects the Olympics as the highest level of sport. We are the second wave; ISF has
been doing this for years. Our goal as a winter-sports association is
to get people in the mountains enjoying winter sports instead of
going to the Caribbean."[18] As the "new sensation," and compared
to the stagnating sport of skiing, snowboarding currently offers the
FIS a viable means to attract people to the ski fields, and hence to
maintain ski industry profits.

However, snowboarders want to control their own activity.
Snowboarders follow lifestyles different from those of skiers. Their
styles have their roots in skating, punk, and grunge and in the bans
that ski fields placed on snowboarding. As ISF negotiator and rider
Mark Fawcett puts it,

> Some people choose to do the FIS tour because that's
> how they can compete [at the Olympics]. In the long
> term, what are you doing to the sport? You're giving
> control to skiers, and calling your sport a discipline of

skiing. Snowboarding was developed by surfers and skateboarders, not skiers ... And now everything we've all
worked for, you're giving to them on a silver platter.
You're jumping on your knees in front of the dictator.[19]

In reality, most snowboarders have ignored the Olympic
squabble. According to Ste'en Webster, "competitive snowboarders ... are Olympic athletes" and "a different breed ... Most
snowboarders couldn't give a hoot."[20] But such acceptance by the
ski federation and the IOC is symptomatic of an activity becoming mainstream. Tom Sims, snowboarding pioneer and manufacturer, has no problem with snowboarding's Olympic status and
increased popularity:

> ... now that it's allowed everywhere, I think it's more
> fun than ever. But it's true some people are bummed
> because they think it makes snowboarding uncool. It comes
> down to why you snowboard in the first place. Do you
> want a cool, underground sport or something that's fun?[21]

All the evidence suggests that it is the underground that the
overwhelming majority of snowboarders desire. Prominent New
Zealand snowboarder Aaron Bolt argues that now that snowboarding
has established itself, riders will have to be wary because "if it
becomes [too] mainstream ... it will stifle the creativity. It'll become like skiing."[22] The authors of *Flakezine* agree:

> In the hands of the 'mainstream' ... snowboarders,
> snowboarding companies and the snowboarding media
> will make a lot more money ... but it will be in ex-
> change for their souls, creativity, and individuality ...
> Snowboarding will become exactly like skiing, golf, in
> line skating, NASCAR and tennis—boring, dull and
> staid.[23]

These anti-commercial sentiments derive from an 'artistic sensibility' that snowboarding shares with other activities such as surfing,
skateboarding, parachuting, and rock climbing. These activities
emerged with the cooperative new leisure movement in the 1960s,
and all are currently undergoing a resurgence as "extreme" sports
in the 1990s.

An Artistic Sensibility

The artistic sensibility in the new leisure movement involved a transfer of an abstract 'art' to the physical realm. Art represents creativity, innovation, freedom of action and expression in every sphere. It is a noncommercial philosophy at odds with capitalism. Good art represents "human expression." It is "the product of genius" and hence, by definition, "original and innovative."[24] New leisure movement activities, while recognizing the brilliance of 'geniuses,' those people who lead the way through originality and innovation, and who are admired, followed, and mimicked, also celebrate a more democratic view of expression. As art historian Arnold Hauser explains, the French Revolution brought democracy to art—artistic freedom was "no longer a privilege of the genius, but the birthright of every artist and every gifted individual . . . All individual expression is unique, irreplaceable and bears its own laws and standards within itself."[25] The social revolution of the 1960s introduced this philosophy into leisure.

In the 1960s, disciples of the counterculture reacted against what they saw as the overarching conformity and stifling nature of society and the mass market. This reaction was epitomized by student spokesman Mario Savio, who called for a rebellion against a world that treated people as "cogs" in a machine. The counterculture followed the Beats' philosophy that "every person is entitled to act and believe as he wants to."[26] The counterculture inspired individuals to see themselves as original works of art and to act accordingly—to be true to one's self.

The new leisure movement also embodied this philosophy by rejecting the unplayful, unexpressive and "overly rationalized, technologized, and bureaucratized"[27] world of traditional sport, preferring activities that were free, fun, cooperative, and individualistic. For example, the philosophical tenets of rock climbing advocated "liberty, individualism and a lifestyle independent of the conformist and reactionary middle classes."[28] Not surprisingly, then, new leisure movement activities are often referred to as art. As one skateboarder puts it, a lot of skaters " 'are really involved with artistic endeavours . . . it's a kind of freedom of expression . . . How do you express yourself playing football, playing basketball? When you are skating it's . . . definitely . . . a way to express yourself. Many athletes, and indeed sport sociologists, claim that players express themselves in traditional sports. However, the point is that the lack of formal structures convinces skaters that they have more creative freedom than that available in codified traditional sports, with its compulsion, rigid rules, codification, institutionalization, competition, and training."[29] One skateboarder summed up the new leisure movement's attitude toward competition in the following remarks: " 'Who's to say what trick is better? I like to do stuff that feels cool, that gives me butterflies in my stomach.' "[30] The philosophy of music has many parallels with the artistic sensibility of the new leisure movement. As a member of Gus Gus, a group consisting of nine musicians, put it, "There is no leader in this band . . . there is never a problem of competition . . . This is art, and you never compete in art."[31]

In the 1970s and 1980s punk further influenced the artistic sensibility of the new leisure movement. Punks appropriated the principle tenet of the counterculture philosophy, a principle as stated by Yippie leader Jerry Rubin: "People should do what ever the fuck they want."[32] The political failure of the counterculture to deliver the promised Utopia disgusted punks.[33] Malcolm McLaren, manager of the Sex Pistols, summed up this disgust when he declared that "the philosophy of the Sex Pistols . . . was never to trust a hippie."[34]

In the eyes of punks, distrust stemmed not so much from the failure of the counterculture's social agenda as from the fact that many of its disciples appeared to renege on the values they once vociferously espoused. It seemed to many youth that the 1960s generation had performed a philosophical and political about-face, abandoning the Left for the New Right. Yippies, including Abbie Hoffman, became yuppies; communists, such as David Horowitz, became neoconservatives; everywhere materialism replaced idealism.[35] Those who dismantled the welfare system in the 1980s were part of the same generation that had exploited it to drop out in the 1960s. Determined not to fail like their countercultural parents, punks built their value system around personal honesty and integrity. Furthermore, although post-Fordism brought greater choice to consumers, punks retained the countercultural critique of late capitalism—that mass communication and mass consumption produced a blandness in the quality of life.[36] As a result, punks emphasized originality, arguing that people should be innovative in every sphere of daily life. Punks found a succour and philosophical ally in the art world. Their politics and philosophies—both based on personal honesty and nonconformist innovation—were best explored and articulated through the tenets of art. In a sense, their very lives were art. Yet initially, punks rejected art as a class-based and elitist institution.

Punks did, initially, celebrate the counterculture's democratic philosophy. But as early as the late 1970s, their high ideals about nonconformity meant that punk norms shifted to those found in the elitist world of art, which they had previously rejected. Punk quickly became a competition about individualism, and, as Gavin Hills argues, it became "one of the most discriminating youth cultures . . . Punk was obsessed with its own authenticity."[37] Where the counterculture celebrated universal free expression, punks emphasized an individuality based on truly original expression. This meant that doing what you wanted, in punk terms, often required being as socially different and offensive as possible, even to fellow punks. American journalist Charles Young captures the essence of the punk attitude toward clothing: "True punk fashion is determined by your attitude toward the apparel, not by the apparel per se. If you wear it to conform to other punks, you're an asshole. If you wear it to offend other people—even other punks—you're really an asshole, and that's cool."[38] This was a world where the "best" art was the most original: original to the point that it alienated people. An example of this attitude comes from Holger Czukay, a member of the German band Can: "I remember once we played in a big hall and made it completely empty. When we finished there was nobody anymore. No housemaster, just total silence. I thought it was a great success."[39]

Later, in the early 1980s, a "postpunk" movement emerged. By this time punk had divided along two philosophical and political lines. Pioneer punks continued to equate their lifestyle with "artful" offensiveness; new punks saw themselves as vehicles for social change. Penny Rimbaud, a member of Crass, a postpunk band which took the Sex Pistols anarchist tenets literally, says, "When Johnny Rotten proclaimed that there was 'no future,' we saw it as a challenge to our creativity. We knew there was a future if we were prepared to work for it."[40] Crass was

> crucial in drawing a large contingent of post-punks towards the idea of punk as a way of life, rather than a mere lifestyle: pro-squatting, nuclear disarmament, feminism and animal liberation. Following their inspiration, punks were taking on board sixties ideals, and slowly mutating into the hippie continuum.[41]

Both of these punk strands affected the new leisure movement, which became an uneasy mix of democratic countercultural beliefs, boosted by politically anarchist postpunks and the high individualism of the "art" punks. Interestingly, both versions of the artistic sensibility fueled an almost universal opposition to commercialism, and even to popularity.

Selling Out

To contemporary artists, art that has "sold out" or gone "commercial," is "inauthentic, . . . lightweight and insubstantial and, by definition, not worth serious consideration. Similar judgements are made of the artist or artists who created it."[42] This concept influenced both schools of punk. Among punks, "selling out" denotes an overdependence on capitalism to support one's lifestyle. More specifically, to pioneer punks it means a lack of innovation with respect to music, fashion, or attitudes; to postpunks, selling out means to give up punk politics and philosophies. Among the latter, capitalism does more than create blind followers of fashion: it fosters greed and causes rifts in society. One anarchist describes capitalist social relationships as conniving with "coercion . . . You don't want that Jeep Cherokee anymore, you need it, and therefore you will step on anyone that gets in your way . . . Capitalism is not about desires, but about compulsions and control."[43] Both coercion and excess materialism are deemed abhorrent. Describing rampant materialism, punk, hip-hop, and skateboard photographer Glen Friedman pointedly declares,

> I don't care if you are an artist, a stockbroker, a musician, I don't care what you're doing, no one deserves a million dollars a year . . . If you're a pro athlete and the owner's making that much, yes. You should take a smaller wage and force him through your union to lower ticket prices. It makes good business sense: these greedy fucks are going to make the people who support them go broke . . . and soon their fans won't have any money left to spend on these diversionary, mind dulling games. Maybe we should just watch it eat itself.[44]

In the wake of these developments, 'punk rock' became an adjective to describe the 'purity' of one's actions. It expresses punks' condemnation of the "materialist superficiality" of life under capitalism. It emerges in comments such as "Oh, you bought new shoes, that's not very punk rock," and in public criticisms of those who are, for example, distributed by a major label or interviewed in a mainstream music magazine; even those who eat at McDonalds are said to be supping "with the devil."[45]

In addition to these criticisms of capitalism, both artists and punks consider the commercial sphere as bland. They reject it because, as Bill Ryan argues, "the conservative bias in marketing . . . pressures artists to temper the type and degree of their originality, to create upon themselves and in their work, signs drawn from the languages of style already spoken in the market; i.e. to develop a commercial idiolect."[46] "Art," Ryan says, "transcend[s] the earthly, utilitarian realm . . . It offends the supposedly finely-tuned sensibilities of artists, critics, collectors and audiences to speak of their subject in the same breath as they speak of money."[47]

While punk influenced the philosophies of the new leisure movement, punk's philosophical outlook is much more politically motivated and confrontational. Remaining separate from the commercial mainstream constitutes the core of punk identity. Hence, boarders and other disciples of the new leisure movement followed punk's anti-commercial sentiments, but did not respond to commercialism with the same intensity and vehemence. For example, in 1992, a visiting Swiss snowboarder attracted criticism after he won a New Zealand competition because he returned his prizes complaining that he came to win money, not T-shirts. A writer for *New Zealand Snowboarder* responded, "If you ever start thinking this way I suggest you take up pro golf or tennis."[48] Furthermore, the quasireligious views of countercultural soul-surfers are still present in some sectors of snowboarding. Soul-surfers saw surfing as a religious experience; some viewed it as a means of getting back to nature.[49] Similarly, one correspondent to *Transworld Snowboarding* described snowboarding as "a spiritual act . . . When one is snowboarding they're not simply manipulating the snow and the mountain, they're trying to become one with the large being of the mountain."[50] Clearly, in these contexts money and spirituality do not mix. Snowboarding is about fun, self-expression, and getting back to nature, not making money. Obviously this philosophy is idealistic, and it raises critical issues about the opportunities that snowboarding provides for professionalism. These issues will be discussed later.

According to this perspective, if snowboarding is perceived as becoming too mass produced and embroiled in commercialism, it loses its "soul." It would be seen as "typical and conventional, rather than as innovative and original." Snowboarding would "appear instead as an object of no particular uniqueness and of relatively little artistic significance."[51] This explains why snowboarders and skateboarders believe that activities like skiing and Rollerblading have sold out. Skiing is seen as rigid and as a symbol of the elite. One ski racer-turned-snowboarder argued that snowboarding rejuvenated her passion for winter sports: "I love snowboarding so much because there is not all these rules. There's still a little of a young feeling to it."[52] Skiing is also seen as an impersonal money-making machine: "The ski industry stagnated because they became so wrapped up in the carbon paper of business that they forgot who was even on their skinny planks."[53]

Rollerblading is also seen as having sold out because of its popularity among the wrong types: it has been embraced by the body-beautiful Lycra set as a means of aerobic exercise, and by ice skaters, and cross-country and downhill skiers as a training tool. Although young adherents perform tricks,[54] skaters sneer at them. As Craig Harris, owner of a Wellington, New Zealand, skate-snowboard shop says, Rollerblading is "stupid because everything that they are doing has been done on rollerskates and skateboards . . . it's pathetic, it's a stolen sport. It seems to me that it's just trying to make money. They will never get respect from skateboarding."[55] Rollerblades "are like Billy Ray Cyrus or Beverly Hills 90210, popular with no class." On the other hand, skateboards may not be popularly respected but are "cultural classics nonetheless."[56]

Debates over selling out pervade the new leisure movement, and especially its professional wing. Rockclimber Tim Fairfield claims that climbing is "packaged radicalism. It's anti-police, anti-ranger, anti-land management. It's anti-authority. But it's not anti-money. That's why we have to learn how to sell it."[57] However, this is not a commonly held, or at least a commonly expressed, view. Andrew Morrison, a former New Zealand skateboard professional, recalls the dilemmas of being paid to ride: "Even though I didn't feel like going, I still did, because it was my job, and the better I got, the more money I got, which is a shit way to look at it. You should skate for fun. That's why I am so happy now, not being a pro skater."[58]

Here is the paradox of the new leisure movement professional: no matter how esoteric they believe their activity to be, professionals cannot not separate themselves from the reality of capitalism. "There's all this talk about selling out, but what have snowboarders gained? Their own home? Ability to support their families? Yeah, real big sellout."[59] In order to follow a credo which, in Craig Harris's words, "is doing what you want to do and not being restricted,"[60] professional snowboarders still have to rely on financial support from commercial manufacturers, filmmakers, photographers, and the like. This creates a fine line between credibility and sell-out. Snowboarders deemed "too commercial," who overactively search for money, or who receive support from the "wrong source," like a traditional ski company or a business that breaches the punk code of ethics, are sell-outs.

However, unlike most professional surfers, professional snowboarders do not have to compete. Success in competition is not a necessary prerequisite for skate or snowboard professionals. The latter can promote their sponsors, and themselves, through videos, photographic shoots, snowboard camps and simply by riding at their local mountain. Unlike professional surfers who had to be photogenic and articulate well to gain public acceptance, the majority of snowboard professionals did not have to change their image.[61] Professional snowboarders do not have to promote a clean and healthy image because they rarely deal directly with the public. Their primary interaction is with other snowboarders. Furthermore, the Professional Snowboarders Association (PSA), which formed in 1990, recognized the problems that had occurred in other activities such as surfing. Riders set up the PSA in order to "promote and protect the rights and personalities of its members."[62] Hence, to a significant degree, snowboarders could promote whatever images took their fancy.

However, the sponsor-professional relationship is ultimately an employer-employee relationship. Employers demand that employees satisfy their needs. Professionals must deal with the concrete world of commercialism, as opposed to the abstract, idealistic world of art. Ultimately, professionals in the new leisure movement find it increasingly difficult to indulge in endless play. A similar problem occurs when musicians become successful, and therefore, in a sense, "professional." Jazz historian Andre Hodeir argues that

> the history of both jazz and jazzmen is that of creative purity gradually corrupted by success. . . . First, the young musician expresses himself freely, breaks the rules, disconcerting and even shocking his listeners; then the public adopts him, he attracts disciples and becomes a star. He thinks he is free, but he has become a prisoner.[63]

Nonetheless, professional snowboarders, like jazz musicians, still enjoy substantial freedoms. Howard Becker, in his study of professional jazz musicians in the 1940s and 1950s, concludes that no one could tell them how to play, and "logically . . . no one can tell a musician to do anything. Accordingly, behavior that flouts conventional social norms is greatly admired."[64] Indeed, as one young musician said, "The biggest heroes in the music business are the biggest characters. The crazier a guy acts, the greater he is, the more everyone likes him."[65] Becker concludes that "people with such gifts cannot be subjected to the constraints imposed on other members of society; we must allow them to violate the rules of decorum, propriety, and common sense everyone else must follow."[66]

But what happens when such freedoms are taken to the extreme? A letter, reprinted in *Transworld Snowboarding* from the manager of a motel used by professional snowboarders, suggests one common answer. According to the manager, "from the minute they arrived, it was total chaos":

> They were rude to all of the employees, and showed absolutely no respect for our hotel. . . . The following day, I was bombarded with complaints of obscene and illegal acts that were committed by a few of the boarders. . . . Why they need to conduct themselves in such a manner is incomprehensible. . . . If the professionals cannot act like adults, how can we expect all the young kids learning the sport not to do the same?[67]

Similarly, the *San Francisco Bay Guardian* recently painted a disturbing picture of the darker side of such attitudes in skateboard professionalism: Josh Swindell was awaiting trial for murder, Jeff Phillips committed suicide, and Mark Rogowski was in jail for rape and murder.[68]

As these examples demonstrate, philosophies of unbounded freedom are impossible to contain within specific activities. And while they may be the basis of artistic freedom, and hence contribute to greater innovation within an activity, when extended to public behavior they can be irresponsibly and dangerously antisocial. Violating the rules of decorum, propriety and common sense is one thing; damaging people and their property is another.

The Olympics or Exploring Mickey Mouse's Sexual Preferences: Which Way Snowboarding?

Snowboarding's inclusion in the Olympic Games represented a new high in the commercial appropriation of the activity. The games, which embody traditional modernist sport, pose additional problems for new leisure movement and punk-influenced snowboarders. The long-term impact of the Olympics on snowboarding will emerge slowly. Prior to the Nagano Olympics, snowboarders had four main concerns. First, the Olympics advocate rigorous competition. Although Todd Richards, a leading ISF half-pipe contender, is a seasoned competitor, his experience in the sphere of the relatively relaxed snowboard competitions did little to prepare him for the high competition of the Olympics. Before Nagano he predicted that: "it'll be way weirder than we're used to dealing with. It's going to be superserious and not as much fun as it has been. Training has always been a joke to me, but now I'm thinking about lifting weights, running, training."[69] Even though Richards was competing against the same people who take part in ISF events, the very structure of the Olympics imposes intense competition on snowboarders. Additionally, professional snowboarder Dave Downing argued that, "after the Olympics I think a lot more focus will be on contests. The world is going to look at snowboarding as racing or halfpipe riding and confine it to those to areas, instead of about just going riding."[70]

Second, some snowboarders fear the rigid rules that inevitably accompany such competition. Paul Trapski, a New Zealand snowboarder, is afraid that, "by putting [the half-pipe] in the Olympics, it'll become a structured event with strict guidelines. . . . Hopefully it won't end up like freestyle skiing or something, with people telling you what trick you can or can't do."[71] *Flakezine* also expressed these fears:

> Those who think the Olympics are actually cool should remember what happened to 'freestyle' skiing, which garnered the same kind of media attention in the 70s as snowboarding is enjoying presently. The mogul competitions have turned into a race where the only way you can win is by looking just like everyone else. Not only that, but skiing with style and personality means a loss of points.[72]

Third, many snowboarders fear that their governments will use them as tools to promote excessive nationalism. Fourth, there is the problem of conflict between sponsors, for example, between uniform suppliers and personal sponsors. One well-known case involved the United States Olympic basketball team at the 1992 Olympics.[73] It is a problem that has not been fully resolved. Also, many snowboarders oppose the conformity that uniforms represent. As ISF coach Rob Roy puts it:

> I have this image of some of the best snowboarders in the world riding in uniforms in a halfpipe. The youth of the world seeing their heroes giving in to conformity. If that's the one image they see, it would be devastating to the sport. That's not why the youth of the world has embraced snowboarding. The youth of the world will say, 'Uh-oh. Our parents have a hold of this sport now.'[74]

World half-pipe champion Terje Haakonsen sums up the feelings of these snowboarders: "Snowboarding is about fresh tracks and carving powder and being yourself and not being judged by others. It's not about nationalism and politics and money."[75] Haakonsen refused to compete at the Olympics, in part because this would have compelled him to compete at FIS-run events. Interestingly, Haakonsen also likened the IOC to the Mafia, that is, to "people who take over control but never let anyone have an inside look at what they are doing . . . The fact is that the big wigs ride in limousines and stay in fancy hotels while the athletes live in barracks in the woods."[76]

While Nagano has finished, and it seems that Olympic snowboarders have taken the games in their stride, the problems are long-term and will unravel only slowly. The antics of the competitive snowboarders at Nagano proved that no matter how smooth the transition to competitive snowboarding appears, competitive snowboarders are leagues removed from traditional athletes. For example, an Austrian snowboarder was sent home after causing US$4,000 worth of damage to a hotel room after a party. When asked what level of drug testing there was during pre-Olympic qualifying rounds, American Adam Hostetter replied, "Testing? I say try them all! They're all great!!"[77] Indeed, the very first gold medal ever awarded to a snowboarder, won by Canadian Ross Rebagliati in the giant slalom, was removed after drug testers found traces of marijuana in Rebagliati's urine sample. Although the IOC reinstated him,[78] the event caused some snowboarding commentators considerable mirth, considering the IOC and FIS's push to have snowboarding included in the Olympics and their stand on drugs in sport. As one commentator laughed,

> Perhaps it's karmic justice that the gold-medal winner is a pot smoking fool . . . The money-grubbing soul-less peons of FIS . . . [stole] snowboarding from behind the sports back before the snowboarders could put down their collective pipe and figure out what happened. It's sweet revenge that the rebels of snowboarding have had the last snickle.[79]

Whatever the effect of the incident on the IOC and its campaign against drugs, it will not affect snowboarding's burgeoning popularity: "There might be a few more figure skaters turning up their noses at those peasants in snowboarding" but "in fact the whole incident will probably spawn a great advertising campaign for Pepsi or some other hipper-than-thou brand."[80]

In the short- to medium-term at least, the Olympics will exert little influence on snowboarding because they have essentially broadened the gulf between competitive and ordinary snowboarders. World champion snowboarder Michele Taggart sees a split: "It's almost like there's going to be a different sport—freeriding is one thing, and training and competing and now going to the Olympics is going to be another."[81] Yet, snowboarding's acceptance by the FIS and inclusion in the Olympics show just how popular snowboarding has become.

Not surprisingly, snowboarders have responded to this 'crisis' of popularity along the two different philosophical lines of punk. The first group laments snowboarding's popularity because, by definition, when snowboarding was new, snowboarders were innovative and trendsetting. But, as snowboarding became more popular, participants lost their source of individuality. Today, few people notice snowboarders or consider them abnormal. Some snowboarders responded by moving on to new, less popular activities or by trying to make snowboarding more individualistic. The latter typically involved offensive behaviour. A letter to *New Zealand Snowboarder* in 1993 complained about the lack of unity amongst snowboarders and warned of the dangers posed by image-conscious snowboarders: "Until last season there was a kind of common bond between boarders; all happy to meet other boarders and share stories. But this seems to be ebbing away with time, and being replaced with the 'I'm soooo cool,' bad attitude syndrome."[82] The response was vitriolic: "What the hell is this shit about... manners on the mountain?" wrote one correspondent to *Transworld Snowboarding*:

> I thought snowboarding was about tattoos, body piercing, and punk music, not being all nice and shit. What is this, the Brady Bunch girls with snowboards? We should be able to cuss and smoke anywhere we want. And I like pants so big you can carry Greyhound buses in your pockets and no one knows it.[83]

A similar reaction occurred in skateboarding after its commercial appropriation: "As the mainstream absorbs rebel sportswear, rebel sportswear is busy running, kicking and screaming away from the mainstream." Various skate companies' exploration of themes (printed on shirts and boards) "as diverse as female masturbation and Mickey Mouse's sexual preferences," in other words, skateboarding's "adoption of outrage and bad taste is in some ways an attempt... to make something the mainstream can't simply snap up in its next summer fashion special spreads."[84]

The second group genuinely cares about the detrimental effect of overcommercialization as well as the obnoxious and offensive behavior promoted by 'image' snowboarders. Unfortunately, they have become bogged down in political disputes and, paradoxically, contributed to the institutionalization of boarding. Ironically, it was the absence of institutionalisation that first attracted this group to snowboarding. New Zealand professional Dani Meier's fears are well-founded: "The more we worry about these politics, the more we'll become involved in them and the less we'll be snowboarding. What a shame our sport has to become so prostituted by office jerks."[85]

There has also been a third reaction. Although these boarders appear overtly apathetic to traditional forms of politics and protest, they too are concerned about capitalism's negative impact on snowboarding. However, they have no confidence in interventionist strategies that they believe capitalism will only subvert. In this sense, they see commercialization as an inevitable process. Thus, they refuse to get involved in the politics and administration of snowboarding, and concentrate on maintaining their own personal space through "soulboarding" (riding for intrinsic pleasure). Soulboarders apply the punk 'do it yourself' (DIY) ethic, and prefer to ride in the backcountry, or at small, low-key, club fields. DIY soulboarding meets the high ideals of the artistic sensibility as the backcountry is removed from the world of commercialism and popularity. In this manner this group follows the sentiments of Craig Kelly, a top professional with Burton, who, when asked what he considered his favorite trick, retorted, "Avoiding all public snowboarding."[86]

It seems that this is the only real option available to snowboarders who wish to keep their activity, or at least their physical space, underground and unsullied by commercialism. Snowboarding is no longer new or shocking. By trying to preserve snowboarding with its original philosophies, especially with respect to competition, the second group of snowboarders has become more involved in administration, and has less time to ride. The fact is that snowboarding is no longer a small activity, enjoyed by a few enthusiasts who all know one another, but a multimillion dollar, front-cover fashion magazine, overhyped commodity.

Nonetheless, snowboarders have changed the face of skiing forever. No longer are snowboarders in revolt against snotty upper-class skiers. The latter still exist, but they are no longer the raison d'être of ski fields. Ski fields must now appeal to two markets: those who can afford outrageously priced day-lift tickets, and regulars who capitalize off cheap season passes. Snowboarding revived skiing spiritually; it reminded skiers that the rationale of skiing is to have fun, and snowboarders injected a healthy dose of street fashion style to the mountains. Overall, snowboarding has maintained—and will continue to maintain—its philosophies. Snowboarding has appeared on the British television show *Absolutely Fabulous*, and dozens of corporations use snowboarding images to promote their winter products. As Aaron Bolt says, "It will destroy its underground cool image, but it will always be there. Just like skateboarding. Just like surfing."[87]

Notes

1. Steve Wulf, "Triumph of the hated snowboarders," *Time*, 29 Jan 1996, p. 69.

2. Elif Sinanoglu, "Snowboarding: It's cool! It's hot! It's even pretty safe!," *Money*, Jan 1996, p. 124.

3. Douglas Booth, "Surfin' 60s," *Australian Historical Studies*, No. 103 (1994), p. 276.

4. Charles Gant, "Teenage lust," *The Face*, May 1996, p. 108.

5. "The 100 greatest things that ever happened to skiing," *Ski*, Jan 1993, p. 84.

6. Billy Miller, "Who's afraid of the FIS?," *Transworld Snowboarding*, Jan 1997; www.twsnow.com/snowboarding/html snow_oly_afraid_fis_0197.html

7. Michael Farber, "Snowboard nation," *Sports Illustrated*, 23 Jan 1995, p. 83.

8. Dana White, "Surf and turf," *Skiing*, March/April 1993, p. 95.

9. *NZ Skiing Annual and Guide*, 1997, p. 1.

10. Ste'en Webster, interview, 25 June 1995.

11. Miller, "Who's afraid of the FIS?"

12. Ste'en Webster, "The Olympic question," *New Zealand Snowboarder*, July/Aug 1997, p. 28.

13. Martin Hamilton, "Separate snowboard circuits could be headed for board war," *Summit Daily News*, 12 March 1995, p. 18.

14. Miller, "Who's afraid of the FIS?"

15. Ibid.

16. J. P. Martin, "Nagano: Before and after the Olympics," *Transworld Snowboarding*, 15 Jan 1998; www.twsnow.com/olympics/html/oly_politics_nagano1.html

17. "Rant-o-rama: Getting FISted," *Flakezine*, No. 2.3 (18 Nov 1995); users.aol.com/angerinc/rant23.html

18. Quoted in Miller, "Who's afraid of the FIS?"

19. Miller, "Who's afraid of the FIS?"

20. Ste'en Webster, interview, 25 June 1995.

21. Farber, "Snowboard nation," p. 81.

22. Aaron Bolt, interview, 13 June 1995.

23. "The destructive power of mainstream press and advertising," *Flakezine*, No. 1.3 (5 Oct 1994); users.aol.com/flakezine/fz13.html

24. Bill Ryan, *Making Capital from Culture: The Corporate Form of Capitalist Cultural Production* (Berlin: Walter de Gruyter, 1991), p. 39.

25. Arnold Hauser, *The Social History of Art*, Vol. 3 (New York: Vintage Books, 1958), p. 153.

26. Howard Becker, "The professional dance musician and his audience," *American Journal of Sociology*, Vol. 57, No. 2 (1951), p. 138. Forerunners to the counterculture, the Beats of the late 1950s to mid to late 1960s held the notion of gaining "individual enlightenment through the rejection of bourgeois society and the embracing of a rootless lifestyle, literary romanticism and experimentalism, elements of Eastern religions, and in many cases the use of drugs and alcohol." They also identified with cafe society, modern jazz, and modern art. (Tony Thorne, *Dictionary of Popular Culture: Fads, Fashions and Cults* (London: Bloomsbury, 1994), pp. 20–21)

27. Peter Donnelly, "Sport as a site for 'popular' resistance," in R. Gruneau (ed.), *Popular Cultures and Political Practices* (Toronto: Garamond Press, 1988), p. 74.

28. Tilman Hepp, *Wolfgang Güllich: A Life in the Vertical* (Stuttgart: Boulder Ed, 1994), p. 33.

29. Becky Beal, "Alternative masculinity and its effects on gender relations in the subculture of skateboarding," *Journal of Sport Behavior*, Vol. 19, No. 3 (1996), p. 210.

30. Beal, "Alternative masculinity," p. 210.

31. Grant Smithies, "Gus Gus: Don't eat the yellow snow!," *Real Groove*, Aug 1997, p. 35.

32. J. Clarke, S. Hall, T. Jefferson and B. Roberts, "Subcultures, cultures and class," in S. Hall and T. Jefferson (eds.), *Resistance Through Rituals* (London: Hutchinson, 1976), p. 61.

33. Jeffrey Alexander, "Modern, anti, post and neo," *New Left Review*, No. 210 (1995), p. 81.

34. Paul Kent, "Young, loud and snotty," *The Story of Pop*, Part 30 [radio serial] (British Broadcasting Corporation).

35. Alexander, "Modern," p. 80.

36. David Harvey, *The Condition of Postmodernity* (Oxford: Basil Blackwell, 1989), p. 139.

37. Gavin Hills, "Never mind the Sex Pistols, here's the bollocks," *The Face*, June 1996, p. 136.

38. Charles Young, "Skank or die," *Playboy*, June 1984, p. 190.

39. Marty Duda, "Can in flow motion," *Real Groove*, Aug 1997, p. 16.

40. Quoted in Matthew Collin and John Godfrey, *Altered State: The Story of Ecstasy Culture and Acid House* (London: Serpent's Tail, 1997), p. 187.

41. Ibid.

42. Ryan, *Making Capital from Culture*, p. 53.

43. Newsgroup post, srini, yeah, "nobody here but us capitalists," Anarchy List (anarchy-list@cwi.nl), 22 May 1997. Anarchism is a political and philosophical stance that works towards the abolishment of government and other institutions in favor of individuals governing themselves in a cooperative milieu. It is popular with sectors of postpunks.

44. Interview with Crashsite, 1997; crashsite.com/GEF/gef3.html

45. Jonathan Bernstein, "Anarchy in the USA," *The Face*, Dec 1994, p. 155.

46. Ryan, *Making Capital from Culture*, p. 224.

47. Ibid., p. 53.

48. Ste'en Webster, "Winter of '92," *New Zealand Snowboarder*, May/June 1993, p. 27.

49. Booth, "Surfin' 60s," p. 277.

50. Matthew Rutledge, letter to editor, *Transworld Snowboarding*, May 1995, p. 28.

51. Ryan, *Making Capital from Culture*, pp. 53–54.

52. Miller, "Who's afraid of the FIS?"

53. Billy Miller and Matt Linnell, "The question of soul," *Transworld Snowboarding*, May 1995, p. 24.

54. The discipline is known as 'aggressive' Rollerblading to differentiate it from the less street-credible disciplines.

55. Interview, Craig Harris, 16 June 1995.

56. Daniel Ting, "Why we dislike rollerblades—theories," www.clark.net/pub/len/dan2.htm

57. Stefan Fatsis, " 'Rad' sports give sponsors cheap thrills," *Wall Street Journal*, 12 May 1995, p. B8.

58. Quoted in Ste'en Webster & Phil Erickson, "Crossover," *New Zealand Snowboarder*, July/Aug 1993, p. 40.

59. Miller and Linnell, "The question of soul," p. 24.

60. Interview, Craig Harris, 16 June 1995.

61. Douglas Booth, "Ambiguities in pleasure and discipline: The development of professional surfing," *Journal of Sports History*, Vol. 22, No. 3 (1995), pp. 199–200.

62. International Snowboarding Federation, "ISF Message," 1995, p. 8.

63. Richard Peterson, "Audiences—and all that jazz," *Trans-action*, Oct 1964, p. 32.

64. Becker, "The professional dance musician and his audience," p. 137.

65. Ibid., 138.

66. Howard Becker, *Art Worlds* (Berkeley: University of California Press, 1982), p. 14.

67. Letter to the editor, reprinted in *Transworld Snowboarding*, Jan 1995, p. 66.

68. "Hell on wheels," *San Francisco Bay Guardian*, May 1994, reprinted in *DansWorld Skateboarding*, www.cps.msu.edu/~dunhamda/dw/guardian.html

69. Miller, "Who's afraid of the FIS?"

70. Ibid.

71. Webster, "The Olympic question," p. 30.

72. "Rant-o-rama: Getting FISted," *Flakezine.*

73. Reebok supplied the team uniform while Michael Jordan was personally sponsored by Nike. Jordan did not want to be seen wearing Reebok, and so, at the medal presentation, he wore a towel over his shoulders to cover the Reebok name and logo.

74. Miller, "Who's afraid of the FIS?"

75. Stacy Perman, "The master blasts the board," *Time*, 19 Jan 1998, p. 51.

76. Doug Mellgren, "AP reports Terje boycotting Nagano?" *SOL Snowboarding Online*, 7 Jan 1998, www.solsnowboarding.com/compete/terje.html

77. Ari Cheren, "The press conference," *Explore*, 1 Feb 1998, www.exploremag.com/events/ussnowboardteam/saywhat.html

78. Whilst some claim Rebagliati was reinstated to placate snowboarders, the official line is that the IOC has no rules against the use of marijuana in competition. Rebagliati was, however, interviewed by Japanese police.

79. Andy Hood, "Couch potatoes of the world unite," *Explore*, 19 Feb 1998, www.exploremag.com/xtras/olympics

80. "Drugs in sport," *Carbohydrated*, No. 2, www.carbonplaces.com/zine/imho.asp

81. Miller, "Who's afraid of the FIS?"

82. Letter to the editor, *New Zealand Snowboarder*, July/Aug 1993, p. 7.

83. Letter to the editor, *Transworld Snowboarding*, May 1995, p. 28.

84. Gavin Hills, "Sympathy for the devil," *The Face*, Aug 1995, p. 73.

85. Dani Meier, "Dani's corner," *New Zealand Snowboarder*, July/Aug 1994, p. 16.

86. Burton Snowboards, "Burton Snowboards 1995" [CD-ROM], 1995.

87. Aaron Bolt, interview, 13 June 1995.

Index

429

SUNY series, Sport, Culture, and Social Relations
CL Cole and Michael A. Messner, eds.